THOMAS BECKET:
A Textual History of his Letters

THOMAS BECKET:
A Textual History of his Letters

Anne Duggan

CLARENDON PRESS · OXFORD
1980

Oxford University Press, Walton Street, Oxford OX2 6DP

OXFORD LONDON GLASGOW
NEW YORK TORONTO MELBOURNE WELLINGTON
IBADAN NAIROBI DAR ES SALAAM LUSAKA CAPE TOWN
KUALA LUMPUR SINGAPORE JAKARTA HONG KONG TOKYO
DELHI BOMBAY CALCUTTA MADRAS KARACHI

Published in the United States by
Oxford University Press New York

British Library Cataloguing in Publication Data

Duggan, Anne
 Thomas Becket.
 1. Henry II, *King of England*
 2. Thomas Becket, *Saint*
 3. Great Britain—History—Henry, 1154–1189
 —Sources
 942.03′1′0924   DA206   79–41048

 ISBN 0-19-822486-9

Set, printed and bound in Great Britain by
Fakenham Press Limited, Fakenham, Norfolk

Preface

A full edition of the correspondence of Thomas Becket, in conjunction with Elias of Evesham's *Quadrilogus* Life of Becket, was first published by Christian Wolf (Lupus) in Brussels in 1682, from a Vatican manuscript. Since then, no less than three major editions of the whole or part of Becket's correspondence have been produced, but no attempt has so far been made to collate all the known manuscripts or to elucidate the relationship between the different collections of Becket letters now surviving. Similarly, although the Lives of Becket and the relevant contemporary chronicles have been available in print for many years, no editor has satisfactorily investigated the epistolary sources upon which most of these accounts substantially depend for their versions of the Becket dispute. The exceptional quality of the biographies and chronicle accounts, in contrast with other contemporary hagiographical literature, stems in part from their subject, but mainly from their direct reliance on the surviving records of the dispute. It is this feature which gives an immediacy and authenticity to the works, especially of William of Canterbury and William FitzStephen, Roger of Hoveden, and Ralph de Diceto. This study analyses the twenty-four surviving manuscript collections of Becket correspondence, investigates the principal lines of textual transmission as far as they can now be reconstructed from these sources, and examines in detail the use made of epistolary material by biographers in the late twelfth and early thirteenth centuries.

The author of a book based almost exclusively on the study of manuscript sources owes a very great debt to those Librarians, Archivists, and Keepers of Manuscripts whose learning and labours preserve and make available the materials on which his work depends. Among the many to whom such acknowledgements are due are the Keepers of Manuscripts and their assistants in the Manuscript Room of the British Library in London, the Bibliothèque Nationale in Paris, and the Bodleian Library in Oxford; the Librarians of Corpus Christi College and Trinity College in

Cambridge; the Librarian of Lambeth Palace, London; the Municipal Librarians of Laon and St Omer; the Keeper of Manuscripts in the Biblioteca Vallicelliana in Rome; and the Prefect of the Biblioteca Apostolica in the Vatican. Particular thanks are also due to the late Fr David Knowles, for early encouragement at the beginning of the present venture; to Professor Christopher Brooke and Sir Roger Mynors for generous access to various stages of their work on John of Salisbury's later letters, and to Professor Brooke for his unfailing kindness; to the Central Research Fund of the University of London for the purchase of microfilm; to Professor Stephan Kuttner, for affording the generous hospitality of the Institute of Medieval Canon Law in Berkeley, California, where the work was finalized; and finally, to my husband, Dr Charles Duggan, for valuable advice during all the stages of preparation, and not least for driving me to Laon one stormy September to consult MS 337.

Anne Duggan
Queen Mary College
December 1979

Contents

Abbreviations

BIHR	*Bulletin of the Institute of Historical Research*
Dict. d'hist.	*Dictionnaire d'histoire et de géographie ecclésiastique*
DNB	*Dictionary of National Biography*
EHR	*English Historical Review*
Giles, *EpGF*	J. A. Giles, ed., *Gilberti ex abbate Glocestriae episcopi primum Herefordiensis deinde Londoniensis epistolae . . .*, 2 vols., Patres Ecclesiae Anglicanae, Oxford (1846)
Giles, *EpST*	J. A. Giles, ed., *Epistolae Sancti Thomae Cantuariensis . . .*, 2 vols., Patres Ecclesiae Anglicanae, Oxford (1845)
Giles, *VST*	J. A. Giles, ed., *Vita Sancti Thomae Cantuariensis . . .*, 2 vols., Patres Ecclesiae Anglicanae, Oxford (1845)
Hardy	T. D. Hardy, *Descriptive Catalogue of Materials Relating to Great Britain and Ireland to the end of the Reign of Henry VII*, 3 vols., RS 26, London (1862–71)
JEH	*Journal of Ecclesiastical History*
JL	P. Jaffé, S. Loewenfeld, F. Kaltenbrunner, and P. W. Ewald, edd., *Regesta Pontificum Romanorum*, II, Leipzig (1888)
Ker	N. R. Ker, *The Medieval Libraries of Great Britain*, Royal Historical Society, London (2nd edn., 1964)
Leland	J. Leland, *Collectanea de Rebus Britannicis*, ed. T. Hearne, London (1770)
Lupus	C. Lupus, ed., *Epistolae et Vita Divi Thomae Martyris et Archiepiscopi Cantuariensis*, 2 vols., Brussels (1682)

Mats.	J. C. Robertson and J. B. Sheppard, edd., *Materials for the History of Thomas Becket, Archbishop of Canterbury*, 7 vols., RS 67, London (1875–85)
MB, *Foliot*	A. Morey and C. N. L. Brooke, edd., *The Letters and Charters of Gilbert Foliot*, Cambridge (1967)
MGH	*Monumenta Germaniae Historica*
NMT	Nelson's Medieval Texts
PBA	*Proceedings of the British Academy*
Pat. Lat.	J. P. Migne, ed., Patrologiae Cursus Completus: Series Latina, Paris (1844, etc.)
PR	Pipe Rolls
RH	*Revue historique*
RS	Rolls Series: *Rerum Britannicarum Medii Aevi Scriptores*
Rev. des quest. hist.	*Revue des questions historiques*
TRHS	*Transactions of the Royal Historical Society*
Rev. d'hist. ecclés.	*Revue d'histoire ecclésiastique*
Rymer	T. Rymer, ed., *Foedera, Conventiones, Litterae et Cujuscunque Genera Acta Publica inter Reges Angliae et Alios . . .*, Record Commission, London (1816)

Manuscript Abbreviations

Addit.	Brit. Libr. MS Addit. 1777
AlanT(A)	Brit. Libr. MS Cotton Claudius B.II
AlanT(B)	Vatican Latin MS 1220
AlanT(C)	Cambridge Corpus Christi College MS 295
Arundel	Brit. Libr. MS Arundel 219
Bodl.A	Oxford Bodl. MS 509
Bodl.B, I	Oxford Bodl. MS 937, Part I
Bodl.B, II–III	Oxford Bodl. MS 937, Parts II and III
Cave	Oxford Bodl. MS Cave e Mus. 249
Douce	Oxford Bodl. MS Douce 287
Harl.	Brit. Libr. MS Harleian 215
Lamb.	Lambeth Palace MS 136
Laon	Laon Bibl. de la Ville MS 337
Laud	Oxford Bodl. MS Laud Misc. 666
RC	Paris Bibl. Nat. Latin MS 5372
Rawl.	Oxford Bodl. MS Rawlinson Q.f.8
Roy.	Brit. Libr. MS Royal 13.A.XIII
Trin.	Cambridge Trinity Hall MS 24
Vat.	Vatican Latin MS 6024

Select Bibliography

A. MANUSCRIPTS

CANTERBURY: CATHEDRAL LIBRARY
Cartae Antiquae, A.50
Registers: A, N, and O

CAMBRIDGE: CORPUS CHRISTI
COLLEGE
MS 123
MS 295

CAMBRIDGE: TRINITY COLLEGE
MS B.I.23
MS B.XIV.37
MSS O.5.39–45

CAMBRIDGE: TRINITY HALL
MS 24

CAMBRAI: BIBLIOTHÈQUE
MUNICIPALE
MS 488

DOUAI: BIBLIOTHÈQUE MUNICIPALE
MS 860

DURHAM: CATHEDRAL LIBRARY
MS B.IV.18
MS B.IV.41
MS B.IV.44

ÉVREUX: BIBLIOTHÈQUE
MUNICIPALE
MS Lat. 7

HEREFORD: CATHEDRAL LIBRARY
MS. O.IV.14

LAON: BIBLIOTHÈQUE DE LA VILLE
MS 337

LINCOLN: CATHEDRAL LIBRARY
MS 121

LONDON: BRITISH LIBRARY
Addit. MS 1777
Addit. MS 11506
Addit. MS 16607
Addit. MS 32100

Arundel MS 15
Arundel MS 27
Arundel MS 52
Arundel MS 219
Cotton MS Julius A.XI
Cotton MS Julius D.XI
Cotton MS Claudius B.II
Cotton MS Claudius E.III
Cotton MS Nero A.V.
Cotton MS Otho C.XIV
Cotton MS Vitellius C.XII
Cotton MS Vitellius E.X
Cotton MS Vespasian B.XIV
Cotton MS Vespasian E.X
Cotton MS Titus D.XI
Cotton MS Faustina B.I
Cotton MS Faustina B.VIII
Harleian MS 2
Harleian MS 215
Harleian MS 4242
Lansdowne MS 398
Lansdowne MS 402
Royal MS 9.B.XII
Royal MS 13.A.XIII
Royal MS 13.C.VI
Royal MS 13.E.VI
Stowe MS 52

LONDON: LAMBETH PALACE
MS 135
MS 136
MS 138
MS 157
MS 1212

MONTPELLIER: ÉCOLE DE MÉDECINE
MS 2

OXFORD: BODLEIAN LIBRARY
Bodl. MS 278
Bodl. MS 509
Bodl. MS 937

Cave MS e Mus. 133
Cave MS e Mus. 249
Douce MS 287
Laud Lat. MS 18
Laud Misc. MS 527
Laud Misc. MS 666
Rawlinson MS Q.f.8

OXFORD: CORPUS CHRISTI COLLEGE
MS xxxviii

OXFORD: ST JOHN'S COLLEGE
MS 15
MS 126

OXFORD: UNIVERSITY COLLEGE
MS lxix

PARIS: BIBLIOTHÈQUE NATIONALE
Latin MS 5320
Latin MS 5372
Latin MS 5615
Latin MS 8562

ROME: BIBLIOTECA ALESSANDRINA
MS 120

ROME: BIBLIOTECA APOSTOLICA
VATICANA
Latin MS 1220
Latin MS 1221
Latin MS 6024
Latin MS 6027
Latin MS 6933

ROME: BIBLIOTECA VALLICELLIANA
MS TOM. III
MS B.60

ST OMER: BIBLIOTHÈQUE
MUNICIPALE
MS 710

WINCHESTER COLLEGE
MS 4

B. PRINTED SOURCES

Alan of Tewkesbury: *Epistolae*, Pat. Lat. CXC, cols. 1477–88.
Anecdota Bedae: *Anecdota Bedae, Lanfranci et Aliorum*, ed. J. A. Giles, Caxton Society, XII, London (1851).
Anglia Sacra: ed. H. Wharton, 2 vols., London (1691).
Annales Ecclesiastici: ed. C. Baronius, Lucca (1746).
Annales Monastici: ed. H. R. Luard, 6 vols., RS 36, London (1864–9).
Arnulf of Lisieux: *Arnulfi Lexoviensis episcopi Epistolae . . .*, ed. J. A. Giles, Patres Ecclesiae Anglicanae, Oxford (1844).
—— *The Letters of Arnulf of Lisieux*, ed. F. Barlow, Camden Third Series, LXI, London (1939).
Bernard of Clairvaux: *Epistolae*, Pat. Lat. CLXXXII, cols. 67–662.
—— *The Letters of St Bernard of Clairvaux*, ed. and trans. Bruno Scott James, London (1953).
Bibliotheca Latina: *Bibliotheca Latina Mediae et Infimae Aetatis*, ed. J. A. Fabricius, 6 vols., Hamburg (1734–46).
Breviarium ad Usum Insignis Ecclesiae Sarum, edd. F. Proctor and C. Wordsworth, 3 vols., Cambridge (1882–6).
Codex Pseudoepigraphicus: *Codex Pseudoepigraphicus Veteris Testamenti*, ed. J. A. Fabricius, 2 vols., Leipzig (1713–33).
Concilia Britanniae: *Concilia Magnae Britanniae et Hiberniae*, ed. D. Wilkins, I, London (1737).
Epistolae Cantuarienses: *Chronicles and Memorials of the Reign of Richard I*, vol. II: *Epistolae Cantuarienses, The Letters of the Prior and Convent of Christ Church, Canterbury, 1187–1199*, ed. W. Stubbs, RS 38, London (1865).
Foedera: *Foedera, Conventiones, Litterae et Cujuscunque Generis Acta*

Publica inter Reges Angliae et Alios ..., ed. T. Rymer, Record Commission, London (1816).

Gerhoch of Reichersberg: *Epistolae*, Pat. Lat. CXCIII, cols. 489–618.

Gervase of Canterbury: *The Historical Works of Gervase of Canterbury*, ed. W. Stubbs, 2 vols., RS 73, London (1879–80).

Gesta Regis Henrici II: *Gesta Regis Henrici Secundi Benedicti Abbatis*, ed. W. Stubbs, 2 vols., RS 49, London (1867).

Gilbert Foliot: *Gilberti ex abbate Glocestriae episcopi primum Herefordiensis deinde Londoniensis epistolae* ..., ed. J. A. Giles, 2 vols., Patres Ecclesiae Anglicanae, Oxford (1846).

—— *The Letters and Charters of Gilbert Foliot*, ed. Dom A. Morey and C. N. L. Brooke, Cambridge (1967).

Giraldus Cambrensis: *Giraldi Cambrensis Opera*, edd. J. S. Brewer, J. F. Dimock, and G. F. Warner, 8 vols., RS 21, London (1861–91).

Glanvill: *Tractatus de legibus et consuetudinibus regni Anglie qui Glanvilla vocatur*, ed. G. D. G. Hall, NMT, London (1965).

Guernes de Pont-Sainte-Maxence: *La Vie de Saint Thomas le Martyr par Guernes de Pont-Sainte-Maxence*, ed. E. Walberg, Lund (1922).

Henry II: *Recueil des actes de Henri II, roi d'Angleterre* ... *concernant les provinces françaises et les affaires de France*, edd. L. Delisle and E. Berger, Académie des Inscriptions et Belles-Lettres, Chartes et Diplomes, 4 vols., Paris (1909–27).

Herbert of Bosham: *Herberti de Boseham Opera Omnia*, ed. J. A. Giles, 2 vols., Patres Ecclesiae Anglicanae, Oxford (1845).

Hildebert of Le Mans: *Epistolae*, Pat. Lat. CLXXI, cols. 135–312.

Hildegarde of Mont-St-Rupert: *Epistolae*, Pat. Lat. CXCVII, cols. 145–382

Innocent III: *The Letters of Pope Innocent III: A Calendar*, edd. C. R. Cheney and Mary G. Cheney, Oxford (1968).

—— *Selected Letters of Pope Innocent III concerning England*, edd. C. R. Cheney and W. H. Semple, NMT, London (1953).

Ivo of Chartres, *Epistolae*, Pat. Lat. CLXII, cols. 11–288.

John of Poitiers: *Epistolae*, Pat. Lat. CCIX, cols. 877–82.

John of Salisbury: *Joannis Saresberiensis* ... *Opera Omnia*, ed. J. A. Giles, 5 vols., Patres Ecclesiae Anglicanae, Oxford (1848).

—— *The Letters of John of Salisbury*, I: *The Early Letters*, edd. and trans. W. J. Millor and H. E. Butler, NMT, London (1955); II: *The Later Letters (1163–1180)*, edd. and trans. W. J. Millor and C. N. L. Brooke, Oxford Medieval Texts, Oxford (1979).

Liber Regie Capelle: ed. W. Ullmann, Henry Bradshaw Society, XCII, Cambridge (1961).

Matthew Paris: *Chronica Majora*, ed. H. R. Luard, 7 vols., RS 57, London (1872–83).

—— *Historia Anglorum*, ed. F. Maddon, 3 vols., RS 44, London (1866–9).

Monumenta Germaniae Historica: *Constitutiones et Acta Publica Imperatorum et Regum*, ed. L. Weiland, I, Hanover (1893; repr. 1963), *Legum*, IV, I.

Papsturkunden: 'Papsturkunden in England', I–III, *Abhandlungen der*

Gesellschaft der Wissenschaften in Gottingen (1930–1, 1935–6, and 1952).

Peter of Blois: *Petri Blesensis Epistolae*, ed. J. A. Giles, 2 vols., Patres Ecclesiae Anglicanae, Oxford (1846–7); cf. Pat. Lat. CCVII, cols. 1–560.

Peter of Celle: *Epistolae*, Pat. Lat. CCII, cols. 401–636.

Peter the Venerable: *The Letters of Peter the Venerable*, ed. G. Constable, 2 vols., Harvard Historical Studies, no. 78, New York (1967).

Pipe Rolls: Pipe Rolls 31 Hen. I, 2–4 Hen. II, 1 Rich. I, and 3 John, ed. J. Hunter, *Record Commission*, 2 vols., London (1833–4).

—— Pipe Rolls 5 Hen. II–39 Hen. II, *Pipe Roll Society Publications*, London (1844–1925).

Ralph de Diceto: *Radulfi de Diceto decani Lundoniensis opera historica . . .*, ed. W. Stubbs, 2 vols., RS 68, London (1876).

Recueil des Historiens: *Recueil des historiens des Gaules et de la France*, XVI, Paris (1814); cf. nouv. édn., ed. L. Delisle, 24 vols., Paris (1869–1904).

Regesta Pontificum: *Regesta Pontificum Romanorum*, 2nd edn., P. Jaffé, G. Wattenbach, S. Loewenfeld, F. Kaltenbrunner, and P. Ewald, 2 vols., Leipzig (1885–8).

Richard FitzNeal: *Dialogus de Scaccario*, ed. C. Johnson, NMT, London (1950).

Robert de Torigny: *The Chronicle of Robert of Torigni*, ed. R. Howlett, *Chronicles of the Reigns of Stephen, Henry II and Richard I*, vol. IV, RS 82, London (1889).

Roger of Hoveden: *Chronica Magistri Rogeri de Houedene*, ed. W. Stubbs, 4 vols., RS 51, London (1868–71).

Roger of Wendover: *Flores Historiarum*, ed. H. G. Hewlett, 3 vols., RS 84, London (1886–9).

Sancta Concilia: *Sanctorum Conciliorum nova et amplissima collectio*, ed. J. D. Mansi, XXI–XXII, Venice (1776); facs. repro. Paris/Leipzig (1903).

Scriptores Ordinis Grandimontensis: Corpus Christianorum, Continuatio Mediaevalis, VIII (1968), ed. J. Becquet.

Spicilegium Liberianum, ed. F. Liverani, Florence (1864).

St Hugh of Lincoln: *Magna Vita S. Hugonis episcopi Lincolniensis*, ed. J. F. Dimock, RS 37, London (1864).

—— *Magna Vita Sancti Hugonis*, edd. and trans. D. L. Douie and H. Farmer, NMT, 2 vols., London (1961–2).

St Paul's: *The Early Charters of the Cathedral Church of St Paul, London*, ed. M. Gibbs, Camden Third Series, LVIII, London (1939).

Stephen of Tournai: *Epistolae*, Pat. Lat. CCXI, cols. 309–562.

Suger of Saint-Denis: *Epistolae*, Pat. Lat. CLXXXVI, cols. 1347–1440.

Thesaurus Novus Anecdotorum, edd. E. Martène and U. Durand, 5 vols., Paris (1717).

Thomas Becket: *Epistolae Sancti Thomae Cantuariensis . . .*, ed. J. A. Giles, 2 vols., Patres Ecclesiae Anglicanae, Oxford (1845).

—— *Epistolae et Vita Divi Thomae Martyris et Archiepiscopi Cantuariensis*, ed. C. Lupus, 2 vols., Brussels (1682).
—— *Materials for the History of Thomas Becket, Archbishop of Canterbury*, edd. J. C. Robertson and J. B. Sheppard, 7 vols., RS 67, London (1875–83).
—— *Thomas Saga Erkibyskups*, ed. E. Magnusson, 2 vols., RS 65, London (1875–84).
—— *Vita et Processus Sancti Thome Cantuariensis Martyris super Libertate Ecclesiastica*, ed. Johannes Philippi, Paris (1495).
—— *Vita Sancti Thomae Cantuariensis Archiepiscopi et Martyris*, ed. J. A. Giles, 2 vols., Patres Ecclesiae Anglicanae, Oxford (1845).
Walter of Dervy: *The Letters of Walter Abbat of Dervy*, ed. C. Messiter, Caxton Society, VI, London (1850). This ascription is erroneous; the letters were written by Peter of Celle.
Walter Map: *De Nugis Curialium*, ed. M. R. James, Oxford (1914).
William of Newburgh: *Historia Rerum Anglicarum*, ed. R. G. Howlett, *Chronicles of the Reigns of Stephen, Henry II, and Richard I*, I–II, RS 82, London (1884–5).

C. SECONDARY WORKS

Abbot, E. A., *St. Thomas of Canterbury: His Death and Miracles*, 2 vols., London (1898).
Alexander, J. W., 'The Becket Controversy in Recent Historiography', *Journal of British Studies*, IX, No. 2 (May 1970), pp. 1–26.
Bannister, A. T., *A Descriptive Catalogue of the Manuscripts in the Hereford Cathedral Library*, Hereford (1927).
Borenius, T., *St Thomas Becket in Art*, London (1932).
Brooke, Z. N., *The English Church and the Papacy from the Conquest to the Reign of John*, Cambridge (1931).
—— 'The Register of Master David of London and the part he played in the Becket crisis', *Essays in History Presented to R. L. Poole*, Oxford (1927), pp. 227–45.
Brown, P. A., *The Development of the Legend of Thomas Becket*, Philadelphia (1930).
Canivez, J.-M., 'St Bernard de Clairvaux', *Dict. d'hist.*, VIII, cols. 610–44.
Cheney, C. R., 'Magna Carta Beati Thome: another Canterbury forgery', *BIHR* XXXVI (1963), pp. 1–26.
Cheney, M. G., 'William FitzStephen and his Life of Archbishop Thomas', C. N. L. Brooke, D. E. Luscombe, G. H. Martin, and D. M. Owen, edd., *Church and Government in the Middle Ages*, Cambridge (1976), pp. 139–56.
Classen, P., *Gerhoch von Reichersberg*, Wiesbaden (1960).
Claudin, A., *Histoire de l'imprimerie en France au XVe et au XVIe siècle*, 5 vols., Paris (1901–71).
Cohn, E. S., 'The manuscript evidence for the letters of Peter of Blois', *EHR* XLI (1926), pp. 42–60.

Compton, J., 'Fasciculi Zizaniorum I', *JEH* XII (1961), pp. 35–46.

Constable, G., *Letters and Letter-Collections*, Typologie des sources du moyen âge occidental, fasc. 17, Turnhout (1976).

Dark, S., *St Thomas of Canterbury*, Great English Churchmen Series, London (1927).

Davies, G. R. C., *Medieval Cartularies of Great Britain: A Short Catalogue*, London (1958).

De Beauchamp, R., *Historia Synopsi Franco-Merovingica*, Douai (1633).

Dodwell, C. R., *The Canterbury School of Illumination, 1066–1200*, Cambridge (1954).

Douglas, D. C., *English Scholars, 1600–1730*, 2nd edn., London (1951).

Dugdale, Sir William, *Monasticon Anglicanum*, 8 vols., London (1849).

Duggan, Anne, 'The French Manuscripts of the Becket Correspondence', in R. Foreville, ed., *Thomas Becket*, Paris (1975).

Duggan, C., 'Bishop John and Archdeacon Richard of Poitiers: their Roles in the Becket Dispute and its Aftermath', in R. Foreville, ed., *Thomas Becket*, Paris (1975).

—— 'The Reception of Canon Law in England in the later-Twelfth Century', *Proceedings of the Second International Congress of Medieval Canon Law, Monumenta Iuris Canonici, Series C: Subsidia*, I, Vatican City (1965), pp. 359–90.

—— 'Richard of Ilchester, Royal Servant and Bishop', *TRHS*, 5th Series, 16 (1966), pp. 1–21.

—— 'The Significance of the Becket Dispute in the History of the English Church', *Ampleforth Journal*, LXXV (1970), pp. 365–75.

—— *Twelfth Century Decretal Collections and their Importance in English History*, University of London Historical Studies, No. 12 (1963).

—— and Duggan, A., 'Ralph de Diceto, Henry II and Becket', in B. Tierney and P. Linehan, edd., *Authority and Power: Studies in Medieval Law and Government . . . presented to Walter Ullmann*, Cambridge (in preparation).

Étienne, E., *La Vie de Saint Thomas le Martyr*, Paris (1883).

Eyton, R. W., *Court, Household and Itinerary of Henry II*, London (1878).

Foreville, R., *L'Église et la royauté en Angleterre sous Henri II Plantagenet*, Paris (1943).

—— *Le Jubilé de Saint Thomas Becket du XIIIe au XVe siècle*, Paris (1958).

—— ed., *Thomas Becket: Actes du colloque international de Sédières, 19–24 août 1973*, Paris (1975).

Foss, E., *A Biographical Dictionary of the Judges of England, 1066–1870*, London (1870).

Freeman, E. A., 'St Thomas of Canterbury and his Biographers', *Historical Essays, First Series*, London (1875), pp. 79–113.

Froude, J. A., 'The Life and Times of Thomas Becket', *Short Studies on Great Subjects*, London (1878; repr. Fontana Books, 1963).

Froude, R. H., 'History of the Contest between Thomas à Becket, Archbishop of Canterbury, and Henry II, King of England', *Remains of the Late Reverend R. H. Froude*, Part II, ii, Derby (1839).

Galbraith, V. H., *Roger of Wendover and Matthew Paris*, Glasgow (1944).

Gams, P. B., *Series Episcoporum Ecclesiae Catholicae*, Ratisbon (1873).

Ghellinck, J. de, *Le Mouvement théologique du XIIe siècle*, Bruges and Paris (2nd edn., 1948).

Giry, A., *Manuel de diplomatique*, Paris (1925).

Goldie, F., 'St Thomas the Martyr', *St George the Martyr, etc.*, London (1890), pp. 1–24.

Gransden, Antonia, *Historical Writing in England c. 550 to c. 1307*, London (1974).

Greenway, D., 'The Succession to Ralph de Diceto, Dean of St Paul's', *BIHR* (1966), pp. 86–95.

Halphen, L., 'Les biographes de Thomas Becket', *RH* CII (1909), pp. 35–45.

——'Les entrevues des rois Louis VII et Henri II durant l'exil de Thomas Becket en France', *Mélanges d'histoire offerts à Charles Bémont*, Paris (1913), pp. 151–62.

Hall, M. G. (Mrs M. G. Cheney), 'Roger, Bishop of Worcester, 1164–79, University of Oxford Unpublished B. Litt. thesis, 1940.

Hardy, T. D., *Descriptive Catalogue of Materials relating to the History of Great Britain and Ireland to the end of the Reign of Henry VIII*, 3 vols., RS 26, London (1862–71).

Harris, M. A., 'Alan of Tewkesbury and his Letters, I–II', *Studia Monastica*, XVIII (1976), pp. 77–108 and 299–351.

Hohenleutner, H., 'Die Briefsammlung des sogenannten Walter von Dervy (Montier-en-Der) in der Oxforder Handschrift St John's College, Mrs. 126', *Historisches Jahrbuch*, LXXIV (1955), pp. 673–80.

Holtzmann, W., 'Quellen und Forschungen zur Geschichte Friedrich Barbarossas (Englische Analekten I)', *Neues Archiv*, XLVIII (1930), pp. 384–413.

Hutton, W. H., *Thomas Becket, Archbishop of Canterbury*, Cambridge (1926).

Jacquin, M., 'Alain de Lille', *Dict. d'hist.*, I, pp. 1229–1304.

James, M. R., *The Ancient Libraries of Canterbury and Dover*, Cambridge (1903).

Jayne, S. and Johnson, F. R., *The Lumley Library*, British Museum Publications, London (1956).

Jenkins, C., *The Monastic Chronicler and the early school of St Albans*, London (1922).

Johnson, C., 'The Reconciliation of Henry II with the Papacy: A Missing Document', *EHR* LII (1937), pp. 465–7.

Ker, N. R., *The Medieval Libraries of Great Britain*, Royal Historical Society, London (2nd edn., 1964).

King, H. P., 'The Life and Acts of Robert de Chesney, Bishop of Lincoln, 1148–1166', University of London unpublished M.A. thesis, 1955.

Knowles, M. D., 'Archbishop Thomas Becket: A Character Study', *PBA* XXXV (1949).

—— *The Episcopal Colleagues of Archbishop Thomas Becket*, Cambridge (1951).

—— 'The Humanism of the Twelfth Century', in *The Historian and Character, and Other Essays*, Cambridge (1963), pp. 16–30.

—— and Hancock, R. N. *Medieval Religious Houses: England and Wales*, London (1963).

—— Anne J. Duggan, and C. N. L. Brooke, 'Henry II's Supplement to the Constitutions of Clarendon', *EHR* LXXXVII (1972), pp. 757–71.

Kuttner, S. and Rathbone, E., 'Anglo-Norman canonists of the twelfth century', *Traditio*, VII (1949–51), pp. 279–358.

Laurent, M.-H., *Codices Vaticani Latini*, Vatican City (1958).

Lawlor, H. J., 'Primate Ussher's Library before 1641', *Proceedings of the Royal Irish Academy*, 3rd Series, VI (1902), pp. 216–64.

Leclercq, J., 'La collection des lettres d'Yves de Chartres', *Revue Bénédictine*, LVI (1945–6), pp. 108–25.

Leland, J., *Collectanea de Rebus Britannicis*, ed. T. Hearne, London (1770).

L'Huillier, Dom A., *Saint Thomas de Cantorbéry*, 2 vols., Paris (1891–2).

Lyttelton, Lord G., *History of the Reign of Henry II*, 6 vols., London (1769–72).

Morey, Dom A. and Brooke, C. N. L., *Gilbert Foliot and his Letters*, Cambridge Studies in Medieval Life and Thought, Cambridge (1965).

Morris, J., *The Life and Martyrdom of St Thomas Becket*, London (2nd edn., 1885).

Mynors, R. A. B., *Durham Cathedral MSS to the End of the Twelfth Century*, Durham (1939).

Orme, M., 'A reconstruction of Robert of Cricklade's Vita et Miracula S. Thomae Cantuariensis', *Analecta Bollandiana* 84 (1966), pp. 379–98.

Oppenheimer, F., *The Legend of the Sainte Ampulle*, London (1954).

Pacaut, M., *Alexandre III: étude sur la conception du pouvoir pontifical dans sa pensée et dans son œuvre*, Paris (1956).

—— 'Les légats d'Alexandre III, 1159–81', *Rev. d'hist. ecclés.* (1955), pp. 821–33.

Poillin, P., *Gallia Christiana Nova*, Paris (2nd edn., 1870–9).

Poncelet, A., *Catalogus Codicum Hagiographicorum Latinorum Bibliothecae Vaticanae, Bibliotheca Hagiographica Latina*, II, Rome (1910).

—— *Catalogus Codicum Hagiographicorum Latinorum Bibliothecarum Romanarum*, Brussels (1909).

Poole, R. L., 'The Early Correspondence of John of Salisbury', *PBA* XI (1924), pp. 27–53.

—— 'Two documents concerning Archbishop Roger of York', *Speculum*, III (1928).

Pouzet, P., *L'Anglais Jean dit Bellesmains*, Lyons (1927).

Radford, L. B., *Thomas of London before his Consecration*, Cambridge Historical Essays, VII, Cambridge (1894).

Rathbone, E., 'The Influence of Bishops and of Members of Cathedral Bodies in the Intellectual Life of England, 1066–1216', University of London unpublished doctoral thesis, 1936.

Reuter, H., *Geschichte Alexanders des dritten und der Kirche zeiner Zeit*, 3 vols., Berlin (1845–64).

Robertson, J. C., *Becket, Archbishop of Canterbury*, London (1859).

Russell, J. C., *The Writers of Thirteenth-Century England*, London (1936).

Saltman, A., 'Two Early Collections of the Becket Correspondence and of other Contemporary Documents', *BIHR* XXII (1949), pp. 152–7.

—— *Theobald, Archbishop of Canterbury*, University of London Historical Studies, II, London (1956).

Schmeidler, B., 'Die Briefsammlung Froumunds von Tegernsee: Bemerkungen zur Beschaffenheit frühmittelalterlichen Briefsammlungen überhaupt', *Historisches Jahrbuch*, LXII–LXIX (1942–9), pp. 220–38.

Schramm, P. E., *A History of the English Coronation*, trans. G. Wickham Legg, Oxford (1937).

Simon, G. A., *Recherches . . . sur le séjour de S. Thomas Becket à Lisieux en 1170*, Paris (1926).

Smalley, B., *The Becket Conflict and the Schools*, Oxford (1973).

—— *The Study of the Bible in the Middle Ages*, Oxford (2nd edn., 1952).

—— 'A Commentary on the Hebraica by Herbert of Bosham', *Recherches de théologie ancienne et médiévale*, XVIII (1951), pp. 29–65.

Stapleton, T., *Tres Thomae*, Cologne (1612), pp. 24–80.

Stenton, D. M., 'Roger of Howden and Benedict', *EHR* LXVIII (1953).

Urry, W. G., *Canterbury under the Angevin Kings*, University of London Historical Studies, XIX, London (1967).

—— 'Two notes on Guernes de Pont-Sainte-Maxence: Vie de Saint Thomas', *Archaeologia Cantiana*, LXVII, pp. 92–7.

Voss, L., *Heinrich von Blois, Bischof von Winchester, 1129–71*, Berlin (1932).

Walberg, E., *La Tradition hagiographique de S. Thomas Becket avant la fin du XIIe siècle*, Paris (1929).

Webb, C. C. J., *John of Salisbury*, London (1932).

Wilson, C., 'The Early Biographers of Thomas Becket', *Modern Language Review*, XVIII (1923), pp. 491–9.

PART I

The Collections of Letters
Relating to the Becket Dispute

CHAPTER 1

The Becket Correspondence in the Context of Twelfth-century Collections of Letters

1. GENERAL INTRODUCTION

It is generally acknowledged by medieval scholars that the art of letter-writing reached a very high peak of attainment in the twelfth century, and prolific letter-writers like St Bernard of Clairvaux, Peter of Blois, and John of Salisbury can be cited as outstanding exponents of this achievement. Various factors help to explain this remarkable development, whose origins can be discerned in the previous century, and of particular relevance was the revival of literary studies in the great cathedral schools of north-west France, together with the acceptance of Classical models, especially in the school at Chartres. The revival of the ancient *cursus curiae Romanae* in the papal chancery at the end of the eleventh century was a further development of pervasive importance:[1] the curial style stimulated interest in rhythm and the flow of language, and its influence can be traced not only in the production of formal administrative documents in the ecclesiastical chanceries of Western Europe, but also in the private correspondence of men like John of Salisbury who were well acquainted with the curial practices. In fact many influences combined to produce that flowering of literary skill which characterized the twelfth-century renaissance: dialectic and the practice of textual commentary inculcated care and accuracy in the use of words; the study of ancient Latin literature also promoted an interest in style and rhythmic phrasing; and the papal and imperial chanceries set a very high standard both of verbal formulation and of script in the pro- duction of their legal and administrative documents.[2] Literary

---

[1] Cf. A. Giry, *Manuel de diplomatique*, Paris (1925), pp. 675–6.

[2] For a more general account of the literary achievements of the twelfth century, cf. Dom D. Knowles, 'The Humanism of the Twelfth Century', in *The Historian and Character, and Other Essays*, Cambridge (1963), pp. 16–30.

style was consciously cultivated by writers of all kinds, so that many writers whose skill might be considered deficient found it prudent to apologize to their readers for the inelegance and barbarity of heir compositions. Such seemingly modest disclaimers were often themselves merely literary conventions, but some were sincerely intended, reflecting perhaps the intractable subject-matter with which the writer was dealing. The author of the *Tractatus de legibus et consuetudinibus regni Anglie*, attributed to Ranulf Glanvill, and Richard FitzNeal, author of the *Dialogus de Scaccario*, each expressed regret for his stylistic shortcomings and explained that the technical nature of his subject-matter made good style impossible.[1] In both these instances the plea seems justified, but similar pleas were perhaps less seriously intended by biographers like Herbert of Bosham and the author of the *Magna Vita Sancti Hugonis*, each of whom claimed that his work had no literary merit.[2] Even self-conscious stylists like Arnulf of Lisieux, John of Salisbury, and Peter of Blois offered disarming apologies for their work,[3] though all three considered their letters worth preserving for posterity.

It is clear that, as part of a broader advance in literary and stylistic standards, the writing of letters had become an important and self-conscious genre of literary composition, providing a mode of expression for the culture and learning of their authors. But the letters have also their intrinsic importance in proportion to the significance and purpose of their subject-matter. Many letters therefore acquired a twofold value, derived respectively from their content and form. In the course of the twelfth century many authors, whether for didactic or for literary reasons, caused collections of their most important letters to be compiled and circulated. Several collections of letters of continental provenance suggest a practical rather than a literary purpose in their composition and

[1] G. D. G. Hall, ed., *Tractatus de legibus et consuetudinibus regni Anglie qui Glanvilla vocatur*, NMT, London (1965), p. 3; Richard FitzNeal, *Dialogus de Scaccario*, ed. C. Johnson, NMT (1950), pp. 2 and 5–6.

[2] Herbert of Bosham, *Vita Sancti Thomae, Mats.* III, p. 155; D. L. Douie and H. Farmer, edd., *Magna Vita Sancti Hugonis*, NMT, 2 vols. (1961–2), I, pp. 1–2.

[3] F. Barlow, ed., *The Letters of Arnulf of Lisieux*, Camden Third Series, LXI, London (1939), pp. 1–2; W. J. Millor and H. E. Butler, edd., revised by C. N. L. Brooke, *The Letters of John of Salisbury*, I: *The Early Letters*, NMT (1955), p. 177; J. A. Giles, ed., *Petri Blesensis epistolae*, Patres Ecclesiae Anglicanae, 2 vols., Oxford (1846–7), I, ep. 1.

dissemination, though in some instances their literary interest is considerable nevertheless. The collection of St Bernard's letters is a case in point:[1] this very important collection was made under Bernard's direction and distributed throughout the Cistercian Order and beyond. These letters were concerned principally with spiritual advice and exhortation, ranging widely over matters relating to monastic discipline and the spiritual life; and, though written in a distinctive and impressive style, they were doubtless recorded and circulated for their moral content rather than for their literary merit. Other collections of continental authorship include respectively the letters of Ivo of Chartres, Suger of St-Denis, Gerhoch of Reichersberg, St Hildegarde, Peter the Venerable, and Stephen of Tournai. Each of these compilations was made by the writer of the letters, or under the writer's direction; and the collections of Ivo, Peter the Venerable, and Stephen contain, with very few exceptions, the author's outgoing letters only. The collection of Ivo of Chartres was a conscious selection of letters of canonical or theological interest,[2] whereas Stephen's collection resulted in all probability from a rudimentary form of registration, the letters being preserved for record purposes simply; and there is no evidence to suggest that the collection was designed for general circulation.[3] The other collections mentioned above were compiled by members of religious orders, or at their instructions: St Bernard was a Cistercian, Peter the Venerable a Cluniac, Suger a Benedictine, Gerhoch a Canon Regular, and St Hildegarde a Benedictine nun. Bernard's collection of 235 letters was compiled by his own monks at Clairvaux and under his direction;[4] the basic collection of Peter the Venerable's letters was made at Cluny by his scribe Peter of Poitiers and Brother Nicholas;[5] Suger's collection is for the

[1] For the letters of Bernard of Clairvaux, cf. Pat. Lat. CLXXXII, cols. 67–662; in translation, Bruno Scott James, *The Letters of St Bernard of Clairvaux*, London (1953); and J. Leclercq, C. H. Talbot, and H. M. Rochais, edd., *Sancti Bernardi opera*, Rome, I (1957) proceeding. The basic collection of 235 letters was partly supervised by Bernard's secretary, Geoffrey of Auxerre; cf. James, ed. cit., p. xvii.

[2] Ivo of Chartres, *Epistolae*, Pat. Lat. CLXII, cols, 11–288; cf. J. Leclercq, 'La collection des lettres d'Yves de Chartres', *Revue Bénédictine*, LVI (1945–6), pp. 108–25.

[3] Stephen of Tournai, *Epistolae*, Pat. Lat. CCXI, cols. 309–562.

[4] Cf. J.-M. Canivez, *Dict. d'hist.* VIII, col. 610; a total of 534 letters of St Bernard have survived in various sources.

[5] G. Constable, ed., *The Letters of Peter the Venerable*, Harvard Historical Studies, no. 78, 2 vols., New York (1967), II, pp. 12–13.

greater part a register of his incoming letters, since only twenty-eight of the total 154 are from his own hand;[1] Gerhoch's short register of twenty-eight letters is largely his own record of his theological disputations with Eberhard of Bamberg;[2] and St Hildegarde's collection of 145 items contains a selection of her own correspondence, with the incoming letters and her replies to them arranged in chronological sequence.[3] Stylistic considerations seem not to have been a major factor in the making of any of these collections; and, with the exception of the letters of Ivo of Chartres and of St Bernard, none appears to have been generally known.[4]

But, in comparison with these continental collections, the several famous collections of English or Anglo-Norman provenance to be mentioned below present various contrasting emphases. The authors in question are Arnulf of Lisieux, John of Salisbury, Gilbert Foliot, Master David of London, Peter of Blois, Thomas Becket, and Alan of Tewkesbury. It is a point of interest that all these authors were known to one another, and their collections were all completed within a period of approximately twenty years following c. 1160; and Peter of Celle should also perhaps be associated with them in this context because of his close connections with John of Salisbury, though Peter lived outside the territorial limits of the Anglo-Norman empire.[5] But, despite these personal associations and a degree of interdependence in the contents of some of the collections, the several collections did not result from any single purpose, whether practical or literary. The collections of the letters of Arnulf of Lisieux, John of Salisbury, and Peter of Blois were, *qua* collections, assembled for their literary merits as much as for the subject-matter of the individual letters;

---

[1] Suger of St-Denis, *Epistolae*, Pat. Lat. CLXXXVI, cols. 1347–1440.

[2] Gerhoch of Reichersberg, *Epistolae*, Pat. Lat. CXCIII, cols. 489–618. A very substantial number of additional letters have been recovered from other sources: cf. P. Classen, *Gerhoch von Reichersberg*, Wiesbaden (1960), pp. 327–406.

[3] St Hildegard of Mont-St-Rupert, *Epistolae*, Pat. Lat. CXCVII, cols. 145–382; the replies usually appear with the heading: 'Responsio Hildigardis'.

[4] For further discussions on the origins and formation of twelfth-century letter-collections, cf. B. Schmeidler, 'Die Briefsammlung Froumunds von Tegernsee, Bemerkungen zur Beschaffenheit frühmittelalterlichen Briefsammlungen überhaupt', *Historiches Jahrbuch*, LXII–LXIX (1942–49), pp. 220–38; G. Constable, ed. cit., II, pp. 1–12, and *Letters and Letter-Collections*, Typologie des sources du moyen âge occidental, fasc. 17, Turnhout (1976), esp. pp. 31–8.

[5] Peter of Celle, *Epistolae*, Pat. Lat. CCII, cols. 401–636; for details of Peter's close and enduring friendship with John of Salisbury, cf. C. N. L. Brooke in Millor and Butler, ed. cit., pp. ix–xi and xix.

they were devised to serve as monuments of their authors' literary style, and were intended for circulation as literary models among the writers' friends and admirers.[1] In fact Peter of Blois made a selection of his best letters at the request of King Henry II.[2] On the other hand, there is no evidence in Peter of Celle's short collection to suggest the reasons for its particular selection of letters; and Master David's collection, which survives in a single manuscript, was probably not intended for publication at all, being perhaps simply a register made for record purposes only.[3] The large collection of Foliot's letters was apparently begun towards the end of his life, and abandoned on his death; this important compilation was very probably derived from a series of record files accumulated over the years by that eminent and powerful ecclesiastic; and, although Foliot was by no means without literary renown among his friends, it is unlikely that any merely literary purpose lay behind the compilation of his letters.[4] And this conclusion is certainly true of the Becket collections, which were begun by Becket himself, and continued after his death and brought to impressive completion by Alan of Tewkesbury.[5] The Becket collections were more didactic and propagandist in character than any of the other collections considered here, since they clearly aimed at preserving a full and accurate record of the archbishop's controversy with the king. In this respect, therefore, the Becket collections may be compared with Gerhoch's much smaller compilation among the continental works, and with the *Epistolae Cantuarienses* of the

[1] Arnulf presented the first recension of his letters to Giles de la Perche: cf. Arnulf of Lisieux, ep. 1; and it is very likely that John of Salisbury made the collection of his early letters for Peter of Celle: cf. Brooke in Millor and Butler, ed. cit., pp. x–xi.

[2] Cf. J. A. Giles, ed., *Petri Blesensis Epistolae*, Patres Ecclesiae Anglicanae, 2 vols., Oxford, I (1846), ep. 1.

[3] The MS is Vatican Latin MS 6024, fos. 140ra–154ra; for an analysis of the collection, cf. Z. N. Brooke, 'The Register of Master David of London and the part he played in the Becket Crisis', *Essays in History Presented to R. L. Poole*, Oxford (1927), pp. 227–45. Many of the letters are printed in F. Liverani, ed., *Spicilegium Liberianum*, Florence (1864).

[4] Cf. MB, *Foliot*, pp. 1–16.

[5] Alan of Tewkesbury's collection of the Becket correspondence will be discussed in Chapter 3, below. But it should also be noted that, in addition to the fragmentary collection mentioned in Hardy, II, p. 452 and printed in J. A. Giles, ed., *Herberti de Boseham Opera Omnia*, Patres Ecclesiae Anglicanae, 2 vols., Oxford (1845), II, pp. 313–36 (cf. Pat. Lat. CXC, cols. 1475–88), a new MS of a more complete collection of Alan's own letters has recently been discovered: cf. M. A. Harris, 'Alan of Tewkesbury and his letters, I–II', *Studia Monastica*, XVIII (1976), pp. 77–108 and 299–351.

later twelfth century, recording the vexatious disputes in which the Church of Canterbury was involved at that time.[1]

Much scholarly work has already been completed on the English and Anglo-Norman collections, and it is possible to trace in some cases the process of their compilation or expansion. This is particularly true of the Foliot collections and of the collections of letters of Arnulf of Lisieux and of John of Salisbury. Thus, it has been shown that the final collection of Arnulf's letters, containing 141 items, passed through two recensions: the first was completed in 1166 and sent to Giles de la Perche, while the second was finished by 1180; and when Arnulf undertook the task of gathering together his letters he clearly had inadequate records of his own, for he was constrained to write round to his friends to ask them to return any copies of his letters which they might have.[2] In contrast, John of Salisbury made two separate collections of his letters: the first contained a selection of letters which he wrote as secretary to Archbishop Theobald of Canterbury, together with letters written in his own name at that time, while the second contained letters written in his own name and further letters written on behalf of others from 1162 onwards; the first collection was probably compiled for Peter of Celle,[3] and the aim of the second was perhaps both literary and didactic, since most of these letters were written during the Becket dispute, and many of them are directly concerned with it, including 102 letters which were absorbed into the definitive collection of Becket correspondence assembled by Alan of Tewkesbury in the mid-1170s. The Foliot materials have recently been the subject of a complete and distinguished investigation,[4] while an exhaustive examination of the Becket collections in their origins, manuscript transmission, and later exploitation is the purpose of this present study. All these English and Anglo-Norman collections have their historical and their literary interest, but it is not easy in all cases to assess the extent of the influence in their own time; the only works whose manuscript survivals suggest an

[1] W. Stubbs, ed., *Chronicles and Memorials of the Reign of Richard I*, vol. II: *Epistolae Cantuarienses : The Letters of the Prior and Convent of Christ Church, Canterbury, 1187–1199*, RS 38, London (1865).

[2] Cf. Barlow, ed. cit., pp. lxi–lxiii.

[3] Cf. C. N. L. Brooke in Millor and Butler, ed. cit., p. xi. In contrast, R. L. Poole held the view that at least part of the collection was used as a formulary book: cf. his 'The Early Correspondence of John of Salisbury', *PBA* XI (1924–5), p. 27.

[4] Undertaken by Dom A. Morey and C. N. L. Brooke: MB, *Foliot*.

extensive circulation are those of Arnulf of Lisieux, Peter of Blois, and Thomas Becket,[1] though many of John of Salisbury's letters were widely known through their inclusion in the edition of Becket's letters by Alan of Tewkesbury.

2. THE MANUSCRIPT SOURCES OF THE BECKET CORRESPONDENCE

Many manuscripts survive from the medieval centuries containing substantial numbers of letters written by or to Thomas Becket, or dealing closely with his affairs; and this general corpus of letters together with related records and documents may be designated simply as the Becket correspondence. In the present study only those manuscripts which contain substantial sequences, that is to say containing intentional collections of his materials, have been considered, so that transcriptions of isolated letters or of groups of merely a few letters and charters have been omitted. Nevertheless, no less than twenty-four collections exist to provide a basis for this investigation. The most obvious source of the Becket correspond-ence is the Becket collections properly so-called, that is those collections which include almost exclusively material relating to the period of the well-known dispute in which the archbishop was involved with the king, and derived, in all probability and ulti-mately, from his archives. But, in addition to this source, large numbers of letters concerning the controversy, including letters of Becket himself, are found in a group of collections apparently dependent for this material on the Foliot archives; and still further smaller sequences of the Becket correspondence are found else-where.

Certain features of the collections of the Becket correspondence can be briefly described at the outset. Excepting only the smallest groups of letters, the collections record a two-way traffic of letters, including both incoming and outgoing letters, together with papal letters and copies of letters of other participants in the controversy: the English bishops, the papal legates, the kings of England and France, and so forth. The scope of the collections is narrowed in

---

[1] Arnulf's collection of letters has survived in 19 MSS: cf. Barlow, ed. cit., p. lxxi; and Hardy (II, pp. 553–5) cites more than 100 MSS for the letters of Peter of Blois: cf. E. S. Cohn, 'The Manuscript Evidence for the Letters of Peter of Blois', *EHR* XLI (1926), pp. 42–60. There are 24 MSS containing Becket correspondence.

time, with their concentration on the period of the controversy and its short-term aftermath. The manuscripts themselves are well-preserved copies, varying greatly in the number of letters which each contains. No immediate textual interdependence exists between a single pair of manuscripts, though family connections can be established in many instances. It is not possible to identify or reconstruct a common ancestor or archetype for all these collections, though a careful scrutiny of the survivors reveals a basic group of seventy-nine items including a selection of the most important letters of the controversy, which could possibly be derived from an early collection made by Becket himself or by one of his colleagues; but this early collection no longer survives and its traces are not found in every extant manuscript. The total number of items included in all these manuscripts is 678, of which 189 letters were sent out by Becket and 117 were received by him; there are 98 letters of Pope Alexander III, in addition to those addressed to Becket; 39 were written by various bishops, 16 by King Henry II and 125 by John of Salisbury; and the total is made up with 94 miscellaneous items. The largest single collection was compiled by Alan of Tewkesbury in the late 1170s, containing the very large number of 598 items in its most complete recension, and comprising the definitive edition of Becket's letters; this was in fact the largest collection of letters in the twelfth century. Although eight of the manuscript collections are composite, combining materials from more than one source, it is possible to group them in three principal categories: the Becket Group, the Alan of Tewkesbury edition in its various recensions, and the Foliot Group. The Becket Group can itself be sub-classified into three families: the Bodleian, Vatican, and Lambeth families. Each of these main groups and subsidiary families will be discussed in full detail in the chapters below, but to provide at this stage in the investigation a clear basis for cross-reference a few of the salient characteristics of each group or family are listed here.[1]

THE BECKET GROUP

The Becket Group comprises eleven manuscripts which vary in their contents from 35 to 368 items, and in time of transcription from the late twelfth to the fifteenth century; and though all these

---

[1] For a brief résumé of the chief MSS of the Becket correspondence, cf. MB, *Foliot*, pp. 17–19.

manuscripts do not belong to a single filiation or family, yet they are aptly considered together, since all derive ultimately from records kept in Becket's household. The eleven manuscripts can be divided into three families on a basis of similarities in their arrangements and texts, and all disclose a dependence on the early group of seventy-nine letters of high importance in the Becket dispute, already mentioned above.

(a) *The Bodleian Family*

Four fairly short collections compose the Bodleian Family, each of whose members include the whole or a part of the basic seventy-nine items, which may for convenience be described as the Bodleian Archetype. This family may in its origins record the earliest organization of Becket's correspondence, though the surviving manuscripts are later transcriptions and include additional material. The manuscript details are as follows:

Oxford Bodleian MS 509, fos. 1r–109v; s. xii; 84 letters. Nos. 80–4 possibly derive from Foliot sources.

Brit. Libr. Addit. MS 1777, fos. 1r–47v; s. xiv; 35 letters.

Oxford Bodl. MS Laud Misc. 666, fos. v–liii, 1–190v; s. xiv; 109 letters. Nos. 78–109 derive from Alan of Tewkesbury's Recension III.

Oxford Bodl. MS Rawlinson Q.f.8, fos. 1r–122r; s. xii; 88 letters. Nos. 1–22 and 85–8 possibly derive from the Ely archives; nos. 23–46 possibly derive from Foliot sources.

(b) *The Vatican Family*

The Vatican Family comprises five medium-length collections in medieval manuscripts together with one seventeenth-century transcription.[1] These collections derive from early attempts to organize the Becket correspondence, probably at Canterbury and before the canonization. The compilers used whatever material was at hand, including that in the Bodleian Archetype. In the list below, the Vatican and Royal MSS represent two different and independent attempts to arrange the material; the Laon and Harleian MSS, now incomplete, reflect the arrangement of the Vatican MS, while the St John's MS reproduces that of the Royal MS:

Vatican Latin MS 6024, fos. 72ra–139vb; s. xii; 267 letters (+11 duplicates). Nos. 1–27 and 265–77 possibly derive from Foliot sources.

[1] The transcription is Oxford Bodl. MS 278.

Brit. Libr. Royal MS 13.A.XIII; s. xii; 252 letters. Nos. 188–91 possibly derive from Foliot sources.

Bibl. de la Ville de Laon MS 337, fos. 29r–64v; s. xiii; 78 letters.

Brit. Libr. MS Harleian 215, fos. 1r–101r; s. xiv; 91 letters. Nos. 1–14 (= Rawl. 9–22) possibly derive from the Ely archives.

Oxford St John's College MS 15, fos. 182ra–251vb; s. xv; 252 letters.

(c) *The Lambeth Family*

There are only two members of the Lambeth Family, but they are both very large collections, combining derivatives from the Bodleian and Vatican archetypes with still further material from Becket sources. The manuscript details are these:

Lambeth Palace MS 136; s. xiii; 2+347 letters (+15 duplicates). Nos. 3–6 possibly derive from Foliot sources.

Oxford Bodl. MS 937, fos. 175r–446r (Bodl. B, II and III); s. xiii; 363 letters.

THE ALAN OF TEWKESBURY COMPILATION

A large and comprehensive collection of the Becket correspondence, intended as an authoritative record of the dispute and as a monument to the martyred archbishop, was drawn up by Alan of Tewkesbury; and this is the only collection under review on which there is any contemporary comment. The work was undertaken at Christ Church Canterbury, by Prior Alan, who returned from Sicily in 1174 and was promoted to the abbacy of Tewkesbury in 1186. The basis of the compilation was completed within the limits 1174–6. This was evidently a Canterbury composition, directly dependent on materials available at Canterbury in the years following Becket's canonization. It was later in construction than the collections of the Bodleian and Vatican Families, and was possibly contemporaneous with the archetypes on which the Lambeth Family was based. It will be seen that Alan used the existing collections in the composition of his own work, but his collection contains an additional 185 items unknown to any collections in the Becket Group, of which 96 were taken from John of Salisbury's correspondence, while the remaining 89 relate to the early period of the controversy, in the years 1163–6.

Alan's great work is devised in five books arranged chronologically and provided with two introductions: one by John of Salisbury and the other by Alan himself. The investigation of his sources is a complicated problem, and Alan comments in his introduction that he found the letters in various places arranged in files. Had there been a systematic register of Becket's letters in the archbishop's household, and had it been available in the mid-1170s, it is certain that Alan would have used it; but he did not do so, and there is no independent reference to its existence, so it was only by diligent scrutiny 'in variis locis' that Alan was able to gather together his impressive collection, taking the work of compilation far beyond the earlier anonymous efforts. On the other hand, the chronological systematization of the material obscures the sources on which he drew, except where some very significant correlations exist in the order and arrangement of the letters between Alan's sequences and the earlier Becket collections. Yet it is clear in the earliest surviving manuscript of Alan's collection that he had available to him a number of different versions of many of the letters, and that he took great pains to collate the variant readings in an attempt to produce as accurate a text as possible.

With the expenditure of much effort and scholarly labour Alan's compilation progressed through various stages and recensions. Three major manuscripts survive of his editions, representing with some variations of contents and texts the completed work; and there are in addition four abbreviations or derivative collections. To clarify discussion of these closely related manuscripts, the three major survivors may be designated AlanT(A), AlanT(B), and AlanT(C), in order of their probable derivation, though the completed manuscript of AlanT(B) incorporates material from the year 1220 and is thus later in its completed form than AlanT(C). The three manuscripts are these:

AlanT(A): Brit. Libr. MS Cotton Claudius B.II; s. xii; 598 letters.

AlanT(B): Vatican Latin MS 1220; fos. 54va–254vb; s. xiv; 535 letters.

AlanT(C): Cambridge Corpus Christi College MS 295; s. xii; 569 letters.

But it is easily shown that other versions existed, though they no longer survive, and that the author himself carried through a series of revisions or recensions. The marginal references in

AlanT(A), together with a consideration of the extant manuscripts, disclose at least three principal revisions, and these may be most simply identified as Recensions I, II, and III. Recension I can be reconstructed from the marginalia in AlanT(A): it contained about 535 letters, and its texts agreed with those in the Vatican Family. AlanT(A) was itself derived from this recension, but incorporated further material making up a total of 598 letters; and it was much corrected after its basic transcription by collation with Recension II as well as with the later letters of John of Salisbury. Recension II can also be largely deduced from the marginalia in AlanT(A), and contained 535 letters broadly in agreement with the earlier version, but with important variations of order and significant textual emendations. Of the surviving manuscripts, AlanT(B) appears most closely to resemble Recension II, while Recension III is represented by AlanT(C), which generally follows the order and readings of Recension II, but includes a further thirty-three letters, mostly taken directly from a copy of John of Salisbury's later correspondence; it has also added diplomatic details of dates and protocols omitted from the earlier versions. So it will be seen that these three principal revisions are reflected in the three surviving manuscripts. That Alan's collection enjoyed a wide circulation is suggested by the survival of five abbreviated versions, two derived from Recension II and three from Recension III. The manuscript abbreviations of Alan of Tewkesbury's collection are respectively:

Oxford Bodl. MS 937, fos. 11r–170v (Bodl. B,I); s. xiii; 222 letters. Nos. 1–24 are derived from an unknown source.

Cambridge Trinity Hall MS 24, fos. 113ra–192vb; s. xiii; 168 letters.

Brit. Libr. MS Arundel 219; s. xiv; 375 letters.

Paris Bibl. Nat. Latin MS 5320, fos. 61ra–191rb; s. xiii; 110 letters.

Oxford Bodl. MS Laud Misc. 666, fos. v–liii, 1r–190v; s. xiv; 109 letters. Nos. 1–77 derive from the Bodleian Archetype.

Recension I seems to have been almost immediately superseded. AlanT(A), which was perhaps an autograph copy kept by Alan himself, is its sole surviving derivative, and it records the emendation and correction of Recension I against a copy of Recension II. The production of the third recension cannot be exactly dated, but its earliest surviving derivative belongs to the early thirteenth century,[1] and Recension III was used by Roger of Crowland in the production of his jubilee version of the second *Quadrilogus*[2] which he completed in 1213 and presented to Stephen Langton in 1220. It survives in only two manuscripts:

Oxford Bodl. MS Cave e Mus. 133, fos. 7r–144va; s. xiv; 111 letters and extracts.

Paris Bibl. Nat. Latin MS 5372, fos. 1ra–126vb; s. xv; 240 letters and extracts (+1 duplicate).

THE FOLIOT GROUP

The Foliot Group is made up of two manuscripts, both preserved in the Bodleian Library and dating from the late twelfth century. The members of this group are clearly distinguished from the Becket collections by their contents and arrangement; and where the two groups have material in common there are textual variations between them. There can be little doubt that the Foliot collections were directly derived from records kept in the household of Gilbert Foliot, Bishop of London; and the Becket correspondence incorporated in them records an attempt to construct an epistolary account of the Becket dispute favourable to the position adopted by Foliot in that controversy. The members of the Foliot Group are in the following MSS:

Oxford Bodl. MS Cave e Mus. 249; s. xii; 447 letters.

Oxford Bodl. MS Douce 287, fos. 43ra–101vb; s. xii; 94 letters.

In addition, it is highly probable that portions of five of the collections cited above were ultimately derived from the Foliot archives.[3]

---

[1] Cf. AlanT(C) and pp. 134–7 below.

[2] The *Quadrilogus* is a composite life of Becket, composed of selections from the works of John of Salisbury, Alan of Tewkesbury, William of Canterbury, and Herbert of Bosham, and concluded with extracts from Benedict of Peterborough's *Passio*; it was compiled by Elias of Evesham in 1198–9. Two versions have survived, known respectively as the *First Quadrilogus* and the *Second Quadrilogus*, according to the order of their first printed editions rather than that of the versions on which they were based; thus, *Quadrilogus I* was the first to be printed but it is in fact a thirteenth-century interpolated version (cf. Johannes Philippi, ed., *Vita et Processus Sancti Thome Cantuariensis Martyris super Libertate Ecclesiastica*, Paris (1495); whereas *Quadrilogus II* was first printed later, but appears to be Elias's original composition (cf. C. Lupus, ed., *Epistolae et Vita Divi Thomae Martyris et Archiepiscopi Cantuariensis*, 2 vols., Brussels, (1682), I, pp. 4–172); cf. *Mats.* IV, pp. xix–xxii.

[3] From the Bodleian Family, cf. Bodl.A, 80–4, and Rawl. 23–46; from the Vatican Family, cf. Vat. 1–27 and 265–77, and Roy. 188–91; from the Lambeth Family, cf. Lamb. 3–6. It should be noted that in all these instances, the Foliot derivation forms a separate section, distinguished by a change of hand.

3. THE BECKET CORRESPONDENCE IN THE LIVES AND CHRONICLES

While the Becket correspondence in the Canterbury archives and elsewhere was being sorted and arranged as briefly outlined above, the earliest Lives or biographies of the martyr were also being composed; and it is not surprising to discover that two of the first biographers, William of Canterbury and Edward Grim, writing between 1172 and 1174, relied very heavily on these epistolary sources for their accounts of the career and death of the archbishop. And both of these writers had direct associations with Canterbury. William was present in Canterbury at the time of Becket's murder, but fled from the cathedral at the moment of the attack; later he was given the task of recording instances of miracles alleged to have taken place at the martyr's intercession, and there can be no doubt that he had access to a large supply of letters from which he made his own selection. Indeed William's version is in parts little more than a mosaic of citations from canonical sources favourable to Becket's stand in the jurisdictional conflict[1] together with nineteen letters, some of which are otherwise unknown. Textual collation reveals that William used material from the sources of the Becket Group of collections. In a similar way Edward Grim was working at Canterbury after the murder, and he also used these epistolary sources in his biography, though to a much lesser extent. But it was William FitzStephen, drawing on the Foliot sources in the same period, who made the most striking use of the letters. Although he preserves the full text of only seven short items, numerous brief extracts from the letters are scattered throughout his work, and from such extracts or citations no less than thirty-eight letters and documents can be identified. In contrast with these authors, Herbert of Bosham seems not to have used the correspondence very extensively in the preparation of his account of the life and death of the archbishop, but in personal association he was the closest of all these writers to the archbishop, and he wrote in the knowledge that Alan of Tewkesbury's compendium was already available; indeed on more than one occasion he refers his readers to it. On the other hand, Guernes de Pont-Sainte-Maxence composed rhymed

---

[1] For a detailed discussion of William's use of canonical materials, cf. C. Duggan, 'The Reception of Canon Law in England in the later-Twelfth Century', *Proceedings of the Second International Congress of Medieval Canon Law, Monumenta Iuris Canonici, Series C : Subsidia*, I, Vatican City (1965), pp. 359–90.

French versions of some of the letters in his metrical *Vie de Saint Thomas*. And, in an example already mentioned, when a jubilee version of the Life of Becket was required in the early thirteenth century, Roger of Crowland was commissioned to produce a work which combined the *Quadrilogus* with Alan of Tewkesbury's edition of Becket's letters; and it was this magnificent volume which was presented to Stephen Langton in 1220 on the occasion of the translation of the martyr's relics.[1]

The chroniclers likewise made good use of the correspondence. In the late twelfth century, both Ralph de Diceto[2] and Roger of Hoveden, and the author of the *Gesta Regis Henrici Secundi* who was possibly also Hovedon, drew heavily upon the letters for their accounts of the dispute. And in the thirteenth century, when Roger of Wendover rewrote the earlier history of England at the beginning of a history of his own time, he not only added quotations from seventeen letters to those contained in Diceto's *Ymagines Historiarum*, but he also corrected two of Diceto's texts. In fact the major narrative accounts of the Becket controversy in the chronicles of the late twelfth and early thirteenth centuries were almost all largely dependent on epistolary sources for their information. Gervase of Canterbury alone among the more important chroniclers preferred to use the Canterbury biographies as the basis of his account; but, like Herbert of Bosham, Gervase was writing in the knowledge that Alan's compilation would be available to his readers.

4. THE PRINTED EDITIONS OF THE BECKET CORRESPONDENCE

No less than seven editions of Becket correspondence were published between 1495 and 1875; and individual letters or short groups of letters have been printed in the great source collections such as Wilkins's *Concilia* and the *Thesaurus* of Martène and Durand. But so far no editor has had access to all the manuscripts now known, and until recently no editor had attempted to

---

[1] For a detailed discussion of the biographical use of Becket correspondence, see Chapter 6, below.

[2] A short study of the early chroniclers' use of Becket materials is in an advanced state of preparation and should appear shortly. Meanwhile, see C. Duggan and A. Duggan, 'Ralph de Diceto, Henry II and Becket', in B. Tierney and P. Linehan, edd., *Authority and Power: Studies in Medieval Law and Government . . . presented to Walter Ullmann*, Cambridge (in preparation).

work out systematically the relationship between the various manuscripts available to him.[1] Four of the editions contain very substantial numbers of letters, while three are comparatively short selections. The earliest large-scale edition was undertaken by Christian Lupus and published in Brussels in 1682. That edition was based on the seventeenth-century Vatican Latin MS 6027, which was itself copied from the fourteenth-century Vatican Latin MS 1220.[2] The latter was the transcription made at the request of Pope Gregory XI (1372–8), containing a copy of the *Second Quadrilogus* and the 1220 jubilee version of Alan of Tewkesbury's collection. The Lupus edition included 535 letters and documents; it is a fairly faithful rendering of the fourteenth-century Italian manuscript, except for the introduction of Classical spellings, some very minor rearrangements, and some misreadings and incorrect emendations. It was subsequently judged rather harshly by J. C. Robertson,[3] though most of its blemishes can be explained by its dependence on a single late and faulty manuscript. A later edition of 337 letters was published by Dom Brial in 1814 in Bouquet's *Recueil des historiens des Gaules et de la France*.[4] Dom Brial's edition is rather more defective than that of Lupus, though once more the faults can be attributed to the manuscripts used; the editor's sources were the Lupus edition itself and two imperfect French manuscripts: the thirteenth-century abbreviation of Alan of Tewkesbury's Recension III in the Bibl. Nat. Latin MS 5320, and an early fifteenth-century mutilated copy of Roger of Crowland's adaptation of the *Second Quadrilogus* in Bibl. Nat. Latin MS 5372.

Two of the major editions of the Becket correspondence were produced in England in the nineteenth century: the first was published by J. A. Giles at Oxford in 1845, and the second by J. C. Robertson in the Rolls Series in the years 1881–5.[5] The editing labours of Giles were enormous, his editions and translations including the complete works of Arnulf of Lisieux, John of Salisbury, Herbert of Bosham, and Peter of Blois, the letters of

---

[1] MB, *Foliot,* pp. 17–19.

[2] Lupus, ed. cit.   [3] Cf. *Mats.* V, p. xxi.

[4] M. Bouquet, *et al.*, edd., *Recueil des historiens des Gaules et de la France*, XVI, pp. 208–487.

[5] J. A. Giles, ed., *Epistolae Sancti Thomae Cantuariensis . . .*, 2 vols., Patres Ecclesiae Anglicanae, Oxford (1845), comprising 344 items; and J. C. Robertson and J. B. Sheppard, edd., *Materials for the History of Thomas Becket, Archbishop of Canterbury*, 7 vols., RS 67, London (1875–85), vols. V–VII, containing 808 items.

Foliot, and the Lives and letters of Becket.[1] His work on the Becket correspondence was an imposing undertaking, based on a wide knowledge of the relevant manuscripts; he had the great advantage of having access to almost all the known manuscripts of the Becket materials, as well as to printed editions, and his published list of sources is most impressive.[2] Nevertheless, his use of these rich resources is far from satisfactory, if modern standards of textual criticism are applied to it. The resulting edition has therefore serious faults which Canon Robertson did not hesitate to point out in his turn.[3] The arrangement of the correspondence according to the rank and status of the sender or recipient, with little attempt at a chronological sequence within the categories, is one obvious point of weakness. There is also the lack of a critical apparatus: the manuscripts and printed sources are listed at the end of the work, but there is little evidence of textual collation; the basic texts are not identified for the individual items, nor are the variant readings cited. It does indeed seem that he consulted many of the manuscripts listed, and some of the English manuscripts have an inscription in his handwriting on their flyleaves to record this. He claimed moreover that no letter was printed by him without being first collated with at least one manuscript exemplar;[4] but it seems that the extent of his use of the manuscripts in some instances was simply to check the total contents of the volume, and then to transcribe from it the texts of any new letters which he found there.[5] But Giles was a good Latinist; and, despite its faults, his edition was nevertheless much superior to the two earlier publications, though principally because the manuscripts on which he chiefly relied were much better than those available to his continental predecessors. It is not easy to make a balanced assessment of Giles's merits in this context, yet it is clear that he made a significant contribution in his day, and his work on any single source must be

---

[1] All these editions are found in the series Patres Ecclesiae Anglicanae (Oxford): *Arnulfi Lexoviensis episcopi epistolae* . . . (1844); *Herberti de Boseham Opera Omnia*, 2 vols. (1845); *Vita Sancti Thomae Cantuariensis Archiepiscopi et Martyris*, 2 vols. (1845); *Gilberti ex abbate Glocestriae episcopi primum Herefordiensis deinde Londoniensis epistolae*, 2 vols. (1846); *Petri Blesensis Epistolae*, 2 vols. (1846–7); *Johannis Saresberiensis . . . opera omnia*, 5 vols. (1848). All were reprinted by Migne in Pat. Lat.

[2] Cf. Giles, *EpST* II, pp. 311–13.

[3] Cf. *Mats.* V, pp. xvii–xviii.

[4] Cf. Giles, *EpST* I, p. x.

[5] Cf. his note in Oxford Bodl. MS Douce 287, fo. lv, and p. 159, n. 3 below.

judged in the context of his over-all massive editorial output. His work on the Becket correspondence is easily vulnerable to criticism, but it should be noted that in an important study on the Foliot materials Professor Brooke has seen him in a somewhat more favourable light.[1]

It was Robertson's declared intention to remedy the defects which he recognized in the editions by Lupus and Giles, and his strictures on both these scholars were severe.[2] In his own edition he adopted a chronological plan and used ten manuscripts in addition to the printed editions by Lupus, Brial, Giles, and Liverani. Thus, he used a much more restricted range of manuscripts than Giles, but he used them to better effect. The shortcomings in Robertson's work include misquotations of the manuscript press-marks and some confusion in the identification of the manuscript sources.[3] There is evidence that he sometimes accepted a printed text without reference to its manuscript source;[4] and he did not in fact use many important English manuscripts, of whose existence he must have known from Giles's work.[5] There is no suggestion in his introduction of his criteria of selection in deciding which manuscripts he would use as a basis for his edition, though it must be said that his choice resulted in fairly sound texts. The sources on which he primarily drew were the excellent copy of Alan of Tewkesbury's collection in the Brit. Libr. MS Cotton Claudius B. II, the Vatican Latin MS 1220, the two manuscripts of the Lambeth Family,[6] and two members of the Foliot Group,[7] together

[1] Cf. MB, *Foliot*, p. 22.

[2] *Mats.* V, p. 19.

[3] Thus, a list of sources is provided at the beginning of Vol. I of the letters (*Mats.* V, p. xxviii), citing 10 MSS including the letters of Arnulf of Lisieux, Herbert of Bosham, and Peter of Blois; Oxford Bodl. MS 937 (Robertson's MS O) is cited in this list as Bodl. MS 509 and Vatican Latin MS 6024 (Robertson V*) is cited as Vatican Latin MS 6027 in both the list and the introduction: cf. ibid., pp. xxiii and xxviii.

[4] No MS authority is cited for the following letters: 23, 24, 44, 46, 56, 57, 63, 65, 69–72, 79, 83, 104, 105, 185, 186, 211, 226, 235, 256, 294, 334, 374, 387, 392, 398, 416, 473, 484, 511, 525, 556, 685, 688 (here the lack of a MS authority is acknowledged), 737, 739, 742, 744–7, 749, 755, 773–5, 795, 796, 799, 806, and 808. The MS source cited for ep. 735 is incorrect.

[5] Among the more important MSS not used are: Cambridge Corpus Christi College MS 295, Oxford Bodl. MS 509, and Brit. Libr. MS Royal 13.A.XIII.

[6] Lambeth Palace MS 136 (Robertson A), and Oxford Bodl. MS 937 (Robertson O), wrongly cited by him as Bodl. MS 509.

[7] Oxford Bodl. MSS Cave e Mus. 249 (Robertson C), and Douce 287 (Robertson D).

with the editions by Lupus, Brial, and Giles. In sum, therefore, the merits of Robertson's edition are its comprehensiveness, the chronological arrangement of the contents, and the fair standard of accuracy of its texts. The editorial work is inconsistent in detail and consequently unreliable. Nevertheless, Robertson's edition is certainly the best produced so far.

Among the shorter editions of the Becket correspondence is the fragment published by the German printer John Philipps (Johannes Philippi) in Paris in 1495. This is in fact the earliest of all the printed editions and appears as an appendix to the *First Quadrilogus*. This sequence of sixty-seven items was printed from an exemplar which can no longer be traced, and its sources remain obscure; the text seems somewhat corrupt, but it is impossible now to determine how far this resulted from a faulty source. The edition adds nothing of interest in its readings, but it contains the texts of two letters not known elsewhere.[1] Also of little value is the short appendix of sixteen letters found at the end of the chapter on Becket in Thomas Stapleton's *Tres Thomae* published in Cologne in 1612; these texts also are drawn from an unknown manuscript source, containing in this instance letters of Peter of Blois and Peter of Celle, of which most are found in the manuscript collections of their letters. Lastly, a fragmentary edition of the Becket correspondence, derived from the Vatican Latin MS 6024, is found distributed among other material in Liverani's *Spicilegium Liberianum*, printed in Florence in 1864: in this case the texts are fairly accurate copies from their originals in the manuscript.[2]

In conclusion, it is worth noting certain small groups of letters included in the more well-known source collections. Wharton's *Anglia Sacra* provides the texts of four letters concerning Becket,[3] of which Robertson adopted three in his edition. Two of these

---

[1] Johannes Philippi, ed. cit.; the volume is unpaginated, but for an analysis of the epistolary supplement, cf. Table 7 below. The two new letters supplied by this edition are *Aggredimur rogare* (37), from Becket to Master Fulk of Reims, and *Gratias agimus* (46), from Becket to William of Norwich. The latter was printed by Giles, without MS authority (Giles, *EpST* I, ep. 143), and was then reprinted by Robertson (*Mats.* VII, ep. 688).

[2] F. Liverani, ed., *Spicilegium Liberianum*, Florence (1864). Mgr. Liverani printed 109 items from Vatican Latin MS 6024, largely taken from Master David's Register.

[3] Henry Wharton, ed., *Anglia Sacra*, 2 vols., London (1691), I, pp. 171–2, 628, and II, p. 177.

letters, namely *Vestrorum Eliensis* and *Ad questionem uestrorum*, were addressed to Nigel of Ely,[1] and were preserved in Richard of Ely's twelfth-century continuation of the *Historia Eliensis*; and the third letter is Alexander III's *Constitutus*, being the notification of St Anselm's canonization.[2] The two letters to Nigel are otherwise unknown, but there is no reason to doubt their authenticity. The fourth letter is a very curious forgery purporting to be Alexander III's condemnation and deposition of Becket in the first year of the Pope's pontificate, a clearly impossible date.[3] The spurious character of this letter was obvious to Wharton, and Robertson naturally ignored it. The Becket material in Wilkins' *Concilia*,[4] comprising thirty-two letters in addition to the Constitutions of Clarendon and including the spurious privilege *Preteritorum casus*,[5] was assembled from the following sources: Brit. Libr. MS Cotton Faustina B.I, fos. 2r–11va;[6] Canterbury Cathedral Register A, fos. 12r–15r;[7] Durham Cathedral MS B.IV.18, fo. 99v;[8] and Roger of Hoveden's *Chronica*,[9] with Matthew Paris's *Chronica Majora* providing the text of the Constitutions of

[1] Wharton, I, p. 628; cf. *Mats.* V, epp. 69 and 70.

[2] Wharton, II, p. 177, JL 10886; cf. *Mats.* V, ep. 23. Wharton's text was probably derived from Archbishop Courtney's Register, vol. 8, fo. 48v, preserved at Lambeth Palace. Cf. also Canterbury Register N, fo. 183r.

[3] Wharton, I, pp. 171–2; the document is dated: 'Romae ii die mensis Decembris et nostri apostolatus anno primo'; cf. Brit. Libr. MS Cotton Vitellius E.X, fo. 83r and Hardy, II, p. 319, no. 410.

[4] D. Wilkins, ed., *Concilia Magnae Britanniae et Hiberniae*, London (1737), I, pp. 435–75.

[5] Ibid., pp. 437–8; this piece is taken from Archbishop Courtney's Register, vol. 8, fo. 46v; cf. *Mats.* VI, ep. 555. For a full discussion of this forgery, cf. C. R. Cheney, 'Magna Carta Beati Thome: another Canterbury forgery', *BIHR* XXXVI (1963), pp. 1–26.

[6] From Faustina B. I, in Wilkins, *Concilia*, I, pp. 449–75; *Que uestro pater, Mirandum, Oportuerat uos, Licet commendabiles, Quam iustis, Ab humane pietatis, Vestro apostolatui, Vestre placuit* and *Redolet Anglia* (cf. *Mats.* V, epp. 205 and 224; VII, epp. 700, 701, 723, 734, 740, 736, and 785). The MS is analysed in Appendix VIII below.

[7] Wilkins, *Concilia*, I, pp. 446–61: *In apostolice sedis, Ex commissi nobis* (Wilkins: *vobis*), *Quoniam ad audientiam, Oportuerat uos*, and *Quamuis cure* (*Mats.* epp. 170, 632, 633, 700, and 720).

[8] Wilkins, *Concilia*, I, pp. 459–65: *Illius dignitatis* and *Licet commendabiles* (*Mats.* epp. 169 and 701).

[9] Ibid., pp. 439–74: *Desiderio, Ad audientiam, Fratres mei, Etsi circa nos, Quod circa ea, Mandatum uestrum, Loqui de Deo, Si littere nostre, Satis superque, Quam paterne, Que uestro, Mirandum, Vestram pater, Excessus uestros, Vestram non debet, Ad sanctorum, Magnificentie tue, Licet commendabiles, Ab humane pietatis, Vestro apostolatui, Vestre placuit, Inter scribendum* and *Fraternitati uestre* (*Mats.* epp. 154, 74, 198, 486, 106, 108, 603, 219, 195, 423, 205, 224, 204, 479, 488, 550, 258, 701, 734, 740, 736, 735, and 753).

Clarendon.[1] Martène and Durand's *Thesaurus* provides the texts of seven letters otherwise unknown, all relating to events after Becket's death;[2] and it also supplies a version of John of Salisbury's *Ex insperato* which is found appended to Master Everard's *Passio Sancti Thome* in several French manuscripts.[3] Two of these seven letters were printed from a manuscript from Mont-St-Michel,[4] four from a Grandmont manuscript,[5] and one from a manuscript belonging to the Cistercian house of Fontaines.[6] And all seven were reprinted by Robertson from Martene without reference to the manuscripts. The Grandmont letters, however, purporting to be the correspondence between Petrus Bernardi, fifth Prior of Grandmont (wrongly identified with Bernard de Corilo), and William de Trahinac after the murder of Becket, have been branded by Dom J. Becquet as late concoctions.[7] Certainly, their texts give rise to considerable doubt. Apart from stylistic peculiarities, the first letter (*Anglorum regis*) wrongly claims that its author was the associate of Simon of Mont-Dieu, thereby confusing Petrus Bernardi and Bernard de Corilo; the second (*Cruento reuerendi*) repeats the confusion in the alleged reply of Prior William de Trahinac; and the third (*Ut innumerabilia*), addressed to Henry II, refers to the dead archbishop as 'Reverendus ille pater Becket', a highly unusual form for *c*. 1171. Dom Becquet is wise to regard them as spurious.

---

[1] Ibid., pp. 435–9.

[2] E. Martène and U. Durand, edd., *Thesaurus novus anecdotorum*, 5 vols., Paris (1717), I, pp. 559–70: *Ob reuerentiam, Cum testimonium, Anglorum regis, Cruento reuerendi, Item domine, Ut innumerabilia*, and *In apostolice sedis* (*Mats*. VII, epp. 739, 742, 744, 747, 746, 745, and 755).

[3] Ibid., III, pp. 1746–50: *Ex insperato* (*Mats*. VII, ep. 748). The letter here has an incorrect heading: 'Epistola prioris Sancti Trinitatis Cantuariae ad episcopum Wintoniensem de passione Sancti Thomae martyris'.

[4] Ibid., I, p. 559: 'Ex MS Sancti Michaelis in Periculo Maris': *Ob reuerentiam* and *Cum testimonio*.

[5] Ibid., I, pp. 560–2: 'Ex MS. Grandimontensi': *Anglorum regis, Cruento reuerendi, Item domine*, and *Ut innumerabilia*.

[6] Ibid., pp. 569–72: 'Ex MS. Beatae Mariae de Fontanis': *In apostolice sedis*.

[7] *Scriptores Ordinis Grandimontensis*, Corpus Christianorum, Continuatio Mediaevalis, VIII (1968), ed. J. Becquet, p. 162: 'falsorii cuiusdam Grandimontensis saeculi tertii decimi uel quarti decimi opus uidentur.'

CHAPTER 2

The Becket Group of Collections

As briefly explained in the preceding chapter, one group of eleven interrelated collections can be distinguished from the others as having an especially close connection with the archives in Becket's household. Indeed so close is this relationship that their earliest origins may have existed in the first compilations made in his own lifetime or in his *familia* soon after the martyrdom. In this sense they can be differentiated from those collections which were dependent on the Foliot archives, and from the large compilation by Alan of Tewkesbury, which assimilated many letters written by John of Salisbury. For these reasons the eleven collections can be appropriately named the Becket Group. All but the smallest members of this group are composite works, and it is difficult in some cases to identify precisely the various elements which were combined in their composition. The collections vary in length from 35 to 368 letters, in time of transcription from the late twelfth to the mid-fifteenth century, and in present location from the British Library to the Vatican Library. The larger number of the letters which they contain were either issued by Becket or received by him, but the longer collections also contain a notable selection of letters written on his behalf by lay and ecclesiastical supporters in England and in France, as well as the major appeals by Gilbert Foliot and the English bishops, and most of the surviving papal letters concerning the controversy.

There is significant agreement in contents, order, and texts between the various members of the group, but there are also significant variations; and all but the smallest collection, which is itself merely a fragment, have items and readings peculiar to themselves. Nevertheless, an ultimate common source, or more probably sources, must be assumed to explain the agreements which occur. Three subdivisions of the group, containing respectively 4, 5, and 2 collections, can be differentiated and called the Bodleian, Vatican, and Lambeth Families, the name in each case being adopted from the present location of its most primitive member.

1. THE BODLEIAN FAMILY

The four smallest Becket collections comprise the Bodleian Family, now found in the Oxford Bodl. MS 509, the Brit. Libr. MS Addit. 1777, and the Oxford Bodl. MSS Laud Misc. 666 and Rawlinson Q.f.8; and they contain 84, 35, 109, and 88 letters respectively.[1] All are dependent to some extent on the Bodleian Archetype, but with the exception of the Addit. MS each incorporates further material from other sources.

A. THE BODLEIAN COLLECTION

The earliest surviving member of this family is the Oxford Bodl. MS 509,[2] a carefully written manuscript dating from the late twelfth century. The volume in which it is contained is composed of four sections, of which the letter collection is the third.[3] The first section is a transcription of miscellaneous materials relating to Becket, including John of Salisbury's *Prologus* and *Vita et Passio Sancti Thome*[4] and two poems concerning Becket by the otherwise unknown William, Chanter of Combe;[5] a couplet *Annus millenus . . . Thomas*[6] is inserted after the *explicit* of John of Salisbury's

---

[1] For full details of these MSS see Chapter 1, p. 11 above. The Rawlinson MS contains 88 letters, of which 38 are derived from the Bodleian Archetype; for simplicity the full collection is discussed in this chapter.

[2] $7\frac{1}{2} \times 6$ ins.; 170 fos; cf. Summary Catalogue of Western Manuscripts in the Bodleian Library, no. 2672. The volume was donated to the Bodleian Library in 1605 by Dr William Cotton, Bishop of Exeter.

[3] Bodl. 509 is divided as follows: Part I, fos. 1r–14v: John of Salisbury's *Prologus* and *Vita*, fos. 1r–12r; *Annus millenus*, fo. 12r; William of Combe's two poems, fos. 12r–14v; the *Reuelatio Domini* and two further verses, fo. 14v. Part II, fos. 15r–20r: an anonymous *Passio Sancti Thome* (Anon. IV). Part III, fos. 21r–109v: *Prologus* and *Passio* by Maurinus, fos. 21r–32r; two hymns in honour of Becket, fos. 32v–33r; table of contents, fos. 33va–34va; 84 letters, fos. 34vb–109v; 110 blank. Part IV, fos. 111r–170v: Benedict of Peterborough's *Miracula Sancti Thome*, fos. 111r–130r; the *Liber Cherubim*, fos. 130r–133r; assorted lections and tracts, fos. 134r–170r. For the letters, cf. Appendix I below.

[4] *Mats.* II, pp. 301–22.

[5] Printed by J. A. Giles for the Caxton Society in *Anecdota Bedae, Lanfranci et Aliorum*, London (1851), pp. 191–6. Nothing is known about the author.

[6] This couplet forms the first two lines of a poem on Becket's death ascribed by Giraldus Cambrensis (*Opera*, VII, p. 56) to William Turbe, Bishop of Norwich (1146–74). The same ascription is made in a late MS of Gervase of Canterbury's *Chronica*: cf. ibid., n. 6, 'Unde felicis memoriae Willelmus Torbo Nordwicensis episcopus, literis admodum eruditus, volens beati martyris Thomae annum passionis versifice designare, ait:
    'Annus millenus centenus septuagenus,
    Primus erat primas cum ruit ense Thomas. [*cont.*]

Vita, and the *Reuelatio Domini*[1] and two further verses are added on fo. 14v.[2] The second section, comprising one gathering of six folios only, contains the well-known but anonymous *Passio Sancti Thome*,[3] while the fourth includes a fragment of Benedict of Peterborough's *Miracula Sancti Thome*[4] and the *Liber Cherubim* attributed to Alan de L'Isle.[5] The part containing the letters has ten gatherings of eight leaves each, with each gathering numbered on its final folio verso; it opens with a rhymed *Vita et Passio Sancti Thome*[6] by the monk Maurinus and a hymn and sequence by the same author.[7] The collection of letters is immediately preceded by a full table of contents, written in double columns with red initials and numbers, containing the the headings to the individual letters exactly as they occur rubricated in the body of the collection. In the collection itself the initials and numbers as well as the headings are rubricated, and the only break in transcription occurs after item 79 on fo. 102v, at which point there is a gap of seven lines followed by the concluding five letters. Although found in the index, these final items constitute an addition to the main collection which constitutes the Bodleian Archetype. The arrangement of the archetypal material is broadly chronological, covering the period 1164–70, and its final letter is also the latest in date of issue, being the *Quam iustis* which Becket sent to Alexander III soon after his return to England in December 1170, describing his reception.[8] The absence of the letters of canonization suggests that Bodl. MS

---

[1] Another well-known text: cf. Gervase, *Chronica*, II, p. 283; Grim, *VST, Mats.* II, p. 413; FitzStephen, ibid., III, p. 83. It also occurs in AlanT(A), I.184.
[2] Cf. Giles, *Anecdota Bedae*, p. 196.
[3] Giles, *VST* II, pp. 137–45; cf. *Mats.* IV, pp. 186–95, where it appears as Anonymous IV.
[4] *Mats.* II, pp. 21–72; the MS ends abruptly with the words 'siccam inuenit' in Book II, *cap.* xxi.
[5] *De sex alis cherubim*, lacking the prologue and beginning 'Prima ala', Pat. Lat. CCX, pp. 265–80; cf. M. Jacquin, 'Alain de Lille', *Dict. d'hist.*, I, pp. 1229–1304.
[6] Giles, *Anecdota Bedae*, pp. 170–87.
[7] Ibid., pp. 187–91.   [8] Bodl. 79, *Mats. VII*, ep. 723.

Quinta dies Natalis erat. Flos orbis ab orbe.
Vellitur, et fructus incipit esse poli.'
For a fuller version, cf. Cambridge Corpus Christi College MS 495, fo. 136r. The couplet seems to have had wide currency in the twelfth century: cf. Hoveden, *Chronica*, II, p. 17; FitzStephen, *VST, Mats.* III, p. 154. The couplet also occurs in Cambridge Corpus Christi College MS 130, fo. 222r; Dijon, Bibl. Municipale MS 219, fo. 3; Oxford Bodl. MS Douce 287, fo. 36vb; and the quatrain occurs in Évreux, Bibl. Municipale MS Lat. 7, fo. 83r.

509 derives from an early source, certainly not later than 1172 and possibly completed just before or shortly after Becket's death. Content, character, and handling all point to an archival source close to Becket himself.

The collection consists principally of letters sent by Becket or received by him, to which are added papal letters relating to the controversy: fifty-four of the seventy-nine items were written or received by Thomas;[1] and twenty-two further letters were issued by Alexander III in addition to those which he addressed to Thomas.[2] Only three items do not fit into either category: namely two letters of Henry II, the first was addressed to a cardinal and the second to the Young King,[3] and a petition sent to the Pope on Becket's behalf by Louis VII.[4] The Becket correspondence proper is arranged in four chronological sequences: nos. 1–11, written *c.* June 1165–August 1166;[5] 13–26, dating predominantly from 1167; 27–31, written in 1169–70; and 59–65 and 79 composed after the reconciliation at Fréteval on 22 July 1170. Apart from those addressed to Thomas personally, the papal letters are nearly all commissions to legates and other papal representatives,[6] encyclical letters to the English and Norman bishops,[7] or letters to the king.[8] None of the letters was of a private nature, so it is very likely that copies were available to members of Becket's *familia*; and it is probable that most of them passed through the archbishop's own hands. Throughout his exile Becket was kept well informed of the correspondence between the Pope and his adversaries. His informants were either friends in Normandy, like Nicholas of Mont-St-Jacques near Rouen, who had access to the court of the Empress Matilda,[9]

---

[1] Cf. Appendix I below. From Becket, 38 letters: 1–14, 16–31, 59–65, and 79; to him, 16 letters: 15, 35, 36, 45, 47, 49, 54, 55, 67, and 70–6.

[2] Papal letters (exclusive of those addressed to Becket himself): 32, 33, 37–44, 46, 48, 50–3, 56, 58, 68, 69, 77, and 78.

[3] *Super his que* (34) and *Sciatis quod* (66).

[4] *Tenemus firmiter* (57).

[5] No. 12, Becket's appeal to Robert of Leicester written shortly after his flight in November 1164, is misplaced.

[6] Nos. 32, 33, 37, 41, 42, and 56.

[7] Nos. 38–40, 43, 44, 46, 48, 68, 69, 77, and 78.

[8] Nos. 50–3 and 58.

[9] Nicholas of Mont-St-Jacques was a friend and correspondent of Becket and John of Salisbury throughout the exile. It was he who in December 1164 tried to gain the Empress Matilda's intercession in favour of Becket (*Mats.* V, pp. 146–7); and in contrast with many of the exiles, he enthusiastically applauded the Vézelay excommunications in 1166 (*ibid.*, ep. 209). Four of his letters to

or agents and supporters at the Curia,[1] and perhaps his most important informant was John of Salisbury, in exile at Reims with his friend Peter of Celle, Abbot of St-Rémi.[2] It was in any case customary for copies of the more important papal letters and others of like importance to be passed round to the interested parties.[3]

From the point of view of chronology, the most weighty emphasis is on the final year of the exile, since slightly less than half the total contents date from late 1169 or 1170,[4] from which it seems possible that the greater number of letters were derived from a file of incoming and outgoing letters compiled towards the end of the exile, to which was added a selection of the more significant early correspondence, including three of Becket's most important letters to the king.[5] Thomas's own letters are mostly arranged in correct chronological order in three sequences,[6] beginning with *Loqui de Deo* issued in early 1166, and ending with *Quam iustis*, the last surviving letter from his hand; and the incoming letters also are arranged in their proper sequence. But the papal letters are less correctly organized: one group dating from 1170 (32, 33, and 37–

---

[1] A succession of clerks represented Becket at the Curia: Master Hervey, from September 1163 until his death in ?late 1166 (cf. *Mats.* V, pp. 49, 53, 81, 94, 99, 121, 180, 439, and 447); Gunther of Winchester, in 1164 (cf. *Mats.* V, pp. 81 and 83); Alexander Llewelyn (Walensis), from late 1167 to early 1170 (cf. *Mats.* VI, p. 315, VII, pp. 181 and 219); John, from early 1167 to early 1170 (cf. *Mats.* VI, pp. 150, 315, and VII, p. 219); Hugotio of Rome in 1169 (cf. *Mats.* VII, p. 181); Reginald Lombardus in 1169 (cf. *Mats.* VII, p. 238); and a number of cardinals were very favourable to the archbishop's cause, including Cardinal Albert of St Laurence in Lucina, later Pope Gregory VIII, Bernard of Porto, Boso of St Pudentiana, Henry of Pisa, Humbald of Ostia, Hyacinth of St Mary in Cosmedin, later Pope Celestine III, and Manfred of St George, as well as the notary Gratian, nephew of Eugenius III, and Master Vivian.

[2] John acted as a collector and disseminator of news and of the relevant letters: cf. *Mats.* V, pp. 381, 382–4, 432, 433, and 439; VI, pp. 13, 63, 68–9, 71, 119, 191, 217, 220, 319, 320–1, 323, 341, 370, 393, 417, 482, and 497; VII, pp. 32, 231, and 233.

[3] Copies of many letters also passed through Becket's hands: cf. *Mats.* V, pp. 318, 339–41, and 345; VI, pp. 315 and 316; VII, pp. 51, 179, 259, 262, 264, 318–19, 353, and 410.

[4] Nos. 27–30, 32, 33, 37–42, 52, 53, and 59–79.

[5] *Loqui de Deo* (1), *Desiderio desideraui* (2) and *Expectans expectaui* (5); cf. *Mats.* V. epp. 152, 154, and 153.

[6] Cf. p. 27 above.

Becket (ibid., epp. 76 and 209; VI, epp. 254 and 284) survive among the Becket letters, together with 1 from Becket to him (ibid., V, ep. 184), 3 from John of Salisbury (ibid., epp. 216 and 230; VI, ep. 327), and 1 from Herbert of Bosham (ibid., ep. 271).

42) precedes a large miscellaneous group (43–56 and 58), containing material ranging from 1164[1] to January 1170;[2] and this in turn is followed by further letters issued in 1170 (68, 69, 77, and 78). A possible explanation of this arrangement is that the collection was formed by the integration of three or more chronologically arranged files of letters, of which one contained letters dispatched by Becket, another the letters which he himself received, especially during the last year of the controversy, and a third some relevant papal rescripts. If this suggestion is correct, the compiler was not content simply to transcribe the letters in their original groupings, but attempted to knit them together in chronological sequence, and in so doing misplaced the second group of papal letters. But it is also possible that the papal letters reached him in separate components. Full protocols are preserved in the first half of the collection only;[3] and thereafter, with two exceptions,[4] they are omitted, although the dates of some of the papal documents are given.[5] The group of early Becket letters is thus the most formally arranged of the component sources, which suggests perhaps the existence of an earlier, carefully composed, collection on which the extant manuscript depended.

There are strong reasons for concluding that the Bodleian Archetype (though not of course this particular version of it) derived directly from Becket's own archives. Content, arrangement into 'Becket' and 'papal' sections, and chronological sequence suggest an orderly if primitive system of record-keeping; and the two references to multiple copies of specific items reinforce this impression. The archetype contains three different forms of the papal letter *Nouerit industria* (nos. 38–40),[6] which, in February 1170, ordered the promulgation of an interdict throughout Henry II's territories, if an authentic peace were not secured, addressed respectively to the king's French prelates,[7] to Roger of York and his

---

[1] *Etsi pro animi* (49) was dated 5 March 1164.

[2] *Dilecti filii nostri* (53) was probably dated 19 January 1170.

[3] Cf. nos. 1, 3–16, 18, 19, 21, and 23–31.

[4] Slightly abbreviated protocols are given for nos. 39 and 40: these are different versions of *Nouerit industria uestra*, addressed respectively to the Province of York and the Archbishop of Tours.

[5] Nos. 32, 38, 39, 44, 49, 51, 52, 56, 68, and 69.

[6] *Mats.* VII, epp. 629, 630, and 634.

[7] In ibid., ep. 629, the letter is addressed to the Canterbury bishops; but the Bodleian address to Henry II's French prelates seems to be the more accurate: cf. below, p. 31.

ecclesiastical subjects, and to the Archbishop of Tours. The third version, however, is followed by the record that exactly similar letters were directed to the other metropolitans in Henry's French dominions:

> [fo. 81r]   In eundem modum: Bituricensi archiepiscopo et suffraganeis eius, necnon aliis ecclesiarum prelatis.
> In eundem modum: Burdegal(ensi) archiepiscopo, apostolice sedis legato et suffraganeis eius.
> In eundem modum: Auxitano archiepiscopo et suffraganeis eius.
> In eundem modum: uniuersis episcopis et ceteris ecclesiarum prelatis per Rotomagensem prouinciam constitutis.

And the papal censure of clerics involved in the coronation of the Young King is similarly treated. Two texts of *Quamuis cure* are given in this instance (nos. 77 and 78),[1] followed by the note:

> [fo. 100v]   In eundem modum: Eboracensi archiepiscopo, preterquam de relaxatione suspensionis quam sibi reseruat dominus papa.

These examples indicate the existence of regular archival procedure; and both record the registration or 'filing' of letters which were never, in the event, issued to their intended recipients: in both cases, rapidly changing circumstances rendered them redundant before they could be put into force. The interdict was never promulgated, and *Quamuis cure* arrived too late for use by Becket. It is also highly unlikely that *Gratias habemus* (no. 23), addressed to William of Pavia in mid-1167, was ever sent to its intended recipient. It is the second of two draft replies to a missive from the Cardinal Legate, which Becket submitted to John of Salisbury's diplomatic judgement.[2] Both versions were in the event condemned by John and presumably abandoned. The preservation of this rejected draft in the Bodleian Archetype is a further argument in favour of its archival derivation.

Its record of the *Nouerit industria* letters is equally significant and

---

[1] *Mats.* VII, epp. 720 and 721.

[2] For the first draft, cf. *Mats.* VI, ep. 312: *Litteras celsitudinis.* This letter only entered the textual tradition of Becket's letters at a comparatively late stage; it first appears in the Lambeth Addition: cf. Appendix IV, no. 306. For John of Salisbury's comment on both drafts, cf. *Mats.* VI, epp. 317 and 318.

valuable, though from a different point of view. There is an inherent contradiction between the address and text of version A of the letter (ep. 629) as it occurs in most manuscript sources and in the *Materials*. Canon Robertson, mainly relying on Alan of Tewkesbury's collection, provided the letter with an address to the bishops of Canterbury province, although the text seems to refer only to France. It orders the observance of an interdict to be pronounced by Rotrou of Rouen and Bernard of Nevers in Henry's territories 'citra mare' (on this side of the sea): that is, in France; and such phrasing seems wholly inappropriate to English recipients. Although the legates were instructed to follow the king to England,[1] there was no suggestion that their authority extended to the Provinces of Canterbury and York. On the contrary, the Pope's original commission ordered an interdict on Henry's continental lands only;[2] this was reiterated in a more urgently phrased later mandate, which referred to the sending of appropriate letters to bishops in Henry's French lands;[3] and Becket's own letter to Bernard of Nevers urged the immediate pronouncement of an interdict on Henry's cismarine lands.[4] It was the exclusion of England from the legates' jurisdiction which explains the awkward formulation of version B (ep. 630), which cites the French interdict in the arenga, but orders York and Durham to promulgate the interdict which the Archbishop of Canterbury would issue in his own Province. The pronouncement of an interdict in England was dependent on Becket's own initiative as legate. Hence it is highly unlikely that version A was intended for English recipients. The erroneous heading, which Robertson understandably accepted from his manuscript authorities, was derived from a faulty textual tradition in which the originally accurate reading of the Bodleian Archetype (preserved in Bodl. A, 38) *omnibus episcopis terre regis Anglorum in regno Francorum* was transformed, first into ... *in regno Anglorum*,[5] then into ... *in Anglia*[6], and finally into *omnibus episcopis Cantuariensis prouincie*[7] or a variant of that form.[8] On this

---

[1] Ibid., VII, p. 210.
[2] Ibid., p. 200.
[3] Ibid., p. 211.
[4] Ibid., p. 251.
[5] Rawl. 77.
[6] Bodl. B, II. 38.
[7] AlanT (A) and (C), V. 7, and Laud 38.
[8] AlanT(B), V.7: ... *Cantie*(!) *prouincie*.

evidence, MS Bodl. 509 seems to preserve the soundest version of an (Archetype A) assembled from Becket's own records.

The presence of the *Quamuis cure* texts in the Archetype is also highly significant. These particular papal letters, censuring certain English bishops (and others) for their participation in the illicit coronation, were in fact the second set of such letters issued by the papal Curia. Alexander III had issued *Oportuerat uos* and *Licet commendabiles* on 16 September 1170: the one suspending the Bishops of Exeter, Chester, Rochester, St Asaph, and Llandaff, and excommunicating London and Salisbury; the other suspending Roger of York and Hugh of Durham.[1] To these Becket replied, probably in late October, requesting adjusted letters which should suppress all mention of the customs, the king, and his son, and leave him free to issue sentences at his own discretion according to circumstances.[2] The two versions of the letters were duly issued on 24 November in compliance with Becket's request, but they were too late. Becket left France on 1 December, having sent the first set of papal sentences ahead, and *Quamuis cure* can only have reached him (if indeed they did reach him), in the very last days of his life. They mark the final accession to his archives and provide the *terminus ad quem* for the construction of the Bodleian Archetype. This archetype can only have been completed either just before or, more probably, very soon after Becket's murder, and drew exclusively on his records.

There is another feature of Archetype A which deserves comment. Full protocols are given in the first half of the collection only[3] and are omitted thereafter. This may suggest that the Becket

---

[1] *Mats.* VII, epp. 700 and 701.

[2] Ibid., ep. 716: *Ex quo, pater.*

[3] Full protocols occur in nos. 1, 3–16, 18, 19, 21, and 23–31; cf. for example, no. 1 (*Loqui de Deo, Mats.* V, ep. 152, fo. 34vb): 'Reuerentissimo domino suo H(enrico) Dei gratia illustri Anglorum regi, duci Norm(annorum), comiti Andeg(auie) et duci Aquita(nie)', Thomas eadem gratia Cantuariensis ecclesie humilis minister, salutem et per omnia bene facere'. Only four items appear without full protocols in this section (to no. 31): no. 2 (*Desiderio desideraui, Mats.* V, ep. 154, fo. 35v) has, in place of the usual protocol, the note: 'Hec sunt uerba domini Cant(uariensis) ad regem Anglorum.' Since this is the letter thought to have been received by Henry II at Chinon in May 1166, it may well be that the text was originally intended for oral delivery by Becket if an interview with Henry had been arranged; no. 17 (*Si grandia, Mats.* VI, ep. 269, fo. 63r) and nos. 20 and 22 (*Inter optimam* and *Desiderio magno, Mats.* VI, epp. 288 and 314, fos. 64v and 67v) have the short, cryptic, protocols which Becket (and also John of Salisbury) used in secret or sensitive correspondence with friends

section existed as a formally constructed separate entity before its incorporation into the archetype.

The five letters appended to the Bodleian Archetype in Bodl. A are clearly independent of the main transcription, since they follow in a different hand after a gap of some lines. This additional material contains the bishops' appeal of 1166 and Becket's reply addressed to Foliot;[1] two papal letters, addressed to Henry II and Becket respectively; and a further letter from Becket to Foliot.[2] The first three items are well known in other collections, but the final two (83-4), relating to the dispute between the Priory of Pentney and Earl Hugh of Norfolk and William de Vaux, exist in no other copy. Robertson received the text of the papal mandate *Quoniam nobiles uiri* (pronouncing the excommunication of the Earl and William de Vaux) from Giles's edition;[3] but Becket's accompanying letter *Litteras domini pape*, commanding the execution of the mandate, seems nowhere to have been printed hitherto. A clue to the possible source of the whole appendix is provided by the fact that its version of *Etsi circa nos* has a long passage, also relating to the Pentney dispute, appended to the main text; and that passage is otherwise known only in Oxford Bodl. MS Cave e Mus. 249,[4] the most important collection of the letters of Gilbert Foliot, made in his chancery within the dating limits 1175-89. This unique agreement may therefore suggest that the compiler of the Bodleian manuscript derived the appendix from a Foliot source. And this supposition is strengthened by the fact that its text of *Vestram pater*, the first of the additional letters, agrees with that in the Foliot manuscripts to a marked extent.[5] The combination, in

---

[1] *Vestram pater* (80), cf. *Mats.* V, ep. 204; *Mirandum et uehementer* (81), cf. *Mats.* V, ep. 224.

[2] *Etsi circa nos* (82), cf. *Mats.* VI, ep. 486; *Quonian nobiles uiri* (83), cf. *Mats.* VI, ep. 484; *Litteras domini pape* (84), unprinted.

[3] Cf. Giles, *EpST* II, p. 35, ep. 236. Giles took his text from Bodl. A.

[4] No. 82; the MS has the long addition 'Ad hec . . . abstinere' found also in Cave 151; cf. *Mats.* VI, pp. 555-6.

[5] This has been noted by Morey and Brooke; cf. MB, *Foliot*, p. 220, n. to line 20.

---

who might be open to reprisals from the king. Thus no. 17, sent to Nicholas of Mont-St-Jacques (though in Bodl. A 17 wrongly addressed to Conrad of Mainz), has the inscription 'Suus suo salutem et animi constantiam'; and nos. 20 and 22, sent to Conrad of Mainz, have respectively: 'Anime sue dimidio salutem quam sibi et ampliorem cum sibi sit minima' and 'Anime sue dimidio salutem quam sibi'.

the Bodleian manuscript, of the archetypal material and this appendix is identified in the present investigation as Collection Bodl.A.

Nothing can be definitely established about the medieval provenance of the manuscript, although the introductory material suggests
a connection with the Coventry diocese. Both William the Chanter
of Combe and Maurinus the monk are otherwise unknown, though
they were apparently members of religious communities; but the
second of William of Combe's two poems, *Ara fit a Thoma . . .
uicem*, which celebrates a miraculous cure, is also found in William
of Canterbury's *Miracula Sancti Thome*,[1] where it is associated
with the cure of the Deacon Thomas of Careslege (Keresley) and
with Richard Peche of Coventry's formal authentication of the
miracle, addressed to Richard of Canterbury. These details help
to locate the time and place of composition of the poem: the cure
itself was subsequent to the feast of SS. Philip and James (1 May),
when Thomas was attacked and wounded; and the earliest possible
date for Richard of Coventry's letter is 1174,[2] while the insertion of
the cure in William's *Miracula* provides the *terminus ad quem* of
1175–8 for its notification at Canterbury. On this evidence it seems
likely that the poem was composed *c.* 1176, and perhaps in a
religious house in the diocese of Coventry; and this accords very
well with the identification of Cumba with the Cistercian Abbey of
Combe in Warwickshire.[3] The manuscript as a whole contains
nothing that can positively be dated later than *c.* 1178 in composition; and the greater part of the material, including John of
Salisbury's *Vita*, the fragment of Benedict of Peterborough's
Miracula, and the letter-collection, was ultimately derived from a
Canterbury source.

B. THE ADDITIONAL COLLECTION

Closely related to the archetypal material in Bodl.A is the now
fragmentary Brit. Libr. Addit. MS 1777, fos. 1r–47v: a small, early
fourteenth-century manuscript of unknown provenance, containing only forty-seven leaves; it both begins and ends abruptly in

---

[1] Cf. *Mats.* I, p. 428. The cure occurs in Bk. VI, composed *c.* 1178.

[2] It is addressed to Richard of Canterbury and must therefore be subsequent
to his consecration as archbishop on 7 April 1174 (cf. MB, *Foliot*, p. 531).

[3] Cf. *Mats.* I, pp. xxviii and n.4, and II, p. xlix. It should be noted that the
Cistercian Order was very favourably disposed to Becket during his exile, and
copies of the Miracles were sent to Igny in France by Odo of Battle in the
1180s: cf. *Mats.* II, p. xlix, n. A, for his letter.

mid-sentence. It is clearly in an unfinished form, for it lacks initials, headings, and numbers; and the spaces left for the rubricator are so small that only a very brief form of heading (such as *idem eidem*) can have been intended. The text is transcribed in single columns in a small and clear, though untidy, hand; and common form abbreviations are usual in the papal letters. Beginning in the middle of *Expectans expectaui*[1] and breaking off before the end of *Quoniam de prudentia*,[2] Addit. MS 1777 is identical in order with Bodl.A, 5–41, except that it omits items 11 and 12.[3] This comparatively late, unfinished, and mutilated fragment is significant only in showing that material from the Bodleian archetype was being reproduced in England as late as the fourteenth century.

C. THE LAUDIAN COLLECTION

The third member of the Family is the far more valuable Bodleian MS Laud Misc. 666, fos. v–liii and 1–190v, dating from the late thirteenth century. The MS volume belonged at one time to James Ussher, Archbishop of Armagh,[4] and later to William Laud, Archbishop of Canterbury.[5] It is a fine, carefully executed, manuscript, written in single columns in a large and pointed script, with

---

[1] The MS begins '(imperato)rem excommunicauit et ab ecclesia exclusit'; cf. *Mats.* V, p. 275.

[2] It breaks off with the words 'in his que uobis in(iunximus)'; cf. *Mats.* VII, p. 203; the catchword 'iunximus' is written at the bottom of the folio, indicating that another gathering followed.

[3] Cf. Appendix I below.

[4] James Ussher was Bishop of Meath in 1621–6, and Archbishop of Armagh in 1625–56. A theologian and biblical scholar and an important collector of manuscripts and early printed books, he belonged to the circle of such eminent bibliophiles as Camden, Savile, Cotton, and Laud; and on occasion he borrowed books from the Cotton Library. Most of his books were acquired between 1602 and 1640 during visits to England. The Library was purchased in 1661 with money raised from Cromwell's army in Ireland, and donated by Charles II to Trinity College, Dublin, where it still resides. Some of his books had earlier passed into the hands of friends like John Junius and William Laud, and through them came into the possession of the Bodleian Library. Laud Misc. 666 was one such volume, acquired by Laud from Ussher and given to the Bodleian. Cf. James Compton, 'Fasciculi Zizaniorum I', *JEH* XII (1961), pp. 35–46; H. J. Lawler, 'Primate Ussher's Library before 1641', *Royal Irish Academy Proceedings*, 3rd Series, VI no. 2, Dublin (1900–02), pp. 216–64; D. C. Douglas, *English Scholars 1660–1730*, 2nd edn., London (1951), pp. 25 and 196–7.

[5] Fo. iv has the inscription, 'Liber Gulielmi Laud Archiepiscopi Cantuar(iensis) et Cancellarii universitatis Oxon(iensis). 1633.'

rubricated headings and numbers, and with blue initials decorated
in red scroll-work which occupies much of the margin; capital
initials within the text are overtouched in red. The 244 folios
are arranged for the greater part in gatherings of twelve leaves,[1]
with catchwords at the end of each gathering. The manuscript is
now incomplete, breaking off at the end of a gathering in mid-
transcription of the letter *Licet Anglicane ecclesie*.[2] The manuscript
volume is divided into three parts, with a blank folio side preceding
each of the second and third parts:[3] the first part is formed by Alan
of Tewkesbury's *Explanatio*; the second comprises John of
Salisbury's *Prologus* and *Vita*, the *Reuelatio Domini* and a series of
lections *In translatione beati Thome martiris*;[4] and the third contains the correspondence. All three were written by the same hand,
and the work was conceived as a whole.

The Laudian collection illustrates the way in which an early
work was expanded in the hands of a later compiler. Laud 1–77 is
identical in order and content with Bodl.A, 1–76, except that Laud
inserts one additional letter.[5] But from Laud 78 onwards, the
collections diverge in content and arrangement, although the concluding three letters of the Bodleian Archetype, Bodl.A, 77–9, are
found later in the Laud manuscript.[6] It is clear that Laud was not
directly dependent on Bodl.A over the area of their correspondence, since it has the additional letter *Sepe nobis a pluribus* not
found in Bodl.A, its headings are for the most part peculiar to
itself,[7] and for one letter it has a more correct address.[8] Moreover,

---

[1] The foliation runs in two sequences, v–liii and 1–193, with two consecutive
folios numbered 182. The transcription breaks off on fo. 190v.

[2] The volume ends with the words '. . . ut si alias audita illic . . .'; cf. *Mats*,
VII, p. 524. The catchword 'prouenerint' appears at the bottom of the folio,
indicating that another gathering followed.

[3] Fos. xxvii[v] and liii[v] are blank.

[4] For the nine lections, taken from the Office of Matins for the feast of the
Translation (7 July), cf. F. Proctor and C. Wordsworth, edd., *Breviarium ad
Usum Insignis Ecclesiae Sarum*, III, Cambridge (1886), pp. 445–50: 'Gloriosis-
simi martyris . . . seculorum'.

[5] *Sepe nobis a pluribus* (45); cf. *Mats*. V, ep. 157: from Alexander III to Gilbert
Foliot.

[6] Bodl. A, 77–9 = Laud 86–7 and 91.

[7] Laud has fuller headings in 13–18, 23, 25, 29, 34, 38, 47, 51–4, 62, and
67.

[8] For *Si grandia loquitur* Bodl.A, 17 has 'Maguntino archiepiscopo',
where Laud 17 has 'T. Cant(uariensis) archiepiscopus Nicholao de Monte
Rothom(agensi)'.

it is dependent on a different source for the second part of its contents, since Laud 78–109 closely follow their order in Alan of Tewkesbury's collection,[1] omitting fifteen letters which had already appeared in the Bodleian Archetype.[2] Collation with the Alan of Tewkesbury manuscripts suggests that this group was dependent on Recension III of Alan's work, as represented by Alan(C), and it agrees in content and textual details with Recension III in contrast with Recensions I and II.[3] The letters derived from this source are all concerned with the death of the archbishop and its aftermath, including the appeals to the Pope for vengeance[4] and two accounts of the Compromise of Avranches.[5] It is more than likely that the final gathering or gatherings now missing contained the rest of the last book of Alan's collection, including the bulls of canonization.[6]

The Laudian collection is a hybrid compilation, combining the smallest and earliest Becket collection with part of the comprehensive edition made by Alan of Tewkesbury between 1174 and 1178–9. In script, arrangement, and decoration it closely resembles another collection of Becket letters now preserved in the British Library, namely Brit. Libr. MS Arundel 219; and these two manuscripts seem to have been designed as companion volumes. The Arundel manuscript, which will be discussed in more detail

---

[1] This table shows the relationship between Laud and AlanT(C), Cambridge Corpus Christi College MS 295:

Laud	AlanT(C)
78–9	V. 46–7
80	53
81–2	55–6
83–5	63–5
86–109	68–91

[2] AlanT(C), V. 48–52, 54, 57–62, and 66–7 = Laud 60–6, 72–7, and 69–70.

[3] For example, Laud 82 has the date preserved in AlanT(C), V. 56, but omitted in AlanT(A), V. 58 and AlanT(B), V. 56; Laud 92 includes 'Norfolkie' in the heading, agreeing with AlanT(C), V. 74, against (A), V. 78 and (B), V. 74; Laud 100 has the valediction preserved in AlanT(C), V. 82, but lacking in AlanT(A), V. 86, and (B), V. 81. Similarly, Laud agrees with AlanT(C), V. 81 in the placing of *Ex insperato* (99): in both these MSS the letter appears between *Inter scribendum* and *Vestre placuit*, while in AlanT(A), V. 82, it is placed between *Circa mee uocationis* and *Ab humane pietatis*, and AlanT(B) lacks the letter altogether.

[4] Laud 96–8, 100, and 101.

[5] Laud 107 and 108.

[6] Cf. AlanT(C), V. 92–7.

later, contains an abbreviation of Alan's Recension III, and derives in all probability from St Augustine's, Canterbury.[1]

D. THE RAWLINSON COLLECTION

The remaining member of the Bodleian Family is found in the very complex Oxford Bodl. MS Rawlinson Q.f.8, fos. 1r–122r,[2] a carefully transcribed twelfth-century volume which belonged in the Middle Ages to the Cathedral Church of Ely, and was possibly assembled there.[3] The manuscript deserves special consideration because of its venerable age, the fact that its medieval provenance is identified in the volume, and because in its contents it provides a link between the lines of transmission in the Becket and Foliot Families. The collection as a whole contains eighty-eight items, of which thirty-eight were dependent on the Bodleian Archetype, while other items were derived ultimately from Foliot sources, and the collection includes still further matter of much interest independently of these two components. The collection therefore illustrates very well the way in which a compiler could build up an individual collection by drawing on a diversity of sources.

Five separate elements can be distinguished in the build-up of the Rawlinson Collection,[4] reflecting each a different source, though these have no formal differentiation in the manuscript format. The first part, comprising merely nine items, opens with Stephen's charter conferring the succession to the English crown on Henry, then Duke of Normandy and later Henry II,[5] followed by Alexander III's notification of his own election to Theobald of Canterbury,[6] the formal report of the schismatical Council of Pavia of 1160,[7] and two letters relating to the imperial Council held

[1] Brit. Libr. Arundel MS 219; for a full description of this MS, cf. pp. 137–9 below. The marginalia in the Arundel MS suggest a connection with St Augustine's, Canterbury, and it is possible that both MSS were produced there.

[2] 6 × 4½ in.; iv + 127 leaves; single columns; cf. *Summary Catalogue* no. 27836. For the contents, cf. Appendix II below.

[3] Cf. fo. 122v: 'Iste liber pertinet ecclesie Eliensi'; cf. Ker, p. 43. The books in the medieval library of Ely are noted in J. Leland, *Collectanea*, IV, p. 163.

[4] Rawl. Part I: 1–8; Part II: 9–22; Part III: 23–46; Part IV: 47–84; Part V: 85–6, with 87 appended at a much later date. These five parts are disclosed by an analysis of the contents, but are not evident from the format of the manuscript. Cf. Appendix II below.

[5] *Sciatis quod* (1), cf. Rymer, I.i, p. 18.

[6] *Eterna et incommutabilis* (2), JL 10590.

[7] *Quia sedis apostolice* (3), *MGH, Legum* IV,I, pp. 265–6.

at Würzburg in July 1165.[1] These are followed by an otherwise unknown letter from Henry II to Archbishop Theobald and the English clergy dealing with appeals to Rome,[2] a unique abbreviated version of the Constitutions of Clarendon,[3] and two letters concerning the collection of Peter's Pence, one received by Gilbert Foliot and the other sent by him, written in 1165.[4] Of this small group, the letters dealing with the Council of Würzburg and the Foliot letters are found among the Becket correspondence in a number of manuscripts,[5] but four items (1–3 and 6a) have no connection with the controversy, and find no place in the main traditions of the Becket or Foliot correspondence, although the rescript from the Council of Pavia (3) and a slightly different version of Alexander III's election letter (2) are found at the beginning of a small collection of Becket letters in the fragmentary twelfth-century Brit. Libr. MS Cotton Faustina B.I., which belonged in the Middle Ages to the Cistercian monastery of Byland in Yorkshire.[6] The arrangement of the group in correct chronological sequence may suggest its derivation from archival sources: Stephen's charter, Alexander's letter, the rescript of Pavia, and Henry II's letter to Theobald and the English clergy, are all documents of a type, public instruments or encyclical letters, sent out in numerous copies to widely scattered recipients, which would naturally find their way into the archives of cathedral churches.[7]

---

[1] *Iam dudum* (4), *Mats.* V, ep. 100; *Cum clerum* (5), *Mats.* V, ep. 99.

[2] *Sicut ad uestram* (6a); cf. A. Saltman, 'Two Early Collections of the Becket Correspondence and of other Contemporary Documents', *BIHR* XXII (1949), pp. 154–5.

[3] *De presentationibus* (6b), cf. ibid., pp. 155–6.

[4] *A memoria tua* (7), *Mats.* V, ep. 93; *Mandatum uestrum* (8), *Mats.* V, ep. 108; cf. MB, *Foliot*, ep. 155.

[5] Nos. 4, 5, and 7–8.

[6] For nos. 2 and 3, cf. Brit. Libr. MS Cotton Faustina B.I., 1–2. For a brief discussion of this MS, cf. Chapter 5 below.

[7] Letters dealing with Alexander's election and the schism are found in the Byland MS already cited, and in MSS from Worcester, Bury St Edmunds, and an unknown source. Cf. (i), Brit. Libr. MS Royal 9.B.XII, a twelfth-century collection of documents from Worcester Priory: fo. 2ra–vb, *Eterna et incommutabilis*; fo. 3ra–rb, *Cum Christus*; (ii) National Library of Wales, Harlech MS 21, fo. 3v–4r, *Eterna et incommutabilis*; fo. 4v, *Cum Christus*; (iii) Brit. Libr. MS Cotton Otho C.XIV, pp. 104r–105v (fos. 191r–192v), art. 25, *Eterna et incommutabilis*; pp. 105v–107v (fos. 192v–194v), art. 26, *Quia sedis apostolice*; pp. 107v–108v (fos. 194v–195v), art. 27, *Cum clerum*; and p. 108v (fo. 195v), art. 28, *Cunctorum innotuit* (*MGH, Constitutiones*, I, p. 314). This MS, which was very seriously damaged in the Cotton fire of 1731, contains the letters of Robert Grosseteste in addition to material relating to the Abbey of Fountains.

It is therefore conceivable that this sequence in the collection was assembled from records kept in the Ely archives, since as an entity no parallel group exists elsewhere, though the suggestion is conjectural since there is no internal evidence in the group to establish its place of composition as an entity, or to link it positively with the medieval provenance of the completed volume.

At the same time the abbreviated version of the Constitutions of Clarendon found in this manuscript merits special attention, since it differs considerably from the generally received text which, according to Herbert of Bosham, was copied from the actual chirograph presented to the bishops at Clarendon;[1] it omits clauses 8–16 altogether and, while preserving the general sense of the other seven clauses, considerably abbreviates them, and rearranges them into eight chapters so that the famous third clause dealing with the *privilegium fori* appears split into two parts as items 3 and 5.[2] Saltman suggested that this version probably records a draft of the Constitutions before their formal publication at Clarendon;[3] but it is also possible that this unusual text may derive from notes taken at the council itself or from a copy of the Constitutions. Here again the Ely provenance of the volume may have significance, and it is possible that this interesting version of the Constitutions may preserve a record kept by Bishop Nigel of Ely, or his son Archdeacon Richard FitzNeal, or his successor Bishop Geoffrey Ridel: all three leading royal administrators.

The second component of the Rawlinson Collection, composed of fourteen items, is related to a particular grouping of letters which has left its traces independently of the Ely volume. It is identical in contents, order, and arrangement with the first part of a composite collection now in Brit. Libr. Harleian MS 215,[4] though each completed collection has material not found in the other. This degree of correspondence over the sequence in question suggests

---

[1] *Mats.* III, p. 280. The generally received text from which Herbert quotes in his *VST* is found in AlanT (cf. Lupus, I.12); it appears as the first item in the *Causa exilii et martyrii beati Thome* which is usually appended to the *Quadrilogus* (cf. Lupus, I, pp. 163–7), though often occurring independently of it (cf. Hardy, II, pp. 383–4); it also appears as part of the *Summa cause inter regem et archiepiscopum* (cf. *Mats.* IV, p. 208) as well as in William of Canterbury (*Mats.* I, pp. 18–23), Herbert of Bosham (ibid., III, pp. 180–4), Guernes de Pont-Sainte-Maxence, ed. cit., pp. 80–6, vv. 2396–543, and Roger of Wendover, I, pp. 27–30.

[2] Cf. Saltman, art. cit., p. 154.

[3] Ibid., p. 156.

[4] Nos. 9–22 = Harl. 1–14.

their sharing in a definite line of transmission, despite their differences. The group contains an interesting selection of letters, mainly connected with the events of 1166, beginning with two of Becket's eloquent appeals to the king,[1] the sentences of excommunication which he pronounced at Vézelay in that year,[2] the consequent appeal by the bishops to the Pope,[3] and both of Becket's replies.[4] A letter from Foliot to Nigel of Ely, relating to the bishops' appeal, is found only in this manuscript and in the Harleian MS 215 cited above.[5] The group also contains the text of Henry II's treaty with France in 1160,[6] and two letters from 1165.[7]

An analysis of the contents of Rawl. II reveals an episcopal and royal emphasis in the materials included. Seven of its fourteen items came from Becket himself, and are all addressed to English recipients: two to the king (9 and 11), one each to Robert of Hereford (12), Jocelin of Salisbury (13), Gilbert Foliot (21), the Canterbury suffragans (17), and the clergy of England (22). The remaining seven items include the treaty of 1160 (10) and six letters either sent or received by the king or by the bishops: a letter of Henry II to the Cistercians (14), two letters from the English bishops as a body (15 and 20), two papal letters addressed to Gilbert Foliot and the king respectively (18 and 19), and one letter from Foliot to Nigel of Ely (16). The composition of the group reflects perhaps the interests of the author or the limitations of his sources, or possibly a combination of both these factors. All fourteen items, with the exception of the treaty text and the Foliot letter to Ely, are known in both the Becket and the Foliot traditions, though they do not occur elsewhere in their Rawlinson order, except in the Harleian Collection referred to above; and textually they agree more with the Becket than with the Foliot manuscripts wherever there are significant variants. The two exceptional items provide a possible clue to the provenance of the group as a whole. The text of the treaty of 1160 was first critically examined by Saltman in 1949,[8] when he concluded that the version preserved in

---

[1] *Desiderio* (9), *Mats.* V, ep. 154; *Loqui de Deo* (11), *Mats.* V, ep. 152.
[2] *Fratres mei* (17), *Mats.* V, ep. 198.
[3] *Vestram pater* (15), *Mats.* V, ep. 204; *Que uestro* (20), *Mats.* V, ep. 205.
[4] *Mirandum* (21), *Mats.* V, ep. 224; *Fraternitatis uestre* (22), *Mats.* V, ep. 223.
[5] *Appellationem* (16), cf. MB, *Foliot*, ep. 165.
[6] *Notum sit omnibus* (10), cf. Brial, *Recueil des historiens*, XVI, p. 21.
[7] *Si littere* (12), *Mats.* V, ep. 219; *Quod circa ea que* (18), *Mats.* V, ep. 106.
[8] Saltman, art. cit., pp. 156–7.

this manuscript was the best surviving. It was Saltman's view that this text was probably derived from a copy of the treaty made for the king himself, which suggests that the author of Rawl. II had access to material drawn from royal administrative sources. In isolation this consideration would not identify the probable provenance of the collection, but in a significant way it may complement the presence in the group of the otherwise unknown letter to Nigel of Ely, so intimately involved in royal affairs, particularly in view of the Ely provenance of the manuscript volume in the Middle Ages.

The third stratum in the Rawlinson Collection, Rawl. III, is not directly related to any other surviving compilation, though most of its contents are known elsewhere in both the Becket and the Foliot manuscripts; and it too reveals an episcopal and royal emphasis similar to that in Rawl. II. Five of its twenty-four letters were received by Henry II (27, 29, 34, 41, and 44), two were sent by him (37 and 45), and ten were received by various English bishops (28, 30–3, 36, 38, 39, 42, and 43). The chronological arrangement is haphazard, with material ranging in date from 1166 to 1171; and no logical scheme is suggested by the order of the letters. The source of this section is obscure. It is certainly not dependent on the main Becket traditions as they are known in extant manuscripts. On the contrary, interesting and significant agreements in contents, order, and text exist between it and the two collections of the Foliot Family: eighteen of its items are found either in the Cave or Douce collections in the Foliot Group, of which fifteen appear in both collections in significant groupings;[1] and still more reveal-

[1] Table to illustrate the relationship between Rawl. III and the Foliot MSS: Cave e Mus. 249 and Douce 287.

Rawl.	Cave	Douce	Rawl.	Cave	Douce
23	—	—	35	—	—
24	157	24	36	179	71
25	—	—	37	184	76
26	—	—	38	186	79
27	219	42	39	185	78
28	220a; 161	44	40	187	80
29	220b; 162	46	41	183	75
30	—	48*	42	216	28
31	—	49*	43	217	29
32	172	50*	44	255	15
33	—	—	45	182	74
34	—	66	46	—	—

* Protocol only.

ing, the Rawl. letters have eleven protocols,[1] three dates,[2] and one attestation[3] in common with the Foliot tradition. On the other hand, a close textual agreement cannot be established between them, and Rawl. III cannot be dependent on the known Foliot manuscripts, since it has letters not contained in either of them and its readings and order are peculiar to itself.

Four letters may be selected in support of these conclusions, namely *Vniversis oppressis, Pro amore Dei, Dominus Cantuariensis,* and *Inter scribendum,* being respectively Rawl. III, 42, 45, 23, and 46. In the first instance, the date of *Vniversis oppressis* is lacking in the earliest manuscripts of the Becket tradition and is inaccurate in certain later related compilations, whereas the Rawl. version agrees with the possibly accurate dating in the Foliot collections.[4] Again, the formal résumé of Henry II's Peace of Fréteval in *Pro amore Dei* is found in Rawl. and in the Foliot manuscripts, and in Fitz-Stephen's *Vita et Passio,* but nowhere else.[5] In contrast, the anonymous account of the interview between Becket and the papal commissioners, held between Gisors and Trie in November 1167 and recorded in *Dominus Cantuariensis,* is otherwise unknown in either the Becket or the Foliot traditions.[6] *Inter scribendum,* the letter in the name of William of Sens in early 1171 calling for vengeance on Becket's murderers, is found in Alan of Tewkesbury's collection as well as in Rawl., but their texts are different: the full protocol is found in Rawl., but is lacking in all surviving versions of Alan's work; and the Rawl. version incorporates significant passages which are not found in this letter elsewhere except in Hoveden's

[1] Rawl. III, 27–9, 36–40 and 42–4.

[2] Rawl. III, 36, 42, and 44.

[3] Rawl. III, 37.

[4] The date is lacking in Bodl.A, 43, Laud 43, Vat. 208, Lamb. 49, and Bodl.B, II.43. The date given in Roy. 192, AlanT(A), I.28, and AlanT(C), I.33 is: 'Dat. Senon. v. Non. Maii', that is Sens, 3 May (Alexander III was in Sens on that date only in 1164); and in AlanT(B), I.32 is: 'Dat. Lat. v. Non. Maii', that is the Lateran, 3 May, 1166 (cf. JL 11273). Cf. Rawl. III, 42, Cave 216, and Douce 28: 'Dat. Lat. vii. Idus Aprilis', that is the Lateran, 7 April, 1166.

[5] Rawl. III, 45; cf. Cave 182, Douce 74, and FitzStephen, *Mats.* III, p. 112.

[6] Rawl. III, 23; cf. *Mats.* VI, ep. 334. Robertson took the text of this piece from Giles, *VST,* II, pp. 248–51 and Brial, *Receuil des historiens,* XVI, p. 574, neither of whom had an original MS source for the letter: Giles printed it from the seventeenth-century Cambridge Trinity College MS O.5.42 (which is unpaginated), and Brial reprinted it from R. de Beauchamp, *Historica Synopsi Franco-Merovingica,* Douai (1633), p. 936.

Chronica.[1] Reversing Robertson's conclusion from this evidence that the relevant passages in Hoveden were later interpolations, it now appears likely that both Hoveden and the compiler of Rawl. II had access to a source different from that of Alan's collection, as well as from that of Herbert of Bosham which Robertson had consulted for comparison.[2] It can be shown that for most, if not all, his letters Hoveden was dependent on the archives of the Bishop of London, and it may well have been from such a source that the compiler of Rawl. III also in some way derived most of his material.

Thus, in summation, it appears that the third part of the Rawlinson Collection is independent of the known lines of transmission of the Becket collections, but is related in some way to the sources of the Foliot collections. It may have been assembled in its present form at Ely, or it may have been taken from a compilation made elsewhere. Its precise relationship with the Foliot sources is not easy to identify: it may be that both Rawl. III and the comparable sequences in the Foliot collections were derived independently of one another but from an original common source of supply; and this may well have been in the Foliot household, and may have originated in transcriptions of letters as they were actually received there in one way or another. Foliot's ecclesiastical functions and his familiar role in the Becket controversy well placed him, or his chancery officials, in a favourable position to collect the letters and distribute copies to the bishops of England; and it was probably through Foliot's agency that many of the letters to and from Henry II were made generally known.

The fourth part of the Rawlinson Collection is transcribed in a

---

[1] Rawl. III, 46; cf. AlanT(A), V.85, and (B) and (C), V.80; cf. also Hoveden, *Chronica*, II, pp. 22–5. Cf. Robertson, *Mats.* VII, ep. 735, pp. 429–33; the following textual variants may be noted from Hoveden: *Mats.* VII, p. 430, line 5, insert 'iam' before 'sole'; line 7, ins. 'dumtaxat' before 'qui primi'; lines 9–11, read 'Quorum ut memoria eorum perpetuo in maledictione sit intersero nomina: Hugo de Morevilla, Willelmus de Traci, Reginaldus filius Ursi'; line 15, omit 'sciscitantes'; line 19, 'vendicaret' for 'vendicare'; ibid., p. 431, n.3, ins. 'et Christus . . . complectens'; n.5, ins. 'flexis genibus'; n.9, read 'Cujus . . . saltem'; n.10, read 'ut a multis illesa'; n.13, ins. 'Inter quos . . . dedit'; ibid., p. 432, n.2, 'terris' for 'terra sua'; n.5, om. 'Herodis saevitiam'; ibid., p. 433, n.1, ins. 'vendiderunt'. In all these instances the variant supplied from Hoveden is also found in Rawl. (except that Rawl. has 'amplectens' for 'complectens' on p. 431, n.3). But Rawl. and Hoveden have different endings: cf. ibid., p. 433, n.2: Rawl. has 'pater sancte considera ratione' for Hoveden's 'pater sancte auctoritas . . . sancte', and includes the final sentence omitted by Hoveden: 'praesentium portitores . . . revelanda'.

[2] Cambridge Corpus Christi College MS 123, ep. 33.

different hand from the preceding section, and this development coincides with a clear change in the source of the letters. Rawl. IV is the largest single element in the whole collection, and is the part dependent on the Bodleian Archetype: it is in fact simply an abbreviation corresponding with Bodl.A, 1–65, omitting twenty-one items[1] in addition to six which had already appeared in the preceding sections,[2] although it also includes six others which had already appeared in them.[3] Collation with the surviving members of the Bodleian Family reveals a close correspondence of order and text with them,[4] and from Rawl. IV, 65 onwards, the rubricated headings agree with those found in Bodl.A. The principle of selection appears much the same as in the earlier parts of the collection: the compiler was seemingly more interested in material addressed to English recipients, and tended to omit letters to and from continental ecclesiastics, even if the letters were addressed to or sent by Becket himself.[5] An analysis of the material selected again suggests the interests of the compiler: of the thirty-eight letters taken from the Bodleian tradition, twenty-eight were sent by Becket, nine by Alexander III, and one by the bishops of England; and of these the great majority were addressed to English recipients: four to Henry II, twelve to English bishops (either individually or jointly), two to Geoffrey Ridel (elected as Bishop of Ely in 1173), and one to the Earl of Leicester.[6] The inclusion of three of Becket's letters to William of Pavia may possibly be explained by the fact that he

---

[1] Rawl. omits Bodl. A, 17, 20, 34–6, 40–2, 47, 49, 52–5, and 57–63.

[2] Six of the omitted Bodleian letters had already appeared in the earlier parts of Rawl: Bodl. A, 2 = Rawl. 9; 5 = 41; 43 = 42; 48 = 36; 50 = 27, and 51 = 29.

[3] Bodl. A, 1 = Rawl. 47, 11; 3 = 48, 13; 7 = 51, 12; 8 = 52, 17; 15 = 59, 20; and 16 = 60, 22.

[4] Table to illustrate the relationship between Rawl. and MS Bodley 509:

Rawl.	Bodl.A	Rawl.	Bodl.A
47	1	76–8	37–9
48–9	3–4	79–81	44–6
50–60	6–16	82	56
61–2	18–19	83–4	64–5
63–75	21–33		

Cf. Appendix II below.

[5] Seven letters written by Becket are omitted: cf. Bodl.A, 17, 20, and 59–63; 6 addressed to him are also omitted: cf. Bodl. A, 35, 36, 47, 49, 54, and 55.

[6] To Henry II: Rawl. IV, 47, 69, 73, and 84; to English bishops: 48–54, 60 and 77–80; to Geoffrey Ridel: 55 and 62; to the Earl of Leicester: 56. It is possible that some of the material in Rawl. was supplied by Geoffrey Ridel who had been one of the king's chief agents during Becket's exile; elected to Ely in 1173, he was consecrated in 1174.

was a curial supporter of Henry II during the controversy.[1] On the other hand, six of Becket's letters to the Pope are included.[2]

It seems clear from the present appearance of Rawl. IV that its original transcription ended at fo. 115v with *Nouit inspector cordium* (84), the last item derived from the Bodleian stock, since seven lines are left vacant at the bottom of that folio and Part V follows in yet a different change of hand at the top of the following folio. This final part is composed of two items only: the celebrated letter of John of Salisbury describing Becket's murder and addressed to John of Poitiers in early January 1171,[3] and Alexander III's encyclical *Immensas laudes* announcing the Peace of Venice in 1177.[4] Both were written without headings and a space was left for the initial A at the beginning of the papal letter. There can be no doubt that these items are a later appendix to the rest of the collection. And a final item in the volume is the letter *More pii patris* (87) sent by Innocent III to King John,[5] which was clearly added in an even later hand and has no connection with the collection of letters to which it is appended; it was simply inserted in a convenient space at the end of the manuscript volume. A *terminus ad quem* for the entire collection is provided by the date of *Immensas laudes*, issued at Venice on August 6 1177, but it is probable that the earlier sections, Rawl. I–IV, were completed substantially before that date.

The provenance of the surviving members of the Bodleian Family shows that derivatives from the family archetype were circulating in England within a very few years of the archbishop's murder; and the central importance of the archetype in the transmission of the Becket correspondence can be gauged by the fact that, with the exception of the two manuscripts connected with the Foliot archives, all surviving collections of Becket correspondence of any size are to some extent derivatives from it: the Vatican and Royal Collections have integrated it with other material;[6] the

[1] To William of Pavia: 57, 65, and 67.
[2] To the Pope: 61, 63, 66, 68, 70, and 83.
[3] *Ex insperato, Mats.* VII, ep. 748; this letter was later used by John of Salisbury as the basis of the short Life of Becket which he composed as an introduction to the collection of letters published by Alan of Tewkesbury.
[4] *Immensas* (MS: *Inmensas*) *laudes*, JL 12910, *Gesta*, I, p. 187.
[5] Pat. Lat. CCXV, col. 1535; cf. C. R. Cheney and W. H. Semple, edd., *Selected Letters of Pope Innocent III concerning England*, London (1953), pp. 117–20: 23 January 1209.
[6] Cf. pp. 52 and 56 below.

Lambeth and Bodl. B Collections begin with it;[1] and its influence can be traced in Alan of Tewkesbury's great collection.[2] At each stage of incorporation it was subjected to correction, but the identity of the collection was never entirely lost. This evidence suggests that the Bodleian Archetype was perhaps the first collection of the Becket correspondence to be formally assembled, and that it was from the beginning considered to be important and authoritative by the earliest collectors in the Canterbury circle.

2. THE VATICAN FAMILY

The second family of collections in the Becket Group is the Vatican Family which records a further stage in the formation of a comprehensive compilation of the Becket correspondence. The family comprises five medieval manuscripts and one seventeenth-century copy, in which the Bodleian Archetype is combined with other material which, like itself, seems ultimately derived from the Becket archives. Although the two earliest manuscripts of the group were transcribed after Becket's canonization, they derive from archetypes composed between 1170 and 1173; they are therefore later in date of composition than the Bodleian Archetype (an uncorrected version of which they appear to have used), but earlier than that of the Lambeth Family; and textually they are in agreement with Recension I of Alan of Tewkesbury's collection. The family takes its name from its earliest extant member, the Vatican Latin MS 6024, fos. 72ra–139vb, which contains 267 letters; and the five remaining members are in the Bibl. de la Ville de Laon MS 337, the Brit. Libr. MSS Harleian 215 and Royal 13.A.XIII, the Oxford Bodl. MS 278, and the Oxford St John's College MS 15, containing

---

[1] Cf. pp. 68 and 77 below.

[2] The relationship with Bodl.A is particularly striking in AlanT Books IV and V, as the following select table shows:

Bodl.A	AlanT(B)	Bodl.A	AlanT(B)
27	IV.63*	57	IV.18
32–3	V.3–4	59–65	V.47–52,54
37–9	5,7*,8	66–7	43–4
40–2	10,6,2	68–70	66,67,65*
48	IV.49*	71–3	57–9
50–1	3–4	74–6	60–2
53	V.1	77–9	68–9, 73

The letters marked with an asterisk are not in AlanT(B) but occur in this corresponding position in AlanT(A).

78, 93, 252, 250, and 252 letters respectively.[1] The last two manuscripts in the list can be discounted in any detailed textual study, for Bodl. MS 278 is merely a careless transcript from the seventeenth century, possibly copied from Royal 13.A.XIII, and the St John's MS is a fifteenth-century copy of the Royal MS or of a closely related version of it. Moreover, the Laon and Harleian MSS contain only a small fragment of the common stock, and only two collections provide a sufficient basis for study in the present chapter; but, fortunately, they are the earliest and most important surviving members of the group, namely the Vatican (Vat.) and Royal (Roy.) Collections. The two compilations have 244 letters in common, comprising in each case two separate components of the completed work; and of these two elements one, forming in fact the largest element in either compilation, contains predominantly letters written by Becket or received by him, together with a few items written on his behalf by friends or supporters in England and France, while the other is composed exclusively of letters issued by Alexander III in the course of the controversy. But, although they have the greater part of their contents in common, they are not interdependent, nor are they immediately dependent on a common source, since each has items omitted by the other and diplomatic details and readings peculiar to itself. There is no over-all agreement in their order, though certain groupings of letters appear in both manuscripts suggesting that the collections preserve two different arrangements of a common source. Neither appears to record the earliest stage in the formation of the ancestral compilation.

A. THE VATICAN COLLECTION

The collection of Becket letters in Vatican Latin MS 6024 is only part of a volume of materials transcribed in England during the last quarter of the twelfth century.[2] In addition to the Becket correspondence, the volume includes the letters of Hildebert of Le Mans,[3] the letters of Arnulf of Lisieux,[4] the register of Master

---

[1] For full MS details, cf. pp. 11–12 above.

[2] For an analysis of the whole volume, cf. Z. N. Brooke, 'The Register of Master David of London and the part he played in the Becket crisis', *Essays in History Presented to R. L. Poole*, Oxford (1927), pp. 228–9.

[3] Fos. 1ra–29vb: 82 letters; cf. Pat. Lat. CLXXI, cols. 135–312.

[4] Fos. 30ra–71ra, an expanded copy of the first edition of the letters of Arnulf of Lisieux, compiled within the dating limits 1171–3; cf. F. Barlow, ed., *The Letters of Arnulf of Lisieux*, Camden Third Series, LXI, London (1939), pp. lxxiii and lxxxii–lxxxiii.

David of London,[1] two treatises attributed to Anselm of Canterbury, and a letter of Pascal II,[2] the early correspondence of John of Salisbury,[3] and the letters of Ivo of Chartres.[4] Nothing is known of the medieval provenance of the manuscript, but fo. 1r bears the hand-written inscription, 'Ex libris illustrissimi D(omini) Lelyii Ruini episcopi Balneoregien.', suggesting that it came to the Vatican Library in the seventeenth century from the collection of Laelius Ruini, Bishop of Bagnorea (1612-21). Its single individual feature is the copy of Master David's register which is known only in this volume. Script and contents suggest an English provenance: the writing is in English book-hand throughout, with the exception of Master David's register which is written mainly in English charter-hand. And, with the exception of the letters of Ivo of Chartres which were widely known in the Middle Ages, all its material is connected with the Anglo-Norman, or more precisely Angevin, territories in the twelfth century. In fact the volume contains three of the most important letter-collections of Anglo-Norman provenance briefly discussed in the introductory chapter.

The Becket correspondence is transcribed in several English hands of the late twelfth century;[5] it is arranged in double columns with rubricated headings and initials, and occupies eight gatherings, each of which has eight leaves except the first, which has fourteen, and the last, which has six.[6] It is preceded by a table of contents written in four columns on an inserted leaf facing fo. 72r, but it seems clear that this table was a later addition, since the leaf on which it was written was larger than the leaves in the rest of the volume, and had to be trimmed at the side and folded at the bottom to permit its inclusion. Indeed it may be doubted if the table was designed for the present collection, since it lists almost exclusively

[1] Fos. 142ra–154ra; the register and its relationship with the rest of the volume is discussed by Z. N. Brooke, art. cit., pp. 227–45.

[2] Fos. 155ra–157ra; cf. Liverani, *Spicilegium*, pp. 559–69.

[3] Fos. 158ra–78ra; cf. R. A. B. Mynors, introduction to W. J. Millor and H. E. Butler, edd., *The Letters of John of Salisbury*, I: *The Early Letters*, NMT, London (1955).

[4] Fos. 179ra–211rb; 84 letters; cf. Pat. Lat. CLXII, cols. 11–288.

[5] Z. N. Brooke (*art. cit.*, p. 228) and Mynors (ed. cit., p. lix) suggested that the MS was transcribed in the thirteenth century; but Hardy, II, p. 318, Barlow (loc. cit.), and the author of the *Inventarium manuscriptorum Latinorum Vaticanae*, vol. VI, p. 309, preferred an earlier dating.

[6] 8 × 5 in.; double columns, 44 or 45 lines to the column. Quires II–VII contain 8 leaves each; the first quire has 14 leaves, and the last (fos. 134–9) has only 6, the final two folios having been cut out.

the letters in the second part, though with substantial variations in their arrangement, and it omits the entire papal section as well as all but four of the group of twenty-seven letters with which the collection begins.[1] The collection contains 278 items, including one unnumbered item and eleven duplicates, so that the corrected total number of letters is 267.[2] There is no formal classification of the collection in separate parts, but there are changes of hand and breaks in transcription,[3] and it is possible by an analysis of the subject-matter to show that the compilation was derived from a number of separate sources.

Four principal elements can be distinguished in the build-up of the collection as a whole, the second of which is itself of twofold ancestry; and a palaeographical description of the collection can be summarized in the following way:

Part I: Letters 1–27, fos. 72ra–85vb.

The headings are written in black and the initials are alternately red and green. Letters 26 and 27 (*Excessus uestros* and *Vestram non debet*: cf. *Mats.* VI, epp. 479 and 488) were added in a different hand at the end of fo. 85vb.

[1] Table showing the relationship between the index and the letter collection in MS Vat. Lat. 6024:

Index	Letters	Index	Letters
1–4	4, 11, 13, 12	31–60	88–117
5–7	29, 30, 28	61–94	54–87 (lacking Vat. 70)
8–30	31–53	95–181	118–207 (lacking Vat. 154, 155, 157, 158, 178)

[2] The unnumbered item appears in Appendix III below as 84b. The duplications are: 5 = 170; 10 = 171; 14 = 272; 17 = 249; 18 = 248; 19 = 91; 20 = 266; 24 = 105; 25 = 199; 26 = 84a; and 27 = 84b. In the collection as a whole 28 letters were written to Becket: nos. 11, 46, 102, 196, 197, 200–07, 211, 217, 219–22, 231, 247, 255, 256, 259, 260, 263, 265; of which the 15 from no. 211 onwards were written by the Pope. Letters issued by Becket total 138: nos. 2, 4, 5 = 170, 8, 9, 10 = 171, 12 13, 19 = 91, 24 = 105, 26 = 84a, 27 = 84b, 28, 30, 32–7, 39–41, 43–5, 48–51, 54, 55, 57, 61, 63–6, 71, 72, 74, 77, 78, 81–3, 85, 87–90, 92–4, 97, 98, 101, 103, 104, 106, 109–14, 116–30, 133–7, 139–44, 146–51, 153–69, 172–94; letters issued by Alexander III, in addition to those addressed to Becket, total 56: nos. 6, 14 = 272, 17 = 249, 18 = 248, 20 = 266, 22, 208–10, 212–16, 218, 224–30, 232–46, 250–4, 257, 258, 261, 262, 264, 267, 269–71, and 273–7; 30 letters were sent to the Pope: nos. 1, 3, 7, 15, 16, 23, 38, 42, 47, 56, 58–60, 62, 67, 69, 75, 76, 80, 86, 95, 96, 99, 100, 107, 108, 131, 138, 152, and 198; and there are 15 miscellaneous items: nos. 21, 25 = 199, 29, 31, 52, 53, 68, 70, 73, 79, 115, 132, 145, 195, and 223.

[3] Breaks in transcription occur on fos. 85vb and 129ra; and these breaks correspond with the divisions between parts I, II, and III. Changes of hand occur on fos. 85vb, 86ra, 94va, 116ra, 120va, 130ra, and 139ra.

Part IIa : Letters 28–169, fos. 86ra–120va.

Transcribed by more than one hand; all headings are rubricated and the initials are alternately red and green.

IIb : Letters 170–207, fos. 120va–129ra.[1]

Continuing from IIa without a break in transcription; similar in features with IIa, but 22 headings are lacking in this part, and half of fo. 129 has been excised.

Part III : Letters 208–264, fos. 130ra–137rb.

Written and decorated almost identically with Part IIb.

Part IV : Letters 265–277, fos. 137rb–139vb.

Continuing from Part III without interruption, and almost identical in script and format down to no. 274 on fo. 139ra. Letters 275–7 are transcribed in a different hand, and their headings and initials are lacking; these three items are almost certainly a later addition.

The first part comprises twenty-seven miscellaneous letters, including an anonymous account of the Council of Würzburg.[2] These letters originally formed a separate and coherent sequence, independently of later parts of the present collection. Eleven occur again in later positions, either in full[3] or identified by a heading or protocol and *incipit*;[4] and in each such latter instance a reference back is made to the location of the full text in the first part with the words 'supra in primo quaterno'.[5] In one case the reference back is made to a letter which does not in fact appear in the earlier section,[6] which may suggest either a simple scribal error or the possibility that the opening section is no longer complete. Most letters in this section are found in both Becket and Foliot manuscripts,[7] but collation reveals that where there is significant conflict

---

[1] The letters without headings in this section are: nos. 170–9, 181, 182, 184, and 186–94.

[2] *Cum clerum* (3); cf. *Mats.* V, ep. 99.

[3] Nos. 14 = 272; 19 = 91; 25 = 199; and 10 = 171.

[4] Nos. 5 = 170; 17 = 249; 18 = 248; 20 = 266; 24 = 105; 26 = 84a; and 27 = 84b.

[5] Cf. fos. 98rb–va, 103rb, 120va, 135rb, and 137va.

[6] Fo. 135rb, *Illius dignitatis* (246; cf. *Mats.* V, ep. 169); only the rubricated heading 'Idem Eborac(ensi) archiepiscopo et omnibus episcopis Anglie' and the *incipit* 'Illius dignitatis et maioritatis et cetera' appear here, with the reference to the first part of the volume; but the letter is not found anywhere else in the MS.

[7] All the letters in Vat. I, with the exception of nos. 15, 16, and 19–24, are in one or other of the Foliot MSS; and all except no. 3 are in Alan of Tewkesbury's collection.

between the two traditions, the Vatican text is closer to the Foliot than to the Becket version.[1]

The second and largest part of the collection contains 181 items, the majority of which were issued or received by Becket during his exile. This is the section whose contents are listed in variant order in the index which precedes the whole collection. Collation with other Becket collections discloses that two separate sources lie behind this part: the first 143 letters form a chronologically arranged sequence of Becket's correspondence, including letters written in his favour to the Pope and others;[2] and the concluding group of thirty-eight letters are found in the same order as they appear in the Bodleian Archetype. Collation with Bodl.A shows that this small group contains in corresponding order all the non-papal letters in the Bodleian Archetype which had not been already transcribed in the immediately preceding parts of the Vatican manuscript.[3] The second part of the Vatican Collection is thus seen to have been formed by a combination of two originally separate collections of Becket letters, but their union was almost certainly achieved before the compiler of the Vatican Collection had access to them.

The work is completed with the third and fourth parts, which are composed almost exclusively of papal letters: the third part

[1] E.g., Vat. 5 omits the protocol, which is found wherever the letter occurs in the Becket MSS as also in Vat. 170: cf. Cave 294; Vat. 10 agrees with Cave 295 in omitting the protocol, which is likewise known in the Becket MSS and in Vat. 171; Vat. 18 has the full protocol as in the Foliot MSS (cf. Cave 186), whereas it is omitted in the Becket MSS.

[2] Nos. 38, 42, 52, 53, 58–60, 62, 67, 69, 73, 76, 79, 86, 95, 96, 99, 100, 107, 108, 115, 138, 145, and 152. This section also includes some of the legates' reports to Alexander III: nos. 47, 56, 80, and 131.

[3] Table showing the correlation of Becket letters in Vat. I–IIb and Bodl.A (MS Bodl. 509):

Vat.IIb	*Bodl.A*		*Vat.I–IIa*
170	1	2	4
171–4	3–6	7–8	8–9
		9	32
175–9	10–14	15–16	11–12
180–94	17–31		
195–7	34–6		
198	57	59–65	160–6
199–200	66–7		
201–7	70–6		
		79	168

contains fifty-six papal letters, together with the oath taken by
Gerard la Pucelle on his return from Germany;[1] and the fourth is
composed of ten papal letters which were probably derived from a
non-Becket source, with an appendix of three further letters which
were apparently added later, and which are otherwise known only
in Foliot sources.[2] The date of completion of the Vatican Collection, or of its component sections, cannot be certainly stated: the
latest date that can be assigned to any item in the collection is
27 February 1172, which is the date of issue of the final item
to be transcribed in the appendix;[3] the bulls of canonization of
March 1173 are not included, though there is evidence that the
work was transcribed after the canonization.[4] And no letter in
the whole of the Vatican volume can be positively dated later than
1173.

B. THE ROYAL COLLECTION

The Royal Collection, in the Brit. Libr. MS Royal 13.A.XIII, is a
careful manuscript of the late twelfth century, written in single
columns, with rubricated headings and initials.[5] Its 252 letters are
not numbered in the manuscript, and there is much contemporaneous correction of the text, mostly interlinear, but occasionally in
the margins.[6] The final quire has been damaged by damp,[7] and parts
of the last three folios are now illegible, but the surviving volume
appears complete. According to a note barely visible on the back of
fo. 128, it belonged in the Middle Ages to Merton Priory,[8] and may
have been written there; it later belonged to the library of Lord

---

[1] *Ego Girardus* (223); cf. *Mats.* VI, ep. 421.

[2] The three items are: *Quod tibi ad presens* (275; cf. *Mats.* VII, ep. 627), and
two versions of *Fraternitati uestre* (276 and 277; cf. *Mats.* VII, epp. 753 and
767) addressed to different recipients.

[3] No. 277.

[4] The bulls of canonization are *Redolet Anglia* and *Gaudendum est* (cf. *Mats.*
VII, epp. 785 and 784). Evidence of a post canonization transcription is found in
the rubric to no. 70 which includes the reference 'sanctus Thomas'.

[5] 9½ × 6 in., 128 fos.; single columns, 35 lines to the column. The symbol
'pp' for 'papa' has been erased or crossed out wherever it occurred in the
MS.

[6] Corrections are found on the following fos: 5v, 6v, 9r, 9v, 16r, 17v, 18r, 22r,
22v, 23v, 26r, 28r, 28v, 29r, 30r, 30v, 31v, 37r, 39v, 42r, 43v, 45v, 46v, 47r, 48v,
51r, 52v, 55v, 61r, 62r, 65v, 68v, 69r, 72r, 74r, 75r, 77v, 78r, 81v, 83r, 84r, 87v,
88r, 89r, 91v, 93r, 93v, 95v, 96v, 98v, 102r, 108v, 109r, 109v, 111v, 113v,
115v, 117v, 122r, and 124v.

[7] Fos. 123–8.

[8] 'Ex merton'.

John Lumley.[1] The collection, which forms the entire manuscript
volume, contains almost the whole of Vat. II and III, though in a
different arrangement, with the addition of fifteen letters, seven of
which occur in Vat. I. It preserves the same twofold division into
Becket and papal material,[2] and each part was transcribed separately, the archbishop's correspondence occupying the first thirteen
quires and the papal letters the final two.[3] The eight additional
letters are found in two separate groups of four: the first group is
transcribed on a leaf inserted between the two main parts of the
collection,[4] while the second forms the concluding four items of the
whole work.[5] As far as the first group is concerned, it seems clear
both from its content and the manner of insertion that it was a later
addition to the basic material: none of the four letters is found in
any other manuscript of the Becket tradition; and, while one was
written by Becket (189), three were written by Gilbert Foliot (188,
190, and 191) and probably derive from his archives. And three of
the four which constitute the final sequence almost certainly represent an appendix to the collection as a whole, since no. 250 is the
papal mandate of late 1171 ordering the reconciliation of Canterbury Cathedral, and nos. 251 and 252 are bulls announcing the
canonization of Becket in March 1173. The remaining letter (249),
dated 16 May 1168, was sent to Christ Church, Canterbury,[6] and

---

[1] Lumley's signature is inscribed at the foot of fo. 2r. Cf. S. Jayne and
F. R. Johnson, *The Lumley Library*, British Museum Publications, London
(1956).

[2] Nos. 1–187 are the archbishop's correspondence, including some non-papal
letters concerning the controversy; and nos. 192–252 are papal letters.

[3] The collection divides at fo. 107, the papal letters beginning on fo. 108r. The
gatherings of eight leaves are numbered from I to XIV on their final folio versos,
with the exception of quire V; fo. 105 has been inserted into quire XIII and fo.
107 into quire XIV, so that these two quires have 9 leaves each; XV which has
12 leaves is not numbered.

[4] Fo. 107r–v: 188   *Dominus Cantuariensis* G. of London to J. of Salisbury,
                     March 1169 (first sentence only, ending 'sensisse')

             189   *Nouerit Deus* Becket to Jocelin of Salisbury, June 1166

             190   *Vestram scimus* English Church to Becket, mid-1167

             191   *Multis curarum* G. of London to R. Archd. of Oxford,
                     June 1169

[5] Fos. 126v–128v: 249   *Quoniam ecclesia uestra* Pope to Christ Church, 16
                          May 1168

               250   *Mandamus uobis* Pope to Albert & Theodinus, late
                      1171

               251   *Gaudendum est* Pope to Christ Church, 12 March 1173

               252   *Redolet Anglia* Pope to English people, 12 March 1173

[6] *Quoniam ecclesia, Mats.* VI, ep. 412.

may only have come to light after the compilation of the archetype on which the Vatican collection depended.

With the exception of these items, all the letters in the Royal Collection are found also in Vat., though in a different order; and collation of Vat. II and III with Roy. reveals a complex but definite relationship between them. The material common to Vat. and Roy. can be broken down into twenty-one very unequal components, the smallest containing only one item, but the largest containing a sequence of eighty-two letters. The Becket letters break down into fifteen sections and the papal letters into six.[1] The pattern of relationship discovered by comparing the arrangement of these groups in Vat. and Roy. reveals the process by which the two compilations were formed, and discloses a stage intermediate between the Bodleian Archetype and these two large expansions of it. If the groupings are numbered in order as they occur in both manuscripts, the following relationship is established:

a) *Becket letters:*

Vat. IIa, groups 1–8 = Roy. I, groups 1, 3, 5, 7, 9, 11, 13, and 15

Vat. IIb, groups 9–15 = Roy. I, groups 2, 4, 6, 8, 10, 12, and 14

b) *Papal letters:*

Vat. III, groups 16–21 = Roy. II, groups 16, 20, 19, 17, 21, and 18

The most significant correlation is between Vat. IIa–b and Roy. I, and it is scarcely possible that the pattern disclosed here is the result of mere chance. It is conceivable that the numerous subdivisions

---

[1] This table shows the relationship between Vatican MS Lat. 6024 and Brit. Libr. MS Royal 13. A. xiii.

Vat. Part IIa	*Roy.* Part I	*Vat.* Part IIb	*Roy.* Part I	*Vat.* Part III	*Roy.* Part II
28–30 =	7, 6, 5	170–5 =	8–13	208–10 =	192–4
31–3 =	15–17	176–7 =	19–20	211–13 =	242–4
34–41 =	21–8	178 =	29	215–19 ⎫	
42–53 =	30–41	179–90 =	42–53	246 ⎬ =	233–9, 241
54–134 =	54–135	191–4 =	136–9	220–1 ⎭	
135–7 =	140–2	195–8 =	143–6	222–48* =	195–220
138–64 =	147–73	199–207 =	174–84	249–52 =	245–8
165–9 =	183–7			253–64 =	221–32

N.B. Roy. nos. 1–4, 14, 18, and 240, which are missing from this table, are all found in Vat. I, as follows: Vat. 4, 11, 13, 12, 8, 9, and 22.

* omitting 246, which seems to have been misplaced in Vat. as a result of a change of hand after no. 219.

revealed by collation represent small distinct sources which the compilers of Vat. and Roy. arranged in different orders; alternatively, they could derive from files of letters preserved in Becket's archives after the murder, in which case it would be tempting to see in them the *schedule* to which Alan of Tewkesbury referred in the introduction to his edition of the Becket correspondence. But both these hypotheses are extremely unlikely, and a solution to this problem is provided by comparing the two collections with the Bodleian Archetype. It will be remembered that Vat. IIb contains all the non-papal letters from the Bodleian Archetype which had not already occurred in Vat. I and IIa, and that Vat. II is composed of two separate collections of the archbishop's correspondence, the first comprising a collection of 143 letters arranged in chronological order and having some items in common with the Bodleian Archetype, and the other containing an abbreviation of the Bodleian Archetype itself. Significantly, the collation of Vat. II and Roy. I shows that the division of Vat. II into parts a and b corresponds exactly with alternate groups in Roy. I as shown in the table above, and that, whereas the compiler of Vat. had placed the two sources consecutively, the author of Roy. had achieved a more satisfactory integration of them, knitting the sources together in a better chronological arrangement. In the section of papal letters, the Bodleian derivation is much less certain. Although twenty-six of its letters are also found in the Bodleian Archetype, there are sufficient textual differences to indicate that the Vat. compiler derived his material not from the archetype, but rather from the record-files on which it also depended. This explains why certain sequences of letters occur together in both sources, as well as the textual discrepancies between them.[1]

By such a procedure it is possible not only to explain the relationship between the Vatican and Royal Collections, but also to establish the contents and structure of a second basic collection of Becket materials derived ultimately from his archives: the Vatican Archetype or Archetype B. This is achieved by isolating the material common to Vat. and Roy., eliminating from it the Bodleian derivation, and collating the residue with independently surviving deriva-

---

[1] Vat. 208, 211–13, 215, 217–19, 246, 220, 22, 221, 225, 229, 236–9 241–4, 248–51 = Bodl. 43, 55, 56, 58, 44, [Laud. 45], 45–9, 54, 50, 51, 39, 37, 53, 32, 40, 41, 33, 42, 68, 69, 77, and 78.

tives to establish the original order of the archetype.[1] According to this reconstruction, the Vatican Archetype consisted of:

(i) a more or less chronologically arranged collection of Becket letters augmented by miscellaneous items of correspondence mostly written by authors favourable to his cause, totalling 148 items;[2]

(ii) a similarly arranged collection of papal letters into which Gerard la Pucelle's oath renouncing the papal schism had been inserted, totalling 58 items.[3]

Content and arrangement point to an archival source for both parts of the collection. There is virtually nothing in the Becket section which did not pass through Becket's hands during the exile: out of a total of 148 items, 111 were issued by him,[4] three were addressed to him or his co-exiles,[5] and one was written in the name of the *co-exules*, possibly by John of Salisbury;[6] while no less than twenty-six of the remaining thirty-three miscellaneous items were written in his support by friends in England and France[7] and four are formal reports of negotiations with Henry II sent by papal commissioners to Alexander III.[8] There are only three letters in

---

[1] Collation with the Laon, Harleian, Lambeth, and Bodl. B. II Collections suggests that Vat. Parts II and III preserve the order of the original archetype more faithfully than Roy. Hence the archetype can be reconstructed as follows (using Vat. numeration): Vat. 4, 11, 13, 12 (these four items taken from Vat. I and arranged in this order in agreement with Roy. and the collections mentioned above), 29, 30, 28, 31–82 (a and b), 83–4a, 84b, 85–169, 208–19, 246, 220, 22, (Vat. 22 is inserted here in agreement with Roy.), 221–45, and 247–64. Cf. Appendix III, below. Note that item 82 is a combination of two separate letters, indicated in the numeration by letters a and b in brackets; and that item 84b was omitted from the numeration in the Vat. MS. A change of scribe after Vat. 219 led to the omission of *Illius dignitatis* at that point: a reference to it was inserted at 246.

[2] Cf. Vat. 4, 11, 13, 12, 29, 30, 28, 31–82 (a and b), 83–4a, 84b, and 85–169. It was suggested in an earlier study (Anne Duggan, 'The French Manuscripts of the Becket Correspondence', *Thomas Becket: Actes du Colloque International de Sédières*, ed. R. Foreville (Paris) 1975, p. 2), that Archetype B contained a total of only 190 letters, of which twenty-two were in common with Archetype A; the revised statistics presented here result from a closer study of the texts.

[3] Cf. Vat. 208–19, 246, 220, 22, 221–45, and 247–64.

[4] Cf. Vat. 4, 13, 12, 30, 28, 32–7, 39–41, 43–5, 48–51, 54, 55, 57, 61, 63–6, 71 72, 74, 77, 78, 81–2 (a and b), 83, 84a, 84b, 85, 87–94, 97, 98, 101, 103–6, 109–14, 116–30, 133–7, 139–44, 146–51, and 153–69.

[5] Cf. Vat. 11, 46, and 102.   [6] Cf. Vat. 145.

[7] Vat. 38, 42, 52, 53, 58–60, 62, 67–9, 73, 75, 76, 79, 86, 95, 96, 99, 100, 107, 108, 115, 132, 138, and 152.

[8] Vat. 47, 56, 80, and 131.

Part I which do not fit into these categories, and the presence of all three in a Becket collection can readily be explained. Thus, Henry II's letter to the schismatical Archbishop of Cologne (Vat. 29) was known to the exiled members of Becket's circle and was discussed by John of Salisbury, and the Poitevin petition concerning the degree of consanguinity between Henry II and Eleanor of Aquitaine (Vat. 70) was prepared for a conference between the king and papal legates at which Becket's representatives were present. Similarly, the letter from the Abbot and Prior of St-Victor, Paris, to Robert of Melun (Vat. 31), with its belated congratulations on his elevation to the bishopric of Hereford (which had occurred in 1163) and encouragement to sustain the cause of the Church in its present difficulties (August 1166), resulted from the direct intervention of the Becket party.[1] Like the miscellaneous items in Part I, the majority of the papal letters in Part II were by their nature probably known to the Becket party: thirteen were addressed to Becket himself;[2] fourteen were formal instructions to papal representatives involved in negotiations with archbishop and king;[3] nineteen were addressed to the English and Norman/Angevin episcopate and clergy either collectively or individually;[4] eight were sent to Henry II, two to Louis VII, and one to the royal messenger John Cumin.[5] With the single exception of Vat. 264, which was received by Rotrou of Rouen and Theobald of Amiens in October 1171 and hence marks a late accession to the collection after Becket's death, there is nothing here that one would not reasonably expect to find in Becket's archives.[6] But evidence of archival derivation for the Vatican Archetype is not confined to such speculative considerations. Its dependence on record-files is evidenced by such

---

[1] *Diu desideraui*, Mats. V, ep. 213, cf. John of Salisbury, ibid., p. 433; *Sic computati*, ibid., VI, ep. 335, prepared for the conference between Gisors and Trie on 18 Nov. 1167; *Magnam de promotione*, ibid., V, ep. 220, cf. John of Salisbury's recommendation, ibid., VI, p. 20.

[2] Vat. 211, 217, 219–22, 231, 247, 255, 256, 259, 260, and 263.

[3] Vat. 209, 210, 212, 227, 235, 237, 239, 242–5, 258, 262, and 264.

[4] Vat. 208, 214–16, 218, 246, 226, 230, 232, 234, 236, 240, 241, 248–51, 257, and 261.

[5] To Henry II, Vat. 213, 22, 225, 228, 229, 238, 252, and 254; to Louis VII, Vat. 224 and 253; to John Cumin, Vat. 233.

[6] The interesting suggestion made by Morey and Brooke (*Gilbert Foliot and his Letters*, Cambridge (1965), p. 23 and n. 1), that the papal letters in Vat. and Roy. represented the dossier of materials sent to Master Gratian in late 1170 (cf. p. 85, n. 1 below), is difficult to sustain in the light of the dual origin of these collections and the late date of some of the letters contained in them.

details as its accurate chronological arrangement of letters,[1] its separation of Becket and papal material, and its references to multiple copies of specific letters. In the case of *Vestra discretio* (Vat. 121), for example, the following note is appended to the text:

> [fo. 106ra] Walt(erio) Roff(ensi) episcopo, sic, ubi habetur per episcopatum uestrum per totam Cantiam.
> Sicut H(enrico) Wintoniensi, sic Norwicen(si), Cestr(ensi), Exon(iensi), Wigorn(iensi), Dunelm-(ensi).
> Dauid uero Meneuensi et Nich(olao) Landau(ensi), et Godefr(ido) Lanelu(ensi), sic: per totam terram eius que in episcopatu uestro est, in omnibus ecclesiis;

and *Inter emptorum* (Vat. 125), Becket's letter to Cardinal Hyacinth, is followed by the record that identical letters were sent to Cardinals Albert and Theodinus:

> [fo. 107va] Similiter domino Alberto presbytero cardinali;
> Item: Theodino presbytero cardinali;

and Becket's letter to the sub-prior and monks of Christ Church (*Quot et quantas*, Vat. 156) has the note:

> [fo. 116rb] Similiter abbati de Faueresham et aliis abbatibus et prioribus per archiepiscopatum constitutis, nisi quod non tenentur aliquid percipere decanis.[2]

It is evident either that drafts of letters were kept in Becket's archives, or that copies of important letters were made at the time

---

[1] Cf. Appendix III, below. The generally correct chronology is significantly broken in the Becket section only by the intrusion of the letter to Empress Matilda (40: December 1164) into 1167 material and by the placing of a file of Bangor letters among items from 1169 (nos. 110–13); in the papal section, the only serious chronological errors are: the mixed group of letters relating to Becket's authority (nos. 216–21), themselves chronologically confused and dating from the years 1164–6, placed between materials dated respectively 1167 and 1168; the apparent misplacement of no. 230 (from 1163–4) among 1168 material, and no. 255 (from 1166) among letters from 1170.

[2] Cf. also Vat. 117 [fo. 105ra] Similiter scriptum est omnibus episcopis Norm(annie) ut archiepiscopo, et capitulis ut Rothomag(ensibus); Vat 118 [fo. 105ra] Similiter Ric(ardo) priori et capitulo Dour(ie) et Cantie monasteriis; Vat. 136 [fo. 110vb] Similiter omnibus episcopis; Vat. 154 [fo. 116ra] Eodem modo Sarisberiensi; Vat. 155 [fo. 116rb] Eodem modo omnibus episcopis Anglie et Gualie; Vat. 158 [fo. 116va] Similiter Westmonasterii, Sancti Albani, Sancti Edmundi et Malmesberie abbatibus.

of issue, together with notes of their recipients and textual variants, if more than one version was sent out. And there are indications that papal letters were similarly treated. Versions B and C of *Nouerit industria*,[1] already discussed at some length above in the context of Archetype A, occur also in Archetype B, with notes which equally suggest derivation from an archival source. Version B (Vat. 236), addressed it will be remembered to Roger of York and Hugh of Durham, is followed by two notes:

> [fo. 133va]   Idem scribit in eadem forma uniuersis episcopis et aliis ecclesiarum prelatis per Ang(liam) constitutis. In eadem forma scribit uniuersis archiepiscopis, episcopis et aliis ecclesiarum prelatis per cismarinam terram illustris Anglorum regis constitutis, Nou-(erit) industria uestra, etc.

The second note is in fact inaccurate, since a different variant of *Nouerit industria* (version A)[2] was issued for use in Henry II's cismarine (French) lands. But the confusion of an English scribe in this instance is readily understandable. Writing in England in the early 1170s, he could be forgiven for construing *cismarinam* to mean the English rather than the French side of the Channel. It is to be supposed that the original compiler of the Vatican Archetype, like the compiler of Archetype A, was confronted by three copies of the same letter, and that he contrived to save himself time by suppressing version A and attaching its accompanying explanatory note to version B. There can be little doubt that the fault lay in the archetype itself, rather than in this particular Vat. transcription or in the original archival record. The reproduction of precisely the same error in Roy. 209, which was independently received from the archetype, proves that it existed in Archetype B itself; whereas the reception of the accurate text into the Bodleian Archetype argues for the soundness of the archival source at this point. In this particular instance, Archetype A is more reliable than Archetype B. As we have seen, however, a succession of scribes in the subsequent tradition of Archetype A had difficulty with the correct identification of the intended recipients of version A; and even the meticulous Alan of Tewkesbury retained an inaccurate address. Even in its handling of version C of *Nouerit industria*, the Vatican Arche-

---

[1] Cf. above, pp. 29–31.
[2] Cf. ibid. and *Mats*, VII, ep. 629.

type was slightly flawed. Vat. 241, addressed to the Archbishop of Tours, appears with the following brief appendix:

[fo. 134vb] In eundem modum: Bituricen(si) et suis; Burdegal-
             (ensi) et suis; Auxitano et suis; Rothomagen(si)
             et suis.

This is another example of space- and time-saving, which has again resulted in a slight inaccuracy. This particular text was prepared for issue to Henry II's French metropolitans; but it would have been quite inappropriate to send it to Rotrou of Rouen, since he was one of the legates responsible for pronouncing the proposed interdict. All that was necessary in the case of Rouen province were mandates to the suffragan bishops and their clergy. Once again, the Bodleian Archetype preserves the accurate form, providing the adjusted inscription (fo. 81r), 'uniuersis episcopis et ceteris ecclesiarum prelatis per Rotomagensem prouinciam constitutis', for the Rouen letters, where Vat. simply reads 'Rothomagen(si) et suis'.

At least six further examples could be cited to demonstrate that the compilers of the Vatican and Bodleian Archetypes derived their common papal letters from the same archival sources, independently of one another, and that their agreement in short sequences of letters is not to be explained by the dependence of Vat. on Bodl. (or vice versa).[1] In many cases, the slips made (possibly through haste) by the scribe of the Vatican Archetype were not corrected until Alan of Tewkesbury prepared his second recension.

The Vatican and Royal Collections show that two different combinations of the two basic Becket collections were constructed, independently of one another, after Becket's death. Their independence is demonstrated by their inclusion of material unknown to the other, their variant order for common material, and also, perhaps more significantly, by their contrasting diplomatic details. Vat. preserves thirteen protocols omitted by Roy.;[2] and Roy. contains fourteen protocols[3] and twenty-seven dating

---

[1] The most significant divergences occur in Vat. 211–13, 215, 217, 220, and 221.

[2] Cf. Vat. 123, 137, 153, 181, 184, and 186–93.

[3] Roy. 195, 197, 198, 200, 203–5, 208, 210, 213, 220, 225, 229, and 248 preserve protocols lacking in Vat.; cf. Vat. 222, 224, 225, 227, 230–2, 235, 237, 240, 248, 257, 261, and 264.

clauses[1] which are lacking in Vat.: the omissions from the latter are in fact confined to Vat. III, which preserves only five protocols in its entire transcription.[2] The divergences in order between Vat. Part III and the Royal Collection can be explained by the supposition that the compiler of the latter received the basic archetype in separated sections (quires or quaternions), and either sought to improve its arrangement or simply confused some of the pieces. There can be little doubt that they record the same texts, agreeing with one another in contrast with the Bodleian Archetype and its derivatives; but their divergence in diplomatic details is less easy to explain. Vat. on the whole lacks protocols and dates, and it may be that the scribes of this manuscript suppressed what they might have considered to be unnecessary and time-wasting additions to the texts. On the other hand, Vat. and Roy. are not sister manuscripts, dependent on the same parent; and it is equally possible that the inclusion or exclusion of diplomatic details was determined at a stage between the formation of the archetype and the reception of its derivatives by the respective compilers of the Vatican and Royal manuscripts.

The Becket correspondence in the Vatican manuscript was certainly transcribed before that in the Royal Collection, since it does not contain the bulls of canonization which appear as the last two items in the latter work. At the same time, small groups of letters at the beginning and end of the collection seem to have been derived from a Foliot source, and the material from Becket sources is sandwiched between them. The Royal manuscript was certainly completed after the canonization of the martyr; and its only part that can be connected with the Foliot tradition was added on an inserted leaf which was not part of the main transcription.[3]

C. THE LAON AND HARLEIAN COLLECTIONS

Evidence that Archetype B, or at least a substantial part of it, did indeed exist and circulate as a separate entity, is provided by two

---

[1] Roy. 175, 192, 194, 195, 197, 200, 203–5, 209, 210, 212, 220, 223–6, 228–31, 233, 239, 243, 245, 246, and 248 preserve dates lacking in Vat.; cf. Vat. 200, 208, 210, 222, 224, 227, 230–2, 236, 237, 239, 240, 248 = 18, 255–8, 215, 220, 212, 249 = 17, 250, and 252.

[2] Vat. 208–10, 236, and 264.

[3] Cf. p. 54 and n. 4 above.

manuscripts surviving respectively in Laon and London. The earlier of these copies is Bibl. de la Ville de Laon MS 337, fos. 29r–64v, in a small, carefully written, volume dating from the thirteenth century,[1] which contains a collection of seventy-eight Becket letters as its sixth and last item.[2] The manuscript volume is now only a fragment, whose first surviving quire number is VI, appearing on fo. 19v and so suggesting the loss of four gatherings at the beginning of the volume; and the transcription of the letters breaks off abruptly in the middle of *Sinceritati uestre* (80) at the foot of fo. 64v, indicating the loss of further pages at the end. But numbers and catchwords survive for the remaining quires (VI–X), and show that they are bound up correctly.[3] According to a modern note on the inside front cover, the manuscript belonged at one time to the Cathedral Church of Laon;[4] and the French provenance of the volume is confirmed by its contents which include a formulary book containing letters to and from the Bishop of Thérouanne as well as the *Sompnia Pharaonis* by Jean de Limoges. The letter-collection is written in double columns with rubricated initials and headings; it begins without identification towards the end of quire VII, and continues without interruption to the present end of the volume. Only a few of the letters have been numbered: the second item is clearly marked iiii and items 8–16 are marked x to xviii, in red roman numerals. The scheme of numeration in the manuscript is therefore both inaccurate and incomplete, and an emended scheme of numeration corresponding with the actual arrangement of the manuscript has been adopted in the discussions that follow.

Collation with the Vatican Archetype reveals that the Laon manuscript agrees with it almost exactly in content, order, and text: Laon 1–78 = Vat. Archetype 2–81 (= Vat. 11, 12, 29, 30, 28, 31–69, 71–82 (a and b), 83–84a, 84b–103). Thus, over a sequence of seventy-eight items, the Laon collection follows the order of

---

[1] $8\frac{6}{8} \times 6\frac{7}{8}$ in.; 64 fos.; single columns; 35 lines to the column.

[2] The Becket letters are preceded by the following items: fos. 1r–4v, 'Formulae epistolarum'; fos. 5r–7r, 'Condemnatio imperatoris contra regem Robertum'; fo. 7v, 'Littera domini pape ad imperatorem pro rege Roberto et sententia'; fos. 8r–28r, the *Sompnia Pharaonis* (by Jean de Limoges, cf. J. A. Fabricius, *Codex Pseudoepigraphicus Veteris Testamenti*, I, pp. 441–96 and idem, *Bibliotheca Latina Mediae et Infimae Aetatis*, IV, p. 91); fos. 28r–v,' Formulae epistolarum'.

[3] The numbers for quires VI–X appear in order at the foot of fos. 19v, 31v, 38v, 47v, and 57v.

[4] The inscription reads: 'Ce livre est de l'église de Laon.'

Archetype B, except for the omission of three items. Its omission of
Desiderio desideraui and *Mirandum et uehementer* (Archetype nos.
1 and 3 = Vat. 4 and 13) was evidently by design, since the partially
surviving contemporary numeration indicates the deliberate
omission of two letters from the opening sequence of four. But it is
not possible to determine whether its third omission, of the
Gradus cognationis (Archetype 45 = Vat. 70), was by error or intention, since the original numeration was abandoned as early as no.
xviii. Otherwise, however, the numerical correlation between Laon
and Archetype B is exact. Equally striking is the textual agreement
between them. The Laon Collection has the peculiar texts of
Se ipsum ad penam[1] and *Venientes ad terram*[2] which distinguish the
members of the Vatican Family from all other traditions of the
Becket correspondence. There can be little doubt that the Laon
Collection is a later copy of part of the Vatican Archetype, and
provides evidence of its circulation in France.

The material in the Laon Collection appears as the second constituent in the composite Brit. Libr. MS Harleian 215, already
mentioned above.[3] This manuscript is written in an untidy hand in
single columns, with headings and initials in red. Its ninety-one
items, which were not originally numbered, fall into two distinct
groups:[4] the first fourteen items agree with the Rawlinson Collection Part II, discussed when considering the Bodleian Family,
while the remaining seventy-seven letters correspond exactly in
contents and order with the Laon Collection, except that the
Gradus cognationis (Harl. 57) is not found in the latter.[5] The final
letter is unfinished, breaking off with the words 'faciat imitari'. And
after a gap of two lines only, there then follows an assortment of
items, written in a variety of fourteenth-century hands. This
additional material contains among other items a letter from
Prester John[6] and a description of the basilica of St Thomas in

---

[1] Laon 56 = Vat. 82 (a) and (b); cf. p. 73 below.

[2] Laon 22 = Vat. 47; cf. pp. 73, 110, and 114 below.

[3] Cf. p. 40 above.

[4] The two groups of letters in MS Harleian 215 are: (1) Letters 1–14, fos.
1r–31v; cf. Rawl. II, 9–22; (2) Letters 15–91, fos. 31v–101r; cf. Vat. 28–103. The
volume is completed with the further parts: (3) Letter of Prester John, fos.
101r–106v; account of the basilica of St Thomas the Apostle in India, fos.
106v–107r; assorted letters and tracts, fos. 107r–113v; (4) AlanT, *Explanatio*,
much expanded by interpolations and incomplete, fos. 114r–148v; (5) 'Euangelium Nichodemi', fos. 149r–160v.

[5] Cf. *Mats.* VI, ep. 335.   [6] Fos. 101r–106v: 'Nunciabatur . . . impleti'.

India;[1] and the manuscript is completed with an expanded and interpolated version of Alan of Tewkesbury's *Explanatio* and the 'Euangelium Nichodemi'.

The agreement between the Harleian and Laon Collections is very striking: both omit the rubricated headings to *Inualescunt pater* and *Si unum patitur*, which occur in full in the Vatican Collection;[2] both have the headings to *Honor quem, Inspectis litteris* and *Sinceritati uestre*, which Vat. had omitted;[3] both append an abbreviated list of excommunicates to *Nouerit fraternitas*[4] and both have the mistaken reading 'Rob(erto) Wigorn(iensi) episcopo' in the heading of *Et ratio iuris*.[5] But, most striking of all, both collections break off at exactly the same point in the middle of *Sinceritati uestre*, omitting a substantial part of the generally received text.[6] In the Laon copy, the manuscript concludes with the phrase 'faciat imitari' at the foot of its last remaining folio, and it is possible that the transcription of the letter originally continued on to the final leaf of the quire, which is now missing; but in the Harleian copy, the transcription stops abruptly with the same words in mid-folio, and after a brief gap a new hand begins an entirely different section of material unconnected with the Becket controversy. It would be tempting to assume that the fourteenth-century Harleian version was directly dependent on the defective copy preserved at Laon, but the fact that Harl. has in a significant position the *Gradus cognationis*, which is lacking in the Laon MS,[7] and the full text of *Gratias agimus*, which is abbreviated in the latter,[8] makes this supposition virtually impossible. But it seems very likely that both were dependent upon a common and probably defective parent. The features of these two incomplete descendants from the Vatican Archetype show that they record a derivation from the archetype which had, like itself, an independent existence as a collection, which was known in both France and England in the Middle Ages and was considered worth transcribing as late as the mid-fourteenth century.

---

[1] Fos. 106v–107r: 'Thomas apostolus . . . discernitur'.

[2] Harl. 61b and 86 = Laon 49 and 74; cf. Vat. 75 and 99.

[3] Harl. 60, 88, and 90 = 47, 76, and 78; cf. Vat. 73, 101, and 103.

[4] Harl. 76 = Laon 64; cf. Vat. 89.

[5] Harl. 16 = Laon 4; cf. Vat. 30.

[6] Harl. 90 = Laon 78; cf. Vat. 103.

[7] Harl. 57 corresponds with Vat. and Roy. 70.

[8] Harl. 51 = Laon 39; but Laon 39 lacks 'ut ecclesiam . . . suam'; cf. *Mats.* VI, p. 470.

To complete this survey of the Vatican Family, two copies of the full Royal Collection have survived, but, for reasons sufficiently explained, neither is of much significance. The Oxford Bodl. MS 278 is a seventeenth-century transcript whose details are defective: its scribe was not very familiar with medieval abbreviations and frequently misread his text, while adopting Classical spelling in his copy. The Oxford St John's College MS 15, fos. 182ra–251vb, is a fifteenth-century copy either of Roy. itself, or of a closely related version; it contains the full Royal Collection in exactly the same order, while Bodl. 278 omits *Calamitates matris* and *Fraternitatem uestram* (Roy. 163 and 164), possibly by mistake. The Vatican Family of collections is therefore, like the smaller Bodleian Family with which it is connected, retraceable in its origins to the household of Becket himself, and derives for the greater part from the records kept there. But none of the surviving manuscripts was written in the archbishop's household and all are more than one stage removed from the archetypal arrangement; and all except the fragmentary survivals, incorporate additional letters derived from other sources.

3. THE LAMBETH FAMILY

The two largest surviving collections of the Becket correspondence, with the exception of Alan of Tewkesbury's compilation, are the Lambeth Palace MS 136 (Lamb.) and the Oxford Bodl. MS 937, fos. 175r–446r (Bodl.B, II and III), containing 350 and 368 letters respectively, and these can be considered together and called the Lambeth Family, taking their name from the manuscript which seems to preserve the more primitive form of the collection, although it is probably not the earlier in date of transcription.

For the greater part they agree with one another in order and contents, though it is not easy to determine their exact interrelationship or to distinguish the various elements which were combined in their composition. Both are composite compilations, dependent in some way on more accurate versions of materials in the two family groups already discussed, but they have in addition many other letters derived, as the evidence suggests, from a Becket source. In simple terms, their contents and arrangement can be summarized as follows: each begins with a derivative from the

Bodleian Archetype copied without variation of order,[1] to which each adds a small group of other letters, followed by almost the whole of the Vatican Archetype, for the most part omitting only those items which had already appeared in the earlier sections; and each collection is completed with further matter. The basis of these compilations was clearly provided by a combination of two already-existing collections with yet further letters, and upon examination they are found to agree more faithfully with the Bodleian than with the Vatican Family. Thus, where their order agrees with that in the Vatican Collection, the Lambeth Collections preserve diplomatic details, such as protocols and dates, unknown in either the Vatican or the Royal manuscripts, and there is a closer textual agreement between the two Lambeth Collections than that between either of them and the members of the Vatican Family. In some instances their details are otherwise known only in Recension III of the Alan of Tewkesbury collection.[2] Both manuscripts are far more lavishly produced than any extant member of the Bodleian or Vatican Families, and they probably represent a later stage in the formation of a comprehensive collection of the Becket correspondence.

A. THE LAMBETH COLLECTION

The Lambeth MS 136[3] is a finely written manuscript of the early thirteenth century, with rubricated headings throughout and the initial letters coloured alternately red and blue and decorated in pen-work of the contrasting colour. The folios are paginated; and their numeration, the alphabetical sequence of the gatherings from A to Y, and the numeration of the individual letters are in a post-medieval hand; but medieval catchwords survive to link all the gatherings from B to X[4] and prove that the volume is complete and

---

[1] That is, save for the curious repetition of the letter *Mittimus sanctitati uestre latorem* (Bodl. A 18), which appears as Lamb. 24 and 30, with the consequent omission of *Mittimus sanctitati uestre latores* (Bodl. A 24). The similarity between the address, protocol, and *incipit* of the two letters may explain the confusion.

[2] Cf. pp. 134–7 below.

[3] $12\frac{1}{4} \times 8$ in., 2 fo. + 338 pages; double columns, 36 lines to the column; the papal style and title 'pp' or 'papa', and the descriptions 'sanctissimus', 'summus', etc., as well as Becket's Christian name, have been erased or deleted in the opening part of the MS: cf. pp. 1a, 5a, 8a, 9a, 10a, 14a, 23a, 23b, 29b, 42a, 49b, and 53b.

[4] There is no catchword between the last two gatherings (X and Y), but its absence may be explained by the fact that a different scribe completed quire X.

bound up correctly. But the first gathering, marked A, now comprises two leaves only, containing two letters,[1] and these are foliated 1–2 independently of the subsequent pagination; the two following folios have been cut out, leaving traces of large capitals in red and blue.[2] This fragment is all that remains of what was evidently a separate collection, since the script and decoration of the two folios are quite different from those of the rest of the volume, their numeration is independent of the later pagination, and Lumley's signature appears at the foot of the first folio of quire B. But from page 1 onwards the transcription seems continuous in a single hand to the end of no. 346 on p. 317b in the middle of gathering X;[3] a different hand completes this quire with six letters, leaving spaces for the coloured initials, but the earlier hand resumes for the first six items in the final quire Y, while the last six letters were written by the scribe who completed the preceding gathering, and here again the coloured initials have not been inserted.

With the exception of the first two items, the manuscript as a whole contains 362 numbered letters, of which fifteen are duplicated, so that the corrected total is 347.[4] The collection can be analysed in six parts as follows:

Part I: Letters 3–6, pp. 1a–5a.

This small group of letters is not in either Bodl. B, II or Roy., but they are found among the additions in Vat.,[5] and three are in the Foliot collections.[6]

Part II: Letters 7–86, pp. 5a–98b.

This section corresponds almost exactly with the Bodleian Archetype, except that it repeats item 24 at no. 30, and so lacks Bodl. 30, and (in agreement with all Bodleian derivatives, except the earliest version in MS Bodl. 509) inserts *Sepe nobis* (*Mats.* V, ep. 157) as no. 51.

---

[1] Nos. 1 and 2, *Comitem Flandrensem* (*Mats.* V, ep. 36) and *Diu desideraui* (*Mats.* V, ep. 213).

[2] It is possible to identify the capitals H, P, and I.

[3] The modern numeration of the letters in the MS is faulty and has for convenience been slightly emended in the Tables and Appendices: cf. Appendix IV below. Letter 346 is numbered 345 in the MS.

[4] 24 = 30, 55 = 271, 114 = 182, 119 = 274, 122 = 258, 134 = 343, 140 = 347, 146 = 275, 165 = 249, 234 = 286, 267 = 272, 281 = 352, 316 = 349, 317 = 350, and 325 = 348.

[5] Lamb. 3, 4, 5, and 6 = Vat. 2, 1, 3, and 268.

[6] Lamb. 3, 4, and 6 = Cave 168, 170, and 293 and Douce 13, 14, and 27.

Part III : Letters 87–144, pp. 98b–167a.

Of the fifty-eight letters in this section, only twenty-seven occur in the Vatican archetype, and the section as a whole may represent the exploitation of a source, or sources, other than the two basic collections discussed so far. The derivation of the 'Vatican' letters is uncertain, however, save for Lamb. 89–97, 99, and 101–3, whose order agrees with the Vat. Archetype,[1] and whose texts are virtually indistinguishable from it.

Part IV : Letters 145–245, pp. 167a–263a.

This section agrees closely with the Vatican Archetype, containing in correct sequence an abbreviation of Vat. 31–146, lacking the nineteen items which had already occurred mostly in Part III,[2] omitting four others,[3] and inserting five additional items towards the end of the Vat. derivation.[4]

Part V(a) : Letters 246–346, pp. 263a–317b.

This long section of 101 items includes five duplicates,[5] and its derivation, like that of Part III, is uncertain. Once again there is an admixture of letters which occur also in the Vatican Archetype and reveal a degree of agreement with the archetypal order and text, especially in Lamb. 297–300, 328–30, 335, 336, and 339–45.[6]

V(b) : Letters 347–52, pp. 317b–22b.

There is a clear break in transcription at this point: these six letters occupy the last five pages of quire X; they are written in a different hand; and spaces are left for the insertion of coloured initials. Even more significantly, five of the items have already occurred earlier in the MS.[7] This section was almost certainly a late addition to the MS.: cf. Part VI(b) below. None of the letters is found in the Vatican Archetype.

Part VI(a) : Letters 353–8, pp. 323a–33b.

These letters fill the first part of quire Y, and are written in the

---

[1] Cf. Vat. 30, 28, 35, 36, 38, 40, 41, 48, 51, 65, 63, 66, and 67.

[2] Lamb. omits Vat. 32, 35, 36, 38, 40, 41, 47, 48, 51, 63, 65–7, 82 (a and b), 84a, 95, 105, and 122.

[3] Lamb. omits Vat. 53, 73, 136, and 137. Nos. 136 and 137, however, occur later in Lamb.: cf. Lamb. 260 and 261.

[4] Lamb. inserts nos. 231, 234 = 286, 235, 236, and 238.

[5] Lamb. 249 = 165; 267 = 272; 271 = 55; 274 = 119; and 275 = 146.

[6] Cf. Vat. 214, 222–4, 234, 228, 227, 232, 263 (papal letters); and 147, 153–8 (Becket letters).

[7] Lamb. 347 = 140; 348 = 325; 349 = 316; 350 = 317; and 352 = 281.

same hand as Parts II–V(a). They are concerned with the Peace of Fretéval and its aftermath and the group may have been designed as a separate final section. This would explain the gap originally left at the end of quire X, into which Part V(b) was inserted. All but one occur also in the Vatican Archetype.[1]

VI(b) : Letters 359–64, pp. 333b–38b.

These five items fill the rest of quire Y and are written in the same hand as Part V(b); and as in that sequence, spaces have been left for coloured initials. The letters include an account of the martyrdom sent by John of Salisbury to William, Archbishop of Sens in early 1171,[2] three bulls announcing Becket's canonization,[3] the papal mandate to the legates Albert and Theodinus for the reconciliation of Canterbury Cathedral,[4] and the legates' letter to Christ Church ordering the cathedral to be re-consecrated with all due solemnity.[5]

On the basis of this brief analysis, it is possible to argue that the Lambeth Collection was formed by combining Archetype A, which retained its identity and coherence in Part II, and Archetype B, whose coherence was preserved in Part IV, although it is much less clear in Parts III and V(a), with additional material from another source, or sources. If we eliminate from discussion all the letters derived from the Bodleian and Vatican Archetypes, we are left with a residual collection of 140 items, which for convenient reference can be called the Lambeth Addition.[6] This 'new' material is divided into two parts: Addition (a) forming the coherent sequence Lamb. 87–144, of which twenty-seven letters are found independently in the Vatican Archetype; and Addition (b) comprising the eighty-two items either combined with or appended to the Vatican Archetype, from Lamb. 231 onwards. Although it is unlikely that these letters ever formed an independent 'collection', it is convenient to consider them together as an exceptionally interesting augmentation of the Becket correspondence, which,

---

[1] The exception is Lamb. 358, *Segnius irritant* (*Mats.* VII, ep. 685).

[2] Lamb. 359, *Agonem nostram* (*Mats.* VII, ep. 777).

[3] Lamb. 360–2, *Gaudendum est, Redolet Anglia* and *Qui uice beati Petri* (ibid., epp. 784–6).

[4] Lamb. 363, *Mandamus uobis* (ibid., ep. 787).

[5] Lamb. 364, *Letamur nos* (ibid., ep. 788).

[6] Cf. below, Appendix IV.

despite its degree of overlap with the Vatican Archetype, presents a marked contrast both with it and with the Bodleian Archetype.

Whereas both archetypes are remarkable for the chronologically accurate organization of their materials, the Lambeth Addition is characterized by an almost wholly unsystematic chronology. Except for the transcription of most of the *post mortem* letters at the very end,[1] there appears to have been no attempt (certainly no successful attempt) to arrange the materials according to their time of issue or receipt. Equally striking, however, is the contrast in content. The chronological spread of the letters, from 1161 to 1173,[2] is wider, and the range of authors is greater. Slightly less than half the total (65 out of 140) comprises the Becket correspondence properly so called, that is, letters written or received by Becket himself;[3] there is a very significant concentration in the remainder of the Addition on the letters of the royal and episcopal opposition to Becket. In fact, the greater part of the extant royal correspondence touching the Becket dispute is contained in this group of letters. Twenty-two were issued or received by Henry II (excluding the two letters in this Addition addressed to him by the archbishop),[4] and a further nineteen letters were written or received by the episcopal and clerical opposition in England and Normandy (again, excluding the twelve items in this category which involve Becket himself).[5] This suggests that more varied sources were now being used to expand the collections derived from the records kept in Becket's household; and it is not surprising, therefore, to discover that many of the episcopal and royal letters are found also in the Foliot collections. Yet it is highly unlikely that the texts in the Lambeth Addition were derived directly from a Foliot source, since Lamb. lacks the full protocols

---

[1] Cf. Lamb. 359–64.

[2] The earliest item in the Addition is Lamb. 231, *Quanto per carissimum* (*Mats.* VI, ep. 310), issued on 17 June 1161; the latest are the bulls announcing Becket's canonization, Lamb. 360–2, (*Mats.* VII, epp. 784–6).

[3] For letters to Becket (28), cf. Lamb. 88, 111, 140 = 347, 141, 143, 238, 248, 250, 251, 252, 257, 259, 269, 278–80, 287–9, 305, 309–13, 332, 351, and 355. For letters from Becket (37), cf. Lamb. 89, 90–2, 94–102, 109, 113–16, 134, 139, 255, 268, 291, 292, 294, 301–4, 306, 307, 321, 331, 333, 337, 338, and 353.

[4] For letters issued or received by Henry II (22), cf. Lamb. 87, 108, 117, 120, 131, 136, 234 = 286, 276–7, 281, 283–5, 314–16, 318, 323, 325 = 348, 326, 346, and 354. For Becket's letters to Henry II, cf. Lamb. 331 and 346.

[5] Cf. Lamb. 104–7, 118, 122, 123, 129, 132, 137, 231, 235, 236, 254, 256, 264, 282, 324, and 327. For episcopal letters included in the 'Becket' correspondence in n. 3, above, cf. Lamb 88, 90, 109, 113–16, 139, 238, 259, 278, and 280.

which the Foliot manuscripts alone preserve. Indeed, there are good reasons for arguing that the major source for these letters is to be sought among the surviving Becket records. But, whereas the Bodleian and Vatican Archetypes derived from regularly maintained records, with Bodl. possibly enshrining a special didactic collection assembled by or for Becket himself, the Lambeth Addition depended on the haphazard survival of assorted letters. Many of the groupings in the Addition suggest special 'files', or bundles of letters relating to specific topics. A very good example of such a grouping is provided by Lamb. 276–86, which comprises a highly important batch of materials relating to Gilbert Foliot, Jocelin of Salisbury, and Henry II, dating from 1166 and 1169. But other 'subject files' relating to excommunications,[1] legatine negotiations,[2] or the Canterbury-York dispute,[3] can readily be cited. It is also possible that some of the letters were derived from the authors and recipients themselves: for instance, it is not unlikely that William of Sens furnished the extremely interesting tripartite correspondence between himself, Henry II, and the legates in 1169.[4] It is highly probable that in these uncoordinated batches of letters we have echoes of (if not direct derivations from) the *schedule* described in Alan of Tewkesbury's introduction to his own larger collection.[5] This would explain both the uncertain chronology and the curious repetitions of the Lambeth Addition, as well as its occasional reflection of small sequences found also in the Vatican Archetype. In some such instances, it is virtually impossible to distinguish Vat. from Lamb. on textual grounds; and their agreement can best be explained by common derivation from a specific record file. This seems to be the case in Lamb. 89–97, 101–3, 297–300, 328–30, 339–45, and 353–7. But in certain other exceptionally illuminating instances, it is clear that the Vatican Archetype (together with its derivatives) and the Lambeth Addition belong to different textual traditions. Thus, Lamb. 114 provides the supplementary list of excommunications which is

---

[1] Cf. Lamb. 113–17 for letters relating to the excommunications of 1169.

[2] Cf. Lamb. 123–8, relating to the legation of Cardinals William and Otto, in 1167; Lamb. 132, 133, 138, and 142 relate to the legation of Vivian and Gratian in 1169.

[3] For Canterbury-York, cf. Lamb. 254–7.

[4] Cf. Lamb. 314–17.

[5] *Mats.* II, p. 300.

lacking in Vat.;[1] Lamb. 139 not only contains the full text of *Vobis dilectissimi*, which is highly abbreviated in Vat. 122, but provides it with an alternative and inaccurate address;[2] and where Vat. 82 has conflated the texts of *Se ipsum* and *Sacrorum canonum* to form a single letter addressed jointly to William of Norwich, Nigel of Ely, and his Archdeacon Richard, Lamb. 115 and 116 provide the two letters individually.[3] Even more striking is the example of *Venientes ad terram*. Whereas Vat. 47 gives an abbreviated and slightly variant text, omitting the passage 'Nobis itaque . . . iudicium' and modifying the reading of 'timentes ne pretaxatus . . . attemptaret', Lamb. 110 preserves the full text in its generally received form.[4] The most reasonable explanation is that the Vatican Archetype contained defective versions of some letters, resulting either from haste in its own transcription, or from dependence on carelessly made 'register' copies, while the compilers of the Lambeth Addition had access to the original 'files' and so received the better texts. It was this kind of conflict in his sources which Alan of Tewkesbury tried to resolve. His Recension I (which furnished the basic transcription in MS Cotton Claudius B.II) received the Lambeth texts of four of these letters,[5] but a marginal note records the variant address of the Vatican Archetype for one of them.[6] In contrast, he

[1] Cf. Vat. 27 and 84b. The full text of this letter is given in Vat. 27, with a cross-reference in 84b. In Vat. 27 (and in all Vat. Archetype derivatives: Roy. 85, Harl. 71, Laon 61, Lamb. 182, and Bodl. B, II.189) the appendix 'Hec . . . occupauit' is omitted: cf. *Mats.* VI, p. 559.

[2] Vat. 122 suspends the letter at 'Nec timeatis', omitting the long passage 'eos qui . . . posteros' (*Mats.* VII, p. 110), and addresses the letter 'Hug(oni) decano, archidiaconis et toti clero et populo Londonien(sis) ecclesie' (fo. 106ra), whereas Lamb. provides the full text and addresses it 'priori et R. archidiacono et toti clero et populo Cicestrensis ecclesie' (p. 162b): cf. *Mats.* VII, p. 107. There is clearly some error in this address: there was no Prior of Chichester and no Archdeacon R. in the period. Most difficulties are removed, however, if it is assumed that 'Cicestrensis' was a mis-transcription of 'Cestrensis' (= Chester), where Robert was archdeacon from before 1155 to 1194 or later (cf. *The Letters of John of Salisbury, I : The Early Letters*, edd. W. J. Millor and H. E. Butler, NMT (1955), p. 169, n. 1.

[3] Cf. *Mats.* VI, epp. 489 and 490: addressed respectively to William of Norwich, and Nigel and Richard of Ely. In Vat., the conflated text is produced by adding the final paragraph of *Sacrorum canonum* ('Quod si unus . . . patiatur') to the complete text of *Se ipsum* (fo. 98ra).

[4] This peculiarity is discussed below, pp. 110 and 114; cf. Appendix VII, no. 5, and *Mats.* VI, ep. 342, esp. pp. 283–4. Robertson's notes are incomplete and inaccurate.

[5] For Lamb. 114, 139, 115, and 116, cf. AlanT(A), III. 43, 72, 44, and 45.

[6] Cf. ibid., III.72.

first accepted the Vatican text of *Venientes ad terram*, but preferred the Lambeth version for his Recension II.[1]

It has been suggested that John of Salisbury was the author of this collection,[2] but there is nothing in its content or format to support such an ascription; and textual arguments seem to place it beyond consideration in this context. It will be shown that Alan of Tewkesbury's collection passed through three recensions, undergoing emendation at each stage; and, while Roy. (in company with Vat.) tends to agree with the readings in Recension I, Lamb. (and Bodl.B,II) tends to follow those in Recension II, arguing a comparatively late stage in the transmission of the text. Indeed, if one were to seek a possible candidate among the surviving early collections, one would probably select Roy., with its Merton derivation, its early date, and primitive texts, as a derivative from John's preliminary collection of Becket letters. If this were to be the case, then John of Salisbury did no more than combine two already-existing archetypes into a single collection. It is certainly not impossible that Roy. should represent John's work: it has no medieval descendants, suggesting that, like his own later letters, it was not widely circulated. But it is not easy to reconcile such an identification with the *florilegium* taken by Guy of Southwick from a collection of Becket letters which he had helped John to assemble and correct when they were both at Merton after Becket's murder. The *florilegium* follows the format and order of Alan of Tewkesbury's collection almost exactly, includes a preponderance of John's own letters, and cannot have been derived from either Roy. or Lamb.

B. THE BODLEY B COLLECTION: PARTS II AND III

The second collection in the Lambeth Family is in the Oxford Bodl. MS 937,[3] a large and fine volume from the late twelfth or early thirteenth century, containing 592 letters as well as the *Causa exilii*, with its attendant letters, the *Prologus* and *Vita* by John of

---

[1] Cf. AlanT(A) and (B), II.35, and Appendix VII, no. 5, below.

[2] A modern hand has inserted the following note on the front flyleaf of Lamb.: 'Epistolae sequuntur ordinem a Johanne Saresburiensi concinnatum; cf. W. J. Millor and C. N. L. Brooke, *The Letters of John of Salisbury,* II : *The Later Letters (1163–1180)*, Oxford Medieval Texts, Oxford (1979), pp. lxii–lxiii.

[3] $7\frac{1}{2} \times 5\frac{1}{2}$ in., iii + 450 leaves; single columns, 29 lines to the column. The medieval provenance of the volume is unknown, but it was given to the Bodleian Library by Thomas Draper in 1601; cf. *Summary Catalogue*, no. 3088.

Salisbury, and the *Prologus* and *Explanatio* by Alan of Tewkesbury. It is a composite manuscript of unknown provenance, with rubricated headings and initials coloured alternately red and blue; and the extant volume was formed by the binding together of five separately transcribed codices whose contents can be briefly summarized as follows:

Part I(a) : fos. 1–10r.
> The Constitutions of Clarendon, together with Alexander III's letter absolving Becket from having given oral consent to them, and two royal writs forbidding assistance to the archbishop or his family and ordering the arrest of any who should contravene the king's command;[1] two texts of the royal decree of 1169,[2] and three letters of John of Salisbury.[3]

I(b) : fos. 11r–34va, 3 quires.
> Alan of Tewkesbury's *Prologus*, John of Salisbury's *Prologus* and *Vita,* the *Reuelatio ad beatum Thomam,* Alan of Tewkesbury's *Explanatio* and a table of contents (fos. 30ra–34va), the latter arranged in double columns, with rubricated numbers and coloured initials, containing the addresses and *incipits* of 539 letters arranged in five books corresponding with Alan of Tewkesbury's Recension II.

I(c): Letters 1–220, including two unnumbered items, fos. 35r–170v, seventeen quires.
> 222 letters arranged from no. 25 onwards in the order of Alan of Tewkesbury's collection.

Part II: Letters 1–328, fos. 171ra–426v, 31 quires numbered from 1 (fo. 182v) to 31 (fo. 426v).
> A table of contents (fos. 171ra–173vb) containing the addresses and *incipits* of 328 letters, numbered in red; the *Summa cause inter regem et Thomam* (fo. 174ra–vb) inserted by a modern hand with the heading 'ex vetusto codice manuscripto'; and 328 letters arranged and numbered as in the table of contents, with four inserted items.

---

[1] *Ad aures nostras, Precipio tibi* and *Nosti quam male:* Mats. V, epp. 52, 78 and 77.
[2] Cf. *Mats.* VI, ep. 599.
[3] *Ex quo partes, Ex relatione latoris,* and *Cum dominum papam:* Mats. V, epp. 55, 115, and 85.

Part III : Letters 1–41, fos. 427r–48, three quires.

Forty-one letters, numbered in a modern hand. The letters
end on fo. 446r; the manuscript is completed by the insertion
of three hymns on fos. 446v–47r, and a modern hand has
inserted a notification by the Prior of Beaulieu on fo. 447v with
the heading 'ex libro vetusto manuscripto'.

These separate sections were not written by the same hand, nor on
the same quality of vellum; the parchment of Part I is much thinner
than that of Parts II and III, but there is a similarity of format and
decoration which suggests that they were produced in the same
scriptorium and designed as companion pieces. It seems clear that
Part II was designed originally as a separate composition, since it
has its own table of contents, its letters are numbered in a single
sequence from 1 to 328, and its quires are also numbered in their
sequence from 1 to 31,[1] although it is now found within a larger
volume. The high quality of the transcription and the lack of
repetitions or corrections suggest that this part was a fair copy of
an already-existing, carefully compiled, collection. To this was
then added a supplementary collection of forty-one letters (Part
III), transcribed in a different hand, designed possibly to form
part of the larger work, but too late in execution to be included in
the table of contents preceding Part II; and it was left unnumbered. At that point it seems to have been decided to collate the
now large compilation with a *magnum volumen* of the Alan of
Tewkesbury collection, from which were selected 198 additional
letters, transcribed in their order in Alan's work, and preceded by
a unique collection of twenty-four letters (Part I(c), nos. 1–24).
This magnificent volume was then further expanded with the
addition of three quires at the beginning (Part Ib), containing the
Prologus and *Vita* by John of Salisbury, the *Prologus* and *Explanatio* by Alan, the *Reuelatio ad beatum Thomam*, and a full table of
contents of Alan's Recension II, arranged, like the latter, in five
books. A note was inserted on fo. 29v explaining that the letters

---

[1] Most of the gathering numbers are still clearly visible: cf. i, fo. 182v; iv–vii,
fos. 206v, 214v, 222v, and 230v; x–xvi, fos. 254v, 262v, 271v, 281v, 290v 298v,
and 306v; xix–xxviii, fos. 330v, 338v, 346v, 354v, 362v, 370v, 378v, 386v, 394v,
and 402v; but nine have been excised in binding: cf. ii–iii, fos. 190v and 198v;
viii–ix, fos. 238v and 246v; xvii–xviii, fos. 314v and 322v; xxix–xxxi, fos. 410v,
418v, and 426v.

in the following collection should be placed in their order in this table,[1] and the numbers of the letters as they actually occur in Part III are carefully inserted in red roman numerals by the corresponding items in the table of contents. And finally, yet another section (Part Ia) was added at the beginning of this now very large volume. There can be little doubt that the completed manuscript was intended to form a very comprehensive collection of material connected with the controversy.

The abbreviation of the Alan of Tewkesbury collection in Part I(c) will be more aptly discussed in a later chapter; meanwhile, in the context of the Lambeth Family, the relevant sections of Bodl.B are Parts II and III, which are related to the Lambeth Collection. An analysis of these two parts can be summarized as follows:

Bodl.B. Part II: this part can be broken down into four component sources:

(*a*) Letters 1–81; containing with one exception the whole of the Bodleian Archetype, corresponding with Lamb. 7–86

(*b*) Letters 82–147; this section corresponds almost exactly with Lamb. Part III (87–144), agreeing with it in order, but adding a further eleven items, inserted towards the end of the section,[2] repeating one which had already occurred in (*a*),[3] and omitting three.[4]

(*c*) Letters 148–283; apparently an abbreviation of the Vatican Archetype, containing in correct sequence Vat. 31–264, but omitting those items which had already appeared in (*a*) or

---

[1] Fo. 29v: 'Epistole beati Thome que in hoc volumine continentur non eo ordine scribi debent quo hic scripti sunt, sed eo potius quo subterius in capitulis subiectis anotata inueniuntur. In quibus ut facilius inueniri possint, persone mittentis et eius ad quem mittitur notite sunt, et principia epistolarum, et numerus ubi capitulis apponitur, ad certum locum mittit ubi scribitur epistola ipsa inter alias ad eundem numerum, ordinanda tamen et scribenda iuxta ordinem quem capitula ostendunt.'

[2] Bodl. B, II adds 130–4, 140–3, 145, and 146. Of these, nos. 133 and 134 are found in the Lamb. MS, but not in the related sequence: cf. Lamb 360 and 1.

[3] 95b is a repeat of *Quam iustis* (81); it is unnumbered here and marked 'uacat'.

[4] Bodl. B, II omits Lamb. 98–100.

(*b*), or were to appear in (*d*) and Part III;[1] re-positioning one letter,[2] omitting one item,[3] and inserting no. 216.[4] Although the elimination of material which was also contained in the preceding sections seems to have been fairly successfully achieved, five duplicates slipped through the net.[5]

(*d*) Letters 284–328; apart from the first three items, which occur also in the supplementary material added to the archetype in the Vat. MS[6] and the five Vat. letters omitted from sequence (*c*) and inserted here,[7] none of the letters in this section is found in the Vat. MS or Archetype; all but fourteen occur in Lamb. Parts Va and VI, though in a different order.[8]

Part III: forty-one letters, numbered 1–41.

It is evident that this part formed a separate collection and, in contrast with Bodl.B, II, the majority of its letters were neither written nor received by Becket or members of his household,[9] and only one of them is found in the Vat. Archetype.[10] Most of the letters were in fact written or received by

---

[1] Bodl. B, II (*c*) omits 59 items from the Vatican Archetype, all of which appear elsewhere in the collection as follows:

V	B			
		161=61	218=47	243=33
32=9		162=62	219=48	244=42
35=86		163=63	246=49	247=III.9
36=87		164=64	220=50	248=69
38=88		165=65	22=53	249=70
40=89		166=66	221=55	250=78
41=90		168=68	225=51	251=79
47=102		208=53	226=121	252=82
48=91		209=120	229=52	254=304
51=92		210=104	230=114	260=305
67=95a		211=56	236=39	261=306
84a=105		212=57	237=37	262=307
95=127		213=59	238=54	
122=136		215=44	239=32	
159=303		216=45	241=40	
160=60		217=46	242=41	

[2] Vat. 240 occurs out of sequence as Bodl. B, II. 217.

[3] The item omitted is Vat. 83, *Vestra debuerat*, *Mats.* VI, ep. 480.

[4] *Cum hii qui*, *Mats.* VII, ep. 698. This letter occurs also among the supplementary material in Vat. as no. 274.

[5] 171 = 93; 173b = 94; 187b = 107; 188 = 106; and 207b = 126.

[6] Bodl. B, II. 284–6 = Vat. 265, 270, and 273.

[7] Bodl. B, II. 303–7 = Vat. 159, 254, and 260–2.

[8] Lamb. lacks Bodl. B, II. 284–6, 290, 296, 297, 300, 301, 320, 321, and 323–6.

[9] Only five letters in this section were issued by Becket (12–14, 24, and 25) and five were addressed to him (20–3 and 35).

[10] Bodl. B, III.9 = Vat. 247.

Becket's opponents during the controversy: thirteen were sent by or addressed to Henry II,[1] seven were written or received by members of the English and Norman episcopate,[2] and two were written in support of Gilbert Foliot by the Abbots of Westminster and Ramsey respectively.[3] With only five exceptions,[4] all the letters in this section are included in Lamb., though not in the same order, and there is substantial textual agreement between the two manuscripts. But whereas the letters are concentrated in a single supplement to the main collection of Becket correspondence in Bodl.B, III, they are scattered in Lamb., occurring singly or in small groups throughout the second half of the compilation.

Except where Bodl.B, II follows the Bodleian Archetype in (*a*) or the Vatican Archetype in (*c*), the chronological arrangement of the letters is very haphazard; component (*b*) has items varying in date of issue from 1162[5] to 1173,[6] but there is no apparent attempt to arrange them in logical order: the appeal by the French king to Alexander III after Becket's murder is followed by a papal mandate addressed to the Archbishop of York in early 1165;[7] and one of the bulls of canonization later precedes the report by one of Becket's envoys of his arrival in France in late 1163, which must be one of the earliest surviving letters of the controversy.[8] Similar disorder is found in (*d*), whose contents again range in date from 1163[9] to 1173.[10] Nor is the chronology of Part III more reliable: the letters vary in date from 1165 to 1172, but no. 7 was written in December 1171.[11] The chronology of the Lambeth Collection, outside of its agreement with Bodl.B, II, is hardly more reliable, but in this

---

[1] Nos. 1, 3, 4, 15–17, 26, 30, 31, 33, 36, 38, and 39.

[2] Nos. 2, 7, 9, 10, 32, 34, and 37.

[3] Nos. 5 and 6.

[4] Nos. 6–8, 12, and 40 are lacking in Lamb.

[5] *Peruenit ad audientiam* (140), dated 15 August 1162; cf. *Mats*. V, ep. 14.

[6] *Gaudendum est* (133), dated 12 March 1173; cf. *Mats*. VII, ep. 784.

[7] *Ab humane pietatis* (113), written in early 1171, and *Decet prudentiam* (114), 6 August 1165; cf. *Mats*. VII, ep. 734 and V, ep. 42.

[8] *Gaudendum est* (133: cf. n. 6 above); and *Comitem Flandrensem* (134), late 1163; cf. *Mats*. V, ep. 36.

[9] *Sanctitati uestre* (297), Becket to Humbald of Ostia, written after the Council of Westminster in October 1163; cf. *Mats*. V, ep. 30.

[10] *Redolet Anglia* (328), Alexander III to the clergy and people of England, dated 12 March, 1173; cf. *Mats*. VII, ep. 785.

[11] *Si mihi presto*, Roger of York to the Pope; cf. *Mats*. VII, ep. 765.

case a description of Becket's murder, the letters of canonization, and the mandates for the reconciliation of Canterbury Cathedral are grouped more or less correctly at the end of the collection,[1] following a group of letters written between July and October 1170.[2]

There can be little doubt that the compilers of the collections now surviving in Lamb. and Bodl.B, II and III were using the same range of materials; but, as in the case of the compilers of the Vat. and Royal Collections, they worked independently and assembled their various sources in different ways. It is evident that both had complete copies of the Bodleian and Vatican Archetypes: both also used the assortment of materials designated the Lambeth Addition; and it seems that the author of Bodl.B, II and III had access to still further small groups of letters.[3] It is not possible to establish the form in which the Lambeth Addition first appeared, although it is highly unlikely that it had achieved the status of a formal collection in its own right. Its almost total lack of any kind of organization or order suggests the haphazard assembly of scraps of materials rather than derivation from a regular archival source. Yet the degree of correlation between Lamb. and Bodl.B, II suggests that a portion of the material had been assembled into a specific (if unsatisfactory) order before its incorporation into the two larger collections. Thus, the agreement in content and order between Lambeth Addition (*a*) and Bodl.B, II (*b*) can only be explained by their common use of a collection of assorted letters with a certain episcopal-royal bias, arranged in haphazard chronological order. To this, Bodl.B, II added the curiously obtrusive items, nos. 130–3, relating to events after Becket's death;[4] nos. 134, 140, and 145, received before the exile began;[5] nos. 141–3 relating to the Bangor dispute;[6] and no. 146, a stray letter from Cardinal Otto to Becket, written in mid-1167.[7]

Over the rest of the Lambeth Addition, however, the agreement

---

[1] Lamb. 359–64; cf. p. 70 above.

[2] Lamb. 353–8: *Miserationis oculo, Cognito ex litteris, Anxietate cordis, Quam gratum Deo, Audito et intellecto,* and *Segnius irritant*; cf. *Mats.* VII, epp. 684, 689, 714, 697, 711, and 685.

[3] Cf. Bodl. B, II. 130–2, 134, 140–3, 145, 146, 161, 179, 272, 276, 278–80, 283–6, 290, 296, 297, 300, 301, 320, 321, 324–6; III. 6–8, 12, and 40.

[4] Cf. *Mats.* VII, epp. 740, 736, 750, and 784.

[5] Cf. ibid., V, epp. 36, 14, and 39. Ep. 39 is known only in Bodl. B, II.

[6] Cf. ibid., epp. 117, 119, and 118.

[7] Cf. ibid., VI, ep. 306.

in order between it and Bodl.B, II and III is confined to very short sequences of letters; and it is unlikely that Addition (*b*) had been formed into an integrated group when either compiler began to use its materials. This reinforces the supposition that the more disorderly survivals from Becket's archives were now being used. The appearance of structure, which the Addition acquired through its formation into three coherent sequences in the Bodleian manuscript, is almost certainly illusory. This view is reinforced by consideration of the thirty-seven further letters included in Bodl.B, II and III, either singly or in small groups from II.130 onwards. An analysis of the whole accession reveals a chronological emphasis on early and late material: about half the items were issued either before Becket went into exile or after his death.[1] And, once again, there is no coherent order. The nature of the groupings and the manner of their insertion into the common stock give the impression of the incidental discovery of isolated batches of letters or individual texts as the compilation was under way. It is not without significance that two of these letters are otherwise unknown in manuscript sources,[2] and eight were only received into the Claudius manuscript of Alan of Tewkesbury's collection as a late addition to Recension I.[3]

SUMMARY OF CONCLUSIONS

The three families of manuscripts discussed in this chapter enable us to trace some principal stages in the formation of a comprehensive collection of the letters of Thomas Becket concerning his dispute with Henry II, together with other related correspondence. The Bodleian Archetype has the strongest claim to be regarded as the earliest surviving compilation composed in the household of the archbishop, and in all probability either before or very soon after his murder. It is possible that a still earlier collection of Becket's own letters, conceivably assembled for the archbishop

---

[1] For letters written before the exile began, cf. Bodl. B, II. 134, 140, 145, 284, 296, and 297; for those after Becket's death, cf. ibid. 130–2, 283, 286, 321, 323–6 and III. 7. For the full list of 'new' letters, cf. Appendix V, below.

[2] II. 145, *Vestre discretionis* (*Mats.* V, ep. 39) and II. 300, *Benedictus Deus Qui licet* (Giles, EpST, ep. 374) are both known only in this MS.

[3] II. 140–3 occur in AlanT(A), II. 86, 87, 89, and 88; II. 161 = AlanT(A), I. 180; II. 179 = AlanT(A), I. 181; II. 321 = AlanT(A), V. 82; and III. 8 = AlanT(A), IV. 62.

himself, lies back behind the Bodleian Archetype: the first half of
the latter was certainly more formally arranged than the second,
with the retention of full diplomatic details, and contains some of
the most important of Becket's surviving letters, beginning with the
two appeals to the king in early 1166. But none of the extant
members of the Bodleian Family records the earliest stage of composition: the Bodl. MS 509, which is probably the earliest descendant, was not transcribed until after 1177–8, in a location outside
Canterbury. The Vatican Family may be judged to preserve the
second stage in the evolutionary process, combining the contents of
the Bodleian Archetype with a larger and much more comprehensive collection also derived from the records in Becket's household,
and likewise retaining the marks of its archival derivation. The
Lambeth Family marks the augmentation of the two archetypal
collections with still further material, drawn also from Becket's
records, in the form of small groups of letters and documents
which seem to have been hurriedly assembled in haphazard order
and combined with the two more formally arranged collections. It
is possible that Lambeth Addition (*a*) existed as a roughly formed
compilation, intended to supplement the Bodleian and Vatican
Archetypes, since it is found independently in the two surviving
manuscripts of the family. Lambeth Addition (*b*), however, bears all
the marks of unsystematic and piecemeal accumulation, and it is
unlikely that it received identifiable form as a collection until its
contents were appended in two sections to the Vatican Archetype
in Bodl. B, II and III. The Addition as a whole probably resulted
from the final searchings through Becket's surviving records, made
when John of Salisbury and Alan of Tewkesbury undertook the
preparation of a final tribute to the martyr. This explains its unsystematic arrangement, its repetitions, and its unexpectedly
sounder texts, as well as its agreement with Alan's Second Recension.

These general conclusions are reinforced by a consideration of
the textual evidence assembled in Appendix VII, in which a selection of the original readings in the Claudius manuscript of Alan's
collection are collated with the variants and corrections inserted
into it by a team of correctors, and with the corresponding readings
in the major 'Becket' and 'Foliot' collections. The resulting evidence is sometimes contradictory, but the general distinction
between the Vatican Archetype on the one hand, and the Bodleian

Archetype and the Lambeth Addition on the other, in those letters transmitted independently in both traditions, seems clear enough. The contrast between the Vatican and Bodleian Archetypes is most clearly shown in the texts of *Si curamus esse, Excellentie tue, Quam paterne, Dilecti filii, Karissimus in Christo, Quoniam de uestre, Oportuerat uos,* and *Quam iustis;*[1] that between the Vatican Archetype and the Lambeth Addition in *Venientes ad terram* and *Super discretione.*[2] And in all these examples, the readings of the Vatican Archetype are found in the original Claudius text, while those of the Bodleian Archetype and the Lambeth Addition reflect those of the corrections.[3] The Bodleian Archetype seems on this evidence to have been essentially sound, but the Vatican Archetype was apparently flawed by omissions and misreadings. The Claudius manuscript records the strenuous efforts made by Alan of Tewkesbury and his collaborators to ensure the production of as accurate and faultless a text as possible.

It can be concluded that the Bodleian and Vatican Archetypes were brought to final completion very soon after Becket's death, using the most readily available archival material, already assembled into reasonable chronological order. The nature of these records is uncertain. Contemporary practice differed widely: the papal Chancery kept annual registers, the English Exchequer entered its accounts on 'pipe' rolls (in which bundles of parchment leaves were fastened together at the top); and the English Chancery, slightly later, kept both rolls (in which the leaves were sewn end to end and then rolled up) and files (in which individual documents were strung together on cords). There are no precise references to indicate the nature of Becket's record-keeping. Alan of Tewkesbury described a state of some confusion when, four years after the murder, he began to assemble the materials for his own compilation. The correspondence was distributed in 'schedules'—presumably loose parchment leaves, roughly tied together

---

[1] Cf. Appendix VII, nos. 2 and 13–19.

[2] Cf. ibid., nos. 5 and 10.

[3] The two letters cited in Appendix VII (nos. 1 and 11: *Etsi circa nos* and *Quot et quanta*), which seem to contradict these conclusions, should be discounted. In both cases, the Vatican text cited is not derived from the Archetype but occurs in the supplementary material found with it in that manuscript. *Etsi circa nos* does not occur in the Archetype; the text of *Quot et quanta*, which is found there, is abbreviated in the Vatican version because of its occurrence in Vat. Part I. Hence we have to rely on the Royal manuscript for the Vatican Archetype's text of this letter; and this supports the conclusions given above.

in bundles. It was in this form that William of Canterbury left the
first draft of his *Miracula*, before putting it into a more finished
form for presentation to Henry II in 1174.[1] Yet, as the existence of
so substantial a corpus of epistolary material indicates, some form
of regular record must have been adopted. But we can only
speculate on the exact nature of the devices used.

In the case of letters issued by Becket, we may suppose either
that the original drafts were preserved, perhaps on files, or copied
on to 'schedules'; or that copies were taken from the finished letter
immediately before despatch. Where letters were issued simul-
taneously to a number of recipients, a copy of the basic draft would
suffice for record purposes, supplemented by notes of its intended
recipients. The Vatican Archetype provides ample evidence of this
kind of procedure;[2] but we cannot be certain whether the recorded
copy derived from a draft or from one version of the engrossment.
There are indications that even discarded drafts survived and found
their way into later collections, as in the case of Becket's suppressed letter to William of Pavia, preserved in the Bodleian
Archetype.[3] One of two procedures could be employed in the case
of important incoming letters: either a simple filing of the originals
themselves, if they were addressed personally to Becket; or the
systematic copying on to 'schedules' of these and of papal mandates, passed through Becket's hands but intended for other
recipients. Again, the Bodleian and Vatican Archetypes show that
such practices were followed.[4] If the two primitive archetypes thus
seem to reflect the more orderly survivals from Becket's household,
the Lambeth Addition and the supplementary materials in Bodl.
B, II and III depend on the more irregular residue, augmented as
time went on by the appeals for vengeance, the legatine commissions for the king's reconciliation, and, later still, the accounts
of the agreements at Avranches and the canonization.

---

[1] See below, p. 193, n. 1.
[2] Cf. above, pp. 59–60.
[3] Cf. above, p. 30.
[4] Cf. above, pp. 30 and 60–1.

CHAPTER 3

The Alan of Tewkesbury Collection

1. GENERAL INTRODUCTION

It is not possible on the surviving evidence to establish the precise authorship or provenance of the collections already discussed, though their content and arrangement point to a source close to Becket's household for part at least of their archetypal basis. It is clear from Becket's own words that he was anxious to preserve an accurate record of his dispute with the king,[1] and it is possible that part of the Bodleian Archetype is based on a selection of the most important *pièces justificatives* of the controversy made for the archbishop himself. Now, in approaching what may be regarded as the definitive edition of the Becket correspondence, undertaken at Christ Church Canterbury by Alan, prior from 1179 to 1186 and then Abbot of Tewkesbury (1186–1202), the evidence is far more specific. This large collection, devised in five books and containing in its three major extant versions between 535 and 598 letters and documents, has survived in several manuscript copies in varying degrees of completeness.[2] It is carefully arranged on a chronological plan, combining a large collection of Becket's correspondence with a selection of relevant letters by John of Salisbury taken from collections made by the latter, and including the full texts of the Constitutions of Clarendon and the decrees of 1169 as well as the formal reports of the Compromise of Avranches and the letters of canonization.

The collection is prefaced by the short *Vita et Passio Sancti Thome* written specifically for this purpose by John of Salisbury,[3] together with an addition to the *Vita* composed by Alan himself.[4]

---

[1] In late 1170 Becket wrote to Master Gratian asking him to ensure that the relevant papal letters were inserted into the papal register: 'Provideat etiam vestra discretio ut urgentiores et efficaciores litterae, quas Dominus noster pro ecclesia regi Anglorum transmisit, registro inserantur; quia posteris magnum incitamentum est virtutis, quotiens eos animavarint exempla majorum. Ad negotium vero nostrum spectantes quas accepimus remittimus vobis, ut si forte editorum exemplaria desint, ea mutuare possitis a transcriptis.' Cf. *Mats.* VII, p. 353.

[2] Cf. pp. 13–14 above.   [3] Cf. *Mats.* II, pp. 301–22.   [4] Ibid., pp. 323–52.

It was once thought that John was in fact the author of the collection,[1] partly because of its incorporation of a substantial number of
his own letters, and partly because his *Vita* precedes the collection
in its published form. But the evidence of contemporaries, as well
as in the introductory material, appears conclusive on this point,
and there now seems little doubt that the author of the collection in
its substantially finished form was the Prior of Canterbury. Among
his contemporaries, Herbert of Bosham referred in 1184–5 to
Prior Alan as the composer of this work,[2] as did Gervase of Canterbury;[3] and modern editors have seen no reason to question their
testimony.[4] Nevertheless, Alan's introduction suggests that John
also had some part in the initiation of the work,[5] and his statement
is supported by the evidence of an early thirteenth-century
florilegium preserved now in the library of St John's College,
Oxford.[6] John's precise contribution will be further discussed

[1] This view was held by Baronius (*sub. anno* 1162, no. 21), but Casimir Oudin
(*De Script. Eccles.*, II, cols. 1477 and 1519) suggested Alan of Tewkesbury. Cf.
Brial, *Recueil des Historiens*, XVI, p. 208; Robertson, *Mats.* V, p. xv; and MB,
Foliot, pp. 18–19.

[2] Herbert of Bosham, *Vita Sancti Thome, Mats.* III, p. 396: 'Ex epistolis
quippe a nobis vel propter nos in exsilio nostro confecti grande compactum est
corpus epistolare, ... Compactum est, inquam, corpus ex his multas in se
epistolas continens; quas etiam secundum ordinem historiae venerabilis prior
sanctae Cantuariensis ecclesiae Alanus laboriose quidem et studiose digessit.'

[3] Gervase of Canterbury, *Acta Pontificum*, ed. W. Stubbs, RS 73, London
(1879), II, p. 391: 'Legat et volumen epistolarum ejus quas Prior compilavit
Alanus.'

[4] Cf. Brial, *Recueil des historiens*, XVI, p. 208; Robertson, *Mats.* V, xv–xvii;
and MB, *Foliot*, pp. 18–19.

[5] Alan of Tewkesbury, *Prologus in actus et exitum beati martyris Thomae, Mats.*
II, pp. 299–301; see p. 300: 'Verum quia id operis rem ipsam pertingens rei
formam non explicat per omnem modum, placuit et oportuit illi scripto apist-
olas succedere, in quibus continetur series et ordo universorum, ut qui desiderat
et ad id sufficit, totum habeat, si quis vitam viri, modum exsilii, causae pro-
cessum, vel ipsius re requirit exitum.'

[6] St John's College, Oxford, MS 126, fo. 79r: 'Incipit compendiosa defloratio
ex libro epistolarum magistri Iohannis Saresberiensis, qui postmodum fuit
episcopus Carnotensis, super causa beati Thome martyris, a Guidone priore
Suwicense diligenter excerpta. Que studiose dictare uolentibus tum pro modo
scribendi, tum pro sententiarum elegantia, tum pro causa prescripti martyris
declaranda non erit inutilis. Predictus autem liber epistolarum a prescripto
magistro Iohanne post prefati martyris passionem in unum corpus diligenter et
breuiter est collectus et in quatuor uolumina luculenter ac studiose diuisus.
Porro in eiusdem libri collectione et diuisione ac emendatione iam dictus prior,
tunc canonicus Mereton', memorato magistro Iohanni comes indiuiduus ac
familiaris adhesit.' Quoted also in Giles, JohnS, II, p. 301; Hardy, II, pp.
387–8; and Barlow, *Arnulf of Lisieux*, p. lxxxv, n. 2.

later, and it is sufficient to say here that the work of compilation was probably begun by John, using predominantly his own correspondence and a small number of letters supplied by his friends such as John of Poitiers, but was later taken over and completed by Alan who had access from 1174 onwards to Becket's own epistolary records.

The construction of the first draft of the compilation can be dated within fairly narrow limits. Alan of Tewkesbury became a monk at Canterbury in 1174 and was made Prior in 1179,[1] from which post he was promoted to Tewkesbury in 1186.[2] The earliest independent reference to the completed work occurs in Herbert of Bosham's *Vita Sancti Thome* which was begun at Canterbury in 1184, by which time Herbert assumed that Alan's collection would be available to his readers.[3] The *terminus a quo* for Alan's participation in the work cannot be fixed earlier than his arrival at Canterbury in 1174, and in fact the earliest surviving transcription of his *Explanatio* cannot be earlier than August 1176, since it refers to John of Salisbury's elevation to Chartres.[4] The limits of composition of the earliest draft are therefore likely to be from 1174 to mid-1176.

Only three manuscripts of the unabbreviated collection survive, of which each contains material unknown to the others; and by their collation a collection of 535 items common to all three can be distinguished, providing in all probability Alan's basic compilation, which was subject to expansion and adjustment at various times. The collection was clearly intended as a tribute to the martyr, at once a justification of the cause he defended and a monument to his steadfastness,[5] and it was concerned exclusively with the contro-

---

[1] Gervase of Canterbury, *Chronica*, ed. W. Stubbs, RS 73, London I, (1879), p. 293. For the latest account of his life, with an edition of his personal letters, cf. M. A. Harris, 'Alan of Tewkesbury and his Letters, I–II', *Studia Monastica* XVIII (1976), pp. 77–108 and 299–351.

[2] Gervase, p. 353: 'Prior Cantuariensis Alanus electus est abbas Theokesberiae quasi in poenam suae constantiae'. Cf. *Annales Monastici*, ed. H. R. Luard, RS 36, London, II (1864), p. 244, *sub anno* 1186: 'Alanus prior Cantuariae factus est abbas Theokesberiae.'

[3] *Mats.* III, p. 396: 'In quibus de exsilii nostri laboriosa historia perplurima continentur; unde et, eo quod in epistolis illis diligentius conscribantur, multa in libello hoc brevitatis causa praeterivimus, praesertim quia liber ille epistolaris a multis personis et a multis ecclesiis jam habetur.'

[4] Brit. Libr. MS Cotton Claudius B. ii, fo. 9ra: 'postea carnotensis episcopus'.

[5] Cf. Alan's own prologue, *Mats.* II, pp. 300–1: 'In quibus sedulus lector et devotus viri Dei imaginem inveniet plenius depictam. Insuper operum ejus [*cont.*]

versy that cost him his life. The letters in this basic collection range in date from 1162 to 1174: from the reopening of the Canterbury and York dispute over their relative position and privileges[1] to the restatement of Canterbury's jurisdictional rights at the beginning of the pontificate of Becket's successor, Richard of Dover.[2] There is little doubt that the work was designed to be as comprehensive as possible, and contains letters from the king and the bishops as well as from Becket's supporters and the Pope, together with a substantial number of letters written by John of Salisbury. Nor was their selection slanted: the full texts of the bishops' appeals against Becket[3] and Foliot's various attacks on his integrity are included;[4] the strongly hostile *Multiplicem nobis* is given in full in the earliest surviving copy.[5] But when the collection was being assembled the posthumous triumph of the martyr was complete, at least in externals: the king himself had done humiliating penance at Canterbury,[6] the former enemies of the archbishop had purged themselves of complicity in his death,[7] and pilgrims were arriving

---

[1] Cf. *Quanto personam*, dated 13 July 1162, *Mats.* V, ep. 13; AlanT(B), I. 10.

[2] Cf. *Significauit nobis*, dated 14 April 1174, *Mats.* VI, ep. 408; AlanT(B), I. 27.

[3] *Vestram pater* and *Que uestro pater*, addressed to the pope and Becket respectively on 24 June 1166, and *Sublimitati uestre*, despatched to Alexander III on 29 November 1167; cf. Mats. V, epp. 204–5, and VI, ep. 344.

[4] Eg., *Medicine potius* and *Placuit excellentie*, Mats. V, epp. 73 and 167.

[5] *Mats.* V, ep. 225; cf. AlanT(A), MS Claudius B.ii, I. 126.

[6] For a description of Henry II's penance in July 1174, cf. Diceto, *ymagines*, I, pp. 382–3 and Edward Grim, *Vita*, Mats. II, pp. 445–6.

[7] The papal absolution of Roger of York, Gilbert of London, and Jocelin of Salisbury was granted only after their solemn purgation from complicity in the murder; these three had been the leaders of the episcopal opposition to Becket and were also those most closely involved in the events which led to his death. In letters dated 23 October 1171 (*Et ipsa loci* and *Quia non nunquam, Mats.* VII, epp. 763–4), Alexander III gave careful instructions to Rotrou of Rouen and Theobald of Amiens for the absolution of Roger of York; according to Diceto (I, p. 348), Roger was duly absolved by Rotrou and Theobald at Aumâle on 8 December 1171, but it is clear from a letter written by Roger on 13 December that Theobald of Amiens was not present on that occasion, being represented by other ecclesiastics including the Bishop of Évreux; cf. *Mats.* VII, p. 505. A further commission (*Fraternitati uestre, Mats.* VII, ep. 767) was issued by the Pope to Rotrou and Bernard on 27 February 1172, mandating the absolution of Foliot on condition of his purgation; and a similar commission (*Licet in proposito, Mats.* VII, ep. 768) relating to Jocelin of Salisbury was sent out on 30 March in the same year.

---

vestigia si libet perscrutari, ibi inveniet digito Dei fabricatam armorum copiam. Ibi poterunt sacerdotalis dignitas et auctoritas episcopalis in suae militiae speculo sese recognoscere, ut obsequium reddant Caesari debitum, et Deo honorem.'

from all Christendom to pay their respects at his tomb.[1] In such a situation his followers had no need to manipulate the evidence or suppress unwelcome material. It was sufficient simply to provide a chronological framework, and let the letters and documents speak for themselves. In the climate of opinion in the decade following the canonization, the episcopal appeals told possibly more against their authors than against the archbishop.

The arrangement of Alan's collection was designed with much care, beginning with his *Prologus* explaining the purpose of the collection[2] and its schematic plan; this was followed by the Prologue[3] and the *Vita et Passio Sancti Thome*[4] by John of Salisbury and Alan's additional *Explanatio* intended to fill the gaps in John's account.[5] The latter had done little more than expand his letter *Ex insperato*,[6] so eloquently describing the archbishop's murder to John of Poitiers in early 1171; his *Vita* was far from adequate as a biography of the archbishop or as an account of the dispute with the king; and Alan rightly considered that a fuller description was necessary.[7] As Alan explains in his *Prologus*,[8] the collection was

---

[1] The collections of *Miracula Sancti Thome Cantuariensis*, by William of Canterbury and Benedict of Peterborough respectively (*Mats.* I, pp. 137–546, and II, pp. 21–281) record the beginning of the Canterbury pilgrimages.

[2] *Mats.* II, pp. 299–301. It is conceivable that this *Prologus* was written after the composition of the first recension, since it is lacking in AlanT(A): Brit. Libr. MS Cotton Claudius B.ii. In this, the earliest surviving copy of the work, John of Salisbury's *Prologus* and *VST* have pride of place at the front of the volume, followed by Alan's supplementary *Explanatio*.

[3] Ibid., pp. 301–2.   [4] Ibid., pp. 302–22.   [5] Ibid., pp. 323–52.

[6] *Mats.* VII, ep. 748. Though John did not claim to have been an eye-witness of the murder, his account given in *Ex insperato* is the earliest and best description of it, and there is some independent evidence to suggest that he was present at the time in the Cathedral. According to William FitzStephen (*Vita, Mats.* III, p. 139) John was among those clerks who fled to hiding-places behind the altars, and William of Canterbury records that where William de Tracy thought that he had wounded John of Salisbury, when in fact he had struck Edward Grim (*Vita, Mats.* I, p. 134). Unlike William of Canterbury, who confesses that he fled because he considered himself unfit for martyrdom (ibid., pp. 133–4: 'tanquam peccatorum conscius et minus idoneus martyrio'), John seems to have been reluctant later to mention his own flight, and so did not explain his precise knowledge of the details of the murder.

[7] AlanT, *Explanatio, Mats.* II, p. 323: 'Quia vero quaedam ibi juxta brevitatem historiae ex industria omissa sunt, quae si apposita fuerint legentis et audientis poterunt excitare devotionem, maxime cum ea pertineant ad epistolarum quae sequuntur explanationem, ea duximus summatim adjicere quae a concilio de Clarenduna usque ad discessum domini Alexandri papae de Francia juxta historiam magistri Johannis dicuntur contigisse.'

[8] *Mats.* II, p. 300: 'Distinctae sunt vero per partes secundum progressum negotii. Quarum prima pars continet ab initio exsilii usque ad adventum

devised on a chronological plan, its five books being concerned each with a different phase of the dispute: Book I covers the period from the beginning of the exile to the arrival of the papal legates William and Otto;[1] Book II continues to the coming of Gratian and Vivian,[2] Book III to that of Simon of Mont-Dieu and Bernard de Corilo,[3] Book IV to that of Rotrou of Rouen and William of Sens,[4] and Book V covers the peace with the king, the murder of Becket, his canonization, and the reconciliation of Canterbury Cathedral.[5]

---

[1] The legation of William and Otto was announced to Becket, Henry II, and Louis VII in a series of undated letters (*Mats.* VI, epp. 272–4) despatched probably in January 1167; the legates subsequently received precise instructions in letters dated 7 May and 22 August respectively (*Mats.* VI, epp. 307 and 324), and they were present at the meetings held between Gisors and Trie on 19 November (cf. *Mats.* VI, epp. 331–4) and at Argentan on 27 November 1167 (cf. *Mats.* VI, ep. 339).

[2] The embassy of Gratian and Vivian was announced to Henry II in letters dated 28 February and 10 May, 1169 respectively (*Mats.* VI, epp. 476 and 491), and they had reached Vézelay by 22 July (cf. *Mats.* VII, ep. 532); they were present at the conference at Argentan on 15 August (cf. *Mats.* VII, ep. 560), after which Gratian left to return to Rome, while Vivian remained to attend the meetings at St-Denis on 16 November and at Montmartre on 18 November (cf. *Mats.* VII, ep. 601).

[3] The embassy of Simon of Mont-Dieu and Bernard de Corilo was announced to Henry II in a letter dated 22 May 1168 (*Mats.* VI, ep. 423); their own commission was issued on 25 May (*Mats.* VI, ep. 424), and they were present at Montmirail on 6 January 1169 (cf. *Mats.* VI, epp. 451, 461, and 470–1).

[4] The commission to Rotrou and Bernard of Nevers was issued on 19 January 1170 (*Mats.* VII, ep. 623), and they were present on 16 July at Montmartre and on 22 July at the Peace of Fréteval (cf. *Mats.* VII, ep. 685). On 9 October William of Sens, in association with Rotrou of Rouen, was empowered by the Pope to pronounce an interdict on Henry II's continental lands if the king should fail to restore the sequestered property of the Becket exiles (*Mats.* VII, ep. 710); after Becket's murder William alone carried out the mandate, while Rotrou, in association with other members of the Norman episcopate, appealed to the Pope (*Mats.* VII, ep. 740); the sentence was duly ratified by Alexander III on 14 May 1171 (cf. *Mats.* VII, ep. 755).

[5] Diceto records that the formal reconciliation of Canterbury Cathedral took place with great solemnity on 21 December 1171 (I, p. 349). This followed the command of Alexander III (*Mats.* VII, ep. 787) and the instructions of the

---

Willelmi et Ottonis cardinalium. Quid, quando, ubi, vel per quos actum fuerit, per ipsas epistolas clarius innotescet. Secunda pars ab illis cardinalibus usque ad Gratianum et Vivianum. A quibus tertia pars usque ad Simonem priorem de Valle Dei (correctly: de Monte Dei; cf. *Mats.* VI, epp. 424, 451, and 464) et Bernardum de Corilo. Ab illis etiam quarta pars usque ad Rotrodum Rothomagensem archiepiscopum et Bernardum Nivernensem episcopum: demum etiam Willelmum Senonensem, nunc Remensem, archiepiscopum. Quinta continet concordiam et passionem, ipsius martyris canonizationem et ecclesiae Christi reconciliationem.'

The chronological arrangement within the sections is generally sound, though not invariably so. As entities, Books II and III are in reverse order, since Simon of Mont-Dieu and Bernard de Corilo in fact preceded Vivian and Gratian as ambassadors to the English king: the former pair were commissioned by papal letters dated 25 May 1168, while the appointment of the latter was announced to Henry II in letters dated respectively 28 February and 10 May 1169.[1] The source of this confusion is possibly traceable to William of Canterbury's *Vita et Passio Sancti Thome*, composed at Christ Church and completed in 1173–4,[2] which is the earliest biography to give precise details of the various negotiations during the controversy, and the only satisfactory account of the exile which would have been available to Alan of Tewkesbury when he began his compilation in or after 1174. William placed the legation of Vivian and Gratian some time before the conference at Montmirail on 6 January 1169, at which Simon and Bernard were present;[3] and, although he later placed the conference attended by Vivian and Gratian at Montmartre in its correct order, he did not identify the commissioners.[4] It would have been natural for Alan to rely on a work so recently completed by a monk of his own house, and it was probably from that source that he obtained his chronology with its error.

As Alan records in his *Prologus*, he found his material scattered in various *schedule*,[5] which tends to confirm that earlier attempts had been made at Canterbury, and were possibly still continuing, to assemble the archbishop's correspondence. Moreover, the *Vita et Passio* by William of Canterbury drew heavily on epistolary evidence for its account of the controversy,[6] proving (as might be expected) that at least the most important letters were available in

[1] Cf. p. 90, nn. 2 and 3 above.
[2] *Mats.* I, pp. 1–136.
[3] Ibid., pp. 72–3.
[4] Ibid., pp. 75–6.
[5] *Mats.* II, p. 300: 'Epistolae vero vario et disperso per schedulas collectae corpus rediguntur in unum, sicut pro modo suo fieri potuit, singulae locum suum retinentes et ordinem.'
[6] For a full discussion of the use made by William of Canterbury of epistolary sources, see pp. 183–7 below.

legates Albert and Theodinus (*Mats.* VII, ep. 788); and the canonization of Becket was announced in a stream of letters addressed to various provinces throughout Western Europe: e.g. dated 10–12 March 1173 (*Mats.* VII, epp. 784–6).

Christ Church in the years immediately following the martyrdom. It is more than likely that the Bodleian and Vatican Archetypes were available at Canterbury by the time that Alan of Tewkesbury was preparing his collection, and it is conceivable that they furnished a part of his source-material; but Alan's reorganization of the letters obscures the various sources on which he drew. Collation certainly reveals a definite kinship between Alan's work and these collections, but it is not possible to establish whether their affinity resulted from any dependence of the one on the other or from their derivation from a range of common sources.

With forty-four exceptions,[1] the letters in the Vatican and Lambeth Families are all found in the basic collection made by Alan of Tewkesbury, and the majority are concentrated in Books III to V. Using AlanT(B) as a basis of comparison (because in content it approximates most closely to that basic compilation, although it derives from Recension II), collation of Alan's work with these collections discloses substantial agreements of order, which are all the more significant since Alan was consciously rearranging the material according to his own plan.

In contrast, a high proportion of the letters in AlanT(B) is not found in the sources discussed so far, showing that Alan was able to draw on a wider range of materials. The additional matter comprises 185 letters and documents, scattered throughout the five books but most heavily concentrated in Books I and II.[2] Slightly

---

[1] Vat. 3, 35*, 53*, 55*, 70*, 73*, 88*, 106*, 110*, 111*, 112*, 113*, 143*, 150*, 167*, 169*, 185*, 190*, 201*, 246*, 267*, 275, 276, and 277, Roy. 188–91, Lamb. 130*, 143*, 231*, 294, 321, and 326*, and Bodl. B, II. 140*, 141*, 142*, 143*, 145*, 290*, 300*, 308, 321*, and III.8* are all omitted from the Alan of Tewkesbury collection, although the items marked with an asterisk are found among the additional material added to AlanT(A) and marked 'non est inter ordinatas'.

[2] Of the additional letters, 98 are in Book I and 56 in Book II, while Books III–V have only 8, 9, and 14 respectively. The following table shows the distribution of the additional letters through the five books according to their senders or recipients ('Other papal letters' indicates papal letters not addressed to Becket):

	I	II	III	IV	V	Total
To Becket	32	4	2	1	4	43
From Becket	10	5	2	1	3	21
From JohnS	35	45	4	6	6	96
Other papal letters	12	2	0	1	0	15
Miscellaneous	9	0	0	0	1	10
Total	98	56	8	9	14	185

less than half these additional letters, in fact ninety-six items in a total of 185, were written by John of Salisbury,[1] while the remaining eighty-nine include significant letters from a wide variety of authors.[2] None of the John of Salisbury letters was written in Becket's name and only a few were addressed to him;[3] and, though composed during the exile, they fall more into the category of private correspondence than into that concerned with the great and public issues in the dispute. The majority are letters to close friends, supplying information or soliciting help, or reporting on the progress of the negotiations between the king and the papal representatives and Becket. But it is largely through John's letters to friends like Baldwin and Bartholomew of Exeter,[4] Nicholas of Mont-Rouen,[5] John of Poitiers,[6] and Gerard la Pucelle[7] that we are informed of the varying sentiments of the circle of exiles,[8] their worries, fears, and doubts, as successive appeals and embassies brought new threats to the archbishop, and as the Emperor's successes in Italy threatened to defeat the Pope.

Of the eighty-nine additional letters,[9] twenty-one were issued by Becket and forty-three were received by him,[10] ten were sent by

---

[1] The 96 JohnS letters are as follows (the references are to the Lupus edition of AlanT(B): cf. p. 253 n. 1): Book I, nos. 24, 31, 33, 73, 88, 93–5, 103, 107, 109–11, 130, 133, 140, 141, 147, 150–4, 156, 157, 159, 161, 163, 167–73, and 179; Book II, nos. 8, 15–17, 20, 25, 26, 31, 32, 36–40, 48–53, 60, 61, 63–7, 76–8, 85, 89–93, 95, 96, 102, 103, 105–8, and 110; Book III, nos. 5, 12, 19, and 80; Book IV, nos. 29, 34–6, 39, and 49; Book V, nos. 13, 18, 42, 63, 72, and 90.

[2] Book I, nos. 1–3, 6–9, 12–16, 18, 20, 22, 25, 27, 28, 35, 36, 39, 43–6, 50, 51, 53–5, 60–2, 70–2, 75, 80–4, 86–7, 89–92, 102, 105, 111, 114, 118, 138, 139, 143–6, 164–6, and 178; Book II, nos. 6, 7, 43, 75, 79, 80, 81–3, 109, and 111; Book III, nos. 1, 15, 66, and 77; Book IV, nos. 41, 48, and 50; Book V, nos. 9, 17, 33, 53, 65, 74, 75, and 89.

[3] Only 11 of the 96 JohnS letters were addressed to Becket: I. 24, 31, 33, 147, 150, 161, 163; II. 20, 25, 64; and V. 42.

[4] To Bartholomew of Exeter: I. 130, 140, 167, and II. 61; to Baldwin of Exeter: II. 63, 66, 78, 106, 108, 110; III. 5 and V. 18.

[5] Cf. I. 141, 152, and II. 37.

[6] Cf. I. 73, 103, 151, 179; II. 17, 26, 31, 51, 65, and III. 12.

[7] Cf. I. 159, 168, and 170–3.

[8] One of the most important letters of the controversy is *Expectatione longa* (II. 63, *Mats.* VI, ep. 263), in which John refutes at length the charges made against Becket in the bishops' appeal of 1166.

[9] Cf. Appendix VI, below.

[10] For letters written by Becket, cf. ibid., I. 18, 20, 22, 75, 138, 139, 143–5, 165; II. 80–3, 109; III. 15, 66; IV. 50; V. 9, 74, and 75. For those received by him, cf. I. 1–3, 6–9, 14, 25, 28, 35, 36, 43–6, 50, 51, 53, 54, 84, 86, 87, 89, 91, 105, 111, 114, 118, 146, 164, 178; II. 6, 7, 79, 111; III. 1, 77; IV. 48; V. 17, 33, 53, and 65.

various other authors,[1] and fifteen were issued by Alexander III to recipients other than Becket.[2] The emphasis here differs considerably from that in the earlier Becket collections, which were composed markedly of letters dispatched by Becket himself. The general character of these letters is private and unofficial, particularly so with those received by Becket, of which twenty are the private reports of friends and messengers, clearly not intended for circulation. They include five letters from John of Poitiers,[3] two from Master Hervey (who died during an embassy to the Pope), four from Nicholas of Mont-St–Jacques,[4] and the rest from anonymous messengers identified simply as 'nuntius', 'suus', or 'amicus'.[5] The early date of the letters provides another striking point of contrast. Although their total range is from 1162/63 to April 1174,[6] the majority were written in the early years of the controversy, between 1163–4 and 1166,[7] and fifteen were written before Becket went into exile.[8]

2. THE LETTER-COLLECTIONS BY JOHN OF SALISBURY

The letter-collections by John of Salisbury are so important in this context that it will be useful to comment briefly on them at this point. Two separate collections of John's own letters have survived, containing respectively 135 early letters, written mostly in the name of Archbishop Theobald of Canterbury between 1153 and 1161,[9]

---

[1] Cf. ibid., I. 12, 13, 15, 16, 70–2, 102, 166, and V. 89. This list includes both the Constitutions of Clarendon and the decrees of 1169 (I. 12 and 16), as well as two imperial letters (I. 70 and 71) and an anonymous report of the Council of Würzburg (I. 72).

[2] Cf. ibid., I. 27, 39, 55, 60–2, 80–3, 90, 92; II. 43, 75; and IV. 41.

[3] Ibid., I, 1, 2, 25, 35, and 164.

[4] Ibid., I. 9, 45, 46, 50, 53, and 146.

[5] Ibid., I. 3, 6–8, 14, 36, 46; II. 6; IV. 48, and V. 33.

[6] Cf. ibid., I. 114, which dates from the beginning of Becket's pontificate, and I. 27, which was issued on 14 April 1174, immediately following the consecration of his successor.

[7] Cf. I. 1–3, 6–9, 12, 13, 15, 18, 20, 22, 25, 28, 35, 36, 39, 43–6, 50, 51, 53–5, 60–2, 70–2, 75, 80–4, 86, 87, 90, 92, 102, 105, 111, 114, 118, 138, 143–6, 178; II. 75, 79–82, and 111.

[8] Cf. I. 1–3, 6, 7, 9, 12, 18, 20, 22, 25, 75, 91, 114, and II. 111.

[9] The earlier letters have survived in three MSS only: Paris, Bibl. Nat. Latin MS 8562, Cambridge University Library MS Ii. 2. 31, fos. 119–31, and Vatican Latin MS 6024, fos. 158–78; cf. W. J. Millor and H. E. Butler, edd., *The Letters of John of Salisbury*: I, *The Early Letters*, NMT, London (1955), pp. lvii–lxii.

and 169 later letters, covering the period of the Becket dispute and ending with John's own elevation to the bishopric of Chartres in 1176.[1] The second collection is naturally more private in character, though a few of its letters were written for Bartholomew of Exeter in the period following the martyrdom.[2] This later collection has survived in two manuscripts only and these are interrelated: the Brit. Libr. Addit. MS 11506 and the Bibl. Nat. Latin MS 8562, both written in the late twelfth century.[3] The British Library manuscript is now only a fragment, breaking off in the middle of its 119th item,[4] but agreeing completely in order and reading with the manuscript now in Paris, and they were probably derived from a single archetype. The majority of John's letters incorporated in Alan's collection are found in this work, though in a different order, and there is a close textual correspondence between their versions. Whether the original selection for Alan's collection was made by Alan himself or by John is not easy to determine, but a *defloratio* or *florilegium* from a *Liber epistolarum magistri Johannis Saresberiensis* provides important evidence on John's precise contribution. The *florilegium* was made by Prior Guy of the Augustinian Priory of Southwick in the early thirteenth century and now forms part of the St John's College MS 126 in Oxford. It fills two gatherings of a volume of Southwick provenance which also contains a copy of Arnulf of Lisieux's letters,[5] and a selection of the letters of Peter of Celle, which was once thought to have been a collection of the correspondence of Abbot Walter of Dervy

---

[1] Cf. the excellent new edition by W. J. Millor and C. N. L. Brooke, *The Letters of John of Salisbury*, II : *The Later Letters (1163–1180)*, Oxford Medieval Texts, Oxford (1979).

[2] Cf. ibid., epp. 312, 319, 321, and 322. Two of the letters were written in the name of the Prior and Convent of Canterbury: epp. 311 and 320.

[3] There is in addition the badly burnt fragment in Brit. Libr. MS Cotton Vitellius E. xvii, fos. 8ra–17vb: a late twelfth-century manuscript containing a collection of John's later letters, which seems to have been produced by collating the complete collection (as preserved in the two manuscripts just mentioned) with Alan of Tewkesbury's Becket collection and transcribing from the former all the letters which were not found in the latter.

[4] The text breaks off at the foot of fo. 65vb within the letter *Tempora si numeres* at the words 'quiete ipsius audeant apparere qui ui . . .', and the catch-word 'dentes' at the foot of the fo. indicates that the MS once contained the rest of the letter.

[5] Fos. i–iir: defective list of Arnulf of Lisieux's letters; fo. iiv: list of sermons; fos. 1–69r: letters of Arnulf of Lisieux; fos. 69v–70v: ruled but otherwise blank; fos. 71r–78v: four sermons of Arnulf of Lisieux. Cf. Barlow, *Arnulf of Lisieux*, p. lxxxxiii.

(Montier-en-Der).[1] The *florilegium* makes reference to 112 letters, defectively numerated to item 110, and breaks off abruptly at the end of the second gathering in the middle of a letter.[2] Slightly less than half the letters were written by John of Salisbury in his own name;[3] and, of the remainder, thirty were issued by Becket,[4] ten were addressed to him,[5] and twenty-three are attributed to various other writers.[6] And it is possible that some of these other letters were also in fact composed by John. But, although letters written by John of Salisbury in his own name or in that of Becket's supporters formed a substantial element in the collection on which the *florilegium* was based, it also contained many other letters which suggest that John had access either to Becket's own records, or more possibly that he kept copies himself of many of the important letters which were circulated during the controversy. Thus, the very revealing reports by John of Poitiers before the exile began could have been acquired by John of Salisbury from the bishop himself.

Now, when the *florilegium* is compared with Alan of Tewkesbury's compilation and with the collection of John of Salisbury's later letters, it is seen to agree more closely with the former than with the latter: the *florilegium* agrees with Alan's order almost completely, except for the displacement of two small groups of letters, and their book divisions correspond exactly. This evidence therefore reveals at once a relationship between Guy of Southwick's *florilegium* and Alan's collection, though Guy asserts at the outset that the *florilegium* was composed from a book of letters in

---

[1] Fos. 92r–144r: letters of Peter of Celle. These letters were attributed to Walter of Montier-en-Der by C. Messiter, ed., *The Letters of Walter of Dervy*, Caxton Society Publications, 6 (1850); but Heinrich Hohenleutner has more recently shown that they derive in fact from the collection of Peter of Celle's letters: cf. Hohenleutner, 'Die Briefsammlung des sogenannten Walter von Dervy (Montier-en-Der) in der Oxforder Handschrift St John's College, Mrs. 126', *Historisches Jahrbuch*, LXXIV (1955), pp. 673–80.

[2] The *florilegium* breaks off in the letter *Licet Anglicane* at the words 'Christi cuius', and with the catchwords 'nomen judeis'; cf. *Mats.* VII, p. 525. The items are numbered 1–110 in a modern hand, but 2 letters, 17b and 87b, were missed by the numerator, so that the correct total is 112.

[3] Nos. 1, 13–16, 17b, 18, 20–7, 29, 33–6, 39–41, 44–52, 54–9, 67–70, 81, 82, 86, 88, 101, 106, and 110.

[4] Nos. 4–6, 8–10, 17, 28, 30–2, 37, 38, 42, 62–4, 73, 78, 83, 85, 89–92, 96–9, and 105; 91 was written by the 'coexules sancti Thome'.

[5] Nos. 2, 3, 11, 12, 74, 79, 84, 93, 102, and 104.

[6] Nos. 7, 19, 43, 53, 60, 61, 65, 66, 71, 72, 75–7, 80, 87a, 87b, 94, 95, 100, 103, and 107–9.

four volumes relating to the cause of Blessed Thomas the Martyr compiled by John of Salisbury immediately after the murder, with the assistance of Guy himself who was then a canon at Merton.[1] It is on such evidence as this that the supposition was made that John of Salisbury was the author of the work attributed to Alan; but it is more likely that this interrelationship and Guy's comment throw light on the origins than on the authorship of Alan's completed work. His authorship is indeed attested in the writing of contemporary witnesses such as Herbert of Bosham and Gervase of Canterbury;[2] he implicitly claimed the work as his own in the introduction to its published version;[3] and Henry of Eastry refers to Alan's book of letters in his catalogue of volumes belonging to the library of Christ Church Canterbury in the mid-thirteenth century.[4] The most probable solution to this problem is that John of Salisbury did in fact make a collection of letters relating to the Becket controversy and arranged it according to a chronological plan in five books distributed in four *volumina,* and that Guy's *florilegium* is based on the contents and order of that work; but Alan of Tewkesbury apparently took over the collection later and used it as the basis of his own much more ambitious compilation, while preserving its order and general plan for the most part, as well as keeping the *Vita et Passio Sancti Thome* which John had written as the introduction to his collection. If this interpretation is correct, then Alan continued and brought to completion the work conceived and first undertaken by John.

No copy of John's preliminary collection is known to survive, but its general scope and character can be deduced from the *florilegium* briefly described above. His own letters formed a substantial part of the collection, and at least some of the letters issued in Becket's name, and probably some others in the names of French ecclesiastics, were also written by him. The existence of two other collections of John's letters suggests that he kept copies of important letters from the time of his service in Theobald's Curia, and most of the letters in the *florilegium* could have been preserved in his personal files. For, although he was not present in

[1] Cf. p. 86, n. 6 above.　　[2] Cf. p. 86, nn.2 and 3 above.
[3] Cf. *Mats.* II, pp. 300–1.
[4] Cf. M. R. James, *The Ancient Libraries of Canterbury and Dover,* Cambridge (1903), p. 52, no. 358: *Epistole Sancti Thome Alani Prioris.* This reference is ambiguous: it may refer to the collection made by Prior Alan: but it may equally merely designate the volume of Becket letters which he owned.

Becket's circle for most of the exile, many of the letters issued or received by the archbishop were sent to him, and in this way much of the important correspondence passed through his hands.[1] In these circumstances, there is no need to suppose that he derived the material for his collection from the Canterbury records after the murder, since the whole character of the *florilegium* suggests its dependence on his own records, with a primary emphasis on letters composed by himself. At the same time, John's records were probably not his only source of supply, for Guy's comments suggest their collaboration in the accumulation of letters, implying perhaps their acquisition from various sources. It is not possible to determine whether the *florilegium* contains a reference to every letter in the collection from which it was derived, so there remains some doubt as to its full contents. But since Guy was occasionally content to cite only the protocol of a letter, without either *incipit* or indication of contents,[2] it may be assumed that he was providing a digest of the whole work as he had it before him.

Thus, when Alan of Tewkesbury took up the task of preparing a comprehensive edition of the Becket correspondence, he had the advantage of having available not only whatever material survived in the Canterbury archives, but also a preliminary collection composed by John of Salisbury. It is clear from the resulting compilation, as well as from the marginalia in Brit. Libr. MS Cotton Claudius B. II, or AlanT(A), that he drew significantly on the later letters of John of Salisbury, especially for material relating to the first eighteen months or so of the dispute. Although attempts have been made to identify John's 'Becket' collection,[3] his precise contribution to Alan of Tewkesbury's finished product remains uncertain.

3. THE MANUSCRIPTS OF ALAN OF TEWKESBURY'S COLLECTION

Either the whole or part of Alan of Tewkesbury's collection has survived in the following manuscripts: Brit. Libr. MSS Arundel 219 and Cotton Claudius B.II, the Vatican Latin MSS 1220 and

---

[1] John of Salisbury's own letters contain many references to letters which passed through his hands; for references to transcripts, cf. *Mats.* V, pp. 381 and 439; VI, pp. 71, 319, 320–1, 323, 393, and 482; and VII, p. 233. For further references to John's possession of letters, cf. ibid., V, pp. 383–4, 432, 433, and 439; VI, pp. 13, 63, 68–9, 119, 191, 217, 220, 341, 370, 417, and 497; VII, pp. 32 and 231.

[2] Cf. nos. 23 and 87b.   [3] Cf. above, p. 74 and n. 3.

6027, the Cambridge MSS Corpus Christi College 295, Trinity College O.5.40–44 and Trinity Hall 24, the Oxford Bodl. MS 937, Part I (fos. 35r–170v), and the Paris Bibl. Nat. Latin MS 5320.[1] The Cotton Claudius MS B.II, the Vatican Latin MS 1220 and the Corpus Christi College MS 295 have been identified above as AlanT(A), AlanT(B), and AlanT(C) respectively, and the Oxford Bodl. MS fos. 35r–170v is identified as Bodl.B, I. Two of the nine manuscripts are of little importance since they are post-medieval transcripts of earlier collections still surviving: the Vat. Lat. MS 6027[2] is a careful copy of Vat. Lat. MS 1220, transcribed in the seventeenth century, and the Trinity College volumes date also from the seventeenth century and were transcribed by and for Thomas Gale in preparation for a full edition of the Lives and Letters of Becket which was never produced. The Gale transcripts fill six large folio volumes, and contain collated texts of the Alan of Tewkesbury collection, the letters of John of Salisbury, and the *Vita Sancti Thome* by William FitzStephen.[3] Gale's basic manuscript source for the Becket correspondence, identified as A in his transcript, appears to have been the Corpus Christi College MS 295, collated with the Cotton MS Claudius B.II, identified as 'Cott' in his annotations, and with the texts preserved in Roger of

---

[1] Cf. above, pp. 13–14.

[2] 10 × 7 in.; 617 fos.; double columns with 29 lines to the column; written on paper. This MS seems to be an exact copy of the Vat. Lat. MS 1220, and is the transcript from which the Lupus edition of the Life and Letters of Becket was printed.

[3] The Gale transcripts comprise 6 large folio volumes (8 × 12½ in.), very carefully written in more than one hand of the seventeenth century, in the Cambridge, Trinity College MSS O.5.40–45. Their contents are as follows: Vol. I, neither foliated nor paginated, the AlanT *Explanatio*, followed by AlanT, Book I (the letters in this and subsequent volumes were transcribed separately with a blank leaf inserted between each letter); Vol. II, foliated 1–235, AlanT, Book II; Vol. III, foliated 1–434 with one unnumbered leaf at the end, containing 235 letters, of which the majority were written by John of Salisbury (the authors of this part clearly had access to MSS of both the early and the later letters of John of Salisbury, but they did not use all their contents or preserve their order of items); Vol. IV, neither foliated nor paginated, AlanT, Books III and IV; Vol. V, neither foliated nor paginated, AlanT, Book V and a few additional letters; Vol. VI, paginated to p. 94, containing William FitzStephen's *Vita Sancti Thome*, copied as its heading indicates from a MS in the Cotton Library: 'Vita Thome Beket per Gul. FitzStephenum scripta, et ex codice manuscripto Cottoniana desumpta manu cujusdam Galli'; the MS source was almost certainly Brit. Libr. MS Cotton Julius A. XI. For an account of the careers of Thomas and Roger Gale, cf. D. C. Douglas, *English Scholars, 1660–1730*, 2nd edn., London (1951), pp. 59–65 and 168–75.

Hoveden's *Chronica*. Thus, each of his sources is still extant, and there is no evidence that Gale had access to any manuscript which has since been lost. Only three of the medieval manuscripts contain substantially the complete collection,[1] and these three versions differ in both contents and detail, indicating that the collection passed through various recensions. The other four copies are all to some extent abbreviated: the Trinity Hall MS is now only a fragment, breaking off towards the end of Book I,[2] though there is evidence to suggest that it once contained the full collection,[3] while the Arundel, Bodleian, and French manuscripts were abbreviated by design.

A. ALANT(A): BRIT. LIBR. COTTON MS CLAUDIUS B.II

The earliest and best version of the full collection is in the Cotton MS Claudius B.II,[4] that is AlanT(A), a fine manuscript of the late twelfth century, very carefully written in double columns in a well-formed book-hand, with the headings of the individual letters rubricated throughout. The initials are coloured in either red, blue, green, or gold, and those at the beginning of the different parts are quite elaborately decorated: thus, the capital I on fo. 214va has a design incorporating three historiated roundels showing the interview between Becket and the knights, the murder, and the interment of the archbishop.[5] In addition to these embellishments there is one illuminated drawing on fo. 341r which depicts the interview between Becket and the knights and his subsequent murder. The medieval provenance of this beautiful manuscript can almost certainly be ascribed to Canterbury: N. R. Ker in his lists of medieval manuscripts was apparently hesitant on this point, and there is some conflict in his references;[6] but C. R. Dodwell con-

[1] Cf. p. 13 above: AlanT(A), AlanT(B), and AlanT(C).

[2] The MS breaks off in the middle of *Plenam deuotionem*, I. 167.

[3] The MS contains marginal references to letters which it does not itself include, but which are found in later positions in the complete collections; see p. 130 and n. 4 below.

[4] 8 × 12¾ in.; 356 fos.; double columns with 36 lines to the column; arranged in gatherings of 8 leaves each.

[5] Further illuminated capitals occur on fos. 2rb, 2va–b, 9ra, 142ra, 268ra, and 300ra. Some of the smaller initials towards the end of the book are attractively decorated in red, green, and blue; cf. fos. 347rb, 348vb, 353va, 353vb, and 354ra.

[6] In the first edition of N. R. Ker's *The Medieval Libraries of Great Britain*, Royal Historical Society, London (1961), the MS was placed among the 'rejected' Canterbury books; in the second edition (1964) it is found in neither the 'accepted' nor the 'rejected' lists, but it is ascribed to Canterbury in the general index of MSS; cf. ed. cit. (1964), pp. 35 and 356.

cluded, after a close palaeographical and artistic study of the manuscript, that it was in fact produced at Christ Church in the late 1170s or early 1180s;[1] and this conclusion would fit in very well with certain internal evidence.

It is evident from the present appearance of the volume that the Claudius manuscript was not the first exemplar of Alan's collection, nor was it an editor's basic working copy; on the contrary, the high quality of its script and fine illumination suggests that it was originally intended as a presentation volume of some kind. But the presentation seems never to have been made: the decoration of the book is incomplete,[2] and its text has been subjected to a degree of meticulous critical scrutiny going far beyond the correction of ordinary scribal error. Despite the high quality of its original production, nearly every folio contains contemporary corrections, cross-references, and notes, testifying to an exhaustive comparison of the whole work with relevant texts. Equally significant is the fact that this work was begun before the decoration of the manuscript was fully completed, and every attempt was made to preserve the aesthetic integrity of the finished book. Some of the notes are provided with initials and coloured borders which match the main transcription, and some of the major textual emendations are inserted in a hand very similar to, if not identical with, that of the principal scribe. Similarly, where corrections are inserted over erasure, they were written by the main scribe in such a fashion as to be virtually indistinguishable from what he had written before. It is this last feature which fixes the beginning of the collation/correction process before the completion of the volume as a whole. At least three main hands, in addition to the principal scribe, participated in the labour of collating its order, content, and readings with other variously identified *libri*, and one of the four pro-

---

[1] C. R. Dodwell, *The Canterbury School of Illumination, 1066–1200*, Cambridge (1954), p. 112, n. 1, '. . . This is clearly a Christ Church manuscript, an attribution which is confirmed by the fact that the marginal drawings of animals and human heads are copied from one of two Christ Church MSS, either the Eadwine Psalter or the Dover Bible. The book was probably written in the 1170's or early 1180's, and the representation of Becket's death on folio 341 is probably the earliest illustration of that event'. Cotton Claudius B.ii is listed by Dodwell as a Christ Church book, with the date 1170–1200, on p. 122.

[2] Cf. fo. 2ra, where a later hand has filled in the originally blank first column with a roughly executed pen-drawing of an archbishop, surmounted by a title frame composed of four winged-cherubs' heads.

vided the letters with a systematic apparatus of cross-references, in addition to identifications of persons and some comments. An analysis of this editorial material—for such is what it seems to be— reveals the simultaneous existence of two additional versions of Alan's collection (an 'alius emendatior liber' and the 'liber exemplaris'), as well as various books imprecisely described as 'alius liber', including the later letters of John of Salisbury. And it was with these that the Claudius manuscript was collated. But the question remains: why was so fine a volume subjected to such extensive annotation at so early a stage in its existence? The most satisfactory explanation, and one which most adequately seems to fit the evidence provided by both text and marginalia, is that while this manuscript was in process of transcription as a *de luxe* edition of the first state of Alan's collection, a companion version was undergoing correction and rearrangement to become the 'alius emendatior liber', which rendered the former textually obsolete before its ink was dry. It was this circumstance which caused the intermission of decoration at a very late stage and provided both the need and the opportunity for a thorough overhaul of the whole work in the light not only of the now updated text, but through comparison with still further copies of particular letters.

What is revealed in the Claudius manuscript is a complex process of textual purification under the scrutiny of a meticulous editor. Four main hands were engaged in the work:

Hand A, the main scribe, in a careful, well-formed, and skilfully abbreviated book-hand, was responsible for the basic text, all corrections over erasure, occasional superscript insertions of what may have been the original reading, some additions to the text, and some alternative texts.

Hand B, very similar in form to Hand A, and often difficult to distinguish from it: a well-formed book-hand, responsible for the bulk of the interlinear variants and some marginal notes. It is probable that Hands A and B were engaged in the work of correction before the decoration of the volume was completed, since some of their comments are provided with coloured initials and line borders.[1]

Hand C, a fine, slightly more mannered, hand, with distinctive seraphs, responsible for most of the marginalia in the John of Salisbury letters, including numerical cross-references to a manu-

---

[1] Cf. fos. 35vb, 80ra, 82ra, and 160ra.

script of his later letters, as well as occasional variants and comments elsewhere.

Hand D, a more florid, occasionally almost cursive, script, reminiscent in some respects of a charter-hand found in some of Henry II's writs, generally using a heavy black ink, responsible for numerous cross-references to letters, identifications of persons mentioned in the text, and occasional highly significant notes and comments. This is in all respects the most individualistic of the hands and seems to have had a long-standing and authoritative association with the manuscript.

In addition, a later hand (E) has contributed canonical references to two letters at the end of Book V.[1] But he was certainly not part of the editorial 'team', and has been ignored in the discussions that follow.

The Marginalia in AlanT(A).

The annotation in the Claudius manuscript can be most satisfactorily considered in ten main categories:

I. *Order*. There are thirteen highly significant notes in Hands B and D scattered through the volume, describing the variant arrangement of a second version of Alan's collection, which is identified as the 'liber emendatior', 'alius liber', and 'exemplar emendatior'. In nine cases, the variation involves no more than the re-positioning of one letter,[2] but in three instances the change is considerable, involving between five and twenty-four items.[3] Under the opening phrases of *Tanta nos* on fo. 82ra, for example, Hand B has written: 'Hec secundum librum emendatiorem scripta fuit inferius post epistolam Multa quidem scribenda'; to which Hand D has added the numerical reference, 'i(nfra) cxxxiij'; and on fo. 154 vb, Hand B has inserted a list of twenty-two *incipits* under the letter *Nec priorum*. In this instance, too, Hand D has inserted further information in the form of two additional notes inserted respectively above and below the list: 'Ab hac epistola Nec priorum usque ad epistolam Qui amicis in alio libro ita fuerunt epistole ordinate' and 'Qui amicis nec in sal(utis uoto) et cetere epistole sicut in hoc libro ordinantur'.[4] From such references it is possible to deduce the order of letters in the corrected version of AlanT. It is significant that the

---

[1] Cf. fos. 354rb–vb.
[2] Cf. fos. 82ra, 103rb, 160ra, 177vb, 190va, 206rb, 277rb, 279rb, and 294va.
[3] Cf. fos. 101vb, 154vb, and 177rb.
[4] Hand D has inserted the *incipit* of *Nec priorum* above Hand B's list.

fine Claudius manuscript should by implication be described as the less perfect text, that the tense used in the two examples cited and in two others, should be past ('fuit', 'fuerunt'), and that the majority of such notes should be in the hand of the principal collator (Hand B), carefully inserted on specially ruled lines, occasionally with coloured initials, and frequently with numerical identification entered later by Hand D. Such details suggest that this stage of correction was undertaken very soon after the original transcription of the manuscript and that the 'alius emendatior liber' was already in existence at that time.

II*a. Content.* In a similar way, Hand C for the most part, and Hand D in certain special circumstances, has inserted the comment 'Hec non fuit inter ordinatas' or 'Hec non est inter ordinatas' by the side of forty-six letters, while Hand C has written 'hic ponantur epistole que desunt' under a further two items.[1] Such notes identify those items which were added later to the basic collection and which were found neither in the exemplar from which the Claudius manuscript was copied nor in the 'emendatior liber'. They mostly occur at the end of Books II, III, and IV and,

[1] The following letters are marked 'non est (*or* non fuit) inter ordinatas':

AlanT(A)		Mats		AlanT(A)		Mats
I.121	Mandatum domini	107	101	Relatum est		65
130	Omnia nostra	247	102	Cum non ignoretis		159
II.24	Desiderio magno	314	103	Rerum subite		—
30	Vestri similes	410	104	Si consentientes		—
39	Vestra fraternitas	357	IV.4	Placet nobis		396
68	Etsi paruitas	426	8	Gratias non		468
82	Quanta mentis	120	45	Quanto per carissimum		310
86	Peruenit ad	14	49	Illius dignitatis		169
87	Si quanta	117	60	Trecensis comes		394
88	Si quanta	118	61	Illustri Flandrorum		559
89	Quia ex defectu	119	62	Difficile est		619
90	Nouit inspector	129	63	Breuiloquio		603
91	Ad aures nostras	130	64	Facies celi		—
92	Cui plura	125	65	De munere		429
93	Mater tua	127	66	Lator presentium		—
94	Quia ecclesiam	126	67	Quanta fide		377
95	Apostolicis sine	358	68	Quas referre		—
98	Preter eam	364	69	Sobrii moris		383
120	Magnum frater	—	70	Fidem esse		428
123	In te omnium	191	71	Liberalitatis tue		425
124	Doctissimi uiri	432	V.76	Quanta mala		160
126	Si salutationis	333				
129	Quoniam ecclesia	412		Letters marked 'desunt'		
III.99	Scripseramus	578	II.130	Sic computati		335
100	Regium dilectissimi	433	131	Scio pater		—

save for the letters by John of Salisbury, they were probably acquired piecemeal, individually, and in small groups, while the transcription of Claudius was in progress. Out of the eighteen letters written by John of Salisbury, no less than fourteen occur in the surviving manuscripts of his later letters,[1] and were almost certainly derived immediately from that source. But it is the remaining thirty items which reveal most about the process of collection at that stage in Alan's work. The large accession to Book II,[2] for example, is all related to the dispute over the election of the Bishop of Bangor and spans the years 1162-9, with a numerical emphasis on 1166. The insertion of such a group of letters, of virtually no significance in the conflict with Henry II (though important in showing the extent to which Becket was able in certain respects to exercise his metropolitical functions during the exile), indicates the survival of record files in which material relating to specific business was kept together for easy reference. In this respect, the Bangor file invites comparison with the Pentney file;[3] and both probably exemplify the *schedule* to which Alan referred in his introduction and which, as we have argued above, formed the major source both of the Lambeth Addition and of the 'new' letters in Bodl.B, II and III. The remainder of the batch of 'non est/desunt' letters is made up of eight isolated letters of Becket himself, two from Gilbert Foliot, five from Alexander III to various recipients, two anonymous letters, and one from John of Naples to Henry II.[4] Among these, only the group of papal letters calls for special consideration, since their dating and subject-matter are of some interest. Although they were not inserted as a group, but distributed through Books II, III, and IV, they also have something of the character of a special file, this time of materials relating to the rights and privileges of the Church of Canterbury and its archbishops, and span the years from 1161,

---

[1] Cf. p. 95, n. 1, above. John of Salisbury's letters are: II. 30, 68, 98, 120, 123-4, 126, 131; III. 103 and 104; IV. 64-71. All but II. 30, III. 104, and IV. 70-1 are found in the MSS of John's later letters.

[2] Ibid., nos. II. 39, 82, and 86-95.

[3] Cf. *Mats.* VI, epp. 485-7 and 489-90, and AlanT(A), II.74, I. 38, III. 25, 44, and 45.

[4] For the Becket letters, cf. AlanT(A), I.130; II.24; III.99; IV.8, 60, 61, 63; and V.76; for the papal letters: II.129; III. 101, 102; IV. 45 and 59; for the Foliot letters: I.121 and III.100; for the anonymous letters: II.130 and IV.62; and for the letter from John of Naples: IV.4.

before Becket's elevation, to 1174, some years after his murder. In order of issue they are as follows:

Quanto per carissimum, addressed to Roger of York in 1161, granting permission for him to crown Henry II's eldest son;[1]

Illius dignitatis, addressed in 1166 to Roger of York and the Canterbury, suffragans, confirming that the right to crown kings in England belonged to the see of Canterbury and forbidding any infringement of that right;[2]

Quoniam ecclesia uestra, sent to the Chapter of Holy Trinity, Canterbury, in 1168, confirming Becket's right to appoint their prior;[3]

Relatum est auribus, addressed to the Archbishop of Canterbury, protecting his jurisdictional rights against their diminution by his suffragans or by archdeacons during appeals to the Curia;[4] and

Cum non ignoretis, addressed to the Canterbury suffragans, asserting the archbishop's legatine rights in their respect. The present manuscript alludes to the archbishop as 'uenerabilem fratrem nostrum T. Cantuariensem archiepiscopum', apparently linking the letter with Becket, but this is a mistaken attribution.[5]

Of these five letters, two can be safely assigned to the period of Becket's pontificate, namely *Illius dignitatis* and *Quoniam ecclesia uestra*, whose dates are preserved in AlanT(A). The dating of *Quanto per carissimum* has been the subject of some debate, but can confidently be placed in 1161, and therefore before Becket's elevation, by combining the evidence of a dating clause in certain decretal collections with a careful consideration of its text and the arguments advanced in objection to Roger of York's coronation of the Young King in 1170.[6] But *Cum non ignoretis* and *Relatum est auribus* were sent to Becket's successor, Archbishop Richard. *Relatum est auribus* was addressed by Alexander III to Richard after the conferment of his legation in May 1174: the siglum R. for Richard is found in five decretal collections.[7] Moreover, *Significauit nobis*, found elsewhere in Alan's collection, is a complemen-

---

[1] *Mats.* VI, ep. 310. [2] Ibid., V, ep. 169.
[3] Ibid., VI, ep. 412. [4] Ibid., V, ep. 65.
[5] Ibid., ep. 159; cf. AlanT(A), fo. 266va.
[6] Cf. A. Heslin (Anne Duggan), 'The coronation of the Young King in 1170', *Studies in Church History*, II (1965), pp. 165–78.
[7] Cf. *Appendix Concilii Lateranensis* 10.29 in Lincoln Cathedral MS 121, fo. 18r; and four printed collections: *Bambergensis* 42.28; *Compendiensis* 42.29; *Lipsiensis* 47.31; and *Compilatio I* 2.20.25.

tary text, addressed to all Canterbury suffragans, mandating them to observe the archbishop's judicial rights. A single decretal collection identifies the recipient archbishop as R., while the date 14 May at Anagni is found for the same letter in AlanT(A).[1] Alexander III was at Anagni on that date in 1174 and 1176, the former date matching the conferment of Richard's legation. The identity of context of *Relatum est auribus* and *Significauit nobis* is clear, and the date 14 May 1174 can be assigned to both. The date of *Cum non ignoretis* is less certain, except that it also was sent to Richard, on the evidence of one canonical source, and was therefore issued in or after 1174.[2] An earlier tradition assigning this letter, like *Relatum est auribus*, to Becket must be discarded,[3] and *Cum non ignoretis* can certainly be placed within the dating limits 1174–81, and possibly assigned to the opening year of Richard's primacy, 1174–5. Clearly, such letters could not have formed part of the Becket archives. Their inclusion in Alan's collection demonstrates his interest in the privileges of Canterbury and his readiness to admit new letters as they became available, though their immediate source remains to be established. Their simultaneous survival in decretal collections suggests possible derivation from an early canonical source.

For the most part, the insertion of these forty-eight additional letters seems to have been decided on early enough for their inclusion in the tables of contents preceding Books II to V.[4] But five were added considerably later in the day. It is clear that Book II was intended to end with no. 128, since its final word was written in the characteristic spaced style (exhi b e r e) indicating the end of a section, while no. 129, marked 'non fuit inter ordinatas', is squeezed into the space remaining at the foot of the folio, and nos. 130 and 131, marked 'hic ponantur epistole que desunt', are

---

[1] AlanT(A), I. 23, *Mats*. VI, ep. 408. Cf. *Appendix Concilii Lateranensis* 10.24, editio princeps, ed. J. Mansi, Sancta Concilia, XXII, cols. 318–19.

[2] The siglum R. is found in the Fountains Collection, *Font*. 2.52: Oxford Bodl. MS Laud Misc. 527, fo. 39v.

[3] Jaffé assigned *Relatum est auribus* and *Cum non ignoretis* to 1162–70 and 1166–70 respectively (JL 11661 and 11665), and correctly dated *Significauit nobis* 14 May 1174 (JL 12378). Robertson assigned *Relatum est auribus* to the limits of Alexander III's pontificate, 1159–81 (*Mats*. V, ep. 65), thus allowing the possibility of its reception by Theobald, Becket or Richard; he accepted the Becket context of *Cum non ignoretis* (*Mats*. V, ep. 159) and argued, against Jaffé, that *Significauit nobis* was addressed to Becket in mid-1166 (*Mats*. VI, ep. 408).

[4] Cf. AlanT(A), fos. 141ra–vb, 213vb–214rb, 267va–vb, and 299rb–vb.

inserted in paler ink by Hand A into an originally blank column preceding Book III's table of contents on the verso.[1] And, while the rubricated number cxxx occurs at the end of the table to Book II, the *incipit* of 130 together with the number and *incipit* of 131 are missing.[2] In Book III, where the whole 'non est/fuit' accession was appended to the end of the Book in three stages,[3] the final two letters, nos. 103 and 104, are wanting in the table.[4] Similarly, Hand C has indicated the originally intended end of Book IV by inserting an *explicit* at the appropriate point, preceding the group of 'non est/fuit' letters.[5]

There seems to be little doubt that these forty-eight letters mark a distinct addition to Alan's collection, inserted in stages as the transcription of the Claudius manuscript was in progress.

II*b*. It is clear from the manuscript format that there were yet further additions to the basic collection which, perhaps through error, were not marked in any way by the scribes. Five new texts were inserted by Hand A at the end of Book I and three were added in stages to the end of Book V.[6] In order of appearance, this final accession comprises: two letters from Louis VII written probably in 1169, two relating to the rights of the Archbishop of York, respectively from 1175 and 1161, a version of Becket's prophetic vision at Pontigny, Alexander III's mandate on the Pentney case, sent to Richard of Dover, part of Alexander III's decretal on the penalties for Becket's murderers addressed to Bartholomew of Exeter on 31 January 1172, and Peter of Blois' *Benedictus Deus* addressed to Walter of Palermo *c.* 1180.[7] As with the majority of

---

[1] Ibid., fo. 213rb–va.   [2] Ibid., fo. 141vb.

[3] Ibid., fos. 265vb–267rb; the letters were inserted as follows: III. 99–100, with the final word of 100 written in spaced style (expaues c i t e); 101–2, lacking the initial A in the heading of no. 101; and 103–4, lacking the initial R to *Rerum subite* (103).

[4] Ibid., fo. 214rb.   [5] Ibid., fo. 294vb.

[6] Ibid., I. 180–4 and V. 103–5. V. 103 and 104 are written by Hand A in the usual fashion, and rubricated; but the absence of the initial A for Alexander in both letters suggests slightly later insertion, though the *incipits* of both letters are found in the appropriate place in the index to Book V. However, V. 105 was inserted by a different hand after a gap of 24 lines; it is lacking in the index and lacks coloured initials.

[7] The final (unmarked) addition to AlanT's collection consists of the following letters:
I.180   *Honor quem* Louis VII to Manual of Constantinople, 1169
I.181   *Honor quem* Louis VII to William of Sicily, 1169
I.182   *A memoria uestra* Alexander III to Roger of York, 1175
I.183   *Antiquam Eboracensis* Alexander III to R. of York, 22 Jan. 1161.
I.184   *Dum beatus Thomas* Pontigny vision, *c.* 1166–71 [*cont.*]

the 'non est/desunt' letters already discussed, these also were a piecemeal addition inserted as space allowed. The York letters are associated with the Canterbury file mentioned above, and help to round off the Becket phase of the Canterbury-York dispute; the Vision account, which gained wide currency in the late twelfth and early thirteenth century,[1] adds some colour to the martyrdom concept, and the three letters appended to Book V conclude some of the contentious issues still outstanding: the Pentney affair, the punishment of Becket's assassins, and the determination of his status as a martyr.

III. *Corrections over erasure.* Scattered through the manuscript, there are about 145 carefully inserted corrections over erasure, entered in slightly paler ink by the principal scribe A, and now often barely distinguishable from the remainder of the text. They vary in extent from single letters and syllables to substantial passages, and while many, as would be expected, are simply corrections of slips in transcription made by the scribe himself, a significant number seem to represent textual emendation: an improving or at least changing of the reading as a result of collation with an alternative version or versions. An entirely characteristic emendation of this kind is found on fo. 160vb, where the word 'taliter' is written in pale ink over an erasure, while Hand A or B has inserted 'uł ita' above the corrected reading.[2] Comparison with other versions of the letter reveals that the two later manuscripts of the complete AlanT collection (in company with Lamb., Bodl.B, II, and the 'Foliot' Douce collection) agrees with the correction, while derivatives from the Vatican Archetype agree with the alternative. It is possible that this example, together with the thirty-

---

[1] This brief text is found also in: Oxford Bodl. MSS 509, fo. 14v (s. xii); 937, fo. 18v (s. xiii); Laud Misc. 666, fo. xlvi^v (s. xiii–xiv); Paris, Ste-Geneviève MS 1370, fo. 68v (s. xiii); and Rome, Bibl. Alessandrina MS 120, fo. 83v (s. xiii). A close but not exact copy occurs in the Douce MS of FitzStephen's *VST* (cf. *Mats.* III, p. 38), where its oral source is alleged to be Guichard, Abbot of Pontigny, who witnessed the experience and revealed it after Becket's death. The same story is related, though in different words, by Grim (ibid. II, 418–19), who mistakenly places it in the context of Becket's residence at Sens; and it also occurs in Guernes de Pont-Sainte-Maxence (op. cit., p. 129), and in Gervase of Canterbury's *De Vita Sex Episcoporum Coetaneorum* (*Mats.* II, 283).

[2] Cf. Appendix VII, no. 5.

V.103   *Ad aures nostras* Alexander III to Richard of Canterbury, 1174–5.
V.104   *Sicut dignum est* Alexander III to Bartholomew of Exeter, 31 Jan. 1172.
V.105   *Benedictus Deus* Peter of Blois to Walter of Palermo, *c.* 1180.

four similar corrections in the manuscript,[1] merely indicates scribal hesitation about the appropriate expansion of an abbreviated form. But the superscript (or occasionally marginal) insertion of what seems to have been the original reading in these cases strongly suggests that the first reading was not a mistake, in the sense that it was wrongly copied or wrongly expanded from the exemplar being used, but rather that it was rejected after collation with what was considered to be a better or more authoritative text.

In the majority of corrections over erasure, however, the original reading has not been preserved and can now be recovered only conjecturally by collation with related manuscripts. On fo. 18rb, for example, towards the end of *Vix mihi domine*, a long emendation filling $10\frac{1}{2}$ lines was inserted by Hand A over erasure. It is clear that the original text must have been far shorter than the correction since the latter has been highly abbreviated and closely written to make its inclusion in the original space possible; and even so, the correction spreads somewhat awkwardly into the right-hand margin. Comparison with related texts of the letter shows that AlanT(B), which will be discussed in detail later, lacks four lines of the Claudius correction.[2] In this instance, the omission arose from the commonplace scribal error of *homoeoteleuton*, where the copyist's eye passed from one word of his text to another of similar form (in this case from 'pollicitatione' to 'contemplatione'), omitting in consequence the intervening passage. Similar examples are found in *Venientes ad terram*[3] and *Transacta dominica*.[4] In each

[1] Cf. also the examples of such corrections in ibid., nos. 11, 15, and 19.

[2] The correction (over erasure) reads: 'donec ad eas rescripsisset conseruaret nullius oculo nisi sepedicti G. illas inspecturo. Et is, quantum mihi uidetur, compatitur iniuriis que ecclesie Dei irrogantur, etsi non usquequaque forsitan contemplatione diuina, respectu tamen ut existimo affectionis domini sui cui quantum animaduertere possum, timet ne forte in his que agit a deo, quem offendere uidetur, percutiatur. Ego uero dominum Ebroic(ensem) et illos qui cum eo preibant litteris tantum prosecutus, incepto itineri institi, et ab eodem castro, id est a Luchiis, presentium latorem ad uos remisi. Premisi autem cursorem per quem abbatem Pontin(iacensem) ut mihi in curia occurrat inuito, qui'; cf. *Mats.* V., p. 41. AlanT(B) lacks 'donec ad eas . . . contemplatione'.

[3] AlanT(A), fo. 161ra. The correction reads: 'ad iudicium prouenirent nec ad concordiam, nec aliqua ratione uellet causam intrare, ea que nobis innotuerant regi manifestare curauimus, plura siquidem prout decuit reticentes et temperantes audita. Nobis itaque locutioni finem facientibus, rex et magni uiri qui secum aderant ceperunt asserere quod esset deinceps absolutus, ex quo archiepiscopus recusabat iudicium. Cum ergo post multam regis'; cf. *Mats.* VI, p. 283. The MSS of the Vatican Family all lack the sentence 'Nobis itaque . . . iudicium' cf. Vat., fo. 91ra, Roy., fo. 30r–v, and Harl., fo. 56v. Cf. also Appendix VII, no. 5.

[4] AlanT(A), fo. 316rb. The correction reads: 'ut magis timeatur, sed non

of these instances it is likely that the mistake existed in the exemplar from which Claudius was copied; and the corrections result from comparison with more complete versions of the letters in question.

But the most illuminating example, which demonstrates the process of textual purification very clearly, occurs in the letter *Quam iustis*. On fo. 339ra, part of the original text was erased to make way for a slightly longer version, occupying an extra line at the foot of the folio, while Hand A has inserted an alternative reading, carefully surrounded by a border in green ink and supplied with a heading, also in green, 'nunc exemplari ita inuenitur.' Collation reveals that the corrected reading agrees with all surviving AlanT manuscripts, while the reading attributed to the exemplar occurs, significantly enough, only in manuscripts in the Vatican Family.[1] This is another example of something far more significant than the correction of scribal error. The editor (or corrector) was evidently confronted by two versions of the text in question but, while he preferred one, and contrived to have it inserted into the main text, he was yet scrupulously reluctant to discard the first version entirely.

IV. *Variants ascribed to other exemplaria.* Though comparatively few in number, the citations of volumes variously described as 'emendatior exemplar', 'alius exemplar', 'unus exemplar', and

---

[1] AlanT(A), fo. 339ra–rb

Main text	*Variant*
[fo. 339ra] nos pro pace ecclesie et reuerentia domini regis *cum consilio ipsius et domini Wintoniensis et aliorum fratrum nostrorum, subiceremus periculo, et faceremus inde quicquid possemus* [fo 339rb] *salua reuerentia uestra, et eos tanquam fratres in Christo karissimos diligeremus, et in omni mansuetudine et humilitate tracteremus. Quod cum* [The passage in italics is written over an erasure. For this reading, cf. AlanT(B), fo. 246va and AlanT(C), fo. 198va]	[*Bottom margin*] Nunc exemplari ita inuenitur: Nos pro pace ecclesie et reuerentia domini regis, etiam cum periculo nostro diximus, paratos esse absoluere eos, et exinde tanquam fratres in Christo karissimos diligere, et in omni mansuetudine et humanitate tractare. Quod cum, et cetera. [This variant form is now found only in MSS of the Vatican Family: cf. Vat, fo. 120rb, and Roy., fo. 105r]

ueniet quamdiu pacem regis Francorum habuerit. Mandauit etiam Ricardo de Humez quod filiam regis Francorum cum regina Cadomi morantem uestibus, equitaturis et familia decenter instueret, ad transfretandum quando ipse mandaret. Hoc autem'; cf. *Mats*. VII, pp. 316–17. AlanT(B) lacks 'pacem regis . . . Humez quod'.

'liber exemplaris', are extremely valuable in establishing the relationship of Claudius to the rest of the AlanT filiation. In five cases Hand C has cited the variant reading of an 'emendatior liber' or an 'emendatior exemplar', either in the margin or interlineally, according to the length of the variant. For example, on fo. 224va, by the clause 'aut episcopis obedire', Hand C has inserted in the margin: 'In emendatiori exemplari aut episcopis obedire non habetur'.[1] In this, as in the four similar references, AlanT(B) and AlanT(C) agree with the variant form derived from the 'emendatior liber'. In all five cases, the original reading in Claudius now only occurs in manuscripts of the Vatican Family, suggesting that the exemplar from which it was copied was in some way dependent upon the Vatican archetype for those texts.[2] In four further instances, Hands C and D cite the reading of an 'alius exemplar', and again the later AlanT manuscripts agree with the variants inserted by Hand C.[3] Additionally, there is a single reference by Hand C to the reading of a volume simply identified as 'unus exemplar', with which the later manuscripts again concur.[4] It is more than likely that these different forms of citation all refer in fact to the same alternative version of Alan's collection; and it is arguable that most, though certainly not all, of the minor unspecified variants to be discussed below were derived from the same corrected text.

Finally, in this category, there are three interesting citations by Hand C of the exemplar from which Claudius was presumably copied (in addition to the example discussed in *Quam iustis* above). They occur in close proximity and refer to personal names: beside 'Henrico', on fo. 44ra, Hand C has written 'in exemplari tantum h'; beside 'Radulfum' on fo. 47vb, he has written 'in exemplari tantum R'; and beside 'Gillebertus' on fo. 49rb, he has written 'in exemplari tantum G'. Slight and seemingly insignificant as these examples are, they suggest personal knowledge of these names on the part of the principal scribe, who was able to fill in the correct proper names in place of the initials provided by his exemplar; or equally, his consultation at that point in his work with a know-

---

[1] Cf. Appendix VII, no. 11.   [2] Ibid., nos. 11, 13, and 14.

[3] Cf. AlanT(A), fos. 216ra, 347va, and 348ra. An exception is provided on fo. 127va; here, AlanT(B) and AlanT(C) agree with the original reading, and no version corresponding with the variant (inserted by Hand D) has been discovered. Cf. p. 129 below.

[4] AlanT(A), fo. 293ra.

ledgeable confrère. It also testifies to the meticulous attention to detail of the correctors who recorded the exemplar's readings in the margin. Among derivatives, AlanT(B) has received the initials only for all three examples, and AlanT(C) has wrongly expanded h to 'hereberto', while retaining the other two initials. The John of Salisbury letters provide two further examples of late checking against the exemplar by Hands C and D. On fo. 116rb, beside the words 'sua sunt', Hand C has written 'in ex(emplari) non habetur sua';[1] while on fo. 180ra, Hand D has attempted to resolve the doubt about the rubricated address to *Expectatione longa* by inserting the original reading: 'In ex(emplari): Baldewino exoniensi archidiacono'.[2]

Taken together, these citations of different 'exemplaria' argue the existence at Canterbury of at least two supplementary versions of Alan's collection during the final stages of the preparation of AlanT(A): the exemplar from which it was immediately copied, and an edition with an emended order and corrected texts. The existence of two versions of the same work, even one so large as Alan of Tewkesbury's collection, need not surprise us. It is likely that the assembly and transcription of the Becket materials—Lives, Letters, and Miracles—formed the major activity of the Canterbury scriptorium during the years 1172–80; and when Alan took charge of the epistolary work in late 1174, it may at that stage have taken pride of place. The Canterbury Lives (by Grim, William, and Benedict) and Miracles (by William and Benedict) were already in existence in first-recension form by that date; and preliminary work on assembling Becket's surviving correspondence was almost certainly completed. In fact, apart from the 'Becket' output and Gervase's *Chronicle*, there is little else surviving from Canterbury in those years.

V. *Variants ascribed to 'alius liber'*. Apart from seven such references in the John of Salisbury letters, which will be discussed later, there are fourteen citations of an 'alius liber' scattered through the manuscript in Hands A, C, and D.[3] But it is highly unlikely that they all derive from the same source. In five cases, the variation is extremely slight, being no more than the omission of a word, as on fo. 151va, where Hand D records: 'in alio libro non habetur non'; or the inclusion of a word, as on fo. 327rb, where Hand C notes:

[1] Cf. Appendix VII, no. 3. [2] Ibid., no. 7.
[3] For examples, cf. Appendix VII, nos. 5 and 20.

'al(ius) l(iber): euenerit quod die' as a correction for the original
reading of 'euenerit die'; or the alteration merely of a syllable or
letter, as on fo. 147ra, where Hand D noted: 'In al(io) l(ibro):
quem' as a variant for 'quam.' These may possibly indicate no
more than slips made in a particular transcription, but the attention of the correctors to such details is a further proof of the very
special critical care which was given to the text of this manuscript.
The corrected forms occur neither in the Vatican Family nor in the
later AlanT manuscripts, and their source remains a mystery.
Similarly, although the reading attributed to the 'alius liber' on
fo. 138rb is found in AlanT(C), and may therefore have been
derived from the 'emendatior liber', and that inserted by Hand D
on fo. 329va may have been taken from the exemplar, the source of
the incorrect address cited on fo. 227va for *Post nuntiorum* can no
longer be traced.[1]

In the remaining six examples of more substantial variants,
however, AlanT(B) and (C) agree with the alternative texts against
the original reading, suggesting that in these cases at least the
'alius liber' cited is in fact the 'emendatior liber' of category IV.
The most striking example occurs in *Venientes ad terram* where, on
fo. 161ra–rb, a long variant version of part of the letter has been
inserted in the bottom margin by Hand A and marked 'alio libro'
by Hand D. The original reading is now only found in manuscripts
of the Vatican Family, while AlanT(B) and (C) agree with the
variant.[2] The term 'alius liber' seems to have been used to mean
different things at different times to the correctors of the Claudius
manuscript, and, save in a minority of cases where the corrected
version of AlanT itself seems to have been intended, it is no longer
possible to identify the book or books being cited under this general
term.

VI. *Variants marked al(ius), al(iter) in alio, aliter.* These are
similar in form to category V and present similar difficulties, since
the identification of source is so imprecise. For the most part, they
were written in the margins by Hand C, and for the most part also

---

[1] AlanT(A), fo. 138rb, original reading, 'et de crastina uere'; variant (attributed by Hand D to the 'alius liber'), 'et uereor crastinam'. Fo. 329va, original
reading, 'tanquam fratri *karissimo* (karissimo is written over erasure) uestro
desiderio respondere'; variant, 'tanquam fratris karissimi desiderio respondere'.
Fo. 227va, original reading, 'Alexandro pape Bernardus Niuernensis episcopus';
variant, 'Alex(andro) pape Norwic(ensis) episcopus'.

[2] Cf. p. 115, opposite, and Appendix VII, no. 5.

they consist of no more than single word, or even single letter, variants, though a few are more substantial. On fo. 85vb, for example, the text reads 'defixisti', while Hand C has written 'al-(iter) defixsisse' in the margin; and on fo. 91ra, the difference is no more than a change from capital to small letter. It is probable that the fourteen (out of a total of thirty-three) which agree with the readings in AlanT(B), were in fact taken from the 'emendatior liber', and the five which occur as alternatives to correction inserted over erasure possibly record the original reading in

---

Part Collation of Venientes ad terram, *AlanT(A), fo. 161ra-rb*

Main Text

[fo. 161ra]

[Hand A] timentes

       quoniam nostra talis inutilis erat presentia, et ad tutelam contra archiepiscopum minime sufficiens, unanimiter sumpto consilio, tam pro personis suis quam pro uniuerso regno, ad uestram conuertunt audientiam, prefigentes terminum appellationi in hiemali festo sancti Martini; interim se et sua sub apostolica protectione ponentes.

Denique nos, negotium istud in maximum detrimentum ecclesie uergere cognoscentes, supradicto archiepiscopo auctoritate uestra et nostra prohibendo mandauimus ne de cetero

in prescriptum regnum uel personas uel ecclesias regni, aliquid quod excommunicationem saperet aut interdictum, [fo. 161rb] more solito attemptaret, tum quia uestris litteris erat inhibitum, tum quia sollempniter fuerat appellatum; nec abiecto iudicario ordine, sicut alia uice fecerat, in aliquas regni personas sententiam interdicti uel excommunicationis exerceret. Apostolice itaque . . .

Variant

[fo. 161ra: *margin*]
[Hand D] al(io) l(ibro)

[Hand A] timentes ne pretaxatus archiepiscopus, abiecto iudiciario ordine sicut alia uice fecerat, aliquibus regni personis grauamen inferret, quoniam nostra sibi taliter inutilis erat presentia, et ad tutelam contra archiepiscopum minus sufficiens, unanimi sumpto consilio

ad uestram communiter audientiam appellauerunt, appellationi terminum prefigentes in hiemali festo sancti Martini; interim se et sua sub apostolica protectione ponentes, et [fo. 161rb: *margin*] quaslibet regni personas necnon et uniuersum regnum sub eiusdem appellationis includentes edicto.

Denique nos, negotium istud in maximum ecclesie detrimentum uergere cognoscentes, supradicto archiepiscopo auctoritate uestra et nostra prohibendo mandauimus ne de cetero, tum quia uestris erat inhibitum litteris, tum quia sollempniter fuerat appellatum, in prescriptum regnum uel personas uel ecclesias regni, aliquid grauaminis

attemptaret.

Apostolice itaque. Et cetera.

Claudius, and hence the version derived from its exemplar. But the source of the remaining fourteen variants is somewhat conjectural. Collation with all surviving manuscripts, however, suggests a common denominator for eight of them in the Vatican Archetype, and the evidence is particularly arresting in the case of one variant address. In *Vobis dilectissimi* on fo. 251ra, the protocol addresses the letter (wrongly) 'priori et R. archidiacono et toti clero et populo Cicestrensis ecclesie', while a corrector has inserted in the top margin 'Al(iter) Hugoni decano, archidiacono et toti clero Londoniensis ecclesie',—an alternative now found only in the Vatican Archetype.[1] It is certainly arguable that in these instances the correctors were, for whatever reason, going back to the basic source from which many of the letters were originally derived. And such a theory finds ample support in the treatment of John of Salisbury's letters. But little can be established for the last six examples in this category, since an independently surviving reading which agrees with the correction can only be found for one of them. The rubricated heading of *Euocati a domino* reads (correctly) 'Alexandro pape Rotrodus Rothomagensis archiepiscopus', by which, in the opposite margin (fo. 227rb), Hand C has written simply: 'al(iter) Rogerus Wigorn(iensis) episcopus'—an inaccurate attribution now known only in the short introductory section which precedes the transcription of the Vatican Archetype in Vat.[2] The origin of that section is itself in doubt, though derivation from Foliot sources can be urged. It is not possible, therefore, to establish a single source for the variants marked 'al(iter)' and 'in alio' in the Claudius manuscript, though a substantial minority seem to have been derived from the 'emendatior liber', and a smaller minority from the Vatican Archetype or its sources. The puzzling variant noted by Hand C for *Euocati a domino* indicates that less immediate sources may also have been available at later stages in the collation process.

VII. *Variants marked uel, ul, or l.* Numerically, these variants form the largest single element in the editorial apparatus, comprising 391 examples, independently of corrections to the John of Salisbury letters. To these should perhaps be added the thirty-eight changes of word order, indicated by transfer signs or superscript letters,[3]

---

[1] Cf. Vat. 122 and Roy. 123. For a further discussion of this letter, see above, p. 73, n. 2.

[2] Cf. Vat. 16.   [3] Cf. for example, Appendix VII, no. 11.

and a further thirty-eight variants inserted without any form of identification. As with the corrections discussed so far, the overwhelming majority of variants in this category are merely of one syllable within a word, very often of one of the contracted and frequently misread abbreviations for *que, quod, qui, quia, per, pre, pro,* etc.; or confusions between the singular and plural forms of a verb through the omission or insertion of the horizontal line over the final vowel which indicates the absence of an 'm' or an 'n'. Hence, *habēt*, meaning *habent*, can be misread *habet*, and *cred'ent*, meaning *crederent*, can be misread as *credent*. Errors such as these are commonplace in medieval Latin texts. In the Claudius manuscript, however, the insertion of the correction or variant in a careful book-hand (usually Hands A or B) matching the basic transcription, only occasionally in Hand C and rarely in Hand D, suggests that the variants were intended to be preserved alongside the original readings, and were not intended to supersede them. For example, on fo. 21vb 'ł (uel) reddentur' is written above 'redderentur'; and on fo. 22ra, 'uł (uel) decernamus' is inserted above 'demamus.' This feature suggests a degree of uncertainty on the part of the correctors at this stage, when confronted by conflicts of reading.

In contrast with categories V and VI, where sources other than the AlanT tradition itself seem to have been employed, it is likely that by far the greater number of variants here were derived from the 'emendatior liber', and that this stratum of emendation, in company with the corrections relating to content and order, represents an attempt to bring the Claudius text into line with its more accurate sister, though without spoiling the appearance of the finished volume or eliminating the original text. AlanT(B) agrees with 216 out of a possible total of 355 *uel* variants (this total is reached by subtracting from the full total of 393, the five variants which occur in letters not found in AlanT(B), together with the thirty-one which occur in conjunction with corrections over erasure and therefore probably record the original Claudius text and not the reading of the 'emendatior liber'), and with twenty-eight of the word transfers and twenty-two of the unspecified variants.

VIII. *Variants marked with the symbol /.* The majority of these corrections occur in the John of Salisbury letters and will be discussed more appropriately in that context. For the remainder of the manuscript, they form an interesting group of variants, clearly distinguished from the categories discussed so far, both in their form and intention. In contrast with the earlier examples, these corrections were mostly written in the margins, almost exclusively by Hands C and D, and often with less apparent care and less concern for the aesthetic appearance of the page. It is clear that the symbol /., sometimes written simply as an oblique stroke without the dot (/), sometimes replaced by two dots (:), indicated that the new reading was to be inserted into the main text; and it is likely that these marginal corrections were intended for subsequent deletion when the work of correction was complete. This explains the placing of such emendations in the margins and the hurried and untidy appearance of most of them. Out of the total of eighty-five such notes, forty-four seem to be no more than the correction of simple omission,[1] though in one of these cases the omission involves a substantial passage.[2] Whether these omissions resulted from the error of the principal scribe or from the defects of his exemplar, it is now almost impossible to establish with any assurance; but where the omission also occurs in the main later derivatives of Alan's collection, it may be assumed that the fault lay with the exemplar and not with the scribe, and that the corrections were in this case derived from a source or sources other than the AlanT tradition. And, in fact, the majority of cases fall into this category. In striking contrast with most of the corrections discussed so far, where the later derivatives agree more consistently with the variants than with the original reading in Claudius, in this instance the evidence is reversed: AlanT(B) agrees with only eleven of these corrections of omission. The remaining forty-one examples in this category comprise thirty-three emendations, four corrections of the spelling of Cardinal Otto's name (from *Oddo*, and its variants, to *Otho*), and four clarifications of the expansion of the abbreviated form *spale* (to *speciale* or *specialiter*, avoiding the possible misreading of *spiritualiter* or *spirituale*). Once again, collation with AlanT(B) shows that it agrees only with a minority of these corrections: nine of the emendations, none of the corrections of Otto's name, and three of the expansions.

---

[1] Cf. for example, Appendix VII, no. 19, where 'et saresberiensis' is inserted by Hand D. Cf also ibid., no 20, for the insertion of 'suam'.

[2] AlanT(A), fo. 347rb: the passage 'De nuntiis . . . fiet', which is inserted in the margin, is omitted from all surviving 'Becket' manuscript copies of the letter *Nouerit uestra*; cf. *Mats.* VII, p. 475, n. 4.

It has not been possible to establish the source of these corrections with any certainty. If the corrected AlanT is eliminated, as it must be, there remain only the ranges of materials on which Alan drew, including the Bodleian and Vatican archetypes and files of assorted letters. We shall see that in the case of the John of Salisbury letters the correctors C and D had recourse directly to a manuscript of his later letters, bypassing both the exemplar and the 'emendatior liber' in their attempt to secure the most authoritative texts. And it is more than likely that a similar procedure was followed by the same correctors here, although the source they used has long disappeared. The corrections to two letters in particular provide a clue to what was happening. Four of the errors of omission occur in *Imperator cum principes*, a letter which has survived independently in the Cave MS of Gilbert Foliot's letters. Although these emendations were not received into later recensions of Alan's collection, all four are found in the Cave MS.[1] It is possible that Hand C in this instance went back to the original source text as preserved in Becket's archives; and the same may well be true in his treatment of *Sepius nuntios*, where three omissions and three alternative readings are noted.[2]

IX. *Corrections to the John of Salisbury Letters.* The treatment of John of Salisbury's letters is in some ways the most illuminating feature of the whole textual apparatus, for it enables us to trace one of the processes of correction with some security. For the most part, they correspond with the emendations discussed immediately above. The majority are written in the margins, principally by Hand C, and preceded by the omission sign (/), indicating that they were to be properly integrated into the text by the appropriate scribe. Whereas there is considerable uncertainty about the source of the corrections in category VIII, no such doubt need be entertained in this case. Hand C has conveniently provided an almost complete system of numerical cross-reference to John's letters, which enables us to trace the source he was using. If his numbers are compared with the contents of the two surviving manuscripts of John's later letters (London Brit. Libr. MS Addit. 11506 [JS] and Paris Bibl. Nat. Lat. MS 8562 [JS^x]), it is found that they correspond exactly except for about ten items; and the discrepancy can be explained by the assumption that Claudius was compared with

[1] AlanT(A), fo. 58ra–va; cf.
[2] Alan T(A), fo. 226ra–vb.

a fuller version of the letters than has been preserved for us in the
two interrelated manuscripts now available. Even more striking,
however, is the degree of textual conformity between the corrections and those manuscripts. Collation reveals that in virtually
every case the word omitted or the corrected reading is found in one
or other of the surviving copies of John's collection.[1] The total
number of corrections (including those inserted over erasure) is
355, of which fifty-three occur in letters not now found in the
JohnS manuscripts; and of the remaining 302 all but forty-three,
that is 259 out of 302, are found in the John of Salisbury manuscripts. There seems to be no doubt that the corrector had access to
a manuscript very closely related to an ancestor of the surviving
JohnS collection. The following examples of correction to addresses
will serve to bring out the relationship more clearly. The address in
rubric for *A sapiente* in AlanT(A)[2] appears as 'Johannes Saresberie
cuidam amico suo', with the variant 'J. Magistro Hunfrido de Boui'
inserted in the margin; collation reveals that only the JohnS
manuscripts preserve the alternative form. Again, the original
address for *Inhumanus est* in AlanT(A)[3] was 'Johannes Saresberiensis Roberto de Fauresham', but the recipient's name was
later deleted in black ink, and the variant 'Reginaldo archidiacono
Saresberiensi' was inserted in the margin by Hand C. Once more,
the JohnS manuscripts alone preserve the correction. In the case of
Honor cinguli, the heading has been partly erased, the marginal
emendation 'Baldewino' agreeing with the form in JohnS.[4] The
address of *Expectatione longa* provides a particularly interesting
example. The original rubric has been partially erased, now reading
'Ba(   ) Exoniensi (   ), and Hand C(?) has inserted the emendation
'Bartholomeo' from the JohnS manuscript, while Hand D has
written beside it the reading of the Claudius exemplar.[5] And, in
one final example, we find similar evidence of an unresolved conflict
of textual sources. The heading of *Puer meus* in AlanT(A) is written
over an erasure and is itself partly erased, now reading 'Johannes
Saresberiensis (   )uensi archidiacono', while Hand C has inserted
the JohnS variant in the margin: 'Magistro Reimundo Pictauensi
cancellario', and Hand D has again recorded the AlanT version,

---

[1] Cf. for example, Appendix VII, nos. 3, 4, 6–9, and 12.
[2] Cf. AlanT(A), fo. 67ra.   [3] Ibid., fo. 121rb.
[4] Ibid., fo. 188rb; cf. no. 9 in Appendix VII, below.
[5] AlanT(A), fo. 180ra; cf. no. 7 in Appendix VII, below.

this time ascribed to the 'alius liber': '(al)io libro: Ric(ardo) Pictauensi archidiacono'. The two later recensions of AlanT contain conflicting addresses for this letter: AlanT(B) has 'Johannes Saresberiensis Ricardo Pictauensi archidiacono', agreeing with the partly erased rubric in AlanT(A) and with the reading ascribed by Hand D to the 'alius liber'; in contrast, AlanT(C) has 'Magistro Raimundo Pict(auensis) cancellario', agreeing with the reading in the JohnS collection.[1] But 'Magistro Raimundo', etc., was not the original reading in AlanT (C): it was inserted over an erasure in accordance with a marginal correction which seems to have been derived from JohnS.[2] This set of corrections is significant from two points of view. In conjunction with the numerical references and the weighty textual evidence already cited, it proves the utilization of a John of Salisbury manuscript by the correctors of the Claudius manuscript. But it also suggests that Alan's original source for his JohnS letters differed in some respects from the independently surviving collection of the letters. Alan's texts do not seem to have derived directly from John's collection in the form in which it has been preserved, although it was to that source, with its generally more accurate texts,[3] that he had recourse in the final checking and emending of Claudius.

X. *The Notes and Corrections in Hand D.* We have already noted that Hand D occurs throughout the manuscript, often adding details to notes inserted by Hands A, B, and C. In addition, however, he provided an apparatus of cross-reference between the letters,[4] and a series of identifications and comments.[5] While the

---

[1] AlanT(A), fo. 131va.

[2] The marginal correction in AlanT(C) reads: 'Magistro Ra(imun)do Pict-(auensis) ec(clesie) cancellario'.

[3] In the corrections of address just cited, all save one seem to be more accurate than Alan's original reading. The one exception occurs in *Expectatione longa.* That letter was almost certainly sent to Baldwin the Archdeacon and not to Bartholomew the Bishop of Exeter: in this case, the JohnS tradition was faulty.

[4] Cf. AlanT(A), fos. 48vb, 82vb, 115rb, 122vb, 128vb, 148va, 150vb, 151ra, 151rb, 152vb, 153va, 154vb, 159ra, 159va, 160ra, 160vb, 167vb, 175rb, 177rb, 180vb, 190ra, 190va, 191ra, 207rb (unfinished), 212ra, 220va, 228va, 234vb, 244va, 245ra, 247ra, 247rb, 248rb, 248vb, 255rb, 256va, 265ra, 269rb, 269vb, 270vb, 271ra, 272vb, 273ra, 273rb, 274rb, 274va, 279ra, 280vb, 281va, 282ra, 282rb, 283rb, 287ra, 287vb, 288va, 289vb, 290ra, 290vb, 291ra, 291rb, 291va, 292ra, 294va, 296rb, 304va, 308ra, 308va, 308vb, 309rb, 309va, 310rb, 311vb, 313va, 313vb, 315va, 317ra, 318ra, 319va, 320vb, 321va, 322rb, 324ra, 325va, 325vb, 326va, 327va, 328rb, 331rb, 331va, 335va, 338rb, 346ra, 347vb, 349ra, 352rb, and 354rb.

[5] Cf. AlanT(A), fos. 27vb, 'Quando hec constitutiones constitute sint, patet

collations and corrections show a profound concern with the text, the cross-references testify to a degree of interest in their content and argument going far beyond that of an ordinary scribe; and, most illuminating of all, seven datable comments demonstrate a long-term association with the manuscript spanning a period of years from possibly late 1176 to 1190 or even 1199. The earliest datable comment (on fo. 155va) describes Henry of France in the words: 'Iste fuit Henricus, prius monachus Clareuallensis, postmodum episcopus Belluacensis, et nunc archiepiscopus Remensis, frater illustris regis Francorum'. Its use of *nunc* in the final phrase seems to imply that Henry was believed to be still alive when the note was inserted. Such an interpretation would argue an almost impossibly early date, since Henry died on 13 November 1175,[1] and his death would almost certainly have been known at Canterbury by the end of that year. If the *nunc* is emended to *tunc*, then the difficulty is removed, and with it the chronological significance of the note itself, which would become wholly retrospective. A second note, however, on fo. 281ra referring to William of Sens, argues an almost equally early date, in mid-1176. It reads: 'Nota quod quando hec epistola missa fuit Willelmus Senonensis archiepiscopus, qui multum laborauit pro causa sancti Thome, nondum fuit archiepiscopus, sed cito post'. William aux Blanchesmains was appointed to Sens in 1168 and succeeded Henry at Reims in August 1176. If his identification as Archbishop of Sens is taken to imply that his final elevation was at that moment unknown to Hand D, then this entry would be dated to August–September 1176, at the latest. There would be no obvious objection to such a date, were it not for the fact that Alan's *Explanatio* contains on fo. 9ra the comment that John of Salisbury, author of the preceding *Passio*, later became Bishop of Chartres. John's election to Chartres was notified to him at Canterbury on 22 July 1176; he was consecrated at Sens on 8 August and installed at Chartres on 15 August.

---

[1] P. B. Gams, *Series Episcoporum Ecclesiae Catholicae*, Ratisbon (1873), p. 608b.

infra in parte iiij[a], epistola uel capitulo liiij[o]'; 28rb, 'anno dominice incarnationis mclxix,' added to a note on the promulgation of Henry II's 1169 decrees written by Hand C; cf. also, fos. 106va, 126ra, 131rb, 132vb, 133va, 134va, 135rb, 136ra, 137va, 139rb, 145rb, 151va, 154vb, 155va, 158ra, 159va, 169rb, 175rb, 178rb, 179rb, 182ra, 183va, 183vb, 184va, 185va, 186rb, 190ra, 199rb, 202rb, 205va, 206ra, 206rb, 207rb, 208rb, 212rb, 212va, 214va, 217rb, 234vb, 241ra, 244va, 245rb, 248vb, 249rb, 255rb, 255va, 255vb, 260rb, 263va, 277vb, 281ra, 285rb, 289va, 292rb, 292vb, 295va, 298rb, 308ra, 308va, 312va, 313ra, 320ra, 320rb, 320va, 328rb, 334va, 337va, 339rb, 344rb, 351rb, 352rb, and 354rb.

It is hard to reconcile knowledge of John's elevation in the text on fo. 9ra with supposed ignorance of William's translation to Reims (which was finalized in the same month) on fo. 281ra, unless it be argued that the first two quires of the manuscript were transcribed after the rest of the volume, enabling the insertion of 'postea Carnotensis episcopus' in Quire II. The five remaining datable comments point to a much later period. The caustic comment on Richard of Dover can hardly have been written before his death in 1184,[1] a date supported by a reference elsewhere to Baldwin of Ford's elevation to Canterbury;[2] while the notes on William of Northal's appointment to Worcester must post-date his election to that see in 1186.[3] Finally, the two references to Richard I must have been written after his accession in 1189.[4] Such comments bring the *terminus ad quem* down at least to 1189–90; and indeed, if the full force of the past tense employed in all the comments is accepted, then the notes on Baldwin of Ford and William of Northal could have been inserted after their respective deaths in 1190, and those on Richard I could have been inserted as late as 1199–1200. There is, however, no reason to suppose that all Hand D's references were inserted at the same time. On the contrary, the evidence suggests a long-term, even proprietary, association with the manuscript; and it is hard to avoid the conclusion that Hand D is none other than that of Prior Alan himself, appropriating for his own use a super-seded copy of his major work. Such an identification would explain the peculiar character of this unique volume, reinforcing the conclusions already suggested. The Claudius manuscript emerges as a projected fair copy of Alan of Tewkesbury's collection of Becket letters which the editor kept for himself, while ensuring that its defects of content, order, and text were eliminated and admitting new letters as they became available, down to 1179–80. It is this circumstance which explains the high quality of the resulting text and its highly individual character: Claudius B.II preserves the most perfect version of Alan's collection in the form in which it finally left his own hands.

---

[1] Fo. 354rb: 'Iste fuit successor beati Thome, et re et nomine episcopi indignus; Cantuariensis ecclesie monachus, sed prior de Doura'.

[2] Fo. 106va: 'Hic fuit postea Cantuariensis archiepiscopus'.

[3] Fo. 234vb: 'Iste fuit postea Wigorn(iensis) episcopus'; fo. 298rb: 'Hic fuit postea episcopus Wigorn(iensis)'.

[4] Fo. 186vb: 'Hic postea erat gloriosus rex Angl(orum)'; fo. 244va: 'Iste fuit postea rex Anglorum'.

B. ALAN T(B): VATICAN LATIN MS 1220

The exemplar from which the Claudius manuscript was copied must be assumed to be lost; so too the 'emendatior liber' with which it was collated and whose contents, order, and text can be reconstructed from its marginalia. Among derivatives, however, the version most closely resembling the 'emendatior liber' is the late copy in Vatican Latin MS 1220, that is to say AlanT(B), which according to a rubric at the beginning of the work was made for Pope Gregory XI at the close of the fourteenth century.[1] The script and illumination of the volume, as well as its ancient provenance, support this supposition. The script is almost certainly North Italian, of the late fourteenth century, the spare decoration entirely in conformity with contemporary taste[2] and, perhaps more significantly, the manuscript is found fully described in the 1411 catalogue of the papal library in Avignon.[3] Unfortunately, it is not now possible to trace the exemplar(s) used. In addition to Lives and Offices in liturgical books, the papal library contained a number of 'Becket' manuscripts at the beginning of Gregory's pontificate,[4] but, save for the one which has survived, and has been

---

[1] Cf. AlanT(B), fo. 1ra: 'incipit uita beati Thome martiris de plurium narratione collecta [MS: colecta], magis extensa, quam sit infra, quam scribi fecit do(minus) Petrus Rogerii, Gregorius Papa undecimus'; cf. Lupus, I, p. 1. The 'vita' referred to here is the *Quadrilogus II* which precedes the letter collection. It is an interesting detail that, like Becket himself, Gregory XI had once been Archdeacon of Canterbury.

[2] $13 \times 8\frac{7}{8}$ in.; double columns, 49 lines to the column; blue capitals with red pen-work throughout. The illumination is sparse, repetitive and undistinguished, consisting of stereotyped busts of saintly archbishops incorporated in some of the larger initials; cf. fo. 1ra: historiated initial P with small bust of a saintly archbishop (Becket?), with halo, mitre, and pallium; fo. 14vb: historiated initial E, with profile of mitred archbishop; fo. 24va: historiated initial P with profile of mitred archbishop wearing the pallium; fo. 32vb: historiated initial C with three-quarter miniature of an archbishop wearing the pallium.

[3] Cf. Anneliese Maier, 'Der Katalog des päpstlichen Bibliothek in Avignon vom Jahr 1411', *Archivium Historiae Pontificiae*, Pontificia Universitas Gregoriana (1963), p. 155: 'No. 451—Item vita beati Thome martiris cop. pelle rubea et inc. in 2° folio *succedente* et finit in penultimo *immensitas tam*'. AlanT(B) fits this description exactly: cf. fos. 2ra and 261vb; its cover is (now faded) red leather.

[4] Cf. F. Ehrle, *Historia Bibliothecae Romanorum Pontificum*, Rome, Vatican Press (1890):

(1) p. 62, *Recensio Assisiensis* (1339): no. 382—'It. alium libellum de vita b. Thome martiris';

(2) p. 310, *Recensio Librorum Palatii Avenion.* (1369): no. 314—'Item vita, persequcio et passio sancti Thome Cantuariensis, cooperte corio rubeo, que incipiunt in secundo corundello primi folii post diversas tabulas: *nore*, et finiunt in ultimo corundello penultimi folii: *tan*'; [*cont.*]

traced in the Bibl. Alessandrina in Rome,[1] it is impossible to say what they contained. Yet it is unlikely that Gregory XI would have ordered the transcription of a work which he already possessed, and an exemplar outside the papal library should be sought.[2]

The manuscript as it survives is an integer, complete and prop-

[1] Rome Bibl. Alessandrina MS 120. This MS, which can be traced in the papal library from 1369 (cf. p. 124, n. 4, no. 3), was described in the 1411 catalogue in the following words: 'no. 597—Item vita beati Thome martyris per Herrebertum compilata. cop. pelle alba et inc. in 2° folio *fiducia* et finit in penultimo *contrahere*'; cf. A. Maier, op. cit., p. 167. The ascription to Herrebertum (Herbert of Bosham) seems mistaken: the text in question is an expanded *Quadrilogus II*(A) into which parts of Grim ('Electus igitur . . . augusto': *Mats.* II, pp. 356–8) and Bosham ('Deposito igitur . . . cum Christo': ibid., III, pp. 318–22) have been interpolated. The *Quadrilogus* is followed by an assortment of items, including (fos. 123–65) a fragmentary collection of the letters of Gilbert Foliot, corresponding to Cave 2–106. For a full description of the MS, cf. E. Narducci, *Catalogus manuscriptorum praeter orientales qui in Bibliotheca Alexandrina Romae adservantur*, Rome (1877), pp. 91–3; for the Becket section, cf. A. Poncelet, *Catalogus Codicum Hagiographicorum Latinorum Bibliothecarum Romanarum*, Brussels (1909), pp. 184–6; and for the Foliot section, MB, *Foliot*, pp. 11–12.

[2] For the contents of the library in Gregory's pontificate, cf. Ehrle, op. cit.:
  (i) p. 471, no. 245—'Item in volumine signato per XXI vita et passio sancti Thome martiris episcopi Cantuariensis'.
  (ii) ibid., no. 246—'Item in volumine signato per XXII vita et passio etiam Cantuariensis'.
  (iii) p. 528, no. 1222—'Item in volumine signato per LXI cronica Martiniana, item vita sancti Thome Cantuariensis, item cathalogus pontificum et imperatorum, item Lucanus cum suis glosis, item de regimine sanitatis (= Galen), item nomina omnium episcoporum Tholosanorum et Lemovicensium' (*auct.* B. Guidonis): (identified as no. 4 in no. continued below from previous page).
  (iv) p. 532, no. 1304—'Item in volumine signato per CXLIIII vita beati Thome Cantuariensis' (= Bibl. Alex. MS 120).

  (3) p. 380, ibid.: no. 1246—'Item vita sancti Thome Cantuariensis, cooperta corio albo, que incipit in secundo folio *fiduciam*, et finit in penultimo folio ante tabulam in nigro: *carmina*';
  (4) p. 385, ibid.: no. 1328—'Item liber intitulatus *Cronica Martiniana* cum aliis in eodem volumine, coopertus postibus sine pelle, qui incipit in secundo folio: *imperatores*, et finit in penultimo folio in textu: *usus*'; (it is possible that this MS is the same as the one noted in the 1295 catalogue: cf. A. Pelzer, *Addenda et Emendanda ad F. Ehrle Hist. Bibl. Rom. Pont.*, I, Rome, Vatican Library (1947) p. 19: no. 321—It. cronica fris Martini (Poloni sive Oppaviensis)');
  (5) p. 430, ibid.: no. 2023—'Item alius parvus liber, continens vitam sancti Thome martiris, cooperto corio rubeo, qui incipit in secundo folio post tabulam: *nota*, et finit in penultimo folio: *de*'.
For the library in 1411, cf. A. Maier, op. cit.:
  (a) p. 135, no. 146 [identified as no. 4 above]
  (b) p. 148, no. 379 [identified as no. 5 above]
  (c) p. 155, no. 451 [cf. p. 124, n.3 = AlanT(B)]
  (d) p. 167, no. 597 [identified as no. 3 above].

erly bound up,[1] with catchwords for all save Quire 5 (fos. 40–52a), which seems to be a later insertion containing a descriptive index to the letters. It is composed of two sections: the first contains the *Second Quadrilogus*, followed by its usual appendix of Herbert of Bosham's *Catalogus eruditorum*, the *Causa exilii*, and three letters announcing the canonization of Becket,[2] while the second contains a version of the Alan of Tewkesbury collection, preceded by Alan's *Prologus* and *Explanatio* and the short *Prologus* and *Vita* by John of Salisbury.[3] There is no doubt that the two parts were intended to form a single unit.

The letter-collection comprises 535 letters, set out in five books containing respectively 179, 111, 98, 51, and 96 items, and each book is furnished with a complete table of contents consisting of the rubricated headings within the book. Collation with the marginalia in AlanT(A) shows that in all cases but one it corresponds exactly with the variations of order and content ascribed to the 'emendatior liber': it lacks the forty-eight letters marked 'non est/desunt',[4] together with the unmarked supplements to Books I and V,[5] and agrees with the adjusted order of the corrected recension.[6] In addition, however, it lacks six letters which occur without comment scattered through the main text of AlanT(A),[7]

---

[1] The MS comprises 23 quires, all but no. 4 containing 12 leaves, with two inserted folios: fos. 39a and 52a.

[2] AlanT(B), fos. 1ra–39ra; cf. Lupus, I, pp. 4–172.

[3] Summary of the contents of Part II: fos. 40ra–52rb, descriptive index of the introductory material and of Book I of the letters (apparently inserted later); fos. 53ra–54vb, short index to the introduction and Book I; fos. 54va–55ra, AlanT, *Prologus*; fos. 55ra–rb, JohnS, *Prologus*; fos. 55rb–58vb, JohnS, *Vita et Passio Sancti Thome*; fos. 58vb–63vb, AlanT, *Explanatio*; fos. 63vb–254va, the AlanT collection arranged in five books. The main text is followed by: fos. 254va–256va, *Misero uerba, Mittimus sanctitati,* and *Raritas intermeantium,* with a note that they had been omitted from Book II; fos. 256va–57ra, Honorius III's Translation Bull; fos. 257ra–62vb, Stephen Langton's sermon delivered on the occasion of Becket's Translation on 7 July 1220.

[4] Cf. p. 104 n. 1, above.

[5] AlanT(A), I. 180–4 and V. 103–5.

[6] With one exception: AlanT(B) does not repeat *Quanta mala* in the text of its Book IV, although the *incipit* of the letter appears in the appropriate position in Book IV's index.

[7] The omitted letters are AlanT(A):

    I.126   *Multiplicem nobis* Gilbert Foliot to Becket
    II.4   *Magnificentie tue nuntios* Alexander III to Henry II
    V.56   *Exhortationis uestre* Becket to Giles of Évreux
    V.65   *Illum circa personam* William of Pavia to Becket
    V.82   *Ex insperato* John of Salisbury to John of Poitiers
    V.92   *Non ignorat* Roger of York to Hugh of Durham

and it is difficult to determine whether or not they were included in the 'emendatior liber'. The evidence of other known derivatives, however, seems to argue that they were not: five of the six occur nowhere else in the AlanT tradition, and the sixth (John of Salisbury's *Ex insperato*) is found only in the two closely related representatives of Recension III, which is distinguished by its inclusion of a significant number of additional JohnS letters.[1] It seems reasonable to assume that all six were added to Alan's basic collection, in company with the others already discussed in category II*b* above, while the Claudius manuscript was being transcribed. There remains, however, one difficulty, as far as AlanT(B) is concerned. One of the six letters, the highly significant *Multiplicem nobis*, containing Gilbert Foliot's attack on Becket, is twice mentioned in the index to Book I, though there is no trace of it in the following text.[2] Lord Lyttelton argued that the text was consciously suppressed by AlanT(B)'s scribe on account of its hostility to Becket, but the manuscript evidence is less than conclusive on this point. *Multiplicem nobis* did not appear in the Becket collections prior to AlanT(A),[3] and, apart from the tantalizing references in AlanT(B)'s index, there is no evidence that it passed into Alan's second recension and thus into the main line of textual transmission. In any event, correlation between the indices and subsequent letters in AlanT(B) is not exact apart from this example.[4]

The Vatican manuscript is completed with a short section concerned with the translation of Becket's relics in 1220, appended to Book V and containing Honorius III's bull *Rex celestis*,[5] authoriz-

---

[1] Cf. below, pp. 135–9.

[2] In the index to Book I, the *incipit* occurs at nos. cix and cxxix. For discussions of this letter, cf. D. Knowles, *The Episcopal Colleagues of Archbishop Thomas Becket*, Cambridge (1951), pp. 171–80; and A. Morey and C. N. L. Brooke, *Gilbert Foliot and his Letters*, Cambridge (1965), pp. 166–87.

[3] Apart from AlanT(A), the letter only occurs in 'Foliot' MSS: cf. Cave 447 and Douce 18.

[4] A comparison between the indexes and texts in AlanT(B) reveals the following conflicts: for Book I, the index omits AlanT(B), 13–16 and 18; for Book II, AlanT(B), 48 appears as item 89 and the index is defectively numbered from that point; for Book III, AlanT(B), I.128, having already appeared in the index as I.128, is repeated in the index at III.92, and the numeration of the index is defective from no. 87; for Book IV, AlanT(B), I.90, having already appeared as index no. I.89, is repeated in the index at IV.51; and for Book V, the numeration of the index is defective from no. 72. Cf. Hardy, II, pp. 316–17, n. x.

[5] *Mats.* VII, ep. 807.

ing the translation, and Stephen Langton's sermon composed for the festival.[1] These items were obviously not contained in the 'emendatior liber' mentioned in AlanT(A)'s marginalia, and mark a later addition to the basic material in Recension II; they suggest that the Vatican manuscript was derived from a copy of Alan of Tewkesbury's collection made in or after 1220, or possibly that the later copy conflated two earlier sources.

It has been suggested above that AlanT(B) corresponds with Recension II of the AlanT collection, and an examination of the textual evidence supports this supposition, reinforcing the evidence of order and content already cited. Except in the case of the John of Salisbury letters, which were subjected to special treatment, AlanT(B) tends to agree with the variants and corrections attributable to the 'emendatior liber' in preference to the original reading of the Claudius manuscript. It does not, and as a late Italian derivative could not be expected to, reproduce all the variants noted; but the degree of correlation is such that only ultimate dependence on the 'emendatior liber' can explain it. It is just conceivable that AlanT(A) in its corrected state was AlanT(B)'s remote ancestor, but the failure to receive most of the JohnS corrections, as well as the absence of the unnoted additions to the basic collection, seems to rule out that possibility.

The least satisfactory evidence is provided by categories V, VI, and VIII, where the identifications of sources are inexact or non-existent, and where it is probable that sources other than the 'emendatior liber' were being employed, especially by Hands C and D. It is not surprising to find that in these cases AlanT(B) agrees only with a minority of the corrections. Nevertheless, AlanT(B) agrees with six citations of 'alius liber' in category V, including the long variant in *Venientes ad terram*,[2] with fourteen of the thirty-three variants in category VI, and with twenty-three of the eighty-five emendations in category VIII. The evidence for ultimate dependence on Recension II is much more persuasive in categories III, IV, and VII, when due allowance is made for the possibility of faulty textual transmission between the late twelfth and the late fourteenth century. In category III (corrections over erasure), AlanT(B) agrees with 106 out of a possible 146 instances; and twenty-one of the forty cases of conflict are errors of omission, a

---

[1] Cf. Lupus, II, pp. 885–905; and Giles, *VST* II, pp. 269–97.
[2] Cf. pp. 114–15 above, and no. 5 in Appendix VII, below.

form of mistake so commonplace in this manuscript as to render arguments based on its occurrence uncertain and possibly misleading. More significant is the fact that it agrees with the majority of such corrections and with the major emendations in *Venientes ad terram* and *Quam iustis*.[1] In category IV, AlanT(B) agrees with the five specific citations of the 'emendatior exemplar', three of the four readings from the 'alius exemplar', and with the single reference to 'unus exemplar'. The only exception in this category is where AlanT(B) agrees with the original reading of *Edwardum* in conflict with the variant 'Edwinum' ascribed to 'alius exemplar'.[2] Again, in category VII, AlanT(B) agrees with 212 out of a possible 357 variants, twenty-eight of the thirty-eight word transfers and twenty-two of the thirty-eight unspecified variants. AlanT(B) emerges as a late and in some respects defective derivative from AlanT''s Recension II, as far as it can be reconstructed from the marginalia in the Claudius manuscript.

Two further manuscripts survive containing part of the material from Recension II, namely the fragmentary Cambridge Trinity Hall MS 24 and the abbreviated version (Bodl.B, I) in Oxford Bodl. MS 937. The Trinity Hall manuscript was transcribed in the mid-thirteenth century and fills the last ten quires of the extant volume.[3] The medieval provenance of the volume is unknown, but it belonged to Robert Hare in 1562[4] and was consulted by J. A. Giles in August 1844.[5] It is clear from the manuscript's features that the collection of Becket letters was originally a separate entity, since its script and decoration distinguish it from the other material with which it is now bound up in the single volume, and the numeration of its gatherings also shows that it once had a separate existence.[6] It is carefully written in a small book-hand, with initials alternately coloured in red and blue, and decorated in penwork of the contrasting colour. The work of rubrication was never

---

[1] Cf. ibid., nos. 5 and 19.   [2] Cf. AlanT(A), fo. 127va.

[3] Fos. 113ra–192vb; 9¾ × 6¾ in.; double columns.

[4] The top of fo. 1r bears in a bold hand the signature 'Roberti Hare 1562'; Robert Hare was an important Elizabethan antiquary and collector of MSS in the service of William Paulet, the Lord High Treasurer; he gave many volumes to Trinity Hall. Cf. *DNB, sub nomine.*

[5] The following note appears on the flyleaf opposite fo. 1r: 'They are all printed in the collection edited by Lupus, but this MS supplies many corrections of the text. J. A. G. Aug. 5. 1844'.

[6] Its first and tenth quires are not numbered; its other quires are numbered from ii to ix independently of the rest of the volume.

completed; the last rubricated heading was entered on fo. 128va, from which point the spaces for headings remain unfilled through the rest of the manuscript, though the rubric guide-phrases are clearly visible in the margin in most cases. The manuscript is damaged by damp in its final folios, and is defective at the end, breaking off in mid-item 167 with the words 'conscientiam christianorum. Absit . . .' at the end of fo. 192vb.[1]

A modern hand has numbered the letters from 1 to 167, but two items were overlooked in the numeration,[2] and the introduction to the Constitutions of Clarendon and the Constitutions themselves are given two numbers instead of one,[3] so that the corrected total is 168. The manuscript in fact contains the greater part of Book I of Alan of Tewkesbury's collection, finishing with AlanT(A), I. 170. Apart from the obvious fact that the transcription ends in mid-sentence, there is internal evidence in the surviving fragment to suggest that it was originally part of a larger collection: thus, on fo. 170va there is a marginal reference to two letters,[4] of which one is not found in this manuscript, though it appears elsewhere towards the end of AlanT, Book II. And it is very likely that the Trinity Hall manuscript is now merely a small part of what was formerly a complete collection.

When the fragment is collated with other collections of the AlanT Family, it is seen to correspond more closely with the 'alius liber' of the AlanT(A) marginalia than with its basic transcription, that it to say it agrees more closely with Recension II or AlanT(B). It follows the order of the latter fairly consistently for the most part, omitting two of its letters,[5] re-positioning three[6] and inserting one item which occurs among the additional material in AlanT(A).[7] But it has details also which are peculiar to itself: it has seven protocols[8] and one valediction[9] which are otherwise unknown; it has one individualistic heading[10] and minor peculiarities of order.

[1] Cf. *Mats.* VI, p. 425.   [2] Nos. 50b and 156b.   [3] Nos. 12 and 13.

[4] The references are: 'Concordare Placuit excellentie' (= Trin. 123) and 'Concordare Quando dominus Willelmus Papiensis' (= AlanT(B), II.84); cf. also fo. 153va: 'Concordare Audio pater et' (= AlanT(B), II. 92).

[5] Trin. omits AlanT(B), I. 90 and 128.

[6] Cf. AlanT(B), I. 1–170: AlanT(B), I. 100 and 101 = Trin. 96 and 97; AlanT(B), I. 142 = Trin. 95.

[7] Trin. 123; cf. AlanT(A), I. 130.   [8] Cf. nos. 40, 44, 54, 60–2, and 67.

[9] Trin. 45: 'Valeat iterum et semper'; cf. *Mats.* VI. ep. 253.

[10] Trin. 101: '(E)pistola legacionis'; the usual heading for this letter (*Misimus tibi*) is 'Thomas Cantuariensis archiepiscopus Gaufrido Cantuariensi archidiacono'; cf. AlanT(A), I. 96, AlanT(B), I. 99, and AlanT(C), I. 100.

An attempt has been made at a later time to date some of the letters in pencilled notes in the margin, as instanced by the insertion 'Pascha secundi anni ab exilio' by the letter *Vix apud dominum.*[1] And in many such instances the dating is approximately correct.[2]

Bodley MS 937 is a large, carefully produced, volume of the early thirteenth century, of unknown provenance, containing a selection of materials relating to the Becket controversy in four separately transcribed components, including two major collections of the Becket correspondence together with material derived ultimately from the Foliot archives. A general description of the volume with palaeographical details has already been given above when discussing the collections Bodl.B, II and III, a member of the Lambeth Family, which forms its third and fourth parts.[3] The second component, which can be named Bodl.B, I, is an abbreviation of the Alan of Tewkesbury collection. It begins with the usual preface to that collection, exactly as preserved in AlanT(B),[4] and a full table of contents or index written in quadruple columns and containing the *incipits* of 536 letters, together with their addresses. The collection represented by the index is a version of Recension II of Alan's collection, reflecting with very few variations the contents and order of the 'alius liber' referred to in the marginalia of AlanT(A);[5] but the collection of 221 letters which

---

[1] Fo. 130ra. For further examples, cf. fos. 137vb, 140rb, 154va, 156va, 157vb, 161vb, 162rb, 162vb, 164vb, 165va, 172va, 173vb, 174va, and 190rb.

[2] Eg., fo. 156va at *Fratres mei* (*Mats.* V, ep. 198; *c.* 12 June 1166): 'postquam Johannes de Oxeneford et Ricardus de Iuelcestr' iurauerant in Alemannia'; fo. 162rb at *Fides et deuocio* (*Mats.* VI, ep. 228: late 1166): 'post excommunication-em aulicorum'; fo. 172va at *Multa quidem* (*Mats.* VI, ep. 252: November–December 1166): 'Statim post factam appellationem'; fo. 174va at *Ecclesiam Anglorum* (*Mats.* VI, ep. 249: November–December 1166): 'Biennium ab exilio'; and fo. 190rb at *Quod dilectioni* (*Mats.* VI, ep. 270: November–December 1166): 'Circa festum omnium sanctorum tertio anno exilii'.

[3] Cf. pp. 74–7 above.   [4] Cf. p. 126 above.

[5] The index in Bodl. B, I follows exactly the order of the 'alius liber' cited in the marginalia of AlanT(A), omits all the letters marked 'non est (*or* non fuit) inter ordinatas', and lacks the 18 further letters omitted from AlanT(B), thus agreeing with Recension II. But it does not exactly follow the order of any extant copy of Alan's collection: compared with AlanT(A), it re-positions AlanT (A), I. 127 and 159, repeats I. 179 and V. 77, and omits II. 42, III. 97, and V. 82, in addition to the categories of letters already cited; compared with AlanT(B), it re-positions AlanT(B), I. 108, 128, 159, and II. 48, repeats I. 90, 179 and V. 73, and omits II. 36 and III. 97; compared with AlanT(C), it re-positions AlanT(C), I. 159, 178, III. 18 and 50, repeats V. 73, and omits II. 32, 46, 98, III. 19–42, [*cont.*]

follows is a composite work, whose opening twenty-four items reflect neither the order nor the text of Alan's collection.

This unique grouping falls into two parts.[1] Part I, nos. 1–16, comprises an assortment of letters relating to the Becket controversy, lacking any coherent order. All the texts are known in other collections, though this manuscript provides one date (8) and one inscription (9), which are not found elsewhere. Only three of the letters were written by Becket (2–4), five were received by him (1, 8–9, 13, and 15), and eleven were written by Alexander III (6–16). It has not been possible to establish a secure textual affinity with any line of transmission, and the source of Part I remains unknown. Part II, nos. 17–24, is even more puzzling, for it is wholly unique. None of its eight letters is known in any other manuscript source;[2] and, although Becket received two of the letters (18 and 24), and is named in two others (20 and 22), the connection of the group as a whole with the Becket controversy is slight. Nos. 17 and 18 (the latter addressed to Becket) relate to the papal confirmation of the marriage of Philip of Flanders and Elizabeth of Péronne; no. 19 is a judicial mandate addressed to Hugh of Durham; nos. 20 and 21 refer to the case of Richard, son of Henry, a Canterbury citizen, exiled by Henry II; no. 22 requests patronage for Herbert of Bosham from the Bishop of Troyes; no. 23 requests a prebend for John, Dean of Orleans, from Bishop Manasser; and no. 24 is a letter of friendship from an unidentified R. to Becket.

[1] Oxford Bodl. MS 937, fos. 34r–43v:

		Mats.			Mats.
1	Feruentis et	403	13	Si quanta	117
2	Satis superque	195	14	Si quanta	118
3	Satis superque	196	15	Etsi aduersitatum	397
4	Sicut nouit	201	16	Inter ceteras	136
5	Letamur nos	788	17	Quod superna	JL 11288
6	Per uenerabilem	635	18	Fraternitatis tue	232
7	Quanta mala	182	19	Significatum est	JL 13867
8	Ex rescripto	193	20	Veniens ad nos	90
9	Perlatum est	180	21	Iustis petentium	89
10	Quia ex defectu	119	22	Commisse tibi	132
11	Quante auctoritatis	647	23	Dilectus filius	JL 14210
12	Decet prudentiam	42	24	Quod uobis	—

[2] All printed versions derive ultimately from this manuscript, through Giles, *EpST*.

44–6, 78, 126, V. 10 and 82, and inserts a reference to a third version of *Nouerit industria uestra* which is not found in AlanT(C) but is found in AlanT(A) and AlanT(B): cf. AlanT(A) and (B), V. 10.

The ultimate source of the whole group of letters cannot be established. Its position in Bodl.B, I, however, between the index to Alan of Tewkesbury's collection and the opening sequences of the abbreviation itself, strongly suggests that it had been inserted into the front of the volume containing Alan's work, which the compiler of this particular manuscript had before him. Although in this version the twenty-four letters almost exactly fill an eight-leaved quire, it would not have been difficult to transcribe them into the space of three or four large, double-columned leaves at the beginning of an existing volume.

However, from item 25 onwards, the letters follow the order of Alan's Recension II, with minor variants,[1] and there is evidence of their textual agreement with the AlanT 'alius liber'. But this is a heavily abbreviated version of the collection, containing only 197 letters from a total of 535;[2] and it would appear from the contents of Bodl.B, II and III, which is bound up with it, that its very numerous omissions from the AlanT stock are explained by the complementary nature of these component parts of the single volume: only sixteen items are common to both collections,[3] and with four exceptions the abbreviation of Alan's collection omits only those letters which are in fact found in Bodl.B, II and III.[4] It seems likely that Bodl.B, II and III were collated with a version of Recension II of Alan of Tewkesbury's collection, and that the

---

[1] Bodl. B, I. 25–220 agrees exactly with the order of the preceding index, except that it includes only one copy of the letter *Quanta mala* (no. 202), which in the index and in some instances elsewhere appears twice; cf. AlanT(B), index I. 89 and IV. 51; and AlanT(C), I. 91 and IV. 50.

[2] Letters 25–220; nos. 59 and 60 refer to one letter and 176b and c are un-numbered. The following 338 letters have been omitted from the relevant sequence (the references in brackets indicate where the letter is found elsewhere in Bodl.B, I or among the introductory material on fols. 1r–8r): AlanT(B), I. 4, 5, 13(fo. 3), 15(fo.3), 19, 21, 23, 24(fo.5), 26, 31(fo. 8), 32, 33(fo. 8), 34, 37, 38, 40–2, 47, 49, 52, 56–9, 60(=23), 61(=16), 63–8, 74, 78(=12), 82, 85, 96–100, 106, 108, 112, 113, 116, 117, 119–29, 131, 132, 134–7, 138(=2), 139(=3), 142 (=9), 143(=4), 148, 149(=8), 155, 158(=1), 160, 162, 174–7; II. 2–5, 9–12, 14, 18, 19, 22–4, 27–30, 33–6, 41, 42, 44–7, 54–9, 62, 67–74, 84, 86–8, 94(=15), 97–101, 104; III. 2–4, 6–11, 13, 14, 16, 17, 20–32, 34–9, 42–65, 68–76, 78, 79, 81–98; IV. 1–16, 18–28, 30–3, 37, 38, 40, 41(=11), 42–7, 51; V. 1–8, 10, 12, 14–16, 17(=6), 19–32, 34–41, 43–52, 54–62, 64, 67, 69–71, 73, 76–82, 84–8, and 92–6.

[3] Bodl.B, I. 1 = Bodl.B, III. 22; I.5 = III.41; I.12 = II.114; I.10 = II.142; I.13 = II.141; I.14 = II.143; I.15 = II.313; I.52 = III.26; I.82 = II.10; I.92 = II.277; I.122 = II.56; I.131 = II.20; I.186 = II.223; I.212 = II.69; I.213 = II.78; and I.217 = II.132.

[4] The exceptions are: AlanT(B), I. 33, 82, 148, and II. 36.

substantial derivation of 197 items from that source was transcribed in their AlanT order, together with its full introduction and table of contents. A note inserted on fo. 29v, facing the beginning of the index, in a hand that does not appear elsewhere in the volume, provides the reason for the inclusion of this otherwise superfluous table and implies that the two distinct collections were intended to be placed together in this volume, since it states that the letters should be arranged in their order in the table and not as they appear in fact on the following folios.[1] It is improbable that this note refers to Bodl.B, I only, which immediately follows it, since with the exception of the opening twenty-four items its letters are transcribed in the index order, and it seems much more likely to refer to both subsequent collections.

c. ALANT(C): CORPUS CHRISTI COLLEGE MS 295

Three manuscripts survive recording an expansion of Recension II of Alan of Tewkesbury's collection, though it is not possible to establish whether they represent Alan's own further work or that of a continuator. The manuscripts in question are the Cambridge Corpus Christi College MS 295, or AlanT(C), the Brit. Libr. MS Arundel 219 and the Paris Bibl. Nat. Latin MS 5320, the first containing a complete collection in five books, and the other two containing abbreviations only. The Corpus MS, AlanT(C), is a fine, late twelfth-century volume, carefully written in a small book-hand, arranged in double columns and occupying twenty-six gatherings of eight leaves each.[2] The headings and numeration are in red throughout, and the initials are coloured alternately red and blue and decorated in brown and green with gold leaf added in some instances.[3] The letters are preceded by a full and accurate table of contents, written in double columns and filling the whole of the first gathering. The medieval provenance of the volume is unknown, but the rubricated heading at the beginning of the volume, 'Epistole Sancti Thome martyris ecclesie Christi Cantuarie', indicates that it belonged at least at some stage to Christ Church, Canterbury; and it was donated to Corpus Christi College by Archbishop Parker. Among related manuscripts, it is second only to AlanT(A) in the quality of its production.

[1] Cf. p. 77, n.1 above.
[2] 10 × 6¾ in.; 208 + viii folios; double columns with 46 lines to the column.
[3] Cf. especially fos. 1ra, 71vb, 103ra, 114ra, and 185va.

Collation of AlanT(C) with other collections in the AlanT
Family shows that it generally follows the order of arrangement and
textual forms of AlanT(B) rather than of AlanT(A), and therefore
agrees more closely with the 'alius liber' of the marginalia in
AlanT(A) than with the original transcription, but it has also
individual features of order, contents, and text which distinguish it
from both. Compared with AlanT(B), it omits two letters, repeats
one, includes seven in non-corresponding positions,[1] and has an
additional thirty-three, the latter arranged singly or in groups as
follows: three in Book II, twenty-eight in Book III, and two in
Book V;[2] and none of these additions appeared in Recension II, so
far as it can now be reconstructed. All but three of the additional
letters were written by John of Salisbury in the course of the
Becket controversy,[3] and form part of his private correspondence
with friends in England and France; and no less than twenty-six
are found in the manuscripts of his later letters where they occur
in very close sequence.[4] On this evidence, it seems almost certain
that the twenty-six letters were directly derived from a collection
of John's later letters, especially since their texts in AlanT(C) are
virtually identical with those in the John of Salisbury manuscripts.
On the other hand, eleven of these letters are found in AlanT(A),
but were apparently not in the earliest AlanT archetype, since ten
are marked 'non est (*or* non fuit) inter ordinatas'; and it is possible
that the author of the AlanT(A) version likewise derived the
letters from a manuscript of John of Salisbury's later letters.[5]

The letters of John of Salisbury make up the major component of
the additional material in AlanT(C), but they were not the only
source of supply. One letter from Arnulf of Lisieux suggests a
possible derivation from the collection of his letters. The letter in
question is *Personam domini* (III. 78), and appears in AlanT(C),

---

[1] AlanT(B), II.36 and V.10 are omitted; AlanT(B), I.90 appears twice as
AlanT(C), I.91 and IV.50; and 7 letters are re-positioned as follows: AlanT(B),
I.108 = AlanT(C), I.127; (B), I.128 = (C), III.18; (B), I.159 = (C), II.37; (B),
II.15 = (C), II.9; (B), II.48 = (C), II.91; (B), III.12 = (C), III.50; and (B),
III.80 = (C), III.18.

[2] AlanT(C), II. 32, 46, and 98; III. 19–42, 44–6, and 78; V. 10 and 81.

[3] AlanT(C), II. 46, III. 46 and 78 were written by John of Poitiers, Alexander
III, and Arnulf of Lisieux respectively.

[4] Cf. Paris Bibl. Nat. Latin MS 8562, nos. 92, 102, 106, 108, 110–13, 115, 116,
114, 117–26, 128, 129, 131, 132, and 135.

[5] Cf. AlanT(A), II. 30, 68, 126; IV. 64–5, 67–71 (all marked 'non est (*or* non
fuit) inter ordinatas), and V. 82.

fos. 134vb–135rb, with two additional passages added as marginal corrections.[1] Collation with the manuscripts of Arnulf's letters shows that the original shorter text (dated in the summer of 1169) in AlanT(C) is found only in two other manuscripts, namely the Foliot collection in Cave 249 and the copy of the first recension of Arnulf's letters in Vatican Latin MS 6024;[2] and the longer version (dated in December 1170), incorporating the marginal additions in AlanT(C), with necessary changes of tense in the earlier part, was included in Arnulf's second recension, which was completed by 1180.[3] Thus, it is clear that the corrector of AlanT(C) had access to the later version of this letter.

But it is not only the additions and rearrangements which distinguish AlanT(C) from the earlier AlanT recensions: some of its letters were subjected to textual emendation, and a substantial number of protocols and dates were inserted. It has thirty-nine protocols[4] and seven dates[5] lacking in both AlanT(A) and AlanT(B), though six of these protocols[6] and five of the dates are found also in the manuscripts of the Lambeth Family.[7] On the other hand, Alan-T(C) has omitted a small number of protocols and dates which are found in AlanT(A) and AlanT(B),[8] while in some instances its dates[9]

---

[1] Fo. 134va: 'ut nullum litigium nulla iudiciarii forma processit'; fo. 135r: 'Siquidem . . . reduxerunt'; cf. *Mats.* VI, pp. 637–9, and n. 6.

[2] Cf. *Arnulf of Lisieux*, ep. 54a, pp. 97–9.

[3] Ibid., ep. 54b, pp. 106–10; cf. also ibid., p. 97, n. a, and p. 106.

[4] Cf. AlanT(C), I. 19–23, 25–7, 33, 36, 54, 77, 87, 88, 90, 92, 116, 134, 138, 139, 142, 150, 158; II. 5, 80, 83, 84, 89, 106, 111; III. 9, 57, 95, 106; IV. 5, 9, 49; V. 34 and 97. Of these, 17 have preserved only part of the protocol: e.g. I. 21 has 'Salutem et debitam reuerentiam', and I. 23 has 'Salutem et cum summa deuotione reuerentiam': cf. also I. 20, 22, 36, 77, 87, 88, 90, 142, 150, 158; II. 84, 85, 111; IV. 49 and V. 34.

[5] Cf. AlanT(C), I. 92, 142, 148, 149; III. 1, 57, and V. 56.

[6] Cf. AlanT(C), I. 134 and Lamb. 252; II. 89 and Bodl.B, II.290; III. 9 and Lamb. 332; III. 57 and Lamb. 325; IV. 5 and Lamb. 331; IV. 9 and Lamb. 333.

[7] Cf. AlanT(C), I. 142 and Lamb. 287; I. 148 and Lamb. 288; I. 149 and Lamb. 289; III. 57 and Lamb. 325; V. 56 and Lamb. 356.

[8] AlanT(C) omits 5 protocols: cf. I. 79; III. 67; V. 28, 73, and 94; and 3 dates: cf. I. 115, V. 3, and 94.

[9] AlanT(C), I.41 and Arundel I.36 have the date 'Datum in gradu mercurii ix kalendas Septembris', while all other copies of the letter read 'xi': cf. AlanT(A), I.37, (B), I.41, Trin. 42, Cave 148, Douce 8, Harl. 10, and Rawl. 18. AlanT(C), I.176 and Arundel I.68 have 'Datum apud Montem Pessulanum viii idus Augusti', where AlanT(A), I.75 and Roy. 203 have 'Datum Laterani iii kalendas Februarii', and Bodl. B, I.12 has 'Datum Laterani iiii idus Decembris'. AlanT (C), I.174, Arundel I.148 and Bodl.B, II.266 have 'Datum Beneuenti xiii kalendas Iulii', while all other copies read 'Iunii': cf. AlanT(A) and (B), I.175,

or headings[1] differ from those generally received in the other two recensions. There is little doubt that AlanT(C) records a different and probably later recension than that represented by either AlanT(A) or AlanT(B); and it is sufficiently distinguished from both by content and text to be regarded as Recension III. The time and place of its compilation cannot be established with certainty, but there is nothing to exclude the possibility that it was produced in Christ Church during the final decades of the twelfth century. Its acceptance of new JohnS texts directly from a manuscript of his later letters, similar to, if not identical with, that used in the emendation and expansion of the Claudius manuscript, together with the fact that it received many of the JohnS corrections inserted in the margins of Claudius, indicates access to Canterbury materials; indeed it is possible that there were some cross-influences between AlanT(A) and AlanT(C) during the preparation of the latter.

An abbreviation of Recension III is found in the Arundel MS 219, a well-preserved manuscript of the late thirteenth or early fourteenth century,[2] written in single columns in a large pointed hand, with rubricated headings throughout and initial letters coloured alternately red and blue with decorative pen-work of the contrasting colour; and capital letters within the text are over-touched in red. The gatherings (mostly of twelve leaves) are un-numbered,[3] but sufficient catchwords remain to suggest that the extant folios are unbroken in sequence. The marginal references are few; there is little evidence of correction; and the rubricator's guide-phrases are still visible in the margin. The transcription of the letters seems the work of one scribe, excluding the final item,[4]

---

[1] E.g., AlanT(C) and Arundel I.74 have the heading 'Thome Cantuariensi archiepiscopo Aernulfus Luxouiensis episcopus', while AlanT(A), I.83, (B), I.86, Trin. 82, and Bodl.B, I.73 all have 'Thome Cantuariensi archiepiscopo suus Arnulfus'. The correct reading is 'suus Arnulfus', for the letter was not written by Arnulf of Lisieux but by one of Becket's clerks: cf. Barlow, *Arnulf of Lisieux*, p. lxxxvii.

[2] $8\frac{7}{8} \times 5\frac{3}{4}$ in.; 368 fos.; single columns with 27 lines to the column.

[3] Gatherings 1–29 have 12 leaves each; 30 has 11, and 31 has 9.

[4] The last item in the volume, *Quando ego Thomas* (cf. Giles, *VST* II, p. 246), was written on the final folio (fo. 368r–v) after the completion of the main transcription. It purports to be Thomas's own account of a vision at Pontigny in [*cont.*]

Roy. 195, and Lamb. 298. AlanT(C), I.176, agreeing with Arundel I.150, Lamb. 300 and Bodl.B, II.268, is dated 'Datum Beneuenti xiii kalendas Iulii', while the other manuscripts read 'Iunii': cf. AlanT(A) and (B), I.177 and Roy. 197.

and is most carefully executed. This abbreviated version omits the customary introduction, lacks Books IV and V of the collection, and omits no less than forty-four letters from Books I–III.[1] The transcription finishes with AlanT(C), III. 125; a wavy red line drawn across the folio shows that the original transcription did not proceed beyond this point; and the spurious *Quando ego Thomas*,[2] with which the manuscript ends, is clearly a later addition. In arrangement, script, and decoration, the Arundel manuscript is almost identical with MS Laud Misc. 666, already discussed above;[3] and it seems very likely that both manuscripts were produced in the same scriptorium, with the Arundel abbreviation of AlanT designed to supplement the expanded Bodleian derivative in Laud. This supposition would explain the omissions from the Arundel collection, since Laud contains all the letters omitted from AlanT, Books I to III, and much of the material in Book V.[4]

The Arundel collection contains 374 items, set out in three books of 152, 97, and 125 items respectively, closely following the order and contents of AlanT(C). It includes all the items inserted into AlanT(C), and agrees with the latter's additions of protocols and

---

[1] AlanT(C): I. 4, 5, 33, 35, 41, 50, 64–7, 69, 75, 97–102, 113, 119–20, 126, 128, 155; II. 1, 2, 12, 13, 19, 21–3, 36, 42, 43, 45, 47–9, 55, 80, 101; III. 3 and 10.
[2] Fo. 368r–v.   [3] Cf. pp. 35–8 above.
[4] For the letters in AlanT(C), I–III omitted from Arundel, cf. n. 1 above; their corresponding positions in Laud (except that AlanT(C), II.80 is not found in Laud) are as follows: 50, 55, 43, 12, 7, 48, 1–3, 31, 4, 45, 8, 9, 11, 19, 3, 10, 6, 47, 46, 15, 16, 17, 56, 59, 23, 25, 13, 20, 21, 57, 28, 34–6, 18, 14, 24, 26, (—), 30, 53, and 29. With one exception (Laud 44 = Arundel, I.134), the whole of Laud is omitted from Arundel.

---

which the Virgin gave him a miraculous ampulla of oil to be used at the coronations of English kings. The legend is certainly apocryphal; there is no reference to any such occurrence in twelfth-century accounts, and the fabrication of the story seems to be connected with the rivalry between the kings of England and France at the beginning of the fourteenth century. It gained fairly wide currency during the Hundred Years' War, and many fifteenth-century copies of it are known: cf. Hardy, II, no. 11, pp. 382–3. The latest account of the creation of the legend is in the excellent introduction to W. Ullmann, ed., *Liber Regie Capelle*, Henry Bradshaw Society, XCII, Cambridge (1961), pp. 35–9, and 91, n.3. The legend seems first to have been concocted during the reign of Edward II who attempted unsuccessfully to obtain papal confirmation of it from John XXII, and by the end of the fourteenth century English kings were being anointed with this oil contained in an eagle-shaped ampulla. Richard II asked to be re-anointed with it; it was used at Henry IV's coronation, and the fifteenth-century *Liber Regie Capelle* contains a reference (ed. cit., p. 36) to the 'sacra aquila in qua continetur oleum miraculose inventum per sanctum Thomam Cantuariensem'.

dates.[1] The two manuscripts are in very close textual correspondence, the only significant discrepancy being Arundel's inclusion of
a date which AlanT(C) had omitted;[2] it is almost certain that they
derive from the same archetype, although their dates of transcription are widely separated. The forty-four letters which Arundel
lacks do not form a coherent group, but with one exception all are
found in Laud;[3] and, again with one exception only,[4] Arundel
omits the whole of Laud, which can be scarcely a matter of chance
and affords striking support for the suggestion that the collections
are designedly complementary. The few marginalia contain a clue
to the manuscript's provenance: in four places an annotator has
marked references within the text to St Augustine's at Canterbury,
with such phrases as 'nota de Sancto Augustino'[5] or 'nota de
benedictione abbatis Sancti Augustini',[6] and these are the only
references of comparable interest in the whole manuscript. This
evidence strongly suggests that the Arundel manuscript belonged
at one time to St Augustine's and may conceivably have been produced there; and, if these marginal references were made in the
same scriptorium as the main transcription, then both the Arundel
and the Laudian Collections may be of St Augustine's provenance.

Two further manuscripts contain abbreviated derivatives from
Alan's Third Recension: Oxford Bodl. MS Laud Misc. 666 and
Paris Bibl. Nat. Latin MS 5320. In the former, which has already
been discussed above,[7] a fragment of Book V is appended to the
Bodleian Archetype; in the latter, an interesting, though textually
unreliable, abbreviation of the work down to II.19 is associated
with other Becket materials. The Paris manuscript,[8] which once
belonged to the comital family of Béthune, is a composite manuscript of the early thirteenth century, made up of two originally

---

[1] Cf. above, pp. 135–7.
[2] Arundel I.95 has the date, 'Datum Anagnie vii idus Octobris', which is
lacking in AlanT(C), I.115, but which occurs in AlanT(A), I.110, AlanT(B),
I.115, and in the MSS of the Lambeth Family.
[3] The exception is AlanT(C), II. 80.
[4] Laud 44 = Arundel I. 134 = AlanT(C), I. 159.
[5] Fo. 9r.
[6] Fo. 62v; cf. also fo. 10r: 'Nota de Augustinianis', and fo. 63r which has
'Nota' at 'beati Augustini'.
[7] Cf. pp. 35–8 above.
[8] 11¾ × 8½ in.; 191 fos; double columns. Notable coloured initials occur on
fos. 61ra, 69ra, 96vb, and 116rb.

quite separate parts, the first comprising the Life and genealogy of St Servatius and two poems written in his honour,[1] and the second containing an assortment of Becket material.[2] The latter section includes John of Salisbury's *Vita et Passio Sancti Thome*, an abbreviated and partly mutilated version of Benedict of Peterborough's collection of the miracles of St Thomas, an abbreviation of Alan of Tewkesbury's *Explanatio*, and finally a collection of 129 letters corresponding in order with Alan's compilation. It is clear from the manuscript's construction that this unique grouping of material was not fortuitous: though written by more than one hand,[3] all transitions from one part to the next occur in mid-gathering, and the collection was apparently designed as an entity.

A leaf is now missing between fos. 95 and 96, and, in consequence, the account of seven miracles is lost from the manuscript;[4] but this copy of the miracles was rejected by Robertson as of little textual importance,[5] though it seems to preserve in somewhat garbled form the earliest arrangement of Benedict's collection as sent to French Cistercian houses by Abbot Odo of Battle about 1180. It includes 274 cases, arranged in three books of 88, 91, and 95 examples, whereas the later and generally received version was divided into six books of 24, 77, 78, 96, 4, and 7 chapters respectively.[6] The *Explanatio* of Alan of Tewkesbury is also slightly defective in this version, omitting four passages.[7] The text of the introductory material is far from satisfactory, as Robertson discovered, and that of the letters is hardly more reliable.

The letters were not originally numbered, but their numeration has been inserted in arabic numerals by a modern hand. The collec-

---

[1] Fos. 1–60.

[2] Fos. 61–191 comprising: fos. 61ra–69ra, the JohnS *Vita et Passio Beati Thome*; fos. 69ra–142ra, Benedict of Peterborough's *Miracula Sancti Thome*; fos. 142ra–143vb, the two letters *Quam iustis* (*Mats.* VII, ep. 723) and *Redolet Anglia* (*Mats.* VII, ep. 785); fo. 144ra–rb (an inserted folio wrongly bound in reverse order so that the original verso now precedes the recto), a further copy of *Redolet Anglia*; fos. 145ra–151ra, the AlanT *Explanatio*; and fos. 151rb–191rb, the AlanT abbreviation.

[3] Changes of hand occur on fos. 142ra, 144ra, 145ra, 149ra, and 151rb.

[4] This MS lacks 'a languoribus suis in . . . quatuor medullitus'; cf. *Mats.* II, pp. 103–6.

[5] Cf. *Mats.* II, p. xxv.

[6] For a discussion of the relevant MSS of Benedict of Peterborough's *Miracula*, cf. *Mats.* II, pp. xxiv–xxvi.

[7] The 4 omitted passages are: 'Recreatus . . . quievit' (*Mats.* II, p. 326, n.2), 'Verum . . . correctio' (ibid., p. 327, n.6), 'nec . . . video' (ibid., p. 327, n. 11), and 'statimque . . . synagogam' (ibid., p. 328, n.15).

tion is an abbreviation of Alan of Tewkesbury's compilation, but is not divided into books, and includes two letters derived from another source. The work of transcription was apparently interrupted, since it ends abruptly in mid-sentence within the letter *Non credebam me*[1] in the middle of the final folio recto, while the remaining part of the page is ruled, but the folio verso is completely blank. Comparison with the Alan of Tewkesbury manuscripts reveals that this collection is related to Recension III as recorded in AlanT(C): it agrees with the latter in order, and the evidence of its protocols and headings, together with the collation of individual letters, shows that this copy, though corrupt, follows the AlanT(C) tradition more faithfully, where the various recensions diverge in details,[2] though in one instance it agrees with the correct date in AlanT(A) and AlanT(B), where AlanT(C) is inaccurate, perhaps through scribal error.[3]

In many respects the manuscript details are unsatisfactory: compared with related versions, six dates are retained[4] but eleven are omitted;[5] seven headings are lacking,[6] others are incomplete,[7] while many are inaccurate.[8] The omissions and inaccuracies suggest that the rubricator had some difficulty in following his exemplar, most probably through unfamiliarity with the names of persons and places. The manuscript was apparently transcribed in France, as its forms of proper names suggest very clearly in some instances: thus, on three of four occasions when Gilbert of London's name is given in full, it appears in its French form as

---

[1] The MS ends with the word 'examines' in mid-fo. 191rb, omitting 'examinatos, observes . . . valeam'; cf. *Mats.* VI, p. 297.

[2] E.g., the final word in the protocol of no. 7 is 'augustum', agreeing with AlanT(C), I. 9, in contrast with AlanT(A) and (B), I. 9, which end 'obtentum'; no. 9 agrees with AlanT(C), I. 14 in omitting 'apud Marlebergiam' from the attestation: cf. AlanT(A), I. 12b and AlanT(B), I. 13; no. 44 agrees with the unusual text of *Breuiloquio* in AlanT(C), I. 67; cf. AlanT(A), I. 62 and AlanT(B), I. 66. Nos. 12–18, 32, 42, 50, 55–7, 65, 75, 78, 93, 97, 98, 100, 102, 107, and 122 have protocols or parts of protocols preserved only in Recension III: cf. AlanT (C), I. 20–3, 27, 28, 30, 55, 65, 77, 82–4, 99, 114, 118, 134, 138, 139, 142, 144, 158, and II. 5.

[3] No. 115 has the correct reading 'Dat. Beneuent. xiii Kal. iunii' as in AlanT (A), I. 175, while AlanT(C), I. 174 and Arundel I. 148 have 'iulii'.

[4] Cf. nos. 1, 20, 100, 115, 120, and 123.

[5] Cf. nos. 11, 16, 17, 22, 25, 52–4, 61, 75, and 76.

[6] Cf. nos. 28, 34, 47, 58, 69, 72, and 75.

[7] Cf. nos. 4, 10, 13, 49, 73, 109, 110, and 117.

[8] Cf. nos. 9, 12, 14, 15, 18, 29, 33, 36–8, 45, 48, 54, 60, 82, 84, 90, 92, 98, 106, 115, and 124.

'Gislebertus',[1] while William of Pavia appears in the heading of item 92 as William of Paris, no doubt through the misreading of 'Papiensis' as 'Parisiensis', though the correct version is found later in the manuscript.[2] It is suggestive too of French provenance that the rubricated heading of John of Salisbury's *Vita et Passio* refers here to the author as the Bishop of Chartres,[3] whereas all the English manuscripts refer to him in this context simply as 'Johannes de Saresberia', or by a variant of that form, while the introduction by Alan of Tewkesbury also names him John of Salisbury, though adding that he later became Bishop of Chartres.[4]

The collection ends abruptly in mid-item 129, corresponding with AlanT(C), II.19, but of the 196 letters contained in AlanT(C) to that point, the Paris manuscript omits sixty-eight,[5] and adds two from a different source.[6] It appears that the author made a careful selection from Recension III, excluding most of John of Salisbury's correspondence and concentrating on letters issued or received by Becket himself and the papal bulls; and in this way he formed a compilation of the pre-Alan of Tewkesbury type. Slightly less than half the total number were issued by Becket,[7] forty-three were sent by the Pope,[8] twenty-two non-papal letters were addressed to Becket,[9] and fourteen letters were despatched by various other authors, including John of Salisbury.[10] In fact, from

---

[1] Cf. nos. 46, 83, and 85, though in no. 18 Gilbert's name occurs in its usual form 'Gillebertus'.

[2] Cf. no. 129.

[3] Fo. 61ra: 'Incipit uita et passio beati Thome Cantuariensis archiepiscopi et martyris edita a uiro uenerabili Iohanne Carnotensi episcopo'.

[4] Cf. *Mats.* II, p. 299: 'postea vero Carnotensis episcopus'.

[5] AlanT(C), 1–3, 10–12/13, 17, 19, 24–6, 29, 32, 34, 37, 39, 45–7, 51, 52, 54, 70–4, 86, 87, 89, 90, 94–6, 103, 107–9, 111, 133, 141, 148, 149, 151–7, 161, 166–72, 176, 178; II. 6, 8–10, 14, 16, and 17.

[6] Nos. 3 and 47; cf. *Mats.* V, epp. 12 and 99.

[7] 49 letters: nos. 12–15, 19, 21, 24, 28, 31, 34–6, 41–4, 46, 49–51, 63–8, 74, 77, 81, 82, 87–9, 94–8, 101–3, 112, 114, and 124–9.

[8] Nos. 1, 2, 11, 16, 17, 20, 22, 23, 25–7, 30, 32, 33, 37–40, 45, 48, 52, 53–7, 60–2, 73, 75, 75a, 76, 78–80, 100, 108, 115, 118–20, and 123. Of these, 17 were addressed to Becket: nos. 1, 2, 11, 16, 27, 30, 32, 53, 61, 75, 75a, 78, 79, 100, 115, 118, and 123.

[9] Nos. 4–7, 9, 58, 59, 70, 71, 84, 86, 93, 104–7, 109–11, 117, 121, and 122; five of these were written by anonymous messengers: nos. 4–6, 9, and 107; and four were written by John of Salisbury: nos. 105, 106, 109, and 110.

[10] The miscellaneous letters can be analysed as follows: 4 from John of Salisbury, nos. 69, 72, 90, and 99; 3 from Gilbert Foliot, nos. 83, 85, and 91; 2 from Henry II, nos. 8 and 10; 1 from Lombardus of Piacenza, no. 113; 2 anonymous letters, nos. 18 and 29; the oath from Gerard la Pucelle, no. 116; and 1 letter from William of Pavia, no. 92.

the sequence of letters down to AlanT(C), II.19, only five papal letters[1] and three letters from Becket[2] are not found in this manuscript. Some of the letters omitted touched on important matters: two of the missing papal letters confirmed Becket's sentences of excommunication on Jocelin of Salisbury and John of Oxford,[3] while two others, addressed to Roger of York, were concerned with the Canterbury and York dispute over the right to crown kings in England.[4] The missing Becket letters were of less importance: the first is one of five letters of recommendation of the messenger Master Hervey; the second is a letter of very general substance addressed to Master Silvester, Treasurer of Lisieux, and the third addresses thanks to Cardinal Otto for past favours and hopes for future ones. The exclusion of such items as these is of little significance, and does not seriously affect the value of the collection as a record of the dispute.

In contrast, about half of the letters addressed to Becket in the relevant AlanT(C) sequence were omitted from this manuscript,[5] as well as most of the John of Salisbury correspondence,[6] and about half of the miscellaneous items.[7] The loss is not very great in many instances, but some of the omitted letters addressed to Becket are of vital importance for the history of the controversy, providing detailed accounts of meetings and negotiations between the various groups of messengers at the beginning of the dispute.[8] But they have little bearing on the character and conduct of the

---

[1] AlanT(C), I. 10, 11, 148, 149, and 176; nos. 148 and 149 were addressed to Becket.

[2] AlanT(C), I. 19, 155, and II. 14.   [3] AlanT(C), I. 148 and 149.

[4] AlanT(C), I. 10 and 11.

[5] Of the 52 letters addressed to Becket, 25 were omitted: 3 from John of Salisbury, AlanT(C), I. 25, 32, and 34; 5 anonymous letters, I. 3, 24, 37, 45, and II.6; 4 from John of Poitiers, I. 1, 2, 26, and 36; 3 from Nicholas of Mont-St-Jacques, I. 46, 47, and 54; 2 from Arnulf, I. 29 and 87; 2 from Alexander III, I. 148 and 199; 1 each from William of Pavia, Master Hervey, Cardinal Otto, Arnulf of Lisieux, Peter of Pavia, and Gerard la Pucelle: II. 10, and I. 51, 52, 86, 90, and 111.

[6] Of 31 letters written by John of Salisbury (excluding those addressed to Becket, which have been discussed above) 27 were omitted: AlanT(C), I. 74, 89, 94–6, 108, 109, 133, 141, 151–4, 156, 157, 166–72, 178; II. 8, 9, 16, and 17.

[7] Of 20 miscellaneous items 10 were omitted: the Constitutions of Clarendon and the 1169 decrees, AlanT(C), I. 12/13 and 17; 3 accounts of the imperial Council of Würzburg, I. 71–3; 2 letters from Gilbert Foliot, I. 39 and 107; one each from Henry II, Rotrou of Rouen, and Ernisius of St-Victor, I. 70, 103, and 161.

[8] Cf. AlanT(C), I. 1, 3, 37, 45, and II. 6 (*Mats.* V, epp. 25, 61, 92; VI, epp. 253 and 339).

archbishop, and this feature may reveal the interests of the compiler of the Paris manuscript and his subsequent choice. This hypothesis would also explain the omission of the Constitutions of Clarendon and the 1169 decrees;[1] and the John of Salisbury letters clearly fall into the category of material of only peripheral interest to such a compiler, for most of John's letters in the group were sent to friends, and were couched in safe and general terms, throwing little direct light on the controversy.

Although the emphasis in contents is on the correspondence of Becket and the Pope, the individual selection is not notably partisan, for some of the letters most unfavourable to Becket are included. The collection contains the papal letter *Receptis litteris* forbidding Becket to utter censures against the king, the two appeals *Veniens ad nos* and *Ad nos usque* of Jocelin of Salisbury and his chapter respectively against Becket's sentence on Jocelin, Foliot's two letters *Seueritatem uestram* and *Seueritatem domine* in defence of the Bishop of Salisbury, the bishops' appeal of 1166, and the anonymous *Medicine potius* attacking Becket, possibly written by Foliot at the beginning of the dispute.[2]

SUMMARY OF CONCLUSIONS

The happy survival of the Claudius manuscript enables us to establish the various stages in the evolution of Alan of Tewkesbury's major work and to go some way towards discovering its filiation with related collections. From its meticulous apparatus of collation and comment it is possible to reconstruct the contents, order, and text of its own exemplar (Recension I), as well as the general features of a companion copy with variant order and corrected texts (the 'emendatior liber') which became Recension II. No manuscript of Recension I has survived, except the much corrected and expanded Claudius, which demonstrates that it was immediately superseded. Except for the possible derivation from it of some details by Roger of Crowland, the Claudius manuscript itself has no extant derivatives and stands to one side of the textual tradition thereafter. It is in all respects a unique volume, recording a key period in the stabilization of the text, as well as the personal interest and attention of Alan of Tewkesbury himself. Recension

---

[1] AlanT(C), I. 12/13 and 17.
[2] Cf. nos. 32, 70, 71, 84, 85, 86, and 18.

II, which is best exemplified by the late AlanT(B) in the Vatican Library, derived from the 'emendatior liber' and became the generally received version of the text, while Recension III was produced by the incorporation into Recension II of thirty-three new letters, mostly from John of Salisbury, and the addition of protocols and dating clauses from unidentified sources. There can be little doubt that Alan was responsible for Recensions I and II, but his connection with Recension III is less easy to demonstrate. The exact nature of John of Salisbury's contribution to the work, however, remains obscure. Alan acknowledged John's strategic influence in the initiation of a major collection of letters; contemporaries like Gervase of Canterbury and Herbert of Bosham recognized Prior Alan as the effective editor, yet Guy of Southwick claimed personal collaboration with John, at Merton, in the gathering of epistolary materials. It is difficult to reconcile these various claims and statements either with one another or with the known tradition of the collections which survive, except by allowing to John an originating initiative, made on the basis of his own records, which Guy's *florilegium* rather tantalizingly describes. Setting aside the uncertainties of John of Salisbury's contribution, the whole character of Alan's collection suggests dependence on a range of materials which included the Bodleian and Vatican Archetypes, and the later letters of John of Salisbury, together with the record files surviving from Becket's exiled household; and the texts were gradually perfected by constant recourse to archival sources for clarification and improvement.

CHAPTER 4

The Foliot Group of Collections

In contrast with the collections of Becket correspondence discussed so far, which derived most of their material from sources close to the archbishop, two further collections reveal a substantial dependence on the records of Gilbert Foliot, Bishop of London, and these are now found respectively in the Oxford Bodl. MSS Cave e Mus. 249 and Douce 287, while part of the contents of a third collection, namely the Rawlinson MS Q.f.8,[1] already discussed above in connection with the Bodleian Family,[2] reveals a possible influence from the same source. Although the Cave and Douce manuscripts are not interdependent, they have a general agreement of content and order over the area of their correspondence, and they preserve diplomatic and textual details which clearly distinguish them from collections made by compilers with access to the material assembled by members of Becket's household.

A. THE CAVE COLLECTION

The manuscript most closely connected with Foliot himself is the late twelfth-century MS Cave e Mus. 249, which belonged at an early date to Westminster Abbey and subsequently to the Benedictine Priory of Belvoir.[3] Most of its contents relate to the various stages in the career of Gilbert as Abbot of Gloucester, Bishop of Hereford, and Bishop of London,[4] and not unexpectedly, some

[1] Cf. p. 38 above and Appendix II below.

[2] Cf. pp. 38–46 above.

[3] The foot of fo. 1r bears the rubricated inscription: 'Hunc librum dedit frater Willelmus de Beluero prior eiusdem ecclesie Deo et beate Marie de Beluero, quem qui alienauerit uel deleuerit anathema sit. Anima dicti Willelmi et anime omnium fidelium defunctorum requiescant in pace. Amen'; cf. fo. 89v: 'Hic est liber sancte Marie de Beluero quem qui alienauerit anathema sit'. The pressmark of Westminster Abbey, 'S. x. pie. et ed. West', appears at the top of fos. 67rb and 205v; cf. N. Ker, *Medieval Libraries* (1964), p. 6.

[4] Gilbert was Abbot of Gloucester 1139–48, Bishop of Hereford 1148–63, and Bishop of London 1163–87; he died on 18 February 1187. Cf. Knowles, *Episcopal Colleagues*, pp. 37–46, *et passim*; Morey and Brooke, *Gilbert Foliot and his Letters*.

letters from the period of the Becket controversy are included within it. But it also contains an early decretal collection, a small group of papal letters, and an unfinished collection of letters and documents concerned with the controversy, and it appears to have been compiled in Foliot's chancery during the closing phase of his life, being possibly completed shortly after his death. The manuscript was evidently the work of a number of scribes, some perhaps working concurrently and others consecutively both on and within its various parts. Thus, of eleven sections revealed by analysis only two were begun by the same hand,[1] and there is wide variety in their rubrication and formal presentation. Scholars have variously analysed the manuscript's contents in several component sections: Dom Adrian Morey and Professor Christopher Brooke have envisaged the whole in six main parts, while Professor Southern has distinguished eight 'new beginnings'.[2] There is no need to examine here in comparable detail the many relevant points so fully discussed by Morey and Brooke in their recent edition of the letters and charters of Gilbert Foliot, but an alternative analysis suggested here is of eleven parts in order of appearance in the manuscript, which can be briefly summarized as follows:

Part I(a): Letters 1–141, fos. 1–47vb.
  Written by a single scribe in double columns, with red, green, blue, and yellow initials. The letters in this part were mostly issued by Foliot, and span his entire career from the time of his appointment as Abbot of Gloucester. The sequence of letters is broadly chronological, but not consistently so.
I(b) : Letters 142–152, fos. 47vb–56vb.
  Written in a variety of hands, again in double columns, but with red initials only. This part contains various letters connected with the Becket controversy, including *Que uestro pater*, in which the bishops notified Becket of their appeal against him, and his reply *Mirandum et uehementer* addressed to Foliot.[3] The main transcription ends with no. 150 on fo. 55rb, and the concluding two letters are appended in a charter-hand (which has interpolated letters in a similar way in other positions in the MS, and is hereafter identified as

---

[1] Cf. Parts IV(*a*) and VI.
[2] MB, *Foliot*, pp. xxxv–li and 2–11; cf. R. W. Southern's review of MB, *Foliot* in *EHR* LXXXIII (1968), p. 786.
[3] Nos. 149 and 150; cf. *Mats*, V, epp. 205 and 224.

Hand C), with gaps left for the insertion of initials, and a gap of eight lines at the foot of fo. 56vb.

Parts I(*a*) and (*b*) together form a continuous run of seven quires (I–VII), the latter being distinguished from the former by a change of scribe and the unvaried use of red for the initial letters.

Part II : Letters 153–162, fos. 57ra–62vb.

Written by two hands in double columns but lacking coloured initials. Letters 155–162 are in Hand C. All letters in this section are connected with the Becket controversy.

Part III : Fragment of a sermon (numbered 163),[1] fos. 63r–65r, followed by three blank pages, fos. 65v–66v. The text is arranged in single columns and transcribed by a hand which does not recur elsewhere in the volume. This part is related neither by parchment, content, arrangement, nor script to the rest of the MS.

Part IV(a) : Summa cause inter Regem Henricum et Sanctum Thomam (164) and letters 165–200, fos. 67ra–106rb.

Written by at least two very similar hands and arranged in double columns, with initials in red, green, and blue; rubricated headings occur in the earlier part of the section, but they are discontinued from fo. 73vb, though two-line spaces are left between the remaining letters. This section includes, as no. 176, the *Causa inter Cantuariensem archiepiscopum et episcopum Londoniensem.*[2]

IV(b) : Letters 201–8, fos. 106va–109vb.

Transcribed by two hands and arranged and initialled in a manner similar to the preceding section, but without the spaces between letters. Most of the letters in this part were issued by Foliot as Bishop of London, but the group includes Alexander III's decretal *Quoniam quesitum* addressed to Rotrou of Rouen, which occurs also in two other places in the volume,[3] and an otherwise unknown letter from the King of Sicily to Henry II.[4]

IV(c) : Letters 209–14, fos. 110rb–111va, followed by three blank folios, 112r–114v.

---

[1] Attributed to Gilbert Foliot; cf. Giles, *EpGF*, no. 287.

[2] *Mats.* IV, pp. 213–43: a rehearsal of the chief points at issue between Becket and Foliot, composed probably *c.* 1169. Cf. p. 153, n. 3 below.

[3] JL 13583: 11 October 1171–80; cf. also Cave 242 and 304.

[4] *In receptione litterarum,* no. 207; cf. Giles, *EpGF*, no. 513.

This section was transcribed by Hand C and arranged in double columns; but all the initials are black, and no decoration of any kind was apparently intended. All the letters here were issued by Foliot as Bishop of London, but are unrelated to the Becket controversy.

Parts IV(*a*)–(*c*) comprise a sequence of six quires (IX–XIV).

Part V : Letters 215–26, fos. 115r–120v.

Written by two hands in single columns. The first four initials are in red, but the work of rubrication was seemingly interrupted, since the spaces for initials are left unfilled through the rest of the gathering. This section is composed almost entirely of letters addressed by Alexander III to English recipients during the dispute between Becket and Henry II. Letters 221 and 226 are in Hand C.

Part VI : The decretal collection *Belverensis*,[1] numbered 227–57, fos. 121r–135rb.

Transcribed by a number of hands and arranged in both single and double columns. Fo. 136r–v is numbered and ruled, but otherwise blank. Items 248–51 and 257 are in Hand C.

Part VII : Letters 258–84, fos. 137ra–144vb.

Written by two hands and arranged in double columns with red and blue initials. The majority of these items date from Foliot's London episcopate, but five belong to the period when he was Bishop of Hereford.[2] Fo. 144rb–vb, containing a series of questions and letters 283 and 284, is written in Hand C.

Part VIII : Letters 285–304, fos. 145ra–152vb.

Written by two hands in double columns, with initials in red and blue; spaces are left between the letters, presumably for the later insertion of rubrics, as at the end of Part IV(*a*). This section contains a varied selection of letters, including papal letters and other letters connected with the Becket controversy, and has as its final item the third copy of *Quoniam quesitum*, written in Hand C.

Part IX : Letters 305–65, fos. 153ra–176vb.

Transcribed by two hands in double columns. The initials down to no. 350 are red, blue, and green, and the arrangement

---

[1] For a full analysis of the contents of this English primitive collection, cf. C. Duggan, *Twelfth-Century Decretal Collections*, pp. 155–62.

[2] Nos. 260, 263, 267, 272, and 276; cf. MB, *Foliot*, pp. xliii–xliv.

is very similar to Part I(*a*). The great majority of the letters in this part were issued by Foliot either as Bishop of Hereford or as Bishop of London,[1] but they include two of Becket's letters, addressed to Henry II and Robert of Hereford respectively.[2] Nos. 332 and 333 (fos. 163vb–164ra) and 363–5 (fo. 176va–vb) are in Hand C.

Part X(a) : Letters 366–83, fos. 177ra–186vb.

Written by one hand in double columns, with initials in red and green, and displaying a unity of execution unusual in this MS. Most of these items were issued by Foliot as Bishop of London but two papal letters are also included.[3] This section was not completed: the final letter breaks off in mid-sentence,[4] and most of fo. 186vb is left blank.

X(b) : Letters 384–9, fos. 187ra–189va.

Written by the same scribe as the preceding sequence in double columns but with black initials only, and containing six Foliot letters written during the Becket dispute.

X(c) : Letters 390–400, fos. 189va–192vb.

Written in Hand C in double columns, without any decoration. With the possible exception of no. 390, all were written after Becket's martyrdom.

Part XI : Letters 401–47, fos. 193ra–205va.

With the exception of the last item in the volume, this section was transcribed by Hand C, and the formal arrangement and presentation are identical with Part X(*c*) down to fo. 198va; but fos. 199r–200r, though written by the same scribe, are arranged in single columns. All the material in this section was issued by Foliot, and dates from his tenure of the see of London. The last letter in the volume is the controversial *Multiplicem* sent by Foliot to Becket in late 1166; it was added to the completed MS by a hand that does not appear elsewhere in the volume, and occupies the last five folios.[5]

Thus, in its surviving form, the Cave MS appears as a rather unsystematic assemblage of material, lacking unity of presentation,

[1] As Bishop of Hereford, nos. 305–26; as Bishop of London, nos. 327–47, 349, and 351–64; cf. MB, *Foliot*, pp. xlv–xlvi.

[2] Nos. 348 and 350.

[3] Nos. 371b and 372.

[4] *Scitis karissime* (383) ends with the words 'gratiam domino usque . . .'; cf. MB, *Foliot*, p. 252.

[5] No. 447; cf. *Mats.* V, ep. 224 and MB, *Foliot*, ep. 170.

script, or decoration. It can hardly have been derived in this form from a single exemplar or designed as a single collection, and its present order of parts does not readily correspond with a coherent plan. Its construction is in fact complex, and an analysis of its contents raises questions which are not easy to resolve. Each principal section as listed above begins on a fresh quire, though their subsections do not. It is possible that the present order of quires does not in all instances preserve their correct sequence, and that errors in binding have resulted in faulty arrangement. But it is probable also that the transcription of the main sections includes some departures from the schematic plan as originally conceived. The contents of the whole can be broadly classified as Foliot materials, Becket materials, a collection of papal letters, a primitive decretal collection, and the fragment of a sermon. Allowing for some intermixture and some groups of varied items, their distribution is as follows: the Foliot items, covering his whole career and written in double columns, are found in Parts I(*a*), IV(*b*) and (*c*), VII–X(*a*), and X(*c*)–XI; the materials connected with the Becket dispute, similarly arranged, are contained in Parts I(*b*), II, IV(*a*), and X(*b*); the decretal collection *Belverensis* is Part VI and the sermon fragment is Part III; a gathering of papal letters sent during the Becket controversy, arranged in single columns, forms Part V, and may have been intended as a supplement to the Becket materials or, less probably, to the decretal collection. The two principal elements are the Foliot and Becket materials, but it will be noticed that their distribution overlaps the main divisions, most notably in Parts I and IV. Part I begins with letters relating to Foliot's career, but its second component contains letters connected with the Becket dispute; and, conversely, Part IV opens with matter relating to the Becket dispute and continues into its second and third sections with items predominantly concerned with Foliot's career. Moreover, the opening folio of Part IV is rather worn and bears a Westminster press-mark, suggesting that it once existed either as a separate entity or as the first section of a composite work.

Again, there are very marked changes in the quality of the transcription and ornamentation in most parts of the manuscript, which begin in careful hands with some ornamentation or rubrication, but, with a change of hand, introduce a more hasty and less ornate format. The general impression is of the various components

being conceived and begun with much care, after which the opening work was interrupted and the several parts completed rather
hurriedly. Yet there is an important unifying element in all parts
except the sermon fragment in the recurrence of the charter-hand,
Hand C, which supplements and completes the various parts and
in some instances transcribes the whole section.[1] The Cave MS
may have begun as a corporate work, or as a group of works, by a
number of scribes working on its several parts; various hands filled
out the constituent sections, but the unity of interest is imparted by
the work of the one scribe who brought most of the separate parts
and the whole to completion. Dom Adrian Morey and Professor
Brooke have suggested that the manuscript was, for the most part,
produced in the chancery of Gilbert Foliot and probably reflected
his personal interest, and in a fascinating exercise have identified
the writer of Hand C as a scribe who also wrote three of Foliot's
charters;[2] in their view the work was completed by *c.* 1180.[3] In
contrast, Professor Southern questions the close personal association with Foliot, as well as the terminal date of *c.* 1180, since many
items in the manuscript are undatable and one item seems more
likely to have been issued in 1185.[4] A distinction might be made
between the date of final completion of the whole and the date of
composition of its various parts, and the work as a whole may very
well have been produced in the course of several years.

Setting aside the decretal collection, the Cave MS contains a
total of 101 letters and documents (including fragments and
duplicates)[5] relating to the Becket controversy, in addition to the
Summa Cause and the *Causa inter Cantuariensem et Londoniensem.*

---

[1] Hand C appears on fos. 55rb–56vb, 58vb–62vb, 106va–107rb, 110rb–111va,
118r–v, 120r–v, 133v–134v, 135v, 144ra–vb, 152vb, 163vb–164va, 176ra–vb, and
189va–220rb, and it inserts headings on fos. 119v, 147va, and 148rb.

[2] MB, *Foliot*, p. 4 and plates II and III, where this hand is identified as Hand
I.

[3] Ibid., p. 8: 'It is difficult to believe that it was compiled much later than
1177; a date later than *c.* 1180 seems virtually inconceivable.'

[4] Southern argues that Foliot's grant of an indulgence in support of the
Knights Templar should be dated in early 1185, and concludes that the Cave
MS was 'a memorial volume put together without Foliot's control and possibly
after his death'; cf. loc. cit., pp. 786–7 and 789; for the indulgence, *Clamat ad
uos,* cf. Cave 122 and MB, *Foliot,* ep. 459.

[5] There are five fragmentary texts (nos. 157, 162, 199b, 278, and 383), of
which three appear in full elsewhere in the volume (162 = 220b, 199b = 201,
and 278 = 387), and there are two further duplicates (161b = 220a, and 292 =
385). The corrected total of letters is therefore 96.

As mentioned above, these items are distributed most significantly through Parts I(*b*), II, IV(*a*), and X(*b*), though some are found scattered among sequences of predominantly Foliot letters. Part I(*b*) provides eleven Becket letters; Part II contains ten and two fragments; Part IV comprises the *Summa Cause* giving details of the controversy,[1] followed by thirty-six items and one fragment (nos. 165–200),[2] in addition to the *Causa inter Cantuariensem et Londoniensem*, a dialogue account of the dispute between Foliot and the archbishop, which appears as no. 176;[3] but the main transcription of this part ended with no. 200, and the rest of the section is made up with various Foliot letters added in at least three stages by different hands,[4] with the final two folios prepared but left blank; Part X(*b*) provides six letters, while a further thirteen compose the papal section (Part V) and twenty-two relevant items are scattered among the Foliot letters.[5] Part IV(*a*) is particularly interesting, being to all appearances a collection of materials relating to the Becket controversy, which breaks off in mid-gathering, to be followed by a section of Foliot materials. Whether this part records an intention to compile a separate collection of Becket materials, or a Becket supplement to the Foliot collection, to be placed in its correct historical sequence among the letters of the 1160s and 1170s, it is now impossible to determine. The worn appearance of the first folio, bearing a Westminster press-mark, has already been cited as evidence of its possible independent existence; and Morey and Brooke have made the interesting observation that the coherence of the manuscript volume would be improved by the omission of this part together with Parts V and VI.[6]

There is little doubt that the contents of the Cave MS were substantially derived from records kept by Gilbert Foliot or

[1] Cf. *Mats.* IV, pp. 201–12, and Giles, *VST* II, pp. 251–61. This account of the Becket dispute appears without a title in Cave; but cf. Douce, fo. 43ra, for the heading 'Summa cause inter regem Henricum et Sanctum Thomam'.

[2] The numeration here is defective: items 178b and 199b are not numbered in the MS and item 176 is the *Causa inter Cantuariensem et Londoniensem*.

[3] 'Archiepiscopus dicit . . . post facto reuni', fos. 79ra–89ra. This composition has no heading in the MS, but Giles gave it the title 'Causa inter Cantuariensem archiepiscopum et episcopum Londoniensem'; cf. *VST* II, p. 211; and this title was subsequently adopted in Robertson, *Mats.* IV, p. 213. No other MS copy of the work has survived.

[4] Cf. MB, *Foliot*, p. xli.

[5] Nos. 133, 201 = 199b, 277, 278 = 387, 283, 285, 286, 290, 292 = 385, 293–5, 301, 331, 348, 350, 353a, 357, 361, 383, 399, and 447.

[6] MB, *Foliot*, p. 5.

members of his household. This conclusion is most obviously true of those parts which are composed very predominantly of Foliot materials; but it is also supported in a significant way by an analysis of the Becket material which it contains, since no less than sixty-four of the letters and documents were either addressed to or issued by the Bishop of London himself or the English or Norman bishops in the course of the controversy;[1] six more were issued in the king's name,[2] and the small groups of papal and Becket letters which were not sent to the English and Norman episcopate (four each from Becket and Alexander III) were addressed to the king,[3] with whom Foliot was in close association through the years of the archbishop's exile. Thus the correspondence relating to the controversy in the Cave MS is drawn mostly from the letters of either Foliot, the bishops, or the king; in fact a total of seventy-eight items in ninety-six is accounted for in this way. Only two letters from Becket to Alexander III are found in the collection;[4] and neither was written during the exile: the earlier letter, *Ad audientiam tuam*, was written in late 1164 before Becket fled from England, and *Quam iustis* was written in December 1170 after his return. Similarly, only one papal letter addressed to Becket is included in the collection, and this also was despatched to England before the exile began,[5] and was probably known outside the archbishop's circle before he went to France. Most of the other letters addressed to the Pope reveal a close connection with Foliot: four were written by ecclesiastical supporters in defence of Gilbert,[6] and two were composed in his favour by curial friends.[7] At the same time, the collection contains items which could not readily be explained

---

[1] Letters issued by Foliot: nos. 133, 147, 152, 155, 156, 161a, 168, 194, 199b = 201, 200, 277, 286, 290, 292 = 385, 301, 331, 353a, 357, 361, 383, 384, 386, 387, 389, and 447; letters addressed to him: nos. 142–6, 148, 150, 153, 178b, 216, 221, 222, 224, 225, and 388; letters to English or Norman bishops: nos. 161b = 220a, 172, 179, 185, 186, 189, 193, 215, 217, 223, 226, 283, 295, 350, and 399; letters from English and Norman bishops: nos. 149, 154, 160a, 160b, 170, 174, 180, 188, and 199a.

[2] Nos. 173, 177, 178, 182, 184, and 198.

[3] From Becket: nos. 181, 183, 294, and 348; from Alexander III: nos. 151, 162 = 220b, 218, and 219.

[4] Nos. 169 and 187.

[5] *Litteras quas nobis* (293): 26 October 1163–4; cf. *Mats.* V, ep. 34.

[6] Nos. 175, 191, 192, and 285, being respectively from Hugh, Dean of St Paul's, William of Ramsey, Stephen of Holy Trinity, and William of Reading.

[7] Nos. 158 and 159, written respectively by William of Pavia and Cardinal Otto.

by such personal associations: such letters are the legates' report of the negotiations with Henry II in November 1167,[1] or the three letters addressed to the Pope in 1171 by Louis VII, Theobald of Blois, and Stephen of Meaux, calling for vengeance on Becket's murderers.[2] One would not assume that such letters would have been readily available to a member of Foliot's household, or welcome to him, and there is no evidence of material being drawn from the collections connected with the household of Becket. One possible source of supply existed perhaps in the archives in the household of Rotrou of Rouen, since a number of letters connected with him (written by him or to him) are scattered through the volume.[3] The three letters relating to the imperial Councils of Pavia (1160) and Würzburg (1165)[4] were widely known and their presence here need have no special meaning: *Cum Christus* was addressed to Henry II on the subject of the Council of Pavia;[5] *Iam dudum* was an imperial encyclical addressed to all the peoples of the empire; and *Imperator cum principes* was an anonymous account of the Council of Würzburg sent to Alexander III. They were possibly circulated through England to support the cause of the orthodox Pope. It is conceivable that Richard of Ilchester,[6] a friend and kinsman of Gilbert's, furnished the highly informative report of the royal embassy to Rome in early 1171.[7] In contrast, one somewhat surprising letter is that of an appeal to the Pope written in Becket's name by John of Salisbury.[8]

In a general way, therefore, it can be said that the Becket materials in the Cave MS consist principally of material revealing some connection with Gilbert Foliot, from whose archives the greater part was almost certainly derived, but that a balance of interest is also achieved by the inclusion of a range of independent items relating to the Becket dispute. On the one hand, there are the

---

[1] *Venientes ad terram* (157); cf. *Mats.* VI, ep. 342.

[2] Nos. 195–7.

[3] Cf. nos. 180, 193, 206 (= 242 = 304), 223, 224, 226, and 283.

[4] Nos. 165–7; cf. p. 39 above.

[5] Cf. W. Holtzmann, *Neues Archiv*, XLVIII (1930), pp, 386–7.

[6] For a recent discussion of the career of Richard, cf. C. Duggan, 'Richard of Ilchester, royal servant and bishop', *TRHS*, Fifth Series 16 (1966), pp. 1–21.

[7] *Nouerit maiestas* (190); cf. *Mats.* VII, ep. 750. A full account of the embassy was sent to Richard of Ilchester by one of the king's messengers (cf. *Mats.* VII, ep. 651), and it is very likely that he had access to the formal report addressed to the king.

[8] *Anima nostra pater* (171); cf. *Mats.* VI, ep. 354.

greater number of letters written or received by the Foliot party, together with the bishops' appeals against the archbishop and Foliot's lengthy exegesis in *Multiplicem*;[1] on the other, there are Becket's letters to the king,[2] his replies to Foliot and the bishops,[3] his account of his reception in England in 1170,[4] the papal sentences of excommunication and suspension issued against the bishops for their participation in the coronation of the Young King in that same year,[5] and the French appeals for vindication of the archbishop's death.[6] In emphasis this collection is clearly distinguished from collections made by members of the archbishop's circle both in contents and textual details. About one third of its items are unknown outside the Foliot group of manuscripts,[7] and where this manuscript has letters also found in collections of the Becket families, it preserves textual variations peculiar to itself. In many instances the Cave MS retains full diplomatic details: most of its letters have full protocols and the majority of its papal letters preserve their dates.[8] And in twenty-five instances it contains details omitted from the main 'Becket' tradition, comprising twenty-two protocols, one date, one valediction, and one attestation.[9] In most places, the textual variations are slight, though significant, but three texts vary considerably from the versions preserved in Becket manuscripts: the texts of *Mandatum uestrum* and *Etsi circa nos* have additions and interpolations,[10] while the version of Henry's Constitutions of 1169 varies markedly from that in the Becket collections.[11] It is useful to consider these three items in greater detail.

---

[1] Nos. 149, 158, and 447.

[2] Nos. 183, 294, and 348.

[3] Nos. 150 and 153.

[4] No. 187.

[5] Nos. 185 and 186.

[6] Nos. 195–7.

[7] Items known only in Foliot MSS: nos. 142–5, 155, 156, 160b, 161a, 165, 175–8b, 181, 182, 189, 191, 192, 194, 197, 198, 199b = 201, 200, 222–6, 277, 278 = 387, 285, 286, 301, 331, 361, 383, 388, 389, and 399. Cave 225 and 226 appear at the end of Vat.: cf. Vat. 275 and 277.

[8] Cf. nos. 133, 142–56, 160a–161b, 165, 166, 168, 172, 174–5, 179, 180, 183, 185–94, 198–201, 215–26, 277, 283, 285, 286, 290, 292, 293, 301, 331, 350, 353a, 357, 361, 383–7, 389, and 399.

[9] For the protocols, cf. nos. 152, 161b, 168, 173, 174, 180, 185–8, 193, 215, 216, 219, 220b, 221, 283, 290, 292, 357, 384, and 386; for the dates, cf. no. 161b; for the valediction, cf. no. 171; for the attestation, cf. no. 184.

[10] Nos. 147 and 151.

[11] No. 177.

The letter *Mandatum uestrum* contains Foliot's report to the Pope of his embassy to Henry II in 1165, and presents a carefully reasoned justification of Henry's case, with a scarcely veiled hint at the danger of the English Church being drawn into schism by the king, should the Pope continue his support of Becket; it advises the Pope to be tolerant and patient in his dealings with the King of England.[1] But the Cave version contains two passages which are not found elsewhere: the one suggesting that Becket might be sacrificed to save the English Church;[2] and the other referring to the difficulties of collecting Peter's Pence.[3] From one viewpoint the first hardly redounds to its author's credit, and its subsequent suppression would cause no surprise, while the second has something of the character of a postscript to the main part of the letter. The omission of the latter passage from the Becket sources could be easily explained on the grounds that it was not immediately connected with the controversy, but it would be curious for a compiler sympathetic to Becket to exclude a passage which could be interpreted in a manner hostile to Foliot, which a member of the bishop's own chancery staff had not hesitated to retain. This is a difficult problem, though it might be explained by the hypothesis that the Cave MS records a draft version which was never in fact sent, while the sources not directly dependent on the Foliot archives may preserve the version as received by Alexander III. No question of a deliberate later suppression would in this eventuality be involved.

However, the textual conflict in the extant versions of the papal letter *Etsi circa nos* could not be explained in this way. In this letter, which Alexander III wrote to Henry II in 1166, the Pope sets out his exposition of the right relationship between the secular and ecclesiastical powers and advises the king to ignore his evil counsellors. But the copy provided by the Cave MS contains a long additional passage, known only in one other manuscript, in which the Pope recommends the Canons of Pentney to the protection of the king, calling upon him to act in their defence against Earl Hugh

---

[1] Cf. *Mats.* V, pp. 203–9.

[2] Fo. 51rb: 'unde bonum est si placet ut sanando uulneri si quod est ad presens operam detis quam ecclesie Dei partem nobilissimam precidendo, que turbata sunt hoc ipso longe supra quam possit exprimi perturbetis.' Cf. *Mats.* V, p. 207, and MB, *Foliot*, p. 205, n. to lines 70–1.

[3] Fo. 51vb: 'De cetero super censu beati Petri . . . pater.' Cf. *Mats.* V, pp. 208–9, and MB, *Foliot*, p. 206.

of Norfolk.[1] A 'Becket' compiler could have no particular reason
for suppressing such a passage except on the grounds of irrelevance
to the Becket dispute, as in the example mentioned above; and as a
matter of fact other letters relating to the Pentney case were
included in collections connected with the archiepiscopal household.[2] It is possible in this instance that two separate letters were
mistakenly conflated in the Foliot records. In the third passage
cited, namely the text of the Constitutions of 1169, the Cave text
has little correspondence with that which gained general currency
through the Becket collections, and was clearly derived from a
different source.[3]

To sum up, the Cave Collection, as far as its Becket correspondence is concerned, records an attempt made within Foliot's circle
or household to produce a record of the controversy, and this is
embodied within a larger collection of materials relating to Foliot's
career. The work of transcription of the Becket materials was
almost certainly undertaken in the closing years of Foliot's life or
shortly after his death, though some important parts of the whole
work may have been composed at an earlier date. Its production
may have been prompted by the knowledge that the Becket circle
were making their own collections at Canterbury, but there is no
evidence that the compiler of the Foliot collection derived any of
his material from a Canterbury source. The compiler in fact relied
very heavily on the records kept within the chancery of the Bishop
of London, though certain elements included in the decretal
collection *Belverensis* were apparently derived from sources elsewhere.

B. THE DOUCE COLLECTION

A further collection of Becket correspondence closely linked with
the Foliot archives is that associated with William FitzStephen's
Vita Sancti Thome in the Oxford Bodl. MS Douce 287.[4] The
manuscript volume was transcribed in England in the last quarter

[1] Fo. 56rb: 'Ad hec fratres de Panteneia . . . optinere.' Cf. *Mats.* VI, pp. 555–6·
This addition is also found in Bodl.A, 82, fo. 108r–v.
[2] Cf. AlanT(A), II. 72 and III. 25.
[3] Cf. M. D. Knowles, Anne J. Duggan, and C. N. L. Brooke, 'Henry II's
Supplement to the Constitutions of Clarendon', *EHR* LXXXVII (1972), pp.
757–71.
[4] $7\frac{1}{2} \times 4\frac{1}{2}$ in.; iv + 114 folios; mostly double columns with 36 lines to the
column; written in several hands. From fo. 3ra to fo. 87ra the headings and
initials are in red; thereafter spaces of two lines are left between the letters for
the rubrics, though the initials are completed.

of the twelfth century, and it belonged in the Middle Ages to the
Augustinian Priory of St Thomas the Martyr at Lesnes in Kent,[1]
a house founded in 1178 by Richard de Lucy.[2] It is a most interesting volume, which was used by J. A. Giles in the preparation of his
editions of the Lives and Letters of Becket.[3] It contains the earliest
surviving exemplar of FitzStephen's Description of London (unfortunately defective at the beginning, through the loss of the first
folios of the manuscript), together with his *Vita Sancti Thome*, the
Summa Cause Inter Regem Henricum et Sanctum Thomam, ninety-
four letters relating to the Becket dispute, and extracts from Henry
of Huntingdon's *Historia Anglorum*.[4] The volume is divided into
two parts: the Becket materials, written in double columns, with
coloured initials throughout and rubricated headings down to
fo. 87ra, forming an integrated first section; and the Henry of
Huntingdon abbreviation, written in single and double columns,
but similarly decorated, filling the remainder of the present volume.
The Becket section was clearly designed as a single unit consisting
of three related parts: the Description of London, ending at the top
of fo. 2vb, followed after a gap of seventeen lines by the rubricated
heading of the *Vita*; the *Vita* itself, followed immediately by
anonymous verses and John of Salisbury's *Passio*, finishing at the
top of fo. 42vb, and leaving a gap of twenty-two lines; and, finally,
the *Summa Cause* and letter-collection, transcribed as a single work.

---

[1] Fo. iv^r: 'Hec liber est beati Thome martyris de Lesnes qui ei abstulerit
anathema sit'; this inscription is repeated four times in various medieval hands,
while a modern hand has added the note: 'Austin canons of Westwood in Lesnes,
in the parish of Eryth, Kent': cf. Ker, *Medieval Libraries*, p. 64; MB, *Foliot*, pp.
14–16.

[2] Diceto, I, p. 425.

[3] Cf. fo. 1v: 'I have collated every page of this MS most carefully (by which a
later hand, perhaps Robertson's, has inserted an exclamation mark!) with
Lupus's edition and Sparke's Scriptor, and I have copied from it 35 new letters
besides the unpublished portions of Becket's Life by FitzStephen and John of
Salisbury.' J. A. Giles, March 1844.

[4] The contents of the MS can be briefly described as follows: Part I, fos.
1ra–2vb, fragment of FitzStephen's *Description of London*, beginning at 'dente
rodant Theonino' (*Mats.* II, pp. 5–13), followed by the rubric, 'Willelmus filius
Stephani civis lundoniensis: De vita et Passione Sancti Thome archiepiscopi et
martyris'; fos. 3ra–42vb, FitzStephen's *Vita* (ibid., pp. 13–154), two verses, and
John of Salisbury's *Passio*; fos. 43ra–102vb, the *Summa Cause* (ibid., IV. pp.
201–12) and 94 letters (Appendix VIII below), with fo. 102, completing the
section, fully ruled. Part II, fos. 103r–108v, selections from Henry of Huntingdon, followed by fos. 109–10, originally left blank, into which has been inserted
on fo. 109v a letter dimissory from the Prior of Beaulieu to a monk wishing to
change to another Order.

That the letters were transcribed in conjunction with the preceding section is evidenced by the curious feature that four of the letters inserted into FitzStephen's *Vita* on attached leaves are represented by their headings and protocols only, suggesting that the scribe found it unnecessary to repeat the full texts of some letters which had already appeared in the foregoing *Vita*.[1] The date of transcription of the letter collection is therefore fixed as later than that of the completion of FitzStephen's *Vita*.

It seems clear that the compiler of the Douce MS obtained much of the material in its first part from a Foliot source: it has the whole of the *Summa Cause* as found in Cave, but unknown elsewhere, together with the peculiar texts of the 1169 decrees as preserved in that source,[2] while the arrangement and texts of its letters agree more with the Cave versions than with the Becket tradition. Of the total of ninety-four items in Douce, seventy-four are found also in Cave, and there are significant agreements of order between them.[3] Again, like Cave, Douce preserves the same protocols and dates which are unknown in the Becket manuscripts,[4] and in one notable instance it preserves the incomplete text of a letter exactly as it is found in Cave.[5] Nevertheless, Douce was not dependent on Cave, since textual collation shows that Douce sometimes has a better version, as instanced by its full text of *Venientes ad terram* which is abbreviated in Cave.[6] At the same time, it omits the insertion and long addition to *Etsi circa nos* which are found in Cave,[7] and has an additional nineteen letters. And, although eleven of these nineteen letters are also found in Becket manuscripts,[8] Douce has textual

---

[1] Nos. 48, 49, 50, and 56: *Excessus uestros, Vestram non debet, Se ipsum* and *Audiui grauamen.*

[2] No. 64a.   [3] Cf. Appendix VIII below.

[4] Nos. 19, 21, 28, 31, 36, 42–4, 46, 47, 51, 52, 54, 57, 58, 72, 78–81, and 91.

[5] Douce 39, fo. 80rb: the letter *Scitis karissime* (MB, *Foliot*, ep. 180) finishes abruptly with the words 'gratiam Domino usque . . .'; the following 15½ lines in the MS have been left blank and the text has been crossed through in black. In Cave (cf. no. 383, fo. 186va–vb) the letter was left unfinished in the same way, with a gap of half a column intervening between the uncompleted letter and the next item. It is significant that in both instances provision was made for the subsequent completion of the text of the letter, though in neither instance was it in fact completed.

[6] No. 24; cf. Cave 157.

[7] No. 45 omits the insertion 'unde bonum . . . perturbetis' and the appendix 'Ad hec . . . optinere'; cf. Cave 151 and MB. *Foliot*, pp. 205–6.

[8] Douce 17 = AlanT(B), I.127; 22 = II. 101; 32 = I.97; 41 = I.132; 48 = III.39; 49 = III.43; 56 = III.47; 66 = III.2; 67 = V. 15; and 83 = V.84; and Douce 40 = AlanT(A), IV.4.

peculiarities in them which suggest a different source; seven of these letters are otherwise unknown,[1] of which five were written in defence of Foliot by English abbots and priors. The emphasis of the additional group is quite clearly episcopal: with two exceptions, all were either written or received by Foliot himself or by English ecclesiastics,[2] and the exceptions were addressed to Henry II.[3] Douce contains nothing which one could not reasonably expect to find among the archives in the household of the Bishop of London, and it was probably dependent at least for its letter section upon an exemplar made in Foliot's circle. However, the surviving manuscript is evidently a fair copy of an already existing collection, and not itself immediately dependent upon archival material.

[1] Nos. 60, 61, 63, 84, 87, 88, and 90.
[2] Letters to English ecclesiastics: 17, 22, 32, 34, 67, and 83; letters from English ecclesiastics: 60, 61, 63 (anon.), 87, 88, and 90; letters to Foliot: 41, 48, 49, 56, and 84.
[3] Nos. 40 and 66.

CHAPTER 5

Minor Collections of Becket Letters and General Conclusions

A. THE FAUSTINA COLLECTION

The three smallest collections of Becket letters contain 15, 23, and 8 items respectively, and appear to be unconnected with the major collections now surviving. Despite their small size, however, they have a particular interest for the student of Becket's cult, in that they demonstrate the circulation of small groups of important letters throughout England from the late twelfth century onwards, reinforcing the evidence provided by the Rawlinson and Harleian Collections, discussed above. The most interesting of the three in terms of content and antiquity is found in Brit. Libr. MS Cotton Faustina B.I, fos. 2ra–11va.[1] This is a carefully-written late twelfth-century fragment originating from the Cistercian monastery of Byland in Yorkshire,[2] which is now bound up with a cartulary from Barlings Abbey. Three different but contemporary hands shared in its compilation, showing that the material was transcribed in at least three stages: letters 1–6, relating to the elections of Alexander III and the anti-Pope Victor IV (Octavian) in 1159,[3] are written in one hand; letters 7–14, connected with the Becket dispute and its aftermath, are written in a second; and a third hand has completed this short collection with a transcription of Alexander III's bull announcing the canonization. A much later cursive hand has completed the manuscript fragment with the insertion of a fourteen-line Latin poem on the final folio verso. The contents of the second component, that is letters 7–14, can be briefly summarized as follows: it opens with the two papal letters of censure on the prelates who participated in the coronation of the Young King,

---

[1] 9¾ × 6¼ in.; 10 fos.; double columns, 40 lines to the column.

[2] Ker, p. 23. The fragment once formed part of Brit. Libr. MS Royal 8.F.xv.

[3] A brief analysis of the whole fragment, together with a discussion of the section relating to the papal schism and an edition of the otherwise unknown ep. 6 (*Sacra scriptura*: a defence of Alexander III's claims addressed to Frederick I), is given in W. Holtzmann, 'Quellen und Forschungen zur Geschichte Friedrich Barbarossas (Englische Analekten I)', *Neues Archiv*, XLVIII (1930), pp. 384–413; cf. esp. pp. 386–7 and 398–400.

followed by Becket's report of his reception in England after his return from exile, the notification of the bishops' appeal of 1166 and Becket's reply to Foliot at that time, and three letters calling on the Pope to avenge the archbishop's murder; and these are followed by the bull of canonization.[1] This group of letters does not occur in this order in any other source, though all nine are found in AlanT, seven in Cave, and five in the early 'Becket' collections Bodl. A and Vat.

It is indeed evident that the compilation was built up in stages, presumably in a monastic scriptorium, as the materials came to hand, over a period of about fourteen years, beginning with the election dispute of 1159 and culminating with Becket's canonization in 1173. The forms of the rubricated headings to the Becket letters suggest accession before the canonization; none refers to him as 'beatus' or 'sanctus': *Oportuerat uos*, for example, has the heading 'Pro Cant(uariensi) archiepiscopo T(homa); *Quam iustis* has 'Epistola uenerabilis T(home) archiepiscopi Cant(uariensis) ad papam Al(exandrum) de iniuriis sibi fac(tis)'; while even *Ab humane pietatis*, Louis VII's appeal for vengeance, has only the simple heading 'Epistola L(udowici) regis Francorum de morte T(home) Cant(uariensis) archiepiscopi'. They have the character of a specially assembled *justificatio*, circulated to secure support for the cause of the murdered archbishop in the course of 1171, combining Becket's defence of his own position with papal condemnation of his episcopal opponents and foreign expressions of dismay and shock at the final outrage. It is probably no accident that they found their way not only into all the letter-collections but also into most of the narrative accounts of Becket's life, in one way or another.

B. THE VALLICELLIANA APPENDIX

The second of these minor collections is a hitherto unknown, small

---

[1] Cf. Appendix IX A, below. The Becket section of Faust. contains:

7.	*Licet commendabiles*	Pope to York and Durham	16 Sept. 1170
8.	*Oportuerat uos*	Pope to London, et. al.	16 Sept. 1170
9.	*Quam iustis*	Becket to the Pope	early Dec. 1170
10.	*Que uestro pater*	Bishops to Becket	24 June 1166
11.	*Mirandum et uehementer*	Becket to Foliot	July 1166
12.	*Ab humane pietatis*	Louis VII to the Pope	Jan. 1171
13.	*Vestro apostolatui*	William of Sens to the Pope	Jan. 1171
14.	*Vestre placuit*	Theobald of Blois to the Pope	Jan. 1171
15.	*Redolet Anglia*	Pope to all England	12 March 1173

and obviously incomplete, collection of twenty-two letters and one fragment, transcribed between thirteenth-century copies of *Quadrilogus II*(A) and part of Benedict of Peterborough's *Miracula* in Rome Bibl. Vallicelliana MS B.60.[1] The manuscript finishes abruptly on fo. 134v with the words 'sequenti incredibiliter' and the catchword 'intumescentibus' in the middle of Benedict of Peterborough's *Miracula*, II, *cap.* 76.[2] Apart from the obvious excision of one folio between the present fos. 72 and 73 (pp. cxliv and cxlv), the manuscript is complete and correctly bound up as far as it goes. Its contents can be briefly described: it consists of three parts, separately transcribed but intended to form a single volume:

Part I : fos. 1–72rb

> *Quadrilogus II*(A) with the usual subsidiary pieces: *Gesta post martyrium,*[3] *Catalogus eruditorum beati Thome,*[4] *Causa exilii,*[5] 1169 decrees, and the letters *Sciatis hunc esse, Gaudendum est, Redolet Anglia* and *Qui uice beati Petri,*[6] and the *De penitencia et morte sacrilegorum militum.*[7] The only difference from the generally received text of the *Quadrilogus II* is the placing of the *De penitencia* at the end of the whole appendix instead of in its usual place in the *Gesta post martyrium*: but that misplacement was evidently a mistake, since the list of chapter headings on fo. 2va gives it in its usual place.

Part II : fos. 73ra–101rb (one folio excised before fo. 73)

> Letters 1–23. This section is written and decorated in a manner identical with the preceding section; indeed, the rubricator has in error inserted the name ALANUS in the

---

[1] 134 fos.; double columns; 30 lines to the column; matching catchwords survive for all but two of the 16 quires (cf. quires 8 and 9). Titles and headings are rubricated, and the capitals are alternately red and blue decorated with contrasting pen-work. There are two systems of numeration: the earlier, a pagination in small roman numerals in unbroken sequence from i to cclxv, and a modern foliation in arabic numerals inserted when the volume was re-bound in the nineteenth century, from 1 to 134, also in unbroken sequence: it is this latter numeration which has been adopted in my discussions of the manuscript. For a full description of the MS, cf. A. M. Giorgietti Vichi and S. Mottironi, *Catalogo dei manoscritti della Biblioteca Vallicelliana*, II, Rome (1961).

[2] Cf. *Mats.* II, p. 116.

[3] *Mats.* IV, pp. 409–22.

[4] Ibid., III, pp. 523–31.

[5] Cf. ibid., V, ep. 45.

[6] Ibid., VII, epp. 599, 598, 601, and 784–6.

[7] Ibid., IV, pp. 422–4.

margin of fo. 77ra, as if identifying the author of part of the *Quadrilogus*: he was evidently misled by a corrector who had inserted 'alterius' for the guidance of the scribe who had been puzzled by his text and written 'ali', followed by a gap.

Part III : fo. 102 inserted; fos. 103ra–134vb
Benedict of Peterborough, *Miracula*, breaking off in II, 76.

Although the letter-collection appears sandwiched between two major narrative sources, it has no necessary connection with either, though it seems to follow naturally upon the *Quadrilogus*, and may be considered an appendix: it is in fact physically separated from each by a blank folio verso (fos. 72v and 101v). There is no reason to believe that these letters were ever particularly associated with the one or the other: the Vallicelliana MS merely indicates the placing together of three important Becket records in a particular scriptorium. It has not been possible to discover much about the provenance of the manuscript, though script and decoration point to an English source in the first quarter of the thirteenth century. An analysis of the epistolary material shows that that too is composed of three parts:

Part 1a, letters 1–9, contains a selection of the most important material from the period 1164–6, beginning with the Constitutions of Clarendon and ending with Henry II's writ ordering the seizure of the revenues of Becket's clerks. The section begins defectively in mid-clause xiii of the Constitutions[1] and ends abruptly towards the end of *Precipio tibi* at the foot of fo. 83rb. It is clear that the transcription was interrupted for some reason at this point, since the following folios (83v–88v) have been prepared to make possible the later completion of the work.

Part 1b, letters 10–13, contains four letters only, relating to the prelude to Becket's murder.[2] It is possible that this little group formed a separate accession to the collection.

Part II, letter 14, John of Salisbury's *Ex insperato*, set out as a *Passio* with the rubricated title *Passio S(ancti) Thome* inserted

---

[1] Fo. 73ra, the text begins 'difforciaret regi' in *cap.* xiii of the Constitutions of Clarendon, owing to the excision of the preceding folio. Traces of the notes *ho tolerauit* and *hoc dampnauit*, which are found with some copies of the Constitutions, survive in the remaining fragment of the lost folio to show that it contained the first part of the document.

[2] *Illius dignitatis, Licet commendabiles, Oportuerat uos,* and *Quam iustis* (*Mats.* V, ep. 169; VII, epp. 701, 700, and 723.)

in the margin. The transcription of this letter follows immediately from Part I*b* and is itself then followed by Part III without any change of style or format.

Part III, letters 15–23, has the character of a *Gesta post martyrium*, consisting of four appeals for vengeance on Becket's murderers, the royal messengers' report on their embassy to Rome after the murder, two papal mandates relating to the reconciliation of censured bishops, a report on the Compromise of Avranches, and the bull announcing the canonization to the people of England.[1] Two of the letters in this part are unknown in letter-collections: *Eram magnificentie*, an anonymous protest to Alexander III, and *Quoniam expectare uos*, the report on Avranches sent by Cardinals Albert and Theodinus to William of Sens in May 1172,[2] while a third, *Fraternitati uestre*, the Pope's instructions to the Archbishop of Bourges and the Bishop of Nevers on the treatment of censured bishops, is otherwise known only in the Vatican Collection, where it occurs in the supplementary material inserted at the end.[3] There are no rubricated headings in this section.

Although it is not possible to establish a direct connection with any surviving collection of letters, an analysis of the epistolary materials in Grim's *Vita* suggests the strong probability of a relationship between the Vallicelliana Appendix and the source (or sources) which Grim used.[4] It is possible that this manuscript records the assembly of a particularly influential collection (or collections) of materials circulated for propagandist purposes after the canonization of Becket.

C. THE TITUS COLLECTION

The third minor collection is found in a small and untidy fourteenth-century manuscript, Brit. Libr. MS Cotton Titus D.XI, fos. 3r–41v.[5] In contrast with the two collections just discussed, this fragment was hurriedly written by a single inexpert hand, and the decoration of the text was never completed. It contains only

[1] Cf. Appendix IX B, below.
[2] *Mats.* VII, ep. 774.
[3] Ibid., ep. 753.
[4] Cf. below, pp. 181–2.
[5] $5\frac{3}{4} \times 6\frac{1}{2}$ in.; 55 fos.; single columns, 24–30 lines to the column. The MS was given to the British Museum by John Selden; cf. fos. 1r and 2r: 'ex dono Johannis Seldeni'.

eight items: two of Becket's letters to the king,[1] the notification of
the bishops' appeal of 1166, and Becket's replies to Foliot and the
bishops respectively,[2] Becket's announcement of the Vézelay
sentences,[3] followed by his letter threatening censures,[4] and,
finally, his absolution of those who had been forced to take oaths
against the Pope and himself.[5] With the exception of the bishops'
appeal, all these letters were written in Becket's own name, and
with the exception of the last item they were all written between
January and July 1166.[6] These letters are widely known in other
sources: all are in Alan's collection, and seven of the eight
are found in the early collections of the Becket Group as well as
in the Douce Collection. The texts however in this manuscript
are careless in detail, and it is not possible to establish their
source.

GENERAL CONCLUSIONS

Apart from the minor collections of Becket correspondence just
discussed, the twenty-one substantial letter-collections reflect two
main lines of transmission, the one deriving ultimately from
Becket sources and the other from the records kept in the household
of Gilbert Foliot; the two lines were not mutually exclusive and
some of the most interesting early collections represent a conflation
of material from both traditions. Naturally enough, the largest and
most widely known collections are those deriving from the Becket
household and, although it is impossible to construct a satisfactory
stemma codicum linking all surviving Becket manuscripts, it is
possible to trace the main stages in the formation of a comprehensive corpus of the Becket correspondence.

The earliest stage that can be identified is found in the Bodleian
Family, which derives from an archetype of seventy-nine letters,
brought to completion either in the closing days of Becket's life
or very shortly after his death. The archetype preserves a record
of the more formal aspects of the controversy, based on a careful

---

[1] *Expectans expectaui* (1) and *Desiderio desideraui* (2); cf. *Mats.* V, epp. 153
and 154.
[2] *Que uestro pater* (3), *Mirandum et uehementer* (4), and *Fraternitatis uestre* (5);
cf. ibid., epp. 205, 224, and 223.
[3] *Fratres mei* (6); cf. ibid., ep. 198.
[4] *Si curamus esse* (7); cf. ibid., ep. 183.
[5] *Sciatis carissimi* (8); cf. *Mats.* VII, ep. 636.
[6] Cf. Appendix IX C, below.

selection of the most important letters written at the time. The fact that every other 'Becket' collection of substantial size is related in some way to the Bodleian Archetype supports the view that it was among the earliest collections made and that it was regarded as having some special authority. The second stage is not recorded in its pure form by any extant manuscript, but its contents can be largely reconstructed from a comparison of the Bodleian, Vatican, and Lambeth Families. It apparently involved the construction of a much larger collection than the Bodleian Archetype, comprising two sections containing 148 Becket and 58 papal letters respectively, and arranged in broadly chronological sequence. This second early collection, which has been identified above as the Vatican Archetype,[1] was perhaps no more than an orderly arrangement of files of letters preserved in Becket's household. With the exception of its very last item,[2] it contained nothing later than December 1170 in date of issue, and was probably assembled soon after Becket's murder. In combination with the Bodleian Archetype, it formed the basis of the Vatican and Royal Collections, whose archetypes were very likely composed by 1171–2 and 1173–4 respectively. The Lambeth and Bodl.B Collections are still later compositions, in which independent conflations of corrected versions of the Bodleian and Vatican Archetypes were combined with material from other sources.

It was Alan of Tewkesbury, working at Canterbury from 1174 onwards, and benefiting from a preliminary draft made by John of Salisbury, who produced the most comprehensive collection of letters relating to the controversy. But, except where he was using John of Salisbury's second letter-collection, it is not possible to trace his sources with much confidence, although, in their common material, the texts, and even to some extent the order, of Alan's first recension reflect the readings and arrangement of the Vatican Archetype.

Only two comparatively small 'Foliot' collections of Becket letters survive, and one of these is bound up with the unfinished manuscript of Foliot's own correspondence in the Bodleian Library. But the influence of the materials assembled by his scribes is in fact far greater than this survival would suggest. Both Ralph de Diceto and Roger of Hoveden among the chroniclers, and William

---

[1] Cf. p. 57, n. 1 above.
[2] Vat. 264, issued by Alexander III in October 1171.

FitzStephen among the biographers, as well as the compilers of five 'Becket' collections, had access to the Foliot tradition for material.[1]

The minor collections, in turn, have a significance far beyond that which their size would seem to merit, for they testify to the compilation and circulation of small collections of particularly important letters, independently of the major compendia assembled in the main centres of Canterbury and London. The Rawlinson Collection is especially valuable in the evidence it provides of the gradual accumulation of materials over a period of time in a provincial episcopal archive, consisting of documents received through ordinary channels of diocesan communication (Part I); a 'Foliot' section of letters possibly circulated by the Bishop of London in his capacity as Dean of the Canterbury Province (Part III); a derivative from the Bodleian Archetype, probably issued from Canterbury (Part IV); and the special *expositio cause* collection which also survives in the first part of Harl. (Part II). Similarly, the Faustina Collection shows the preservation at Byland of important international documents, followed by an accession of *expositio* and *vindicatio cause* texts (from 1166 and 1170–1), supplemented, after an interval, by the triumphant bull announcing the canonization in 1173. The Vallicelliana Appendix also combines an *expositio cause* with a *vindicatio cause* group, while the scrappy Titus manuscript testifies to the existence of the nucleus of an 1166 *expositio*.

It is probable that these small collections mark the beginning of epistolary dissemination on the part of the exiled Becket circle, whereby supporters were kept abreast of the major statements of Becket and his opponents in 1166 and 1169, and of the degree of papal and continental support that Becket secured in 1170 and then *post mortem* in 1171. It is no mere coincidence that the Bodleian and Vatican Archetypes both begin with 1166 material. The critical circumstances of that year: the Vézelay sentences, the bishops' appeal against Becket, and his enforced removal from Pontigny, marked the opening of a new phase in the dispute in which both sides sought publicly to justify their actions through the medium of long expository letters like *Que uestro pater* and *Fraternitatis uestre*, which were widely circulated. The exile of the chief protagonist, together with Henry II's policy of watch and ward over the ports, rendered the maintenance of Becket's cause among ecclesiastics in

---

[1] Texts reflecting the Foliot tradition are found in Bodl.A, Harl., Rawl., Vat., and Roy.

England very difficult, especially in the face of royally disseminated condemnations in 1164, the appeals of 1166, and the severe measures of 1169. John of Salisbury's letters testify to a regular secret traffic in news and letters between England and France; and Becket's show an equal concern that the authentic record of his struggle should not be lost. The survival of these small collections indicates that their efforts were not without some success. It is even probable that Foliot's 'Becket' collection, intended as an *expositio cause sue*, was begun in response to the circulation of collections similar to those represented by Rawl. Part II and the Vallicelliana Appendix, Part I.

The Becket collections therefore stem from four different, but not unrelated, impulses: from the need to maintain fairly systematic records by Becket and Foliot in consequence of their ecclesiastical functions—hence the accumulation of chronological record files from which the earliest formally-constructed collections were derived (the two Becket archetypes and the Foliot Douce Collection); from the need to inform and rally supporters at critical moments in the exile—hence the circulation of the 1166 and 1170 files; from the desire of the Becket party to summon support for the murdered archbishop in early 1171—hence the issue of *Quam iustis* and the continental expressions of horror; and finally from the mature desire, reinforced as the reconciliation between Henry II and ecclesiastical authority was effected from 1172 onwards, to draw up and preserve an authentic record of the entire controversy, using principally (and naturally) Becket's surviving archives at Canterbury, producing perhaps the Lambeth Collection as the first fruit, and Alan of Tewkesbury's more ambitious and wide-ranging compilation as its richer harvest. The final stages of this process of epistolary collection exactly paralleled in time and intention the accumulation of beatification evidence in the form of miracle-records by William and Benedict, and the composition of narrative *passiones* and *vite* by Grim, William, and Benedict: all completed in first-recension form by mid-1174.

It is not easy to identify the instigator of this flurry of literary activity at Canterbury. John of Salisbury was certainly well versed in the practice of literary communication; but he seems to have taken refuge at Merton and Exeter after the murder and, while it is possible that he combined the Bodleian Archetype with its larger Vatican sister to form the Royal Collection, and certain that he had a hand in the early stages of compiling Alan of Tewkesbury's collection, it is not possible to trace his direct influence in the *post mortem* activities, although his was the first detailed description of the murder to be published abroad in his celebrated letter *Ex insperato* to John of Poitiers. Nor did the faithful Herbert of Bosham play any known part at that stage, though he contributed a weighty and important volume to the Becket corpus towards the end of his life. It is perhaps to the succession of Priors, Odo (1168–75), Benedict (1175–7), and Alan (1179–86), and the monks of Christ Church, that one should look for the creation and propagation of the Canterbury portion of the Becket materials.

PART II

The Use of the Becket
Correspondence by Biographers

CHAPTER 6

Becket's Biographers

1. THE TWELFTH-CENTURY BIOGRAPHERS

During the later twelfth century, numerous accounts of the life and martyrdom of Becket were composed in England, among which those by Edward Grim, William of Canterbury, the Lambeth Anonymous, William FitzStephen, Guernes de Pont-Sainte-Maxence, John of Salisbury, Alan of Tewkesbury, and Herbert of Bosham[1] are the most important, and together with the letter-collections they provide a very sound basis for the history of the Becket controversy. With the exception of Herbert of Bosham's long and ponderous Life, which was composed between 1184 and 1187, all were completed by 1176–7, and no less than four were composed at Canterbury within six years of Becket's murder.[2] Not surprisingly, there are striking similarities between these accounts, and the elucidation of the dating and relationship of the various Lives has provided historians with complex textual problems to which many solutions have been proposed.[3] The most comprehensive discussions of the chronology and interrelationship of the early biographies are to be found in the works of E. Walberg,[4] and the conclusions of his intensive investigations can be briefly summarized as follows: Grim, William of Canterbury, the Lambeth Anonymous, Alan of Tewkesbury, and Herbert of Bosham are all

[1] The best edition of these Lives is by J. C. Robertson, *Mats.* I–IV.

[2] Namely, the Lives by Grim, William of Canterbury, Guernes de Pont-Sainte-Maxence, and Alan of Tewkesbury.

[3] E. A. Abbot, *St Thomas of Canterbury, his Death and Miracles*, 2 vols. London (1898), I, pp. 4–26; E. A. Freeman, 'St Thomas of Canterbury and his Biographers', *Historical Essays, First Series*, 3rd. ed., London (1875), pp. 89–94; E. Magnusson, ed., *Thomas Saga Erkibyskups*, RS 65, London, II (1883), pp. lxxviii–xciii; Robertson, *Mats.* IV, pp. xii–xv; L. Halphen, 'Les biographes de Thomas Becket', *RH* CII (1909), pp. 35–45; Claudine Wilson, 'The early Biographers of Thomas Becket', *Modern Language Review*, xviii (1923), pp. 491–9, and R. Foreville, *L'Église et la royauté en Angleterre sous Henri II Plantagenet*, Paris (1943), pp. xxvii–xxxii.

[4] Cf. E. Walberg, *La Tradition hagiographique de S. Thomas Becket avant la fin du XIIe siècle*, Paris (1929). For the latest general discussion of Becket's biographers, cf. Antonia Gransden, *Historical Writing in England c. 550 to c. 1307*, London (1974), pp. 296–308.

regarded as independent authors whose individual compositions were not derived from any other known narrative source. This assessment does not rule out the probability of personal contact between some at least of the authors, but their works do not reveal any significant textual interdependence. In contrast, Guernes de Pont-Sainte-Maxence derived much of his material from Grim and William of Canterbury,[1] while John of Salisbury apparently used the work of William of Canterbury and the Lambeth Anonymous in the composition of his own short Life.[2]

Most aspects of this hagiographical literature have already been carefully studied, but the biographers' use of primary epistolary material has so far not been the subject of any extensive investigation.[3] Yet the most important of the early biographers, namely Grim, William of Canterbury, and William FitzStephen, were substantially indebted to Becket letters, whether for information, or for quotations, or even sometimes for complete texts, and Guernes inserted translations of some of the letters into his metrical Life. Alone of the principal independent biographers, Herbert of Bosham wrote his Life after the completion of Alan of Tewkesbury's collection of the Becket correspondence, and he assumed that it would be available to his readers. Perhaps for this reason, his biography is less immediately dependent upon the letters than are the others, but there can be no doubt of his intimate knowledge of the correspondence. The two short Lives by John of Salisbury and Alan of Tewkesbury, while not revealing any substantial derivation from the correspondence, were in fact compiled as introductions to the largest of the surviving collections, that is to say to Alan's collection.

A. EDWARD GRIM

The earliest and least circumstantial of the Lives was composed by Edward Grim in 1171–2.[4] Very little is known about the author beyond what he himself relates in the course of the Life. He came to Canterbury on Thomas's return in December 1170, with the express purpose of seeing him, and was present in the Cathedral at

---

[1] Walberg, pp. 75–172, esp. p. 134.   [2] Ibid., pp. 173–85.

[3] For a general survey, cf. Robertson's introductions to the Lives, ed. cit.

[4] This date refers only to the composition of the basic text (to 'benedictus in saecula', *Mats.* II, p. 443). There were at least three further additions to the Life: 'Abhinc viduata ... sequamur ad vitam. Amen.' (ibid., pp. 443–8); 'Insimulatione ... fuit visio.' (ibid., pp. 448–50); and a small collection of letters (ibid., p. 450; cf. below, pp. 178–9).

the time of the murder. His courageous part in attempting to defend the archbishop when the others had fled, naturally commended him to the Becket party and earned him a place in Herbert of Bosham's catalogue of the *Eruditi Sancti Thome*,[1] and he was already a Master by that time. But when Herbert's list was compiled in 1186–7, Grim was dead; and, except for Herbert's notice that he was English and came from Cambridge, nothing further is known of him. He was certainly not a member of Becket's *familia* during the exile.

The Life was completed in its first recension in 1171–2, and is the shortest of the major biographies. Despite its chronological priority, it lacks the detail and accuracy of either William of Canterbury or William FitzStephen, although it has its own intrinsic interest. The author's fame and his personal role, and the later use of his work by Guernes and Elias of Evesham, impart a significance to this Life. On some points Grim's record is valuable, as in his account of the murder, of which he was a witness, and on Thomas's period in the service of Osbert Huit-Deniers[2] and of his friendship with Richer de l'Aigle.[3] His record is circumstantial on the election of Becket[4] and on the Councils of Westminster, Clarendon, and Northampton,[5] yet it is surpassed in value by the versions provided by William of Canterbury, William FitzStephen, and Herbert of Bosham. Indeed in certain respects his account is defective: he makes no mention of the legations or interviews with the king during Becket's exile, and he places the coronation of the Young King four years too early, immediately following Becket's arrival at Pontigny.[6] On such matters as these therefore, Grim had seemingly little direct knowledge of the events which he described. But a certain precision is attained in his account by the use of letters and documents to supplement the otherwise sparse details. His is the earliest narrative account to reveal knowledge and use of specific items of correspondence, thus setting a precedent which was followed by later and more eminent writers. It is this feature which lends an additional quality to an otherwise brief and unreliable narrative. Six items, in addition to the earliest known text of Becket's Pontigny vision, are incorporated into the text of the *Vita*. Thus, Grim's selected clauses of the Constitutions of

---

[1] Ibid., III, pp. 529–30. [2] Ibid., II, p. 361. [3] Ibid., p. 359.
[4] Ibid., pp. 365–7. [5] Ibid., pp. 375–84 and 390–8.
[6] Ibid., pp. 406–7.

Clarendon are not taken from the official chirograph but from Becket's Vézelay letter condemning them;[1] his account of the coronation of the Young King contains the papal letter forbidding it;[2] the texts of the bishops' appeal against Becket[3] and the latter's reply to Foliot[4] are included in the meagre account of the exile, together with one of Becket's letters to Henry II;[5] and the archbishop's report to the Pope after his return from France is inserted into the account of the landing in England.[6]

These letters occur in all three complete copies of Grim's *Vita*,[7] and may therefore be regarded as part of his original composition. In one fourteenth-century manuscript three further letters have been inserted into his account of the coronation,[8] but their absence from all other versions suggests that they were added by a later hand. However, the three complete copies have brief interrelated appendices of letters concerning the murder, the Compromise of Avranches, and Becket's canonization. Thus, the mid-thirteenth-century Brit. Libr. MS Arundel 27 has four letters appended to the text,[9] and is itself defective at the end, breaking off abruptly in

[1] Ibid., p. 380, cf. *Fratres mei*, ibid., V, ep. 198, esp. p. 394.

[2] Ibid., II, pp. 406–7: *Illius dignitatis*; cf. ibid., V, ep. 169.

[3] Ibid., II, pp. 408–9: *Que uestro pater*; cf. ibid., V, ep. 205.

[4] Ibid., II, pp. 409–12; *Mirandum et uehementer*; cf. ibid., V, ep. 224.

[5] Ibid., II, pp. 419–21: *Desiderio desideraui*; cf. ibid., V, ep. 154.

[6] Ibid., II, pp. 422–6: *Quam iustis*; cf. ibid., VII, ep. 723.

[7] For MSS of the Life, cf. Hardy, II, pp. 333–4, though he is mistaken in saying (p. 334, n.) that Brit. Libr. MS Cotton Vitellius C.xii contains the same text as MS Cotton Vespasian E.x. The complete text survives only in: Brit. Libr. MSS Arundel 27 (s. xiii), fos. 1ra–48va; Cotton Vespasian E.x (s. xiv), fos. 200r–261r; and Cotton Vitellius C. xii (s. xv), fos. 254vb–280rb. Cambridge Trinity College MS O.5.39 (s. xvii), Part II, is a copy of Arundel 27, and may therefore be discounted. Of the medieval MSS, Arundel 27 and Vespasian E.x are the best, while the otherwise quite good text in Vitellius C.xii is weakened by the interpolation of the 'Saracen Legend' concerning Becket's descent (cf. *Mats.* II, pp. 553–8). Brit. Libr. MS Addit. 16,607 (s. xiii), fos. 1r–16v, is a fragmentary abbreviation of the *Vita*, with interpolations, which is textually unreliable. The fragment contained in Brit. Libr. MS Cotton Julius D.xi (s. xiv), fos. 94r–98r, includes only the account of Becket's birth together with the interpolated 'Saracen Legend': 'Electus igitur . . . gratiosum'; cf. *Mats.* II, pp. 453–8 and 357, n. a. For two further copies of the legend, cf. Brit. Libr. MSS Cotton Julius D. vi, fos. 157v–160v, and Harleian 978, fos. 114va–116rb.

[8] Brit. Libr. MS Cotton Vespasian E. x, fos. 226v–233v: *Licet commendabiles, Oportuerat uos* and *Fratres mei* (*Mats.* VII, epp. 701, 700; V, ep. 198); cf. *Mats.* II, p. 407, n.1: Robertson's notes are slightly inaccurate.

[9] Brit. Libr. MS Arundel 27, fos. 46va–48vb: *Apostolatui uestro, Ab humane, Vestre placuit*, and *Eram magnificentie* (*Mats.* VII, epp. 740, 734, 736, and 737). The MS finishes abruptly with the words 'et porrectum' at the end of fo. 48vb.

mid-sentence; the fourteenth-century Brit. Libr. MS Cotton Vespasian E. X has an appendix agreeing with the Arundel MS, but adding a further group of seven letters, followed by Alan of Tewkesbury's Life;[1] and the fifteenth-century Brit. Libr. MS Cotton Vitellius C. XII has an appendix containing four of the same eleven letters.[2] This group of letters certainly represents an addition to the Life, but whether from Grim's hand or not it is now very difficult to say, especially since there is no twelfth-century manuscript still surviving. Yet, the fact that the three best manuscripts contain the whole or part of the Appendix suggests an early association with the *Vita*, although it is evident that the last two letters in the Vespasian MS must have been added at a later date, since they refer to the translation of Becket's relics in July 1220.[3]

The six letters which formed part of the text of the Life itself are of special interest here. None of the six is peculiar to Grim; and all are found in other narrative accounts of the controversy, including Diceto's *Ymagines Historiarum*, Hoveden's *Chronica*, and William of Canterbury's *Vita et Passio*. But it is evident that these versions were not derived from Grim's texts, for he has many distinctive readings and abbreviations which are not repeated elsewhere. In Grim's Life, the three letters *Illius dignitatis*,[4] *Desiderio desideraui*,[5] and *Quam iustis*[6] are given in full but imperfect versions; the greater part of *Fratres mei* is omitted;[7] and *Que uestro*[8] and

---

[1] Brit. Libr. MS Cotton Vespasian E. x, fos. 254r–271r: *Qui fuerint primi, Fraternitati uestre, Et ipsa loci, Quoniam expectare, Redolet Anglia, Decens credendum* and *Ecclesie uestre* (*Mats.* VII, epp. 751, 753, 763, 774, 785, (—), and 808; *Decens credendum* is apparently still unpublished). The appendix is completed by AlanT *Vita Sancti Thome*.

[2] Brit. Libr. MS Cotton Vitellius C. xii, fos. 278vb–280rb: *Apostolatui uestro, Ab humane, Vestre placuit*, and *Quoniam expectare*.

[3] *Decens credendum* (unprinted) and *Ecclesie uestre* (*Mats.* VII, ep. 808).

[4] *Mats.* II, pp. 406–7.

[5] Ibid., pp. 419–21.

[6] Ibid., pp. 422–6.

[7] Cf. *Mats.* V, ep. 198. Since the standard Rolls Series edition of the Lives is being used in the textual comparisons which follow, the classicized spellings of that work are retained in the footnote references below. In Grim's version the following passages are omitted: pp. 392–4, 'Thomas ... praesertim his', and pp. 394–7, 'Et alia ... instanter'.

[8] Cf. ibid., V, ep. 205; the following passages are omitted in Grim: p. 408, 'Venerabili ... obedientiam'; p. 409, 'et spiritualibus ... sustinuit', 'quo ... omittitis', 'quo ... scribitis', and 'Quod is quam ... concludat'; pp. 409–10, 'Nos quidem ... inuenitur', 'et sic agendo ... obtiniret', 'in familiarem ... complacere et', and 'vos in eam ... gaudere'; pp. 410–11, 'Quas retributionis ... accrescat'; p. 411, 'quam ... regna', 'ipsumque ... sollicitant', 'et totum ...

Mirandum et uehementer[1] are considerably abbreviated by the omission of single words and numerous small sections, and in some passages in these two letters the text is different from the version generally received.[2] In many instances, therefore, the text is so emended that it is impossible to discover its source. But *Desiderio desideraui* is an interesting exception. When Grim's text of this letter is collated with copies in other sources, it is revealed that it has some readings which agree with peculiarities in the Foliot textual tradition.[3] This discovery is surprising in view of Grim's connection with the Becket circle, with ready access to Canterbury sources during the period of composition.

While it has proved impossible to link Grim's letters with any known tradition by textual analysis, comparison with the Valli-

---

[1] Cf. ibid., V, ep. 224; the following passages are omitted in Grim: p. 512, 'et timore . . . postposito', 'homini . . . dejicere'; p. 513, 'quas . . . accepi', 'Ut . . . proferamus', 'Nunquid . . . confugimus', 'nostrorum . . . efficacissimum', 'non . . . exemplo', and 'Sed . . . praesumis'; p. 514, 'Male . . . offendere', 'Et . . . tamen', 'Ad reliqua transeamus', and 'et consiliarii . . . justificatus sum'; p. 515, 'regem . . . correctionis', 'enim patris', 'saevissima', 'clavem teneo', and 'Ut autem . . . (p. 516) religiosis'; p. 516, 'voluisti', 'ipse videris', 'ejus non multum', 'Esto . . . oratio', 'Absit . . . Christi', and 'quam scribis . . . respondeo quod'; p. 517, 'ecclesiasticas . . . solet', 'Cum . . . decidere', 'Praetaxatis . . . cernere', 'Illud . . . praedicare', and 'Sustinete . . . intelligis'; p. 518, 'Sed fortassis . . . sanguine', 'de . . . paucis', 'Verum . . . nimis', 'quis . . . relinquuntur', 'ut dicis', and 'me praeiudicio . . . ardet'; p. 519, 'illis . . . dicit', 'filii . . . omnes', 'ad Moysem', 'Et de eo . . . ad sacerdotes', and 'dominus noster'; pp. 519–20, 'Inde scriptum est . . . alioquin'; p. 520, 'in . . . dicens', 'Ad hoc . . . hactenus', 'rege . . . obsecro', 'et . . . justitia', and 'Valeat . . . vestra'.

[2] E.g., in *Que uestro pater* (ibid., V, p. 411) Grim's version reads 'quod si per vos illum animi sui indignatio subvertat, in threnis totus ire poteritis, et oculis vestris lacrymarum fontem nulla ratione negare . . .', instead of 'Quod si per vos acciderit, in threnos totus ire poteritis, et lacrymarum fontem oculis vestris de caetero negare nulla quidem ratione poteritis.'

[3] Ibid., II, pp. 419–21, cf. *Mats.* V, pp. 278–82. Using this standard edition as a basis of reference, the Foliot MSS and Grim agree on the following textual variants: ibid., p. 278, n. 7, read 'essem' for 'agerem'; p. 279, n. 8, omit 'et obsequium'; n. 9, omit 'teneor'; p. 280, n. 4, read 'conterendos' for 'coercendos'; n. 11, read 'et aliorum' for 'aliorumque'; p. 281, n. 2, read 'totum reducant' for 'totum perducant' (Cave 348 reads 'tota reducant'); n. 11 omit 'etiam'; p. 282, n. 4, read 'quoque' for 'etiam'; n. 5, read 'possessiones . . . pertinentes' for 'possessionesque . . . pertinentes'; n. 8, omit 'que'; n. 10, omit 'officio . . . exigit'; n. 11, omit 'nostras'; and n. 13, omit 'salvo'.

---

subvertere', 'si placet . . . vestrae', 'si placet . . . omnibus', 'vos hac . . . permittunt', 'experiri . . . sunt', and 'Quae . . . formidanda'; p. 412, 'paci . . . populis', 'exhiberi . . . paratus est', 'colla . . . subdentem', and 'Non . . . laudabile est'; p. 413, 'praepostere . . . suspensionis aut', 'ante . . . controversiam', 'Ordo judiciorum . . . cognoscere', 'et commissas . . . sanctaeque', 'et extendere . . . ecclesias', and 'diem Ascensionis . . . parcatis'.

celliana Appendix, discussed above, reveals a striking similarity of content and order between the two. If Grim's letters are divided into two groups, letters included in the text (Grim A) and letters appended to it (Grim B: the Grim Appendix), the following correspondence is discovered:

Grim A, 1–9 = Vall. 3, 10, 4, 6, 2, 13, 11, 12, and 3 (Vall. 1*a* and 1*b*)

Grim B, 1 to 9 = Vall. 15–23 (Vall. III)

Thus, all but nos. 1, 5, 7–9, and 14 in the Vallicelliana Appendix occur either included in, or appended to, the text of Grim; and the absence of Vall. 1 (Constitutions of Clarendon) can be explained by the fact that Grim took an abstract of the Constitutions from *Fratres mei* (Vall. 3). Grim B, nos. 10 and 11, which relate to the translation of Becket's relics in 1220, are evidently a late addition to the common source, and are absent from the Vallicelliana manuscript. We are confronted here with an undoubted relationship between the Grim Appendix and the Vallicelliana Appendix, Part III, and a probable relationship between Grim A and Vall. Parts I*a* and I*b*; but the nature of the relationship is difficult to elucidate, since no manuscript earlier than the thirteenth century survives, and in the case of Grim we have to contend with late and possibly contaminated texts. It is certainly impossible that the whole of the Vallicelliana Appendix could have been derived from Grim; the most likely explanation of their undoubted relationship is that two originally separate small collections lie at the base of both sources: a collection of 'Becket dispute' material, corresponding with Grim A and Vall. I*a* and *b*, and a collection of 'Becket triumph' material, corresponding with Grim B and Vall. III. Such a possibility would explain both the similarities and the discrepancies between them. The discovery of the Vallicelliana Appendix throws light on a highly problematical area of Becket studies, and it is to be much regretted that its fragmentary state, combined with the late date of the most complete version of Grim's *Vita*, makes the attempt to reach any more positive conclusions a perilous undertaking. In the light of the existence of the Vallicelliana Appendix, however, it is possible to argue that Grim made use of two specially assembled collections of Becket materials in the completion of his *Vita*, and it is even possible that the *Vita* was substantially completed before these letters were introduced into it. The structure of the composition seems to be virtually independent of the letters and their omission would hardly be noticeable. It is more likely that relevant texts were inserted into an already-existing narrative than that the narrative was composed around a set of already selected letters.

B. WILLIAM OF CANTERBURY

William of Canterbury began his Life of Becket slightly later than Grim, and made extensive use of epistolary material. In this case too, little is known of the author, except that he was raised to the diaconate by Becket[1] and composed a large collection of Miracles, begun in June 1172[2] and presented to the king some time in 1174.[3] His biography of the martyr was also composed between 1172 and 1174. Magnusson, editor of the *Thomas Saga Erkibyskups*, suggested that William may have been an Irishman,[4] on evidence in the Book of Miracles which suggests an unusual interest in Irish affairs, including the king's campaign in Ireland, and recounts the details of numerous miracles performed through the martyr's intercession in the island. But no more conclusive evidence concerning him has survived.

William's Life of Becket ranks as one of the best of the biographies, written at Canterbury by one who, though he had not known Becket well, yet had access to all the records available after the archbishop's death, and who was a leading member of the group which helped to create the legend of the glorious martyr.[5] He may indeed have witnessed the murder, though he makes no mention of it, and there is no evidence that he had any personal knowledge of the earlier part of the archbishop's career. His work is a combination of documentary evidence and reliable hearsay. He provides a general account of Becket's splendour as chancellor,[6] and is reliable

---

[1] Cf. *Mats.* I, p. 2.

[2] According to the letter of dedication to Henry II, the work of compilation was undertaken seventeen months after the archbishop's murder, in May–June, 1172: ibid., p. 138; cf. Walberg, p. 116.

[3] *Mats.* I, pp. 137–9. The exact date of presentation cannot be certainly established, but Henry II's Canterbury pilgrimage in July 1174 would have provided a suitable opportunity for such a gesture: cf. p. 193 and n. 1, below.

[4] E. Magnusson, ed., *Thomas Saga Erkibyskups*, RS 65, London, II (1883), p. lxxxvi.

[5] The Book of Miracles contains references to 'Brother William' interviewing those who came to Canterbury with tales of miraculous cures effected through the martyr's intercession: *Mats.* I, pp. 227, 395, 397, and 524.

[6] Ibid., pp. 5–6.

and accurate on the Councils of Westminster,[1] Clarendon,[2] and Northampton,[3] though less circumstantial than the eye-witnesses, William FitzStephen and Herbert of Bosham. His account of the exile is fairly full, though the chronology is sometimes faulty: the embassy of John of Oxford and Richard of Ilchester to the Emperor in 1165 is placed too late;[4] and the legation of Vivian and Gratian is inserted before the Conference of Montmirail instead of after it.[5] On the other hand, his accounts of the meeting at Fréteval,[6] Becket's return to England,[7] and the murder[8] are all good, though inferior to those provided by FitzStephen.

But the most significant aspect of the composition for the present study is its reliance upon documentary evidence in one form or another: the greater part of the narrative is closely dependent upon authentic letters of the controversy, some of which are inserted almost in full; and the very interesting exposition of the dispute over clerical immunity, which is introduced into the account of the Council of Clarendon, is an almost verbatim conflation of passages from two of the most important canonical sources of the time, namely Gratian and Rufinus.[9] Substantial parts of no less than nineteen letters and documents have been inserted into the Life, including the full texts of both the Constitutions of Clarendon and the decrees of 1169 and one otherwise unknown letter.[10] A part of *Fraternitatis uestre* is included in the account of the proscription of Becket's family and household,[11] sections from *Mandatum uestrum* are given to illustrate the attitude of Gilbert Foliot,[12] and extracts

[1] Ibid., pp. 13–14.
[2] Ibid., pp. 15–23.
[3] Ibid., pp. 29–39.
[4] Ibid., pp. 52–3; the account of the Council of Würzburg is placed immediately before the text of the royal decrees of 1169.
[5] Ibid., pp. 72–3.
[6] Ibid., p. 84.
[7] Ibid., pp. 86–7 and 99–121.
[8] Ibid., pp. 131–3.
[9] Ibid., pp. 25–8. For a full discussion of this most interesting passage, cf. C. Duggan, 'The Reception of Canon Law in England in the Later-Twelfth Century', *Proceedings of the Second International Congress of Medieval Canon Law, Monumenta Iuris Canonici, Series C; Subsidia*, I, Vatican City (1965), pp. 359–90.
[10] See Table 2, below.
[11] *Mats.* I, pp. 47–8, 'Domino vertente . . . incommodo'; cf. ibid., V, ep. 223, pp. 495–6.
[12] Ibid., I, pp. 38–9, 'Vestrae supplicandum . . . nati sumus'; cf. ibid., V, ep. 108, pp. 206–8.

from *Non ob gratiam*[1] and *Eam quam*[2] record papal support for the archbishop in his relations both with Roger of York and with his own suffragans. Again, selections from relevant letters are inserted into the account of Becket's proceedings at Vézelay,[3] and the account of the meeting of king and archbishop between Gisors and Trie on 18 November 1167 is composed entirely of an anonymous report of the conference, which William has simply divided into sections and provided with rubricated headings.[4] A reference to the appointment of Rotrou of Rouen and Bernard of Nevers as commissioners for the reconciliation between Henry and Becket includes one of the letters of appointment,[5] as well as two versions of the letter *Nouerit industria*, ordering the pronouncement of an interdict in all of Henry's territories should the peace negotiations fail.[6] The papal prohibition of the coronation of the Young King, *Illius dignitatis*, follows a report of the ceremony,[7] and part of Henry's letter to Rotrou of Rouen and Bernard of Nevers is given before the description of the Peace of Fréteval,[8] while the royal writ announcing the peace is placed immediately after it.[9] Finally, the account of Becket's return to England contains the texts of the papal letters of censure, *Oportuerat uos* and *Licet commendabiles*,[10] and a long extract from Becket's own report of his reception.[11]

In addition to these explicit quotations, it is evident from his knowledge of contents and brief excerpts that William made use of many other items of correspondence. His references to the papal

---

[1] Ibid., I, pp. 59–60, 'Sane indubitanter . . . obedire'; cf. ibid., V, ep. 51, p. 87.

[2] Ibid., I, p. 60, 'Alexander papa . . . excessum is . . . (text breaks off here); cf. ibid., V, ep. 158, pp. 296–7.

[3] Ibid., I, pp. 61–3, 'contrarium tam . . . ostendas' from *Fratres mei*: cf. V, ep. 198, pp. 395–7; and 'Quoniam novimus . . . tibi vale' from *Celebre prouerbium*: cf. V, ep. 199, pp. 398–9.

[4] Ibid., I, pp. 66–70, *Quia te super statu*; cf. VI, ep. 332, pp. 256–60. This letter has been attributed to John of Salisbury (ibid., VI, p. 256, n. a), but William ascribes it to 'quidam oculata veritate loquens', and in AlanT(B), II.27 it appears with the heading 'Amicus amico'.

[5] *Mats.* I, pp. 78–9, *Quoniam de uestre*; cf. VII, ep. 628, pp. 210–12.

[6] Ibid., I, pp. 80–1; cf. VII, epp. 629 and 630.

[7] Ibid., I, p. 82; cf. V, ep. 169, p. 323.

[8] Ibid., I, p. 83, 'Sane novimus . . . exsequemur' from *Super his que*; cf. VI, ep. 255, p. 80. The address and date of this letter are uncertain: in AlanT(B), II. 41 it is addressed 'cuidam cardinali vel coetui cardinalium', but in Vat. 195 it is addressed 'Rotroco Rothomagensi archiepiscopo'.

[9] *Mats.* I, p. 85, *Sciatis quod*; cf. VII, ep. 690, pp. 346–7.

[10] Ibid., I, pp. 89–95; cf. VII, epp. 700 and 701.

[11] Ibid., I, pp. 95–9, *Quam iustis*; cf. VII, ep. 723.

requests to Rotrou of Rouen, the Empress Matilda and the Bishops of Hereford and London to approach the king in Becket's favour suggest a knowledge of the letters sent to them;[1] and his account of the mission of William of Pavia and Cardinal Otto is clearly dependent upon reports written at the time, even to the extent of small verbal borrowings from *Solliciti de statu*,[2] *Desiderio magno*[3] and *Post discessum uestrum*.[4] In a similar way, his description of the legation of Vivian and Gratian is derived from three relevant letters,[5] while his account of the legation of Rotrou of Rouen and Bernard of Nevers merely paraphrases the first papal commission addressed to them.[6]

Wherever William inserted complete letters into his narrative, he treated the texts with great respect. Most of such documents are given in full, and *Super his que*[7] provides the only example of drastic curtailment. Even where there is substantial abbreviation, as in *Celebre prouerbium*,[8] *Mandatum uestrum*,[9] *Fraternitatis*

---

[1] Ibid., I, pp. 57–8, 'Sed et eundem super eodem Romanus pontifex per Rothomagensem archiepiscopum, per imperatricem quondam Romanorum matrem ejus, per Herefordensem et Londoniensem, multa prece sollicitavit'; for the papal letter to Rotrou, cf. V, ep. 182; for that to the Bishops of Hereford and London, cf. V. ep. 93. There is no surviving copy of any papal correspondence with the Empress Matilda relating to the Becket dispute.

[2] Ibid., I, p. 64, 'potius elegit . . . consequendo': cf. VI, ep. 322, p. 230; and ibid., I, p. 64, 'dicens quia . . . gloriam', which is a close paraphrase of VI, ep. 322, p. 229, 'Non enim . . . gloria'.

[3] Ibid., I, p. 64: compare 'Adeo autem . . . ingenio' with VI, ep. 314, p. 213, 'quia (novit Deus) . . . ingenio'; and ibid., I, p. 65: compare 'Unde cum in Franciam . . . dejiciebantur' with VI, ep. 314, p. 212, 'videte litteras . . . voluntatem suam'.

[4] Ibid., I, pp. 65–6: compare 'sententiam suam . . . laceraretur' with VI, ep. 307, p. 201, 'eum praedicto . . . laceraret'.

[5] Ibid., I, p. 72: compare 'missis duobus . . . advocato' with VI, ep. 476 (*Magnificentie tue*), p. 538, 'dilectos filios . . . discretos'; ibid., I, p. 72: compare 'Qui cum litteris . . . praedixerat' with VII, ep. 564 (*Sepius nuntios*), pp. 83–4, 'Cum vero . . . dixeramus'; and ibid., I, p. 73: compare 'Quamuis enim . . . consequatur' with VII, ep. 565 (*Euocati a domino*), pp. 86–7, 'Siquidem . . . consequatur'. This last passage was also quoted by Diceto, I, p. 335.

[6] *Mats*. I, p. 76: compare 'Unde . . . restituerat' with VII, ep. 623 (*Carissimus in Christo*), p. 199, 'Quocirca . . . eorum'; and ibid., I, pp. 76–7, 'Archiepiscopum quoque . . . dimittere' with VII, pp. 200–1, 'Archiepiscopum etiam . . . absolvat'.

[7] Cf. ibid., VI, ep. 255; William's version omits: pp. 78–80, 'Super his quae . . . evidentissime', and pp. 80–1, 'Verum ipsum . . . permissum'.

[8] Cf. ibid., V, ep. 199, pp. 397–8; William's version omits 'Thomas . . . permaneat. Unde'.

[9] Cf. ibid., V, ep. 108, pp. 203–6; William's version omits 'Patri suo . . . pollicetur. Unde'.

uestre[1], and *Quia te super statu*,[2] the significance of the letter is not lost, and no charge of suppression can be laid against the author on this score. There is no evidence that William attempted to censor his material, except that his selection of letters tends in emphasis to favour Becket rather than the episcopal opposition, as one would expect. Even so, the royal case is not entirely unrepresented: the king's position is illustrated by the two sets of Constitutions and by the letters *Meminerit excellentia* and *Super his que*, while that of the bishops is reflected in Foliot's letter *Mandatum uestrum*.

William's Life of Becket was composed before the completion of the great collections of the correspondence of Foliot and of John of Salisbury, and before Alan of Tewkesbury had begun the work of editing the letters of Becket himself. But William had evident access to a large supply of Becket materials, and selections from this source formed the major basis of his biography. With the exception of the one item which is peculiar to William's biography, all his letters are found in Alan's compilation and most are found in the Vatican Collection (the principal collection in the Vatican Family discussed above), and about half of them are also found in Foliot manuscripts. It is not surprising to discover, when William's letters are collated with the copies preserved in other extant collections, that his texts almost invariably follow the Becket rather than the Foliot tradition where there is textual conflict between them. The connection is quite unambiguous in the case of the 1169 constitutions,[3] *Mandatum uestrum*[4], and *Quam iustis*;[5] and it is

---

[1] Cf. ibid., V, ep. 223; William's version omits: pp. 490–5, 'Thomas . . . praescitus', and pp. 496–512, 'Si laudas . . . ecclesia'.

[2] Cf. ibid., VI, ep. 332, p. 260; William's version omits 'Illa rogavit . . . triumphabit'.

[3] William preserves in full the Becket version of the decrees as found in AlanT.

[4] Cf. *Mats.* V, ep. 168, pp. 206–8. In both William's text and in the Becket tradition the following textual agreements are found: p. 207, n. 5, read 'sequestrari' for 'projici'; n. 6, insert 'sed'; n. 7, read 'restituit sanitatem vulneri saepe medicantis operatio' for 'cum sanet vulnus saepissime caute'; n. 8, omit 'Unum . . . perturbetis'; n. 10, read 'cito cum volet' for 'tempore accepto'; n. 14, read 'se demum permittit' for 'scit demum'; n. 15, read 'verecundatur' for 'erubescit'; n. 16, read 'tolerandus' for 'leniendus'; p. 208, n. 1, read 'invehit exhibita in tempus' for 'infert vel exhibita vel in tempus exhibenda'; n. 3, read 'Non enim est dubium . . . perduci' for 'Numquid non severitati . . . fluctuum'; n. 7, read 'severitati deservisse' for 'severitatis partibus institisse'.

[5] Cf. ibid., VII, ep. 723, pp. 401–7. In both William's text and in the Becket tradition the following textual agreements are found: p. 401, n. 6, read 'accitis' for 'associatis'; n. 7, read 'initam' for 'initura'; p. 402, n. 11, insert 'potestatis'; p. 403, n. 3, read 'patiebatur' for 'patiebantur'; n. 6, read 'ingrederemur' for

sufficiently clear in all the remaining letters.[1] But this is exactly what one would expect from an author working at Canterbury in the years following the murder. Of more precise interest is the discovery that William's texts tend to reflect readings in the Vatican group of collections rather than those in the more developed edition which Alan of Tewkesbury prepared, thus supporting the view that William used earlier and perhaps less corrected versions than those transmitted by Alan. It is clear from evidence in the Cotton MS Claudius B. II that many letters were still being collated and corrected at a fairly late stage in the preparation of the mature edition. In fact, William of Canterbury's texts do not exactly or consistently reflect the readings of any single collection now extant; but, where there is significant variation between the Vatican Family texts and those in the various recensions of Alan of Tewkesbury's work, William's readings are closer to the former. This is certainly true of extracts from *Fratres mei*,[2] *Celebre prouerbium*[3], and *Quoniam de uestre*,[4] though the evidence is less conclusive in the case of the longer letters included.

C. WILLIAM FITZSTEPHEN

The third of the independent authors to exploit the Becket correspondence in the preparation of a biography was William Fitz-Stephen. Once more, little is known of the author except what he records in his introduction, but this reveals him as a close associate of the archbishop from the time of Becket's elevation to the archiepiscopate. William was his chaplain, sub-deacon, and even

---

[1] With the possible exception of *Oportuerat uos*, where William's text is far from consistent, following now one version, now another; cf. *Mats.* I, pp. 89–92, and ibid., VII, ep. 700, pp. 360–4.

[2] Cf. ibid., V, ep. 198, pp. 395–7. William's text and the Vatican Family agree on the following details: p. 395, n. 5, omit 'penitus'; p. 396, n. 1, read 'detinet' for 'tenet'; n. 4, read 'innodamus' for 'innodavimus'; n. 5, omit 'atque'; n. 6, insert 'et'; n. 8 insert 'apud'; n. 9, read 'severissima' for 'saevissima'.

[3] Cf. ibid., ep. 199, pp. 398–9. William's text and the Vatican Family agree on the following details: p. 398, n. 6, read 'et omni iuri canonico' for 'omnique canonico iuri'; n. 7, read 're etiam ipsa' for 're ipsa'; p. 399, n. 2, insert 'praecipimus et'.

[4] Cf. ibid., VII, p. 210. William's text and the Vatican Family agree on the following details: p. 210, line 19, omit 'litterarum'; p. 211, n. 1, read 'semoto' for 'remoto'; line 3, read 'nobis' for 'vobis'; p. 212, line 8, read 'habeatis' for 'ad hibeatis'.

'ingrederentur'; n. 7, read 'navem' for 'in navem'; p. 404, n. 1, read 'inurere' for 'incurrere'; n. 5, insert 'et'; n. 6, insert 'ad'; p. 405, n. 5, insert 'factum'; n. 6, omit 'se'; n. 8, insert 'nobis'; n. 9, insert 'cum'; n. 10, insert 'inde'.

judicial assistant;[1] he was present at the Councils of Clarendon and Northampton,[2] and was banished with the rest of Becket's household at the end of 1164; but, like Philip of Calne,[3] he earned his pardon from the king by the composition of a rhyming prayer for the king's use, which he presented to Henry in person.[4] He seems to have rejoined his old master on Becket's return from exile in December 1170, since he was a witness of the murder[5] and of the interviews with the knights which immediately preceded it.[6] He certainly had much greater personal knowledge of the beginning of the controversy than either of the authors discussed so far, yet there is no reference to him elsewhere in the Becket literature, either in the letters, the chronicles, or the other biographies, nor does his Life seem to have been used by any contemporary writer, save Ralph de Diceto,[7] though extracts from it were interpolated into Elias of Evesham's *Quadrilogus* at the beginning of the thirteenth century.[8] Although he would obviously have ranked as an *eruditus*, Herbert of Bosham does not mention him in his catalogue of the *Eruditi Sancti Thome*. His subsequent career remains a mystery, unless we accept his identification with the man of the same name who was Sheriff of Gloucester in 1171[9] and an Itinerant

---

[1] Ibid., III, p. 1, 'boni archipraesulis et martyris Thomae vitam et passionem ego, Willelmus, filius Stephani, scribere curavi: ejusdem domini mei concivis, clericus, et convictor; et ad partem sollicitudinis ejus oris ipsius invitatis alloquio, fui in cancellaria ejus dictator; in capella, eo celebrante, subdiaconus; sedente eo ad cognitionem causarum, epistolarum et instrumentorum quae offerebantur lector, et aliquarum, eo quandoque jubente, causarum patronus.'

[2] Ibid., pp. 1–2, 'Concilio Northamptoniae habito, ubi maximum fuit rerum momentum, cum ipso interfui; passionem ejus Cantuariae inspexi; caetera plurima, quae hic scribuntur, oculis vidi, auribus audivi; quaedam a consciis didici relatoribus.'

[3] Ibid., III, p. 101.

[4] Ibid., pp. 78–81.

[5] Ibid., p. 2.

[6] Ibid., pp. 132–5.

[7] Cf. Diceto, I, pp. 342–5.

[8] Cf. *Mats.* IV, pp. 270, 272, 273, 320, 323, 375, 382, 393, and 394.

[9] A William FitzStephen appears in the Pipe Rolls for the reign of Henry II as Sheriff of Gloucester, first in company with his brother Ralph, from Michaelmas 1171 to Michaelmas 1175 (PR 18 Hen. II, p. 118; 19 Hen. II, p. 150; 20 Hen. II, p. 20; 21 Hen. II, p. 35), and then alone, from Michaelmas 1175 to 1189 (PR 22 Hen. II, p. 123; 23 Hen. II, p. 41; 24 Hen. II, p. 55; 25 Hen. II, p. 88; 26 Hen. II, p. 112; 27 Hen. II, p. 117; 28 Hen. II, p. 23; 29 Hen. II, p. 92; 30 Hen. II, p. 59; 31 Hen. II, p. 143; 32 Hen. II, p. 118; 33 Hen. II, p. 135; 34 Hen. II, p. 106).

Justice in 1191;[1] but there is no evidence to decide this question one way or the other.

FitzStephen certainly had close links with London; like Becket, he was born in London, and his description of the city, which sometimes appears prefaced to his Life of Becket and sometimes separately,[2] is one of the best accounts of daily life in the capital surviving from the Middle Ages; and the earliest manuscript of his biography appears as an introduction to a collection of correspondence derived from the archives of Gilbert Foliot, Bishop of London.[3] Nor is it without significance that the only twelfth-century writer to use his work was Ralph de Diceto, successively Archdeacon of Middlesex and Dean of St. Paul's. This obvious association of the author with the circle of the Bishop of London in the years following the murder may explain the silence of Herbert of Bosham and the other biographers, since Foliot was a leader of the episcopal opposition to Becket and was deeply implicated in the events which led to the assassination.

FitzStephen's Life has been widely regarded as the best of Becket's biographies, and it has many claims to this title. It is generally very full and accurate, with a unique and circumstantial account of Becket's early life and training and of his career as chancellor;[4] the destruction of the adulterine castles early in Henry's reign, the rebuilding of the Tower of London, the splendid embassy to France in 1158, in which Becket peacefully gained control of the fortress of Gisors for the king, the Toulouse campaign of 1159, and the grandeur of Becket's court as chancellor are all described in detail. FitzStephen's account of the Council at

---

[1] He also appears as Itinerant Justice in Worcestershire, Shropshire, and Gloucestershire in 1175–6 (PR 22 Hen. II, pp. 36, 57, and 125); in Shropshire in 1176–7 (PR 23 Hen. II, p. 38); in Wiltshire and Oxfordshire in 1177–8 (PR 24 Hen. II, pp. 30 and 119); in Suffolk, Sussex, Essex and Hertfordshire, Buckinghamshire, Kent, and Surrey in 1178–9 (PR 25 Hen. II, pp. 7, 37, 55, 76, 118, and 123); in Worcestershire and Staffordshire in 1184–5 (PR 31 Hen. II, pp. 121 and 166); in Shropshire, Warwickshire and Leicestershire, Herefordshire, Gloucestershire, Staffordshire, and Worcestershire in 1186–7 (PR 33 Hen. II, pp. 64, 120, 132, 138, 150, and 218); and in Staffordshire, Shropshire, and Gloucestershire in 1187–8 (PR 34 Hen. II, pp. 49, 97, and 111). The identification of Becket's biographer with the sheriff and judge of the Pipe Rolls was first suggested by E. Foss in *A Biographical Dictionary of the Judges of England, 1066–1870*, London (1870), pp. 270a–71a, and it was accepted by Robertson (*Mats.* III, p. xv); but there is no evidence to support it.

[2] Ibid., III, pp. 2–13.

[3] Oxford Bodl. MS Douce, 287, fos. 2vb–36vb.   [4] *Mats.* III, pp. 15–35.

Clarendon is not quite as detailed as that given by the Canterbury biographers, but, in contrast, his report of the Council of Northampton is superb. Like Herbert of Bosham later, FitzStephen includes a close account of the day by day developments at the Council; and, though there are some discrepancies between these two versions,[1] their over-all picture is the same, and FitzStephen's dating is the more accurate. His account of the exile is chronologically unsound,[2] but he records most useful information about contemporary events in England[3] and at the royal court.[4]

There is one serious textual problem to be resolved before a final evaluation of this Life can be made, since it survives in two versions, of which one contains much more material antipathetic to the king and to the bishops than the other. One version (A) has no less than thirty-eight passages, varying in length from a few words to four pages in the printed standard edition,[5] mainly reflecting in some way upon the conduct and character of Henry II and the bishops who opposed Becket, in addition to the long poetical

---

[1] Cf. Knowles, *Episcopal Colleagues*, pp. 163–6.

[2] His account of Foliot's excommunication on April 13 1169 (*Mats.* III, pp. 87–92) is placed far too early, before notice of the first sentence against Jocelin of Salisbury in mid-1166 (ibid., p. 92); the meeting between Henry II and some of the exiled clerks of the archbishop at Angers on 1 May 1166 (pp. 98–102) is put after the conferences of Montmirail and Montmartre, which took place on 6 January and 18 November 1169 respectively (pp. 96–7), and it is immediately followed by the account of the coronation of the Young King on 14 June 1170 (p. 103).

[3] Of particular interest are his accounts of the behaviour of Foliot when he heard rumours of his excommunication (p. 88), the dramatic publication of the sentence in St Paul's Cathedral (pp. 89–90), the delivery of papal letters to the Archbishop of York and the Bishop of London forbidding the coronation on the Saturday before the ceremony (p. 103), the inquiry concerning those who had sent money abroad to Becket (p. 106), the alleged confession of Richard de Haliwell (p. 114), the behaviour of Geoffrey Ridel, Richard of Ilchester, and Gilbert Foliot after the arrival of Becket in England (pp. 120–1), Becket's reception in Rochester, London, and Southwark (p. 122), and the inquiry made by Randulf de Broc and Gervase of Cornhill relating to those who had welcomed Becket in London (p. 125).

[4] Cf. his accounts of the suppression of Becket's name in the services in the royal chapel (pp. 83–4), the meeting at Chinon (pp. 98–102), the discussion between Henry and Roger of Worcester (pp. 104–6), and the king's behaviour on learning of the murder of the archbishop (pp. 128–9).

[5] Ibid., p. 9, n. 7; p. 15, n. 2; p. 26, n. 4; p. 36, n. 14; p. 42, n. 1; p. 46, n. 4; p. 47, n. 4; p. 59, n. 3; p. 67, n. 7; p. 77, n. 1; p. 78, n. 2; p. 83, n. 1; p. 85, n. 4; p. 92, n. 3; p. 93, n. 5; p. 97, n. 8; p. 102, n. 7; p. 103, n. 4; p. 109, n. 2; p. 112, n. 2; p. 114, n. 1; p. 115, nn. 3 and 8; p. 125, n. 5; p. 131, n. 7; p. 135, n. 1; p. 136, n. 5; p. 137, nn. 2 and 3; p. 138, n. 4; p. 139, n. 7; p. 140, n. 7; p. 143, n. 4; p. 146, n. 2; p. 149, nn. 12 and 13; p. 152, n. 4; and p. 154, n. 1.

prayer which FitzStephen composed for the king's use.[1] These passages are all missing from the alternative version (B), which also transposes other passages and inserts three small extracts from John of Salisbury's Life of Becket[2] and the first part of the anonymous compilation known as the *Summa Cause inter Thomam et Regem*,[3] found in Foliot sources; moreover, one thirteenth-century manuscript of Version B also contains an inserted reference to Ralph de Diceto as Dean of St. Paul's.[4]

Much of the character of this Life depends on whether or not the thirty-eight passages discovered in Version A, but absent from Version B, were part of FitzStephen's original composition or were inserted by a later hand, or whether indeed they were consciously suppressed in a later recension either by FitzStephen himself or by some other redactor. The problem of dating the Life raises similar difficulties, principally in assessing the significance of the extracts from John of Salisbury's work, the issue here depending on whether they were part of the original Life or whether they were interpolated at a subsequent stage. There is little external evidence, since no references to FitzStephen are found in other twelfth-century writings and the majority of the extant manuscripts are of comparatively late date of transcription.[5] And the internal evidence is scarcely more helpful. Various scholars have in the past accepted the John of Salisbury extracts as part of FitzStephen's original composition and therefore dated his work not earlier than mid-1176. Setting aside this doubtful point, the incidents inserted or omitted in FitzStephen's narrative are equally inconclusive. There are no references to important events after 1171: neither the Compromise of Avranches (1172) nor Henry II's pilgrimage to Canterbury in July 1174 is mentioned; and the elevation of William of Champagne to the primatial see of Reims in 1176 is omitted from

---

[1] Ibid., III, pp. 78–81.

[2] Ibid., III, p. 38, n. 3, 'Cum enim . . . informaret': cf. JohnS, ibid., II, pp. 306–7; III, p. 42, n. 5, 'Nihil . . . regnaturus': cf. II, p. 310; III, p. 71, n. 4, 'Sed haec omnia . . . seipsum': cf. II, p. 316.

[3] Ibid., III, p. 44, n. 1.

[4] Brit. Libr. MS Cotton Julius A. xi; cf. *Mats.* III, p. 59, n. 2.

[5] For a list of the surviving MSS, cf. Hardy, II, pp. 330–1, and for a brief discussion of their contents, cf. MB, *Foliot*, p. 16. For the fullest discussion so far, cf. Mary Cheney, 'William FitzStephen and his Life of Archbishop Thomas', C. N. L. Brooke, D. E. Luscombe, G. H. Martin and D. M. Owen, edd., *Church and Government in the Middle Ages*, Cambridge (1976), pp. 139–56.

the adulatory synopsis of his career.[1] As Mrs. Cheney has pointed out, the argument from silence in these instances is really no argument at all. The latest reference that can be dated is the informed comment that Robert Foliot was afterwards Bishop of Hereford— 'postea episcopus Herefordensis': and Robert was elected in April 1173 and consecrated in October 1174.[2] There is therefore nothing either in the text or in its known textual history which precludes the conclusion that Version A was brought to completion between February/March 1173 and late 1174. The reference to the 'magnus codex' at Canterbury, containing the English miracles of Becket, does not weaken this argument in any way.[3] It is clear from their resulting works that both Benedict (later of Peterborough) and William of Canterbury were engaged on the business of recording the miracles ascribed to Thomas from early 1171 and mid-1172 respectively,[4] although there is some uncertainty about their completion dates. The standard texts, excellently edited by Canon Robertson, properly record the fullest extent of the finished works in their most complete form, and this tends to obscure the intermediary stages of completeness through which essentially compilatory works of this nature evolved. Like most categories of Becket sources, these miracle-collections 'grew', as new material was added either by the original author or by unknown continuators; and the most recent version would naturally supersede its predecessor in later transmissions of the text. Although it is not possible to provide textual evidence to prove the point, it is likely that the canonization itself provoked the production of 1173 'editions' to edify the flood of pilgrims coming to the new martyr's tomb, and that Henry II's spectacular penance in the following

---

[1] *Mats.* III, p. 84.

[2] Ibid., p. 46; cf. M. Cheney, loc. cit., p. 153. This comment may, however, indicate no more than the special interest and knowledge of the scribe. Generally speaking, such prospective notes are conspicuously absent from FitzStephen's Life; and it is significant that the same comment is (again exceptionally) inserted into the rubric of *Non potest mihi* on fo. 84rb of the same manuscript by the same scribe.

[3] *Mats.* III, p. 151.

[4] Cf. *Mats.* I, pp. 137–546 and II, pp. 21–281 for the two texts. Both record the beginning of miracles immediately after the murder; and both comprise nothing more ambitious than the stringing-together of miracle-accounts, with authenticating letters where available. It is probable that Benedict's compilation was begun first, in early 1171, since there are first-person comments datable to Easter of that year (ibid., pp. 57 and 61), while William began his work some 17 months later, acting as chief assistant to an unnamed brother (ibid., I, p. 138).

year provided the occasion for expanded 1174 'editions'. In the case of William of Canterbury, it can persuasively be argued that an 1173/4 version of his *Miracles* existed, on the evidence of Montpelier École de Médecine MS 2; and it was arguably that version which was presented to Henry II at his own request, probably in connection with his Canterbury pilgrimage of July 1174.[1] The dating of Benedict's work is somewhat more problematic: although almost certainly begun before William's, its final completion was not achieved until 1202, by which time the original author was already dead.[2] Nevertheless, its manuscript-survival indicates a similarly evolving text. Walberg envisaged the existence of a first recension by mid-1174 at the latest,[3] and there is much to be said in favour of this theory. Two separate copies of Benedict's *Miracula* were despatched to the Cistercian monastery of Igny (although one never reached its intended recipients) by Odo, ex-Prior of Canterbury, who had left Christ Church in October 1175 to become Abbot of Battle;[4] while the second addition to Grim's *Life*, datable to October–26 November 1175, describes the new Prior

---

[1] For the letter of dedication, cf. ibid., I, pp. 137–9. The prologue to William's *VST* suggests that the *Miracula* was set aside after its initial compilation before being brought to formal completion (ibid., p. 2: 'miracula ejus, quae in schedulis occultabat incorrecta et imperfecta'); and the known textual history supports the view of two stages (at least) in the work. Montpellier École de Médecine MS 2 contains an earlier and shorter version, ending 'auxilium' and lacking more than 60 pages of the standard edition (ibid., pp. 482–546; for Robertson's description of this highly important MS, which derives from Clairvaux, cf. ibid., IV, pp. xxiv–xxvi; for his select collation, cf. ibid., pp. 422–53). There is nothing in the Montpellier copy which can be dated later than early 1174. The only other known text is in Winchester College MS 4, from which Robertson's full text was taken. It contains material dating from 1175–84. The dedicatory letter to Henry II occurs as the prologue to both texts.

[2] Abbot Benedict died in 1193. The latest datable incident recorded in the longest extant text of the *Miracula* (Cambridge Trinity College MS B.XIV. 37) relates to the remarkable appearance at Canterbury of two men and a girl in February 1202, who alleged that they had escaped from Saracenic captivity through the intercession of St Thomas (ibid., II, p. 273). It is conceivable that this story provided the impetus for the concoction of the 'Saracen legend' of Becket's birth and parentage, which was interpolated into Grim's *VST* and found its way into *Quadrilogus I* in the second decade of the thirteenth century (see above, p. 178, n. 7).

[3] For a discussion of the dating of both collections of *miracula*, cf. Walberg, pp. 55–73, esp. pp. 60 and 72. For the date of FitzStephen's *Life*, cf. ibid., pp. 58 and 73, n. 1.

[4] *Mats.* II, p. xlix, n. A, for Abbot Odo's letter. It survived as a preface to Benedict's *Miracula* in the (now lost) Phillipps MS 4622: an important MS from the Monastery of Aulne, thought by Robertson to be a direct descendant from the Igny exemplar, to which the letter refers.

Benedict as already the author of both *passio* and *miracula*,[1] thus pushing the compilation back into the period before his elevation. Indeed, there is no reason to suppose that the main text of Benedict's composition was not in formal existence by 1173/4. There were therefore two miracle-collections at Canterbury, and it is far from certain which 'magnus codex' FitzStephen had in mind. He describes it as containing English material only, regretting the absence of a chronicler for Becket's foreign miracles: a circumstance which induced Walberg to eliminate William's *Miracula* from the discussion on the grounds that it included both English and Irish accounts. But such a description would suit the earlier and shorter version preserved in Montpellier. The bulk of William's foreign miracles are recorded in the last sixty pages of the printed text, in what was arguably a post-1174 addition to the basic text as now found in Montpellier. The whole argument hinges on the identification of the book used for public reading at Canterbury. While it is possible that William's enjoyed that honour, the force of circumstantial argument suggests that Benedict's was in fact the more highly regarded of the two. Much work remains to be done on the textual history of both collections; but it seems, from the fact that only two manuscripts of the work survive,[2] that William's *Miracula* dropped back into obscurity after its presentation to the king. In contrast, Benedict's became the parent of a considerable progeny in France and England,[3] and was the book to which

[1] *Mats*. II, p. 448: 'Beatus igitur Thomas, cujus martyrium et miracula vir iste de quo loquimur (Benedictus), eleganti stilo transmisit ad posteros . . . hac arte reconciliavit regi'. This reference to Benedict's literary work is contained in an account of Becket's miraculous reconciliation of Henry II and the new prior, which can be dated by reference to a more detailed report in the addition to William's *Miracula* (ibid., I, pp. 493–5 and 542).

[2] Cf. p. 193, n. 1 above.

[3] Hardy (II, p. 341) lists 6 MSS (in the following order): Paris BN Lat. MS 5320; Phillipps MSS 4622 and 1842 (now lost); Oxford Bodl. MS 509; Arras Bibl. de la Ville (lacking shelf-mark; untraced); and Lambeth Palace MS 135. Of these, Canon Robertson used the Paris, Bodley, and Lambeth copies in preparing his edition, adding Cambridge Trinity College MS B.xiv. 37. Each contains a different text: Bodley is only a fragment, breaking off at II. 21; Paris terminates with IV. 106; Lambeth has a change of hand after IV. 106, indicating the physical addition of new material, and continues to VI. 3; and Trinity carries the text to VI. 7. The list of known MSS can now be significantly extended, and a definitive conclusion on the text and its date must await a thorough examination of these important MSS: Cambrai MS 488; Cambridge Corpus Christi College MS 464; Charleville MS 222 (from Signy; this may be the MS which Casimir Oudin saw at Signy in the eighteenth century: cf. Oudin, *De scriptoribus ecclesiasticis*, II, Leipzig (1722), pp. 1477 and 1516, cited in *Mats*. II, p. xxi and

contemporaries referred. Whether FitzStephen's 'magnus codex' is finally identified with the *Miracula* of William of Canterbury or Benedict of Peterborough does not materially affect our assessment of date.

The shorter text of FitzStephen's Life, Version B, was apparently the more widely known in the Middle Ages, since it is represented by all but two of the surviving manuscripts.[1] But the earliest extant manuscript, despite its imperfections, records Version A; and the anonymous compiler who expanded Elias of Evesham's *Quadrilogus* in the early thirteenth century would seem to have had access to Version A, since he included one of the passages omitted from Version B.[2] The passages in question have a character suggesting that their author had personal knowledge of the events he describes, and many give precise and accurate details of events in London or at the royal court during the exile, which are found nowhere else in the Becket materials and presumably reflect the direct and personal knowledge of their author. On balance it seems more probable that A is the earlier version and that the thirty-eight passages were deleted for one reason or another in a later redaction. It seems unlikely that a later compiler of A would have kept these many passages of personal interest and experience, while at the same time deleting all the extracts from John of Salisbury and the *Summa Cause* which are found in Version B.

The earliest extant copy is in the Oxford Bodl. MS Douce 287, already discussed in some detail above;[3] this is a late twelfth-century manuscript containing part of the Description of London and the Life of Becket by FitzStephen, together with John of

[1] Oxford Bodl. MS Douce 287 (s. xii), fos. 2vb–36vb, and Brit. Libr. MS Lansdowne 398 (s. xv), fos. 3r–55v, alone contain Version A, while all other unabbreviated copies have Version B: Oxford Bodl. MS Laud Lat. 18, fos. 89r–110v; Brit. Libr. MS Cotton Julius A. xi (s. xiii), fos. 116v–151va; Hereford Cathedral Library MS O.iv.14 (s. xiv), fos. 199r–223r; and Lambeth Palace MS 138 (s. xiii), fos. 205r–13v. Cambridge Trinity College MS O.5.45 (s. xvii), pp. 1–94, is a transcript of MS Cotton Julius A.xi.

[2] *Quadrilogus I* includes the story of the inquiry made in London by Randulf de Broc and Gervase of Cornhill about those who had welcomed Becket on his return (*Mats*. IV, p. 382), which is otherwise found only in Version A of the biography: cf. *Mats*. III, p. 125, n. 5.

[3] Cf. pp. 158–61 above.

n. 3); Douai MS 860 (from Lyre Abbey); Évreux MS Lat. 7; Montpellier École de Médecine MS 2; Paris BN Lat. MS 5615; Rome, Casanatense MS 463 and Vallicelliana MSS Tom. III, and B. 60; and Vatican Lat. MSS 1221 and 6933.

Salisbury's Life, the *Summa Cause*, and a collection of letters connected with the Becket dispute which was certainly derived from the archives of the Bishop of London. The Douce FitzStephen is a somewhat unsatisfactory copy of Version A, careless in detail, with the impression of haste in transcription; seven letters and two passages are inserted into the text on small strips of parchment.[1] It gives the appearance of being a rough copy taken from drafts, lacking chapter-divisions and chapter-headings. Its unfinished appearance contrasts markedly with the rest of the volume. John of Salisbury's Life, the *Summa Cause* and the letter-collection are all furnished with rubrics and coloured initials down to fo. 86vb, at which point the rubrics are discontinued, although sufficient space is left for their later insertion. This feature suggests that whereas the scribe had a finished exemplar before him for the last three items, he was working from a less satisfactory original in the case of FitzStephen's Life. The Douce copy is the closest in time and provenance to FitzStephen himself and, although certainly transcribed *post* 1176 (since it contains JohnS), it is evidently based on a very early form of the text.

It is possible that both versions came from FitzStephen's own hand, with Version A representing the earlier draft, composed within the period 1172–4 and probably after the bulls of canonization in 1173, while Version B is a final corrected text, prepared for publication and slightly expanded by the insertion of a few passages from recent accounts of Becket's career, with the more critical passages touching the king and the bishops diplomatically removed. It is conceivable that in the years of reconciliation between Church and State from 1174 onwards, FitzStephen prudently modified his earlier frankness. Yet it is highly unlikely, as Mrs. Cheney has argued, that FitzStephen would have sacrificed not only his most individual contribution to the record of Becket's life, but also his Description of London, in the interests of either diplomacy or hagiography. On the contrary, the omissions,

---

[1] The passage 'ad lapides platearum . . . constantie se inmiserat' (cf. *Mats.* III, pp. 31–3) is given on the inserted fo. 7ra–vb, and the letters are inserted on strips of parchment as follows, with a symbol indicating their correct position in the text: fo. 18 (a narrow strip of parchment measuring only $1\frac{5}{8}$ in. in depth), *Audiui grauamen* (*Mats.* VI, ep. 505); fo. 22ra–vb, *Excessus uestros, Vestram non debet, Se ipsum ad penas* and the passage 'Unde . . . constitutionis' (*Mats.* VI, epp. 479, 488, and 489, and III, p. 94, n. 2); and fo. 27r–v, *Pro amore Dei, Sciatis quod,* and *Hoc petimus* (*Mats.* VII, epp. 686, 690, and 604).

revisions, and insertions which characterize Version B, smack more of the work of a later redactor than of a politically sensitive author.

In contrast with the Canterbury writers, FitzStephen inserted the texts of only seven very short letters into his Life of Becket, four relating to the excommunication of Foliot,[1] and three to the archbishop's reconciliation with the king.[2] But it is certain that he used many other letters in the composition of the biography. Many of his descriptions and references clearly indicate that he had precise knowledge of the correspondence: his account of the Christmas court at Marlborough in 1164, at which Becket's family and household were proscribed, echoes the writs issued by Henry II at that time;[3] he refers to Becket's appeal to the king by its identifying *incipit*[4] and to otherwise unknown letters from Louis VII to Henry II; and he quotes small passages from Becket's letters to the bishops,[5] as well as from Foliot's letters to the Pope.[6] Similarly, his account of the excommunication of the invaders of

---

[1] *Audiui grauamen*, inserted on fo. 18, *Excessus uestros*, *Vestram non debet* and *Se ipsum ad penas*, inserted on fo. 22.

[2] *Pro amore Dei, Sciatis quod Thomas*, and *Hoc petimus*, inserted on fo. 27.

[3] *Mats.* III, p. 75; for the writs, cf. *Nosti quam male* and *Precipio tibi*, ibid., V, epp. 77 and 78.

[4] Ibid., p. 81; cf. *Desiderio desideraui*, ibid., V, ep. 154. FitzStephen's quotation 'Dominus dicit . . . iniquas' (pp. 47–8) may also come from the same source; cf. ibid., V, p. 281.

[5] Ibid., III, p. 81; the words 'Ut spiritum Dei resumerent, et pro domo Dei, terreno abjecto timore, murum se opponerent' reflect Becket's language in his replies to the bishops' appeal of 1166, namely *Fraternitatis uestre* to all the bishops of England and *Mirandum et uehementer* to Gilbert Foliot (ibid., V, epp. 223 and 224). Cf. V, p. 491, ' . . . exspectans si forte inspiraret vobis Dominus ut resumeretis vires, qui conversi estis retrorsum in die belli; si forte saltem aliquis ex omnibus vobis ascenderet ex adverso, opponeret se murum pro domo Israel . . .' and p. 520, 'Non obliviscamur illum districtum Judicem, ante cujus tribunal constitutos sola nos veritas judicabit, amoto timore et fiducia omnis terrenae potestatis.'

[6] Ibid., III, p. 81; compare FitzStephen's words with those in Foliot's letter, *Mandatum uestrum*: FitzStephen, p. 81, 'saepius pro causa illa etiam domino papae persuadere intendens regium sanguinem, cum vicerit, vinci, ut in partem regis papa ferretur inclinatior, et ne asperum quid adversum regem loqueretur occasione archiepiscopi, ne forte in schismate illo generali rex cum omnibus terris suis parti adversae, cum imperatore apostatam fovente, adderetur; et tunc in threnos, ut verbo ejus utar, dominus papa totus ire posset. Satis invenirentur qui episcoporum regis Angliae ecclesias et baculos de manu et obedientia idoli reciperent'; cf. ibid., V, ep. 108, pp. 207–8, ' . . . et tam regem ipsum quam innumeros cum eo populos a vestra (quod absit) obedientia irrevocabiliter avertatis . . . non deerit tamen qui genu curvet ante Baal, et de manu idoli pallium Cantuariae, non habito religionis aut justitiae delectu, suscipiat.'

Church property contains phrases from the relevant letters,[1] and his reference to Foliot's resignation of the administration of the sequestrated property of the Canterbury exiles reflects the letter sent by Foliot to the king on that occasion.[2] His remark that Becket condemned the Constitutions of Clarendon in writing may well derive from one or other of the documents issued from Vézelay in 1166, in which Becket announced to the bishops and to the Pope the censures promulgated against his enemies;[3] and his references to various papal letters permitting Becket to exercise his authority,[4] granting him the legation,[5] and confirming his primacy[6] suggest an accurate knowledge of them. Yet again, his account of Becket's sending to Foliot the papal letters confirming his own authority is possibly derived from the account of the matter which Foliot sent to the king.[7] Equally precisely, he refers to the letters of excommunication and suspension issued at Clairvaux on Palm Sunday 1169,[8] to the restraining of Becket, following the appointment of Vivian and Gratian as legates,[9] to the king's command that no one should enter the country without royal licence,[10] to the bishops' appeal to the Pope against Becket,[11] to Henry's decrees of 1169 and Becket's letter absolving those who had taken the illicit oaths,[12] to

[1] Ibid., III, p. 82; cf. Becket's letter *Mittimus uobis*, ibid., V, ep. 166, p. 318, and the papal letter *Vniuersis oppressis*, ibid., ep. 178, esp. p. 344.

[2] Ibid., III, p. 82; cf. *Placuit excellentie*, ibid., V, ep. 167; the words 'a domino papa plurimum redargatus' may refer to the papal letter *Vniuersis oppressis* already cited above, in which the Pope unequivocally ordered Foliot and the other Canterbury suffragans to compel the occupiers of the Canterbury lands to make immediate restitution.

[3] Ibid., III, p. 83; cf. the two versions of *Satis superque* and *Fratres mei dilectissimi*, ibid., V, epp. 195–6 and 198.

[4] Ibid., III, p. 85; cf. *Quoniam ad omnem*, ibid., V, epp. 164–5.

[5] Ibid., III, p. 85; cf. *Sacrosancta Romana*, addressed to Becket himself, and *Ex injuncto nobis*, addressed to the bishops of the Canterbury province, ibid., V, epp. 172–3. It is the second of these two letters which occurs in the Foliot sources.

[6] Ibid., III, p. 85; cf. *In apostolice sedis*, ibid., V, ep. 170. This bull does not appear in any of the collections of letters.

[7] Ibid., III, p. 85; cf. *Tanta nos domine*, ibid., V, ep. 208, esp. p. 417.

[8] Ibid., III, p. 87; cf. *Vestram latere*, addressed to the clergy of London, and *Excessus uestros*, sent to Foliot himself, ibid., VI, epp. 488 and 479.

[9] Ibid., III, p. 93; cf. *Ad discretionis tue* and *Illustris regis Anglorum*, ibid., VI, epp. 414 and 491.

[10] Ibid., III, p. 94; cf. VII, ep. 599.

[11] Ibid., III, p. 94; cf. ibid., V, epp. 204 and 205.

[12] Ibid., III, p. 102; FitzStephen's brief account of the decrees is in fact merely a paraphrase of the introduction to the text in AlanT(A), IV. 54 (and also in the fragmentary Brit. Libr. MS Cotton Titus D.xi, fo. 40r): compare FitzS: 'rex

the papal letters forbidding the coronation of the Young King,[1] to the letter suspending Roger of York and excommunicating the bishops of London and Salisbury,[2] and to Becket's report to the Pope of his reception in England.[3] Finally, his account of the conferences of Montmartre[4] and Fréteval[5] reflect the contemporary reports. In fact, in addition to the seven letters inserted into the Life, thirty-one further letters can be identified either from direct citation or quotation, indicating the degree to which FitzStephen relied upon epistolary evidence. There can be little doubt that he had access to a substantial collection of material connected with the Becket controversy, and his known London associations make it highly probable that his principal source was in records kept in Foliot's household. But, since he inserted the full texts of only seven very short letters into the Life, it is not possible to produce conclusive textual evidence to support this view. In one letter only, *Sciatis quod*, is it possible to establish textual relationships with any

[1] Ibid., III, p. 103; cf. *Ex commissi nobis* and *Quoniam ad audientiam*, ibid., VII, epp. 632–3.

[2] Ibid., III, p. 117; cf. *Oportuerat uos* and *Licet commendabiles*, ibid., VII, epp. 700–1. FitzStephen's statement that Bartholomew of Exeter was excluded from the sentences is not entirely accurate, for his name appears with those of the other bishops in the protocol of *Oportuerat uos*, but it suggests knowledge of the fact that Becket regarded Bartholomew as innocent; cf. Becket's letter to Alexander III, ibid., VII, ep. 716.

[3] Ibid., III, p. 119; cf. *Quam iustis*, ibid., VII, ep. 723.

[4] Ibid., III, p. 97; cf. Becket's account and Master Vivian's report (*Impossibile est* and *Omnem operam*, ibid., VII, epp. 606–7). FitzStephen's reference to Henry II's appeal to the judgement of the scholars of Paris (ibid., III, p. 98) may have been derived from Becket's letter (ibid., VII, ep. 606, p. 164).

[5] Ibid., III, pp. 107–9; cf. Becket's report of the meeting to Alexander III in *Miserationis oculo*, ibid., VII, ep. 684.

intelligens, jurare facit omnem Angliam a laico duodenni vel quindecim annorum supra, contra dominum papam et archiepiscopum, quod eorum non recipient litteras, neque obedient mandatis; et, si quis inventus foret litteras eorum deferens, traderetur potestatibus, tanquam coronae regis capitalis inimicus . . . Archiepiscopus hoc audito, tanto compatiens errori et apostasie, missis clam litteris ad aliquos timoratos Dei, omnes qui inviti juraverant a sacramento absolutos pronunciavit' with AlanT(A), fo. 292ra–v: 'Rex Henricus iurare facit omnem Angliam a laico duodenni uel quindecim annorum supra contra dominum papam Alexandrum et beatum Thomam archiepiscopum, quod eorum non recipient litteras, neque obedient mandatis. Et si quis inuentus foret litteras eorum deferens, traderetur potestatibus tanquam corone capitalis inimicus regis. Archiepiscopus hoc audito, tanto compatiens errori et apostasiae, missis clam litteris que sequuntur ad aliquos timoratos Dei, omnes [292rv] qui iurauerant, a sacramento absolutos pronuntiauit.' In AlanT(A) and Titus D.xi this summary is followed immediately by the letter of absolution to which it refers: *Sciatis karissimi* (*Mats.* VII, ep. 636).

certainty, but in this single instance the FitzStephen text agrees
with that in the Foliot tradition, preserving even the attestation
which is otherwise found only in Foliot manuscripts.[1] Moreover,
the letters *Hoc petimus* and *Pro amore* included by FitzStephen are
nowhere found in manuscripts of the Becket tradition; and most of
the letters which can be identified from references in FitzStephen's
Life are also known in Foliot manuscripts; and it is possible that
the Douce Collection, which follows the earliest transcription of
Version A, was his principal epistolary source.

FitzStephen's use of letters is more extensive and certainly more
mature than that of the Canterbury authors discussed above. He
chose not to insert the complete texts of many letters, but he had
epistolary evidence for nearly every statement which was not
derived from his own personal knowledge or experience. His Life
emerges therefore as the most carefully written and most reliable of
the early Becket biographies; and in some respects, at least in
Version A, it is also the most outspoken in its criticism of the royal
and episcopal party.

D. HERBERT OF BOSHAM

The longest and the last of the independent biographies was composed by Herbert of Bosham,[2] and provides many interesting
points of contrast with FitzStephen's work, though in many ways
the two accounts are also complementary. Herbert, like Fitz-
Stephen, had been an important member of Becket's household;
but, unlike FitzStephen, he had remained faithful to the archbishop's cause both during the exile and after it. He wrote his Life
after the publication of Alan of Tewkesbury's collection; but,
again in contrast with FitzStephen, he made minimal use of the
letters as a source for his account of the exile, drawing rather on his
own personal recollection of events. Both provide eye-witness
accounts of the royal councils at the beginning of the controversy;
but, whereas FitzStephen records events in the court and in
London during the exile, Herbert gives details of the affairs and
conversations of the exiles themselves.

A little more is known of Herbert than of the other biographers,

---

[1] Ibid., VII, ep. 690, pp. 346–7. The FitzStephen and Foliot texts agree on the
following details: p. 347, n. 4, insert 'omnes'; n. 5, read 'exiret' for 'recessisset';
n. 6, read 'melioribus' for 'legalioribus'; n. 8, read 'habetur' for 'habeatur'; n. 9,
insert 'Teste Rotroco archiepiscopo Rothomagensi apud Chinum'.

[2] *Vita Sancti Thome, Mats.* III, pp. 155–522.

partly from what he relates himself in the biography, partly from the independent witness of other writers, and partly from the evidence of his own important scholarly works.[1] He was attached to Becket's household from the latter's days as chancellor, attending him on the journey to Canterbury for his archiepiscopal consecration,[2] and throughout Becket's career was his constant companion and secretary, and even his 'master in the Sacred Page'.[3] It was Herbert's great regret that he was at the last deprived of participation in the martyrdom.[4] He was Becket's envoy on embassies to the King of France and the Pope, refused to desert him in the famous interview with Henry II at Angers in 1166,[5] studied canon law with him under Lombardus of Piacenza at Pontigny,[6] wrote letters on his master's behalf to some of the most eminent persons in Christendom,[7] and was present at all the notable events in Becket's life from his election until two days before the martyrdom. Of all the biographers therefore, not excluding the much more celebrated John of Salisbury, Herbert was closest to Becket, and there seems no reason to doubt his testimony as to the secret workings of the archbishop's mind. His Life of Becket is by far the longest;[8] its long scriptural quotations, sermonizings on the marvellous constancy of the martyr, and long passages of apology for prolixity in describing the Passion (in which in fact Herbert is the least circumstantial of all the authors), all these features tend to make his account unattractive and even tedious for many modern readers. Nevertheless, despite such defects and its sometimes misleading chronology, this

---

[1] For a discussion of Herbert's scholarship, cf. esp. B. Smalley, 'A commentary on the Hebraica by Herbert of Bosham', *Rech. théol. anc. méd.*, XVIII (1951), pp. 29–65; idem, *The Study of the Bible in the Middle Ages*, 2nd edn., Oxford (1952), pp. 186–95; and idem, *The Becket Conflict and the Schools*, Oxford (1973), pp. 59–86.

[2] *Mats.* III, p. 186. For a general survey of Herbert's life, cf. Robertson's introduction, ibid., pp. xvii–xx.

[3] FitzStephen, ibid., p. 58.   [4] Herbert of Bosham, ibid., p. 486.

[5] Cf. FitzStephen, ibid., pp. 99–101.   [6] Herbert of Bosham, ibid., pp. 523–4.

[7] The single surviving MS of Herbert of Bosham's letters, Cambridge Corpus Christi College MS 123, contains 45 letters and one fragment, of which 12 were composed 'in persona Thome Cantuariensis archiepiscopi' (HB 2, 3, 8–11, 15, 16, 20, and 26–8). Since only two of these are found in the Becket collections (*Sciatis carissimi*, HB 8 = AlanT(B), IV.47, and *Gratias ago Deo*, HB 9 = AlanT (B), IV.33), it is doubtful whether the others were ever issued to their intended recipients. The same doubt must be entertained in respect of letters written on behalf of French ecclesiastics (HB 4, 24, 25, 32, 33, 37), of which only one was received into the Becket collections (*Inter scribendum*, HB 33 = AlanT(B), V.80).

[8] *Mats.* III, pp. 155–522.

Life remains one of the most important accounts of the controversy. Herbert asserted that he was recording only what he had seen himself or learned from reliable witnesses,[1] and there is no reason to doubt his claim. His Life has the quality of taking us into the secret councils of the archbishop. At every turn we see Becket thrashing out problems with his *eruditi*,[2] with Herbert himself (the 'discipulus qui scripsit haec') constantly intervening to advise his master, as at Northampton,[3] at Montmirail,[4] and on the eve of Becket's return to England.[5] It is in his record of the arguments and discussions within the archbishop's household that the chief value of Herbert's Life lies. On his testimony, only once did Becket act without, and even contrary to, the advice of his *eruditi*, and that was when he issued the Vézelay censures in 1166. Four times in a very brief space Herbert reports that this was done without consultation.[6]

Although his Life was written between 1184 and 1186,[7] after the publication of Alan of Tewkesbury's collection, to which indeed Herbert refers his readers on no less than three occasions,[8] his dependence upon this invaluable source is much less than might be expected. He includes the full text of no letters or documents, though he quotes and comments on six clauses of the Constitutions of Clarendon,[9] and claims that he was using an accurate copy of the chirograph presented to the archbishop at that council.[10] At the same time, although he does not quote any of the letters or use them as the basis of his narrative, he cites directly and precisely a number of letters, referring the reader at times to Alan's collection for the text.[11] Altogether, sixteen letters and documents can

---

[1] Ibid., pp. 161–2, 'Verum cum hujus viri gesta ipso opitulante breviter describenda susceperim, pueritiae pariter et adolescentiae ejus annos impraesentiarum pertranseo; solum ea de viro hoc pro testimonio relaturus, quae ipse vidi et audivi; de quibus dumtaxat verum testimonium est.'

[2] Cf. ibid., pp. 186, 206–7, 226, 236, 268, 289, 290–2, 307–8, 312, 362–73, 376, 377–8, 381–3, 386, 394–5, 398, 399–402, 411–12, 413, 420, 421, 422, 428, 430, 431, 432–6, 439–40, 451, 451–8, 461, 472–3, 473–6, and 485–6.

[3] Ibid., pp. 307–8.   [4] Ibid., p. 422.

[5] Ibid., pp. 473–6.   [6] Ibid., pp. 387–8.

[7] He says that he began writing in the fourteenth year after the death of Becket (ibid., p. 192); but he was still writing in the fifteenth year, when he states that all Becket's household had died (ibid., p. 497); and he refers to the death of Prince Geoffrey (ibid., p. 497): Geoffrey died on 19 August 1186.

[8] Ibid., pp. 315, 395–6, and 463.

[9] Ibid., pp. 280–4.

[10] Ibid., p. 280, 'ut decreti funesti chirographi propriis utar verbis'.

[11] Cf. n. 8 above.

be identified from these references, including the papal letter of absolution of Becket for his weakness in temporarily yielding at Clarendon,[1] the royal letter to Louis VII and Philip of Flanders,[2] the proscription of the archbishop's family and household,[3] the suspension of Jocelin of Salisbury,[4] the bishops' appeal to the Pope against Becket,[5] and the latter's reply to it,[6] the granting of the legation of England to Becket,[7] the appointment of Rotrou of Rouen and Bernard of Nevers as commissioners for the reconciliation,[8] the prohibition of the coronation of the Young King,[9] the papal letters of censure against the bishops who participated in the ceremony,[10] and the papal letter commending Becket for his constancy.[11] But there is no doubt that Herbert was relatively much less dependent upon epistolary sources than the other biographers.

E. GUERNES DE PONT-SAINTE-MAXENCE

In contrast, the earlier metrical *Vie de Saint Thomas*, composed by Guernes de Pont-Sainte-Maxence at Canterbury between 1172 and 1174,[12] incorporated the texts of some letters, as well as the Constitutions of Clarendon and the royal decrees of 1169. And Guernes showed remarkable skill in rendering the Latin into French verse, managing on occasions to preserve even the diplomatic details such as protocol and date. In all, eight letters and documents were incorporated in the work,[13] namely the Constitutions of Clarendon,[14]

---

[1] *Mats.* III, p. 293; cf. *Ad aures nostras*, V, ep. 52.

[2] Ibid., III, p. 323; cf. *Sciatis quod Thomas*, V, ep. 71.

[3] Ibid., III, 359; cf. *Nosti quam male* and *Precipio tibi*, V, epp. 77 and 78.

[4] Ibid., III, p. 392; cf. *Celebre prouerbium*, V, ep. 199.

[5] Ibid., III, p. 394; cf. *Vestram pater* and *Que uestro pater*, V, epp. 204 and 205.

[6] Ibid., III, pp. 395–6; cf. *Fraternitatis uestre*, V, ep. 223, which Herbert describes as 'sensu suo proprio conceptam et proprio stylo exaratam . . . elegantem satis et sufficienter responsalem'.

[7] Ibid., III, p. 397; cf. *Sacrosancta Romana*, V, ep. 172.

[8] Ibid., III, p. 462; cf. *Carissimus in Christo*, VII, ep. 623.

[9] Ibid., III, pp. 458–9; cf. *Ex commissi nobis* and *Quoniam ad audientiam*, VII, epp. 632 and 633.

[10] Ibid., III, p. 463; cf. *Oportuerat uos* and *Licet commendabiles*, VII, epp. 700 and 701.

[11] Ibid., III, p. 463; cf. *Anxietate cordis*, VII, ep. 714. Cf. Table 4 below.

[12] *Vie de Saint Thomas*, ed. E. Walberg, Lund (1922); for a full discussion of the relationship between Guernes's *Vie* and the Latin biographies of Becket, see idem, *La Tradition hagiographique*, pp. 135–68.

[13] Cf. Table 5 below.

[14] Ed. cit., pp. 80–6, vv. 2396–543.

the 1169 decrees,[1] *Expectans expectaui*,[2] *Desiderio desideraui*,[3] *Que uestro pater*,[4] *Mirandum et uehementer*,[5] *Sciatis quod Thomas*,[6] and *Quam iustis*;[7] and, with the exception of *Expectans expectaui*, all occur in one or other of the Latin narrative sources used by Guernes: four were recorded by Grim[8] and four by William of Canterbury.[9] But it is clear that Guernes had access also to a further source of letters: not only does he provide a translation of *Expectans expectaui*, which occurs in neither of the biographies which he used, but he has fuller versions of *Que uestro pater*[10] and *Mirandum et uehementer*[11] than those found in Grim. It is most probable that the source of this additional material would have been in the considerable Becket records preserved at Canterbury after the archbishop's murder. But it is not possible to identify the textual ancestry of Guernes's items.

It is evident therefore that the most important of the Lives of Becket were dependent to varying extents on epistolary sources for their account of the dispute and of the martyr's exile. We have seen that Grim's Life was expanded with an appendix of letters, in addition to those incorporated in the main narrative; the greater part of William of Canterbury's Life was composed of substantial extracts from a large group of letters and documents relating to the controversy, and much of FitzStephen's information was clearly derived from similar sources. Alone of the independent biographers, Herbert of Bosham seems to have been little influenced by letter collections, though he had obvious access to the best of them. But Herbert had been closest of all to the martyr: his companion, friend, and teacher, eye-witness of everything except the martyrdom itself; and he was writing from personal knowledge some fourteen to sixteen years after the murder, in the knowledge that Alan of Tewkesbury's collection was then available.

---

[1] Ibid., pp. 91–3, vv. 2680–731.   [2] Ibid., pp. 97–103, vv. 2851–3040.

[3] Ibid., pp. 103–8, vv. 3048–180.   [4] Ibid., pp. 108–12, vv. 3186–320.

[5] Ibid., pp. 112–20, vv. 3326–565.   [6] Ibid., p. 151, vv. 4498–516.

[7] Ibid., pp. 158–9, vv. 4716–55.

[8] *Desiderio desideraui*, *Que uestro pater*, *Mirandum et uehementer*, and *Quam iustis*; cf. Grim, *Mats.* II, pp. 419–21, 408–9, 409–12, and 422–6.

[9] The Constitutions of Clarendon, the 1169 Constitutions, *Sciatis quod* and *Quam iustis*; cf. William of Canterbury, *Mats.* I, pp. 18–23, 53–5, 85, and 95–9.

[10] Grim's version of *Que uestro* has many omissions (see above, p. 179, n. 8), but Guernes, p. 109, vv. 3201–10, has included a translation of the eleven-line passage 'et spiritualibus . . . sustinuit' which Grim omitted.

[11] Similarly, Grim considerably abbreviated the text of *Mirandum*, whereas Guernes translated a complete version.

2. ROGER OF CROWLAND'S *QUADRILOGUS*

The author who made the most extensive use of the Becket correspondence in the Middle Ages was Roger, monk of Crowland, who undertook the formidable task of combining the extant correspondence with the so-called *Second Quadrilogus* to form one imposing work in which the relevant letters were inserted into the narrative of the controversy. The *Quadrilogus* is a conflation of the Lives of Becket by William of Canterbury, John of Salisbury, Alan of Tewkesbury, Herbert of Bosham, and Benedict of Peterborough, completed in 1199 by Elias of Evesham. It survives in two recensions identified as *Quadrilogus I* and *Quadrilogus II* in order of their dates of printed editions: the former was published in Paris in 1495 by the German printer John Philipps,[1] while the latter was first published in Brussels by Christian Lupus in 1682.[2] But in reality *Quadrilogus II* seems the earlier and more authentic text of the two, for *Quadrilogus I* contains insertions from an expanded version of Grim's Life, including the fabulous story of Becket's Syrian descent, as well as some small borrowings from the Life by William FitzStephen and further extracts from that by Herbert of Bosham.[3] It is now known in two manuscripts only and the time and place of its composition cannot be established.[4] *Quadrilogus II* survives in two slightly differing versions: one of these, for which Hardy cites sixteen manuscripts,[5] is preceded by the prologue 'Post summi fauoris ... nemo tibi',[6] and followed by an appendix of

---

[1] Johannes Philippi, ed., *Vita et Processus Sancti Thome Cantuariensis Martyris super Libertate Ecclesiastica,* Paris (1495); cf. Hardy, II, pp. 345–8.

[2] Lupus, I, pp. 4–156.

[3] For the details of these additions, cf. Robertson's notes to *Quadrilogus II* in *Mats.* IV, pp. 266. n. 1; 270, n. 8; 271, n. 11; 273, n. 14; 320, n. 5; 323, n. 6; 351, n. 4; 376, n. 4; 382, nn. 1, 4, 8, and 9; 385, n. 3: 393, nn. 3 and 7; 394, n. 2; 398, n. 5; 399, n. 7; 412, n. 10; 413, n. 3; and 420, n. 16.

[4] Oxford University College MS lxix, slightly defective at the beginning; and Bibl. de Saint-Omer MS 710. Hardy (II, p. 345) incorrectly cites two further MSS: Oxford Corpus Christi College MS xxxviii and Bibl. de Douai MS 810 (correctly 861); but both MSS contain *Quadrilogus II.*

[5] Hardy II, pp. 348–9, but his references must be adjusted as follows: Brit. Libr. Stowe 52 (not iii. xix), Cambridge, Trinity College MS O.5.39 (not 39–46), Oxford Corpus Christi College MS xxxviii (not 1505), and Bibl. de Douai MS 861 (not 810); and with the addition of Durham Univ. Library Bishop Cosin MS V. iii. 12, Rome Bibl. Vallicelliana MS B. 60, Vatican Latin MSS 1220 and 6027. Trinity College MS O.5.39 is a seventeenth-century transcript of a text closely resembling Brit. Libr. MS Arundel 52, and Vat. Lat. MS 6027 is a seventeenth-century transcript of Vat. Lat. MS 1220.

[6] Cf. *Mats.* IV, pp. 266–8.

material including the *Catalogus eruditorum*, the *Causa exilii*, the
1169 decrees, and the three bulls of canonization;[1] and the other,
less well-known, preserves the letter of dedication *Virorum illustrium* addressed by Elias of Evesham to Abbot Henry of Crowland
c. 1199,[2] in place of the prologue, and inserts an account of the
translation of Becket's relics in 1220 among the supplementary
material;[3] this latter version is now known in three manuscripts
only, of which one is defective at the end.[4] The letter of dedication
which describes the contents of the work does not mention the
supplementary material, but the evidence of nearly all the surviving
manuscripts,[5] the earliest of which can be dated to within a few
years of the original composition of the *Quadrilogus*, suggests that
the supplement was added at a very early date in the thirteenth
century, if not by Elias himself.

It was this quadripartite Life of Becket which Roger of Crowland
adopted in the first decade of the thirteenth century as the basis of
his large volume containing the Life and Letters of Becket. Three
letters survive which enable us to describe accurately the exact
relationship between the work of Elias and that of Roger, and to
give precise dates to their compilations. The dedicatory letter from
Elias to Henry of Crowland cited above shows that Elias, assisted
by Henry, made a conflation of the major authorities for the Life of
Becket; and a further letter, from Roger of Crowland to the same
Abbot Henry, preserved among the introductory material in Paris
Bibl. Nat. Latin MS 5372, shows that the work was first completed
at Crowland in the last year of the reign of Richard I (1198–9),[6] that
Roger was responsible for adding to it a selection of letters,[7] and

---

[1] These items are not given in Robertson's edition of the *Quadrilogus*; but cf.
Lupus, I, pp. 156–73.

[2] Cf. Hardy, II, p. 343, n.

[3] 'Anno quinquagesimo . . . supportavit', cf. *Mats.* IV, pp. 426–30.

[4] Cf. Hardy, II, p. 342; but note that the two Vatican MSS (Vatican Latin
MSS 1220 and 6027) are wrongly listed here by Hardy, since they contain the
complete text of the other version of *Quadrilogus II*.

[5] All the surviving complete MSS, with the sole exception of Brit. Libr. MS
Cotton Nero A. v, contain the basic supplement.

[6] Paris Bibl. Nat. Latin MS 5372, fo. lvb: 'facta autem prima illa compilatio
hortantibus uobis pariter et cooperantibus apud Croilandiam anno Regis Ricardi
ultimo'. For the full text of this letter, cf. Giles, *VST* II, pp. 42–5.

[7] Bibl. Nat. Latin MS 5372, fo. 1va: 'Sed qui restabant epistole ab ipso uiro
Domini, uel ad eum uel de eo a uiris auctenticis scripto, aduertit prouidentia
uestra quod si ipse locis competentibus predicto inserentur compendio, ex hinc
et plurimum auctoritatis hystorie et non parum utilitatis procuraretur.'

that this second version was finished at Crowland in the fourteenth year of the reign of King John (1213).[1] Further, a copy of this conflation by Roger of Crowland was sent to Stephen Langton, Archbishop of Canterbury, on the occasion of the translation of Becket's relics in July 1220, and its accompanying letter of dedication from Abbot Henry to Stephen Langton is also preserved in the Paris manuscript.[2]

Roger's version of the *Quadrilogus* exists in two manuscripts only: Bodl. MS Cave e Mus. 133 and Paris Bibl. Nat. Latin MS 5372. Both are to some extent defective: the Bodleian copy contains less than half the work, breaking off with the *explicit* of Book III, while the Paris manuscript is slightly mutilated at the beginning and lacks the opening five chapters of Book I, starting abruptly on fo. 11va with the words 'per annos xxij strenue et prudenter rexisset' in the middle of chapter 6;[3] this lacuna is explained by the fact that fos. 9 and 10 are missing from the manuscript. Both manuscripts are fairly late copies: the Bodleian MS was transcribed in the early fourteenth century, while the Paris volume was, according to a note on fo. 1rb, written in 1411.[4] Although later in date of transcription, the Paris MS is much superior to the Bodleian copy, not only in containing almost the entire work, but also because of the care with which it was transcribed. It is a handsome volume,[5] with rubricated headings and blue initials elaborately decorated in red ink, and fine capitals illuminated in blue and gold at the beginning of each book.[6]

Although Elias of Evesham's *Quadrilogus II* and its thirteenth-century expansion in *Quadrilogus I* have both been printed,[7] Roger

---

[1] Ibid., fo. 1vb: 'apud Croiland. anno regni regis Johannis xiiii^mo, qui fuit annus ab incarnatione Domini iuxta Dyonisium millesimus ducentesimus tertius decimus'.

[2] Ibid., fo. 1ra–rb; cf. Giles, *VST* II, pp. 40–2.

[3] *Mats.* IV, p. 274.

[4] 'Incipit prologus in uitam sancti Thome archiepiscopi Cantuariensis et martyris, ex diuersis opusculis excerptam, sumptus anno Domini millesimo quadringentesimo undecimo, finitus in profesto Lucie uirginis per me Johannem Waning de Almania.' Cf. Giles, *VST* II, p. 42.

[5] 14¾ × 10½ in.; double columns, 68–9 lines to the column.

[6] Cf. fos. 1va, 26ra, 46ra, 64va, 80va, 96vb, 111ra, and 125ra.

[7] For editions of the *Second Quadrilogus*, cf. Lupus, I, pp. 1–163, Giles, *VST* II, pp. 192–208 (in part), and *Mats.* IV, pp. 266–424. *Quadrilogus I* has not been re-edited since its first publication by John Philipps in 1495, but Giles printed five short extracts from it in *VST* II, pp. 45–50.

of Crowland's interesting version has not yet been edited,[1] perhaps
because of its great length, or perhaps because it is a conflation of
two sources already well known in their separate forms. But it has
a high degree of individuality; Roger was not content simply to
insert groups of letters haphazardly into the existing text. The
original *Quadrilogus* was in any case not a very good framework for
the letters; it had to be considerably rearranged to make their
inclusion intelligible; and Roger performed the task with much
skill both in the adaptation of the original text and in the selection
and insertion of no less than 240 relevant letters and documents.[2]
The three books of the *Quadrilogus* were re-divided and expanded
into seven by the introduction of new chapters designed to provide
a general background to the letters; and the letters themselves
were arranged according to an accurate chronological plan. By
his skilful combination of the original *Quadrilogus* with a large
selection of letters and documents, Roger thus produced a well-
balanced account of the Becket controversy, including also the full
texts of the Constitutions of Clarendon, the 1169 decrees, and the
details of the Compromise of Avranches,[3] in addition to the letters
of appeal and counter-appeal and papal commissions to legates and
representatives.[4] His adaptation of the *Quadrilogus* has in fact many
claims to be regarded as one of the best accounts of the Becket
dispute composed in the Middle Ages.

The narrative source of Roger's work is explicitly identified in
his letter to Abbot Henry, but he did not identify the source of his
additional letters. Collation with the surviving collections of
Becket's letters reveals that, in all probability, Alan of Tewkesbury's
compilation was Roger's principal source: 238 (including one
duplicate) out of the total 241 documentary items in Roger's work
are found in Alan's collection, and despite the rearrangement of
these letters, either to improve the chronological order or to bring

[1] Although the Paris MS, Bibl. Nat. Latin MS 5372, was used by Brial in the
preparation of his edition of the letters of Becket and John of Salisbury in the
Recueil des historiens, he did not publish the whole work; and it was from this
MS that Giles took the letters of Elias of Evesham, and of Henry and Roger
of Crowland: cf. Giles, *VST* II, pp. 33–44.

[2] Cf. Table 6, below.

[3] Constitutions of Clarendon, no. 1b; two versions of the 1169 decrees, nos.
1d and 187b; Compromise of Avranches, no. 232.

[4] For the bishops' appeal of 1166, cf. nos. 70 and 71; for the papal commissions, cf. nos. 98–9, 128, and 192.

together items of cognate interest, Roger's order reflects that in Alan's collection to a marked extent.[1] Unfortunately, a more accurate identification of the source or sources used by Roger is very difficult. Roger's texts sometimes appear to follow one recension of Alan's work, and sometimes another; and it is conceivable that Roger had access to more than one copy of Alan's collection. Thus, there are four occasions on which Roger's text follows AlanT Recension II,[2] but there are six protocols[3] and a version of one letter[4] which reflect the readings of Recension III. Moreover, Roger's selection includes three of the letters marked 'non est inter ordinatas' in the corrected version of Recension I (preserved in Brit. Libr. MS Cotton Claudius B. II),[5] together with one further letter known only in the same source.[6] On the other hand, Roger's compilation contains eight protocols which are not found in any version of Alan's work,[7] though two of these are preserved in Roger of Hoveden's *Chronica*[8] and one is also contained in a manuscript of Herbert of Bosham's letters.[9]

It seems most likely therefore that Roger derived most of his letters from one or more manuscripts in the Alan of Tewkesbury

---

[1] Although the letters in the MS are numbered 1–236, the actual number of items is 241, including one duplicate (170 = 182): no. 72 has no accompanying letter (the number was entered by mistake); and items numbered 1b, 1c, 1d, 107b, 125b, and 187b in my lists were missed by the numerator. Cf. Table 6, below.

[2] The text of no. 24 (*Ex relatione, Mats.* V, ep. 115) agrees with AlanT(A), I.29 and (B), I.33; the attestation of no. 26 (*Nosti quam male, Mats.* V, ep. 77) agrees with AlanT(A), I.12b and (B), 1.13; the text of no. 60 (*Loqui de Deo, Mats.* V, ep. 152) agrees with AlanT(A), I.59 and (B), I.63; and the protocol of no. 153 (*Excessus uestros, Mats.* VI, ep. 479) agrees with AlanT(A), III.39 and (B), I.39. For the variants in Recension III, cf. AlanT(C), I.34, I.14, I.62, and III.67.

[3] Nos. 2, 7, 14, 40, 141, and 186 have protocols agreeing with AlanT(C), I.19, 26, 25, 54, III.106, and 95; protocols are missing from the corresponding items in AlanT(A) and AlanT(B): cf. AlanT(A), I.14, 21, 20, 49, III.77, and 66; and AlanT(B), I.18, 25, 24, 53, III.77, and 66. The protocol of no. 9 (*Est unde respirare, Mats.* V, ep. 62) agrees with AlanT(C), I.9; for variants, cf. AlanT(A) and (B), I.9.

[4] Cf. no. 38 (*Mats.* VII, ep. 603). Roger's text agrees with AlanT(C), I.68; cf. AlanT(A), I.62 and IV.63.

[5] Nos. 113, 135, and 107b = AlanT(A), IV.4, IV.8, and II.126.

[6] No. 88 = AlanT(A), II.4.

[7] Cf. nos. 3, 10, 56, 57, 68, 81, 161, and 232.

[8] For the protocols of nos. 161 and 232 (*Mats.* VII, epp. 550 and 772), cf. Hoveden, *Chronica*, I, p. 271 and II, p. 36.

[9] The protocol of no. 232 is found also in Cambridge Corpus Christi College MS 123, ep. 43.

filiation; but these were not his only sources. Three of his items do not occur in any known version of Alan's collection, namely the letters *Litteras uestras* from Henry II to Alexander III and *Potestis recolere* from Louis VII to the Pope, and an unusual form of the 1169 decrees. The two letters are in fact discovered in no other surviving source and their printed versions derive from Roger's work.[1] But Roger's version of the 1169 decrees reflects the Foliot text of those royal constitutions: it preserves both the latter's peculiarities of content and order, together with its eightfold division, although the first clause in Roger's version incorporates a passage from an anonymous letter addressed to Becket in 1169, which is not found in the Foliot text.[2]

In selecting his letters, Roger of Crowland concentrated heavily on letters written by Becket or the Pope: no less than 82(+1) of the total of 237(+1) items in common with AlanT were written in Becket's name,[3] while forty-seven were addressed to him,[4] and a further forty-five were sent by the Pope to recipients other than Becket:[5] thus more than half of Roger's selection falls into the category of Becket correspondence proper—that is, letters to and from Becket himself—supported by about half of the papal letters issued during the controversy. In contrast, only eleven out of a possible 106 letters by John of Salisbury were included,[6] and fifty-

---

[1] For *Litteras uestras* (no. 25), cf. *Recueil des historiens*, XVI, p. 256 and *Mats.* V, ep. 185, pp. 362–3; for *Potestis recolere* (no. 172), cf. *Recueil des historiens*, XVI, p. 269, Giles, *Ep. GF*, II, pp. 307–8, and *Mats.* VI, ep. 294, p. 175.

[2] Cf. no. 187b, cap. 1: 'Si quis inuentus fuerit ferens literas domini pape uel mandatum, aut Cantuariensis, continens in se interdictum christianitatis in Anglia, capiatur et de eo sine dilatione fiat iustitia sicut de proditore regis; itaque si regularis illas attulerit, pedibus truncetur. Si clericus, oculos et genitalia amittat. Si laycus, suspendatur. Si leprosus, comburatur'. This version combines cap. 1 of the Foliot version (for which cf. Knowles, Duggan, and Brooke, 'Henry II's Supplement to the Constitutions of Clarendon', *EHR* LXXXVII (1972), p. 765.) with the passage 'Et si aliquis . . . comburatur' from the letter *Sciatis hunc*; cf. *Mats.* VII, ep. 598, p. 146.

[3] Cf. nos. 2–4, 19, 28–30, 34–9, 51–3, 56–62, 67–9, 73, 74, 82–4, 90, 93–6, 103, 105, 114–16, 119–22, 133–6, 151, 153–6, 161–4, 170 = 182, 171, 183–91, 196–9, 201–6, 215, 224, and 225. No. 135 is marked 'non est inter ordinatas' in AlanT (A), IV.8. In the numbers cited above, + 1 indicates the duplication of one item: no. 170 = 182.

[4] Cf. RogerC nos. 1a, 1d, 6–17, 20–4, 40, 41, 47, 49, 70, 76–8, 81, 87, 92, 101, 104, 111, 118, 129, 141, 142, 158, 177, 208, 211–14, and 217–19.

[5] Ibid., nos. 5, 31–3, 42–5, 48, 50, 79, 80, 86, 88, 98–100, 102, 112, 117, 128, 130–2, 143–8, 178, 192–5, 200, 209, 210, 216, 221–3, and 234–6.

[6] Ibid., nos. 75, 107b–110, 127, 149, 150, 165, 220, and 229.

two out of a possible 114 miscellaneous items.[1] Even in the latter category, the Becket emphasis is equally clear: twenty-four of the miscellaneous items were written in Becket's favour by continental supporters.[2] On the other hand, however, the strongly-worded episcopal appeals against the archbishop are retained, so that a charge of suppression of unwelcome material cannot be laid against the selector.[3]

By such selection Roger succeeded in reducing the great bulk of the Alan of Tewkesbury Collection to more manageable size, by excluding most of the material not immediately relevant to the main lines of his narrative; but his greatest skill was shown in the chronological rearrangement of the letters he selected. It should be remembered that Roger was writing forty years after Becket's murder, when oral tradition was unlikely to have remained reliable, and when his documentary sources were themselves somewhat misleading. The chronology of Alan's collection was fairly accurate, yet it contained serious errors, such as the misplacing of Books II and III; and the *Quadrilogus* was not circumstantial enough in its account of the exile to serve as a reliable guide to the compiler. Thus, the greater part of that work was devoted either to events before the archbishop's flight, or to the circumstances of his return and martyrdom,[4] and only a relatively small proportion of the narrative deals with the exile itself.[5] Again, the various legations and negotiations are given in correct order,[6] but only the legation of

---

[1] Ibid., 1b, 1c, 18, 26, 27, 46, 54, 55, 63–6, 71, 85, 89, 91, 97, 106, 107a, 113, 123, 124, 125a, 125b, 126, 137–40, 152, 157, 159, 160, 166–9, 173–6, 179–81, 207, 226–8, and 230–3.

[2] Ibid., nos. 85, 89, 91, 96, 107, 123, 124, 125a, 125b, 126, 137–40, 152, 173–6, 181, 226–8, and 231.

[3] *Que uestro pater* and *Vestram pater:* ibid., nos. 70 and 71. The following table illustrates the relative proportion of letters selected or omitted by RogerC compared with AlanT(A): Brit. Libr. MS Cotton Claudius B.ii.

	Inserted	Omitted	Total
Letters from Becket	82(+1)	96	178
Letters to Becket	47	67	114
Papal letters[e]	45	41	86
JohnS letters[e]	11	95	106
Miscellaneous letters	52	62	114
Total	237(+1)	361	598

[e] exclusive of letters addressed to Becket.

[4] For events before the flight, cf. *Mats.* IV, pp. 269–326; for the return and murder, cf. ibid., pp. 376–424.

[5] Cf. ibid., pp. 326–76.

[6] Ibid., pp. 356–67.

William and Otto is discussed in detail,[1] while the others are described in vague terms, without the identification of the ambassadors, or reference to the time or place of the negotiations. The Conference at Montmirail on 6 January 1169, at which Simon of Mont-Dieu and Bernard de Corilo were present, is placed under the heading 'De quodam regum colloquio, ubi pacis fuit impedimentum hoc uerbum, scilicet, Saluo honore Dei';[2] the legation of Vivian and Gratian appears under the title 'De legatis secundo missis a domino papa';[3] and, although the location of the Conference of Montmartre, held on 18 November 1169, is identified, the names of the legates are not recorded.[4] Such are the defects in his sources.

Roger's chronology is in fact better than that of either of his principal sources: the various stages in the controversy are placed by him in their correct order, and associated with the relevant letters and documents. There are only two serious mistakes in his arrangement of the letters: firstly, his placing of the account of the Council of Würzburg of 1 July 1165, and the letters connected with it, at the end of Book II, after a series of letters written in 1166,[5] and secondly his linking of John of Salisbury's letter *Expectatione longa* with the second appeal by the bishops in November 1167, instead of with the first appeal in mid-1166.[6] Understandably, there are some minor misplacements, especially of general letters of request or thanks, which it is very difficult to date accurately even now.

This *Quadrilogus* devised by Roger of Crowland is set out in seven books, each composed of numerous chapters; and since the collection has not previously been analysed, the following survey of letters incorporated in it will serve as a basis for our present purpose:[7]

Book I : Letters 1–17, including 3 unnumbered items,[8] making a total of 20 letters.

---

[1] Ibid., pp. 356–8.　　　　　　　　[2] Ibid., p. 361.
[3] Ibid., p. 366.
[4] Ibid., p. 367.
[5] Nos. 65–6; cf. Table 6, below.
[6] No. 108; cf. Table 6, below.
[7] It will be clear from the foregoing discussions that these letters are intermingled in narrative chapters.
[8] Cf. nos. 1b, 1c, 1d. In addition, the AlanT text of the 1169 Constitutions is inserted in the bottom margins of fos. 17va–18rb; but it seems not to have formed part of the original transcription and is not included in this analysis.

This book is concerned with Becket's early life and the beginning of his dispute with the king, down to the Council of Northampton in October 1164. All the letters, excepting the last one, were written before Becket's flight, in the period 1163–4, and the inclusion of one item from early 1165 (no. 17: *Quod minor*) is explained by its direct connection with the sentences passed against Becket at Northampton.

Book II: Letters 18–66.

The 49 letters in this section deal with the period from Becket's flight from Northampton to his exercise of legatine authority in and after May 1166. The general arrangement is good, except for the misplacement of nos. 37, 39, and 40, dating from 1164, which should come after no. 19, and of nos. 64–6, dating from mid-1165, which should follow no. 23. The section opens with the two allocutions, delivered respectively by Henry II's representatives and Becket himself in the papal consistory at Sens in November 1164 (18–19); these are followed by three letters expressing loyalty to Becket (20–2) and two reports from John of Salisbury (23 and 24). Henry II's complaint against papal support for Becket (25) and his letters ordering the expulsion of the Becket party from England (26 and 27) are followed by a series of letters of request and gratitude, written by or on behalf of Becket and his family and household (28–33), dating from early 1165 to 1169 and grouped together after the chapter 'De proscriptione tocius cognationis sancti Thome'. With the exceptions already noted, nos. 34–41 were written between July 1165 and May 1166: in nos. 34–6, Becket calls on the English bishops to support him; no. 38 is his appeal to Henry II; and nos. 40 and 41 are Nicholas de Mont's reports concerning the court at Rouen. Nos. 42–5 appear under the heading 'Qualiter dominus papa pro uiro domini tunc episcopis scripsit'; these are papal letters addressed to various English ecclesiastics and date from 1165, except for no. 44, which can be dated 28 January 1167, but is related to the others in subject matter; and no. 46 is Foliot's report to Alexander III of his negotiations with Henry II. The following 13 letters (47–59) relate to the conferring of legatine authority on Becket and to his exercise of it: no. 47 is the papal grant itself, issued on 24 April 1166; nos. 48–53 are papal and archiepiscopal mandates to English recipients enjoining obedience to the archbishop and restoration of the exiles' sequestrated property; nos. 54 and 55 are Foliot's consequential appeals to the king to be relieved of the task of looking after confiscated Canterbury property; and nos. 56–9 show Becket exercising ecclesiastical authority in England. Three of Becket's letters to Henry II come next (60–2), slightly misplaced here, since they preceded the grant of the legation, and these are followed by two of Henry II's letters expressing hostility to Becket (63–4). The book is completed by two letters relating to the Council of Würzburg of 1165.

Book III: Letters 67–107b.

This section covers the period from the Vézelay sentences on 12 June 1166 to the legation of William and Otto at the end of November 1167. The letters are generally in correct chronological sequence, though with some misplacements, and grouped according to subject-matter. The book opens with three letters in Becket's name (67–9) announcing the Vézelay sentences, followed by two letters of appeal against them (70 and 71), Becket's replies to Foliot and the bishops (73 and 74; there is no letter 72, the number being wrongly given to chapter 8), and two letters of John of Salisbury (75 and 76) discussing the appeal. These are followed by two papal rescripts (77 and 78) confirming Becket's sentences. An account of Becket's constrained departure from sanctuary in the Cistercian Abbey of Pontigny is found at this point, under the heading 'Qualiter rex Anglie uirum domini a Pontiniaco amouere querebat', and this is followed by two papal letters (79 and 80) to the Cistercians, thanking them for their hospitality to Becket, and by Louis VII's offer of accommodation to him (81). Becket's letters of counter-appeal to the Pope and friendly cardinals (82–4) and William elect of Chartres' supporting letter (85) are next grouped together, and round off the material of cognate interest in this book. The rest of the book is concerned entirely with the legation of Cardinals William of Pavia and Otto, beginning with papal letters (86–8) announcing their appointment in December 1166, and a group of letters (89–91) revealing the dismay of the Becket party when they heard (through John of Oxford, returning from the Curia in January 1167) that legates, as yet unidentified, were to be sent with full powers to decide the issue between king and arch-bishop. The description of the arrival of the legates, entitled 'De profectione legatorum morosa et pomposa', is completed with William of Pavia's letter to Becket concerning the legates' commission (92) and Becket's appeals for a reduction of their legatine power (93 and 94). Nos. 95–7 also relate to the legates' appointment, but strictly should come earlier, with nos. 89–91, since they were written before the legates' identity was known in France. Then follow two papal letters reducing and circumscribing the legates' authority (98 and 99), des-patched respectively in May and August 1167. Three letters of credence, addressed to Louis VII, Becket, and Henry II (100–2) appear next, though they were earlier in issue, dating from January 1167 when the legates set out; their sequence in this collection is perhaps explained by their becoming avail-able at the time of the legates' arrival in France. The rest of the book is concerned with various negotiations held by or in the presence of the legates: no. 103 is Becket's account of the meetings held between Gisors and Trie on 18 November 1167; nos. 104–6 concern the appeals made after the failure of the legation; no. 107a is the cardinals' formal report to the Pope; and the book is completed with an extract from a letter of John of Salisbury (107b) in which he criticizes William and Otto severely.

Book IV : Letters 108–50, including 1 unnumbered letter, mak-ing a total of 44 letters.

The letters in this part cover the period from December 1167 to the Conference of Montmirail on 6 January 1169 and its aftermath, and it ends with a group of letters confirming and defining Becket's authority in England. This book is chrono-logically less satisfactory than Book III: it begins by misplacing John of Salisbury's *Expectatione longa* (108), linking it with the second appeal by the bishops *c.* 29 November 1167, instead of with that of mid-1166; no. 116 should appear with nos. 90 and 91 in Book III; no. 117, which is dated 16 May 1166, and no. 142 belong chronologically to the end of Book II; and the final ten letters (141–50), defending Becket's authority, are grouped here by subject-matter rather than date, having been issued at different times throughout the controversy. But apart from these items, the letters are arranged fairly satisfactorily

elsewhere in the book: nos. 109 and 110 are letters of John of
Salisbury written in 1167; no. 111 is a papal letter to Becket
advising moderation; nos. 112–15 and 127 deal with the suspension of Becket's legatine power from 19 May 1168; no. 116
is his plea for more positive help from Rome, delivered earlier
in that year; and nos. 117–18 are papal letters to Rotrou of
Rouen and Becket urging a settlement with the king. These
are followed by nine letters (119–25a, 125b, and 126) written
by Becket, or on his behalf by members of the French royal
family, nobles, and bishops, protesting at this suspension,
which Henry II announced at La Ferté Bernard in July 1168.
The rest of Book IV deals with the appointment of Simon of
Mont-Dieu and Bernard de Corilo as commissioners for the
reconciliation of the king and archbishop, and the progress of
their mission, beginning with their official commission of 25
May 1168 (128), the formal notification to Becket of his suspension, dated 19 May (129), and a further papal letter
informing Louis VII that Becket's full powers would later be
restored (130). No. 131 exhorted Henry II to make peace with
Becket, recommending the special envoys Anthelme, Bishop of
Belley and the Prior of (La Grande ?) Chartreuse, and no. 132
formally announced the appointment of Simon and Bernard,
whose commission occurs as no. 128 above. The seven chapters
on the Conference of Montmirail are followed by eight letters
relating to it (133–40), including Becket's own report of the
proceedings to the Pope (133) and those by Simon of Mont-
Dieu and Engelbert of Val-St-Pierre (139) and by Richard of
St-Victor and Richard, *quondam* abbot of St Augustine's,
Bristol (140). The book ends with a batch of letters of varying
dates, all in one way or another supporting the authority
of the exiled archbishop. In 141–2 Master Gratian promises
his aid and Master Arnulf protests his loyalty; 143–8 are papal
mandates issued at various dates, ordering free elections in
England (143), commanding the return of benefices illicitly
conferred by the king (144), defending Canterbury's metropolitical authority (145: this letter is incorrectly ascribed to
Becket's pontificate by AlanT, although it was received by
Richard of Dover in 1174), mandating the English bishops to
respect the customary rights of Canterbury (146), forbidding
Roger of York to have his cross borne in the Southern Prov-

ince (147), and ordering the monks of Christ Church to assist their exiled archbishop (148); in 149, John of Salisbury reports on the peace prospects to Christ Church, and in 150 he urges the monks to give aid to Becket.

Book V : Letters 151–91.

The fifth book deals with Becket's resumption of his powers at the beginning of 1169, his issue of censures on 13 April and 29 May 1169 against the invaders of Church property, various appeals in favour of those so censured, and the appointment and negotiations of the new legates, Vivian and Gratian. The 42 letters contained in the book are well arranged: all, with the exception of no. 154, which was probably sent to Geoffrey Ridel in mid-1166, belong to the period from March to November 1169, and their general order is broadly correct. Nos. 151–3, 155, 156 and 164 contain various announcements of the sentences and threats issued on 13 April; nos. 157–60 are letters of appeal or complaint by Foliot in connection with this; nos. 161–3 contain the second wave of censures issued on 29 May; nos. 166 and 167 record the reaction of Henry II; nos. 168 and 169 are appeals on behalf of the Bishop of London, and nos. 170–6 are a group of letters written in defence of Becket's action. The book ends with an account of the new legation: nos. 177 and 178 announce the appointment of Vivian and Gratian; nos. 179 and 180 record the reaction of the king and the Norman episcopate to the new commissioners; nos. 181–7 contain various accounts of their negotiations, including the Conference at Montmartre (186). No. 187b is the text of the 1169 decrees; nos. 188–90 are letters of Becket commenting on the failure of the negotiations, and no. 191 is his letter to the people of England releasing them from the oath imposed on them by the king to ignore papal and archiepiscopal commands.

Book VI : Letters 192–224.

The sixth book covers the period from the appointment of Rotrou of Rouen and Bernard of Nevers as commissioners on 19 January 1169 to the censures on the bishops involved in the coronation of the Young King. Its 33 letters are mostly well arranged, even to the extent of placing nos. 200–2, taken from AlanT, Book IV, among materials derived from AlanT, Book V. On the other hand, there are a very small number of misplacements: the three papal letters dated 10 September (218) and 16 September (221–2) respectively, are wrongly placed in October material; but with these minor exceptions the remaining letters are placed correctly. The book opens with the commission to Rotrou of Rouen (192), dated 19 January 1170, and a group of letters concerned with the appointment of Rotrou and Bernard (193–5); nos. 196–9 record Becket's dismay at the legates' absolution of the Bishops of London and Salisbury; three letters prohibiting the coronation of Henry's son in the absence of the Archbishop of Canterbury (200–2) precede an account of the coronation; nos. 203–7 concern the Peace of Fréteval; no. 208 is a papal letter declaring that the rights of Canterbury are not affected by the coronation of the Young King; nos. 209 and 210 order that restitution be made according to the terms of the peace made between Becket and the king; nos. 211–13 are congratulatory letters from friendly cardinals sent to Becket after the news of the reconciliation was made known in Rome; no. 214 warns Becket that all is not well in England; in no. 215 Becket requests milder letters of censure of the bishops by the Pope; and there follow various letters containing sentences against the recalcitrant bishops (216–18 and 221–23); no. 219 is the last recorded letter from Henry II to Becket; and the book ends with the last letter written by Becket to the king (224).

Book VII: Letters 225–36.

This final section deals with Becket's return to England, his murder, and subsequent canonization; it is a fairly short book, and contains only 12 letters, beginning with the last known letter to come from Becket's hand and ending with *Qui uice beati Petri*, the encyclical letter of canonization issued by Alexander III in ? April 1173; the chronology of the letters seems correct. Becket's final letter (225) is followed by a 14-chapters account of the martyrdom and four letters calling on the Pope to avenge the archbishop's murder (226–9). The king's position is defended in a letter of Arnulf of Lisieux (230), and no. 231 is a further call for vengeance. The Compromise of Avranches is recorded in no. 232, and the account is completed with the legatine command for the reconciliation of Canterbury Cathedral (233) and no less than three of the papal bulls announcing the canonization (234–6).

It would appear that Roger took pains to preserve the accuracy of the substantial elements in the letters he used, though their diplomatic details, such as protocols and dates, are often lacking. The majority of the letters are given in full; and, although eighty-three letters have been abbreviated to some extent,[1] in fifteen cases the valedictory clause only is missing,[2] while in a further twenty-three instances the abbreviation is slight, involving merely the final sentence, or a postscript to the main part of the letter.[3] In most such cases the missing matter is not a serious loss, except perhaps in the letter *Sepe nobis* (171), where the list of excommunicates appended to the letter has been omitted, though this is clearly information of much interest. In comparison with

---

[1] Nos. 1, 2, 12, 13, 15, 20, 23, 28, 36, 37, 40–2, 54, 55, 61, 63–8, 70, 73, 74, 76, 82, 84, 91, 93–7, 101–3, 107b, 109, 114–16, 119, 120, 122, 124, 125a, 125b, 126, 133, 136, 139, 140, 142, 150, 155, 157, 161, 163, 170, 171, 182–4, 189, 190, 196–8, 201, 212, 213, 215, 218, 220, 225–7, and 229–33.

[2] No. 61 omits 'Valeatis . . . semper', cf. *Mats.* V, p. 278; no. 67 omits 'Valete . . . instanter', cf. ibid., p. 397; no. 70 omits 'Valere . . . pater', cf. ibid., p. 413; no. 95 omits 'Vale . . . proponuntur', cf. ibid., VI, p. 154; no. 96 omits 'Valeat . . . venturis', cf. ibid., p. 165; no. 97 omits 'Valeat . . . multa', cf. ibid., p. 174; no. 115 omits 'Valeat . . . immerito', cf. ibid., p. 400; no. 124 omits 'Valete . . . subvenite', cf. ibid., p. 469; no. 125 omits 'Valete . . . vestra', cf. ibid., p. 464; no. 170 omits 'Valeat . . . vestra', cf. ibid., VII, p. 123; no. 173 omits 'Valeat . . . vestra', cf. ibid., p. 43; no. 201 omits 'Valete . . . in Christo', cf. ibid., p. 257; no. 220 omits 'Valete . . . caritate', cf. ibid., p. 396; no. 230 omits 'Omnipotens . . . incolumen', cf. ibid., p. 439; and no. 231 omits 'Valete . . . facite', cf. ibid., p. 443.

[3] No. 1 omits 'De caetero . . . remittemus. Bene valete', cf. *Mats.* V, p. 41; no. 37 omits 'Praeterea nuntios . . . promovere. Valete . . . semper', cf. ibid., p. 156; no. 40 omits 'Iterato . . . audacia', cf. ibid., p. 151; no. 42 omits 'Ad haec . . . secretum', cf. ibid., p. 252; no. 54 omits 'Doceat vos . . . angustiam. Valeat . . . carissimus', cf. ibid., p. 418; no. 68 omits 'Excommunicavimus . . . extendunt', cf. ibid., p. 401; no. 91 omits 'Unum pro . . . nescit', cf. ibid., VI, p. 179; no. 94 omits 'De caetero . . . procuretis. Valete', cf. ibid., p. 215; no. 102 omits 'Hoc uero . . . dedi', cf. ibid., p. 126; no. 125b omits 'Alioquin . . . posse', cf. ibid., p. 480; no. 126 omits 'Nec vos . . . separari', cf. ibid., p. 516; no. 139 omits 'respondit quod . . . significabit', cf. ibid., p. 490; no. 142 omits 'Quod ipse . . . domine, bene valete', cf. ibid., p. 28; no. 155 omits 'Diu, et . . . tergiversationes', cf. ibid., p. 573; no. 157 omits 'Quod si . . . carebit', cf. ibid., p. 596; no. 171 omits 'Valeat . . . Cheringis', cf. ibid., VII, pp. 29–30; no. 183 omits 'Nuntii . . . meus', cf. ibid., p. 125; no. 190 omits 'ut timorem . . . posteros', cf. ibid., pp. 99–100; no. 196 omits 'Nomen . . . consoletur', cf. ibid., p. 294; no. 212 omits 'Nos enim . . . accepta', cf. ibid., p. 375; no. 213 omits 'Nos autem . . . concordabimus', cf. ibid., p. 373; no. 225 omits 'Vos si placet . . . pater', cf. ibid., p. 407; and no. 233 omits 'Nos sane . . . faciemus', cf. ibid., p. 552.

the corresponding letters in AlanT(A), Roger's letters lack protocols and dates in fifty letters which have these details in the latter,[1]
but one date and one attestation are found in Roger's collection,[2]
which also has no less than sixty protocols in full.[3] Of the latter,
eight were almost certainly derived from a source other than Alan
of Tewkesbury, since they are found in no extant version of his
work.[4] This lack of a consistent correspondence with any of the
various recensions of Alan of Tewkesbury's collection, despite the
seeming dependence on the AlanT stock, suggests once more a
possible derivation from an AlanT collection which has not
survived.

In a small number of cases material is lacking at the beginning of
a letter; but such omissions are very slight in substance, as with the
first line of *Quando dominus* (63) or the first three lines of *Sanctis
uiris* (140);[5] the first half of *Ad pedes maiestatis* (182) and its final
paragraph are omitted, but in this instance the complete text of the
letter is found earlier in the volume.[6] In forty-one letters the
abbreviation is more notable, where Roger's version tends to omit
part of the text not immediately relevant to the Becket dispute,
such as general references to events in Britain or in the Empire.[7]
The absence of terminal passages in the nature of postscripts has
already been mentioned;[8] in a similar category of omissions are

---

[1] Nos. 5, 6, 10, 28, 34–7, 43–5, 48, 50, 58, 63, 67, 74, 77, 86, 95, 99, 104, 107,
111, 128, 129, 132, 143–5, 147, 162, 166, 167, 176–8, 180, 192, 200, 210, 216–19,
221, 223, 224, 228, and 234.

[2] No. 1c has the date and no. 26 the attestation.

[3] Nos. 1–3, 7–10, 12–14, 20, 21, 25, 38, 40, 46, 56, 57, 59–61, 66, 68, 70, 71,
73, 80, 81, 90, 93, 96, 97, 105, 106, 115, 116, 122, 124, 141, 142, 149, 154, 156,
161, 163, 164, 170, 172, 181, 186–9, 201–3, 226, 229, 231, and 232.

[4] Cf. nos. 3, 10, 56, 57, 68, 81, 161, and 232.

[5] No. 63 lacks 'Quando dominus . . . praesentiam': cf. *Mats.* V, p. 365; no.
140 lacks 'Sanctis viris . . . assistentibus, et': cf. *Mats.* VI, p. 529.

[6] No. 182 lacks 'Ad pedes . . . exemplo' and 'Audite . . . vestra'; cf. *Mats.* VII,
pp. 118–120 and 122–3. For the full text, cf. no. 170.

[7] References to British affairs are omitted from nos. 2 and 41: no. 2 omits 'De
Walensibus . . . valete', cf. *Mats.* V, p. 49; and no. 41 omits 'Longe vero . . .
vestra', cf. ibid., VI, pp. 149–50. The reference to the Empire is omitted from
no. 23, which lacks 'Audivi tamen . . . modesti sunt', cf. ibid., V, pp. 164–5.

[8] But cf. also: no. 12 omits 'et Sancti . . . poterit' and 'Quod vobis . . . vestris',
cf. ibid., V, pp. 113–14 and 114–16; no. 13 omits 'in quo qualiter . . . in carcerem
ire', cf. ibid., p. 95; no. 28 omits 'ex precibus . . . ut nobis. Valete', cf. ibid.,
VII, p. 143; no. 36 omits 'Sic Moyses . . . facias. Vale', cf. ibid., V, p. 359; no. 55
omits 'Superest . . . iubeatis. Valete', cf. ibid., pp. 320–1; no. 64 omits 'Visis
litteris . . . imperatoris', cf. ibid., p. 429; no. 65 omits 'Hi tantummodo . . .
adfuerunt', cf. ibid., p. 188; no. 76 omits 'Ad haec . . . ejus', cf. ibid., VI, pp.

credence clauses referring to the bearer of the letter,[1] or the elaborate expression of gratitude in *Solliciti de statu* (93).[2]

In some instances Roger's version omits substantial passages, varying in length from half a page to four pages in the standard printed edition. But in all such cases but one the omission may be explained by the fact that the information in question is contained in other letters preserved in full elsewhere in the collection. Thus, the greater part of the anonymous letter *Comitem Flandrie* (15) has been omitted.[3] Since this letter recorded the difficulties encountered by Becket's messengers in the papal Curia at Sens in mid-1164 (whether in the negotiations concerning Roger of York's claim to have his cross borne before him in the southern Province, or concerning the professions of Foliot and Clarembald, elect of St Augustine's, and the possible summons of Becket to Alexander's presence), and since in most of these matters Becket's representatives failed to achieve their purpose, the deletion of such information, which could be construed as unfavourable to Becket, might indicate the suppression of unwelcome material in Roger's edition. But such an interpretation would be unwarrantable, since the details are contained in full in John of Poitiers' letter *Excitatus precurrentis* (7),[4] to which the anonymous writer of *Comitem Flandrie* himself referred.[5] Similarly, the greater part of the account of the negotiations between the papal legates Vivian and Gratian and the representatives of Henry II and Becket, at Rouen

---

[1] No. 163 omits 'Caetera in ore . . . de est', cf. ibid., pp. 51–2; no. 226 omits 'Latores vero . . . credite', cf. ibid., pp. 428–9; and no. 227 omits 'Praesentium portitores . . . revelanda', cf. ibid., p. 433.

[2] No. 93 omits 'Multa sanctitati . . . longa', cf. ibid., VI, p. 230.

[3] No. 15 omits 'Eo enim . . . anima mea', cf. *Mats.* V, pp. 59–61.

[4] Cf. ibid., pp. 56–7.

[5] Cf. ibid., p. 59.

20–1; no. 82 omits 'et provideat . . . Dei', cf. ibid., p. 51; no. 84 omits 'Utinam . . . vestrum', cf. ibid., pp. 56–7; no. 101 omits 'De caetero . . . exhibere', cf. ibid., pp. 124–5; no. 109 omits 'Nescitis . . . vestrae', cf. ibid., pp. 304–5; no. 114 omits 'Placeat itaque . . . observari', cf. ibid., VII, p. 244; no. 116 omits 'Haec est . . . ecclesiae', cf. ibid., VI, pp. 161–2; no. 119 omits 'Persecutores . . . rationem', cf. ibid., VII, p. 238; no. 120 omits 'Praeterea . . . suam. Valete', cf. ibid., VI, p. 474; no. 122 omits 'Nuper . . . Cant. et caetera', cf. ibid., pp. 472–3; no. 126 omits 'Nec timeri . . . disponetis', cf. ibid., pp. 466–7; no. 133 omits 'haec enim . . . nostra', cf. ibid., pp. 522–3; no. 161 omits 'Sed quia . . . praescribit. Valete', cf. ibid., VII, p. 49; no. 198 omits 'et nobis . . . nostri', cf. ibid., pp. 282–3; no. 215 omits 'Audistis . . . pater', cf. ibid., pp. 388–9; no. 218 omits 'De caetero . . . perturbandam. Datum . . . Septembris', cf. ibid., p. 359; and no. 232 omits 'Hoc . . . habuerint', cf. ibid., p. 518.

and Caen in early 1169, is omitted from *Inter emptorum* (184),[1] doubtless because the details are found in the immediately preceding letter *Clarissimi oratoris* (183), addressed by Becket to Humbald of Ostia.[2] Two pages of the printed text concerning the excommunications and threatened interdict in early 1170 are missing from *Vobis dilectissimi* (189),[3] but are found complete in the preceding letter *Vestra discretio* (188) to Henry of Winchester;[4] again, the letter *Vtinam dilecte* (197)[5] omits much of the matter which is contained in the letter *Nullus preter* (198) which follows it.[6] The omission of most of *Miseriarum cumulus* (103)[7] may perhaps be explained by the insertion slightly later of the formal report of the discussions which took place in the presence of Vivian and Gratian, sent by the commissioners themselves to Alexander III.[8] The concluding sections of *Fraternitatis uestre* and *Mirandum et uehementer* (73 and 74)[9] are both lacking, but the great length of these letters may have prompted their abbreviation, and nothing of significance is lost in either case. And perhaps for similar reasons, Arnulf of Lisieux's long letter *Magnam mihi* (20)[10] has been cut to about one third of its original length; it contains nothing particularly unfavourable to Becket, but it is very diffuse and prolix. There is only one instance in which either Roger or his source may have deliberately suppressed unwelcome material, in the final page of John of Salisbury's impassioned letter *Agonem nostram* (229) to William of Sens after Becket's murder;[11] the excluded passage contains a fierce attack on Roger of York, a leading opponent of Becket, with serious charges against his moral character while Archdeacon of Canterbury.

In the main, therefore, Roger of Crowland's use of Becket correspondence showed thoroughness and care, with an evident concern for the accuracy of his material. There is no evidence that

---

[1] No. 184 omits 'In quo vero . . . vestri', cf. *Mats.* VII, pp. 126–8.
[2] Cf. ibid., pp. 124–5.
[3] No. 189 omits 'Si recolatis . . . posteros', cf. *Mats.* VII, pp. 109–10.
[4] Cf. ibid., pp. 104–7.
[5] No. 198 omits 'nec ob aliud . . . Deum', cf. *Mats.* VII, pp. 279–81.
[6] Cf. *Mats.* VII, pp. 282–3.
[7] No. 103 omits 'et ita sopitis . . . nostri', cf. *Mats.* VI, pp. 249–55.
[8] *Venientes ad terram* (no. 107), cf. *Mats.* VI, pp. 281–4.
[9] No. 73 omits 'Istae sunt . . . ecclesia', cf. *Mats.* V, pp. 511–12; and no. 74 omits 'Quanto melius . . . vestra', cf. *Mats.* V, pp. 518–20.
[10] No. 20 omits 'Ad summam . . . Milonis', cf. *Mats.* V, pp. 306–14.
[11] No. 229 omits 'Eratis . . . ultioni', cf. *Mats.* VII, pp. 528–9.

he misused his sources in an *ex parte* fashion. The omissions which have been made in the introductions or concluding parts of letters did not result in any loss of substance of interest for the record of Becket's career, and where major abbreviations are found, they seem intended to eliminate needless repetitions.

3. THE APPENDIX TO QUADRILOGUS I

As already explained, the compilation known as *Quadrilogus I* was an anonymous amplification of Elias of Evesham's composition, achieved by the insertion into it of extracts from an expanded version of Grim's Life,[1] from FitzStephen's Life,[2] and with additional passages from Herbert of Bosham.[3] The circumstances of its composition are uncertain, and no manuscript of the work earlier than the mid-thirteenth century has survived;[4] but it has the distinction of being the first account of the Becket controversy to appear in print. It was published in Paris in 1495 from a manuscript now unknown by Master Johannes Philippi, a German printer who worked for the master printer George Wolff, at the sign of St Barbara in the rue Saint-Jacques in Paris. A small volume containing *Quadrilogus I*, under the title *Vita et Processus Sancti Thome Cantuariensis Martyris Super Ecclesiastica Libertate*, and Jean Bertrand's tract in defence of the liberties of the Gallican Church was the first book to be printed independently by him.[5]

[1] From this version of Grim's Life were taken much of the prologue, 'Professores artium ... solliciti sunt' (*Mats.* II, pp. 353–5), and the account of Becket's supposed Syrian descent, 'Pie igitur ... gratiosum' (*Mats.* II, pp. 451–8), and three further short passages; cf. *Mats.* IV, pp. 270, n. 8, and 393, n. 3.

[2] Numerous small extracts from FitzStephen are included: cf. ibid., pp. 270, n. 8; 271, n. 11; 273, n. 14; 320, n. 5; 323, n. 8; 375, n. 2; 382, nn. 1, 4, 8, and 9; 393, n. 7; and 394, n. 2.

[3] Ibid., pp. 376, n. 4; 389, n. 5; 399, n. 7; 413, n. 3; and 420, n. 16. Giles printed a few of the interpolations separately as item XVII in his *VST* II, pp. 181–91.

[4] Oxford University College MS lxix and Bibl. de Saint-Omer MS 710 date from the mid-thirteenth and fourteenth centuries respectively.

[5] Cf. A. Claudin, *Histoire de l'Imprimerie en France au XVe et au XVIe siècle*, 5 vols, Paris (1901–71), II, pp. 235–6. The colophon reads 'Explicit quadripartita hystoria continens passionem sanctissimi Thome martyris archipresulis Cantuariensis et primatis Anglie una cum processu eiusdem super ecclesiastica libertate, que impressa fuit Parisius per Magistrum Johannem Philippi, commorantem in vico Sancti Jacobi ad intersignium Sancte Barbare. Et completa anno Domini millesimo, quadringentesimo nonagesimo quinto, vicesima septima mensis Martii'.

Two copies of this valuable little book are now in the British Library, of which one belonged to Grenville[1] and the other to Lumley.[2] The volume was carefully produced, with the manuscript abbreviations faithfully copied in print and with spaces left for the later insertion of coloured initials; but the curious form of some abbreviations and the rather frequent misreading of 'u' for 'n' suggest that the editor had some difficulty in deciphering his exemplar.

Although so early an edition of the Life of Becket has its own intrinsic merit, this volume has a particular interest because it appends a group of sixty-seven letters and documents to the generally received text of *Quadrilogus I*, as preserved in the surviving manuscripts. The work is devised in five books, of which Books I–IV contain the *Quadrilogus*, together with the *Catalogus eruditorum*, the letters of canonization, the *Causa exilii*, and three further letters; but Book V, beginning with a further transcription of the Constitutions of Clarendon and the 1169 decrees (which had already appeared in the *Causa exilii*), contains the substantial appendix of Becket correspondence. The contents of this supplement can be briefly summarized as follows:[3] nos. 1 and 2 are the Constitutions of Clarendon and the 1169 decrees; nos. 3–19 are papal letters from the period October 1163[4] to October 1171;[5] nos. 20–46 are Becket correspondence, comprising twenty-one letters from Becket,[6] one addressed to him,[7] four to the Pope,[8] and an anonymous account of the negotiations held between Gisors and Trie in November 1167;[9] and nos. 47–67 are a miscellaneous group of letters, including some royal and episcopal letters to the Pope.

The appendix thus forms a fairly well-balanced collection of Becket material arranged in three main sequences: papal letters, Becket letters, and episcopal, royal, and other miscellaneous letters; and in a general way it resembles the Vatican Family in its separation of papal and Becket letters. But collation with other

---

[1] Press-mark, G. 1399.

[2] Press-mark, IB. 40476.

[3] For a full list of the letters contained in Book V, cf. Table 7 below.

[4] No. 3, *Litteras quas* (*Mats.* V, ep. 34), dated 26 October (1163).

[5] No. 19, *Mandamus uobis* (*Mats.* VII, ep. 787).

[6] Nos. 20–3, 25, 27, 29–32, 35–7, and 39–46.

[7] No. 24.

[8] Nos. 26, 28, 34, and 38.

[9] No. 33.

surviving collections of the Becket correspondence reveals that this supplement is directly related to none of them: no single collection contains all the letters in this appendix, although most of them are in Alan of Tewkesbury's collection[1] and a high proportion are in the Vatican and Rawlinson Collections.[2] But the appendix has two letters which are otherwise unknown[3] and records one date unknown elsewhere.[4] Again, collation shows that where there is significant variation between the Foliot and Becket traditions, this collection follows the Foliot rather than the Becket readings: it contains one letter otherwise found only in a Foliot derivative,[5] it agrees with the abbreviated text of *Venientes ad terram* as found in the Cave MS,[6] and it agrees with the Rawlinson Collection in its text of *Inter scribendum*.[7] The most striking correlation is with Part I of the Vatican Collection, since two short sequences of letters are found in this appendix in the same order as in the Vatican MS.[8] The source of the collection remains therefore unestablished; it is unlikely to have been originally intended as a supplement to *Quadrilogus I*, since it does not appear in either of the surviving manuscripts of the work, and its first two items repeat material from the *Causa exilii* which formed part of *Quadrilogus I*, Book IV. It may well have been included with *Quadrilogus I* in a manuscript used by Philipps at the end of the fifteenth century, a manuscript which has not survived but which contained a unique combination of Becket materials. But it is also possible that diverse sources were used by Philipps in the production of his single volume.

CONCLUSION

The dramatic circumstances of Becket's murder—in his own Cathedral by agents of a leading monarch, the European dimension of the controversy in which he had been engaged, the publicity

---

[1] With four exceptions (28, 33, 37, and 46), all are in AlanT(A).

[2] There are 43 in Vat. and 33 in Rawl.

[3] *Aggredimur rogare* (37), from Becket to Master Fulk of Reims; *Gratias agimus* (46), from Becket to William of Norwich (*Mats.* VI, ep. 688).

[4] *Quoniam de uestre* (18) has the date 'Datum vi. idus Maii', that is 10 May (1170).

[5] *Dominus Cantuariensis* (33); cf. Rawl. 23.

[6] The letter ends with 'terminum prefigentes', lacking 'in hyemali . . . timent' (cf. *Mats.* VI, pp. 283–4); cf. Cave 157.

[7] No. 60; cf. Rawl. 46.

[8] Nos. 22–5 = Vat. I, 9–12; nos. 26–31 = Vat. I, 1–5 and 8.

which attended its unfolding, and the unexampled speed of his formal canonization—all these factors combined to make the story of his life and martyrdom a matter of widespread interest throughout the length and breadth of Western Christendom in the last quarter of the twelfth century. The extension of Becket's cult[1] was further facilitated by the geographical extent of the continental Angevin Empire, stretching from Normandy to the borders of Navarre, and its diplomatic and dynastic links with Brittany, Castile, Saxony, and the Norman Kingdom of Sicily. At the same time, Becket's network of friends and supporters, established in key positions, assisted the spread of his cult both within and without the area of Henry II's influence: Archbishop Lukacz of Esztergom in Hungary; Bishop John, first of Poitiers and later of Lyons, in Poitou and the Lyonnais, Archbishop William, first of Sens and then of Reims, in Capetian France; and Archbishop Walter of Palermo, in the Norman Kingdom. Equally, the Cistercian Order became a principal promoter of his cult throughout its far-flung federation of monasteries. This created a demand not only for liturgical materials (lections, sequences, prayers, and music) but also for more substantial and authoritative accounts of his life and struggle. In attempting to provide for this demand, the early biographers turned to the surviving materials of the controversy for the authenticity of evidence which current intellectual fashion demanded. There was thus established a very close relationship between the Becket correspondence and other primary sources. This ensured an accuracy of detail and argument not usually found in works of hagiography, so that even derivative Lives, like the Lambeth Anonymous, which did not themselves include verbatim texts, achieved a high standard of authenticity through dependence on those which were steeped in the evidence of the letters. Even if the letter-collections had not survived, much of the essential flavour of the controversy, and certainly its essential features, would have been reliably transmitted in the works especially of William of Canterbury and William FitzStephen, whose access to materials from the archives respectively of Becket and Foliot made possible an approach to true historical writing.

---

[1] A full study of the European expansion of Becket's cult is being prepared.

PART III

Appendices and Tables

For economy in typesetting, the following abbreviations of personal names and titles have been adopted in the Appendixes and Tables:

A(bel), Abbot of St Osyth's
A(imar), Abbot of Chertsey
Albert, (Cardinal Priest of St Laurence in Lucina)
B(aldwin), Bishop of Noyon
Bernard (de Corilo, Prior of Grandmont)
B(ernard), Bishop of Nevers
C(lement), Prior of Llanthony
Engelbert, (Prior of Val-St-Pierre)
G(ilbert), Bishop of London
H(ugh), Bishop of Durham
Humbald (Hubald), Cardinal Bishop of Ostia
L(aurence), Abbot of Westminster
M(aurice), Bishop of Paris
Nicholas de Mont, (Prior of Mont-St-Jacques, Rouen)
Otto, (Cardinal Deacon of St Nicholas in Carcere Tulliano)
R(ichard), Bishop of Coventry-Lichfield-Chester
R(ichard), of Ilchester, Archdeacon of Poitiers
R(eginald, Rainald), Archbishop of Cologne
R(obert), Bishop of Hereford
R(oger), Bishop of Worcester
R(oger), Archbishop of York
R(otrou), Archbishop of Rouen
Simon, (Prior of Mont-Dieu)
S(tephen), Prior of Holy Trinity London
S(ilvester), Treasurer of Lisieux
T(heobald), Bishop of Amiens
Theodinus, (Cardinal Priest of St Vitalis)
W(illiam), Abbot of Ramsey
W(illiam), Archbishop of Sens
William of Pavia, (Cardinal Priest of St Peter ad Vincula)

APPENDIX I

The Bodleian Archetype

This table is dependent on Oxford Bodl. MS 509, which contains a fair copy of Archetype A: the earliest formal collection of Becket letters to be assembled. The numeration is taken from this MS.

			Mats.	Date*
1.	*Loqui de Deo*	Becket to Henry II	152	early 1166
2.	*Desiderio desideraui*	Becket to Henry II	154	April–May 1166
3.	*Celebre prouerbium*	Becket to Jocelin of Salisbury	199	*post* 12 June 1166
4.	*Licet tibi*	Becket to Gilbert Foliot	155	August 1165
5.	*Expectans expectaui*	Becket to Henry II	153	early 1166
6.	*Quanto uobis*	Becket to Henry of Winchester	144	June 1162–Dec. 1164
7.	*Si littere nostre*	Becket to Robert of Hereford	219	*c.* 1165–6
8.	*Fratres mei*	Becket to Canterbury suffragans	198	*c.* 12 June 1166
9.	*Si curamus*	Becket to Canterbury suffragans	183	*c.* June 1166
10.	*Super prudentia*	Becket to the Salisbury Chapter	200	May 1166
11.	*Expectauimus*	Becket to Geoffrey Ridel	237	Aug.–Sept. 1166
12.	*Expectabam litteras*	Becket to Robert of Leicester	80	*c.* Nov.–Dec. 1164
13.	*Non credebam*	Becket to William of Pavia	349	Dec. 1167
14.	*Misero uerba*	Becket to all cardinals	287	*post* 2 Feb. 1167
15.	*Que uestro*	Canterbury suffragans to Becket	205	*c.* 24 June 1166
16.	*Fraternitatis uestre*	Becket to Canterbury suffragans	223	July 1166
17.	*Si grandia*[1]	Becket to Silvester of Lisieux	269	*c.* Jan. 1167
18.	*Mittimus sanctitati*	Becket to the Pope	286	*post* 2 Feb. 1167

* The establishment of the true chronology of these letters must await the completion of a new edition of Becket's correspondence (in preparation). The dates given in these lists are therefore provisional.

[1] Wrongly addressed in this MS to Conrad of Mainz.

			Mats.	Date
19.	*Misimus tibi*	Becket to Geoffrey Ridel	238	Aug.–Sept. 1166
20.	*Inter optimam*	Becket to Conrad of Mainz	288	*post* 2 Feb. 1167
21.	*Solliciti de statu*	Becket to the Pope	322	*c.* Sept. 1167
22.	*Desiderio magno*	Becket to Conrad of Mainz	314	July 1167
23.	*Gratias habemus*	Becket to William of Pavia	313	July 1167
24.	*Mittimus sanctitati*	Becket to the Pope	348	*post* 14 Dec. 1167
25.	*Ex litterarum*	Becket to William of Pavia	329	Sept.–Oct. 1167
26.	*Remittimus sanctitati*	Becket to the Pope	407	July–Aug. 1167
27.	*Breuiloquio*	Becket to Henry II	603*	Nov. 1169
28.	*Celebre prouerbium*	Becket to the Pope	646	late Feb. 1170
29.	*Habita ratione*	Becket to Master Vivian	602	*ante* 11 Nov. 1169
30.	*Verbum euangelicum*	Becket to John of Naples	617	Nov. 1169
31.	*Breuiloquio*	Becket to Henry II	603*	? early 1166
32.	*Karissimus in Christo*	Pope to R. of Rouen & B. of Nevers	623	19 Jan. 1170
33.	*Quoniam de uestre*	Pope to R. of Rouen & B. of Nevers	628	April–May 1170
34.	*Super his que*[1]	Henry II to a cardinal (or all cardinals)	255	Aug.–Sept. 1165
35.	*Mandauit mihi*	Empress Matilda to Becket	275	*c.* 1165
36.	*Cum in mente*	Rotrou of Rouen to Becket	276	1165–7
37.	*Quoniam in aliis*	Pope to R. of Rouen & B. of Nevers	631	23 Feb. 1170
38.	*Nouerit industria*	Pope to Henry II's French bishops	629	18 Feb. 1170
39.	*Nouerit industria*	Pope to R. of York & H. of Durham	630	18 Feb. 1170
40.	*Nouerit industria*	Pope to Josius of Tours	634	18 Feb. 1170
41.	*Quoniam de prudentia*	Pope to Bernard of Nevers	625	*c.* 19 Jan. 1170
42.	*Quoniam de persona*	Pope to Rotrou of Rouen	624	*c.* 19 Jan. 1170
43.	*Vniuersis oppressis*	Pope to Canterbury suffragans	178	7 April/3 May 1166
44.	*Eam quam*	Pope to all English bishops	158	28 Jan. 1167

* There are two different versions of this letter, which are combined in the text published by Robertson in *Materials*.

[1] Wrongly addressed here (and in Vat. 195, 143, and William of Canterbury, *Mats.* I, p. 38) to Rotrou of Rouen.

			Mats.	Date
45.	*Quoniam ad omnem*	Pope to Becket	164	7 April/3 May 1166
46.	*Quoniam ad omnem*	Pope to prelates of Canterbury province	165	7 April/3 May 1166
47.	*Quod minor*	Pope to Becket	94	early 1165
48.	*Illius dignitatis*	Pope to all English Bishops	169	5 April 1166
49.	*Etsi pro animi*	Pope to Becket	50	5 March 1164
50.	*Excellentie tue*	Pope to Henry II	395	19 May 1168
51.	*Quam paterne*	Pope to Henry II	423	22 May 1168
52.	*Magnificentie tue*	Pope to Henry II	476	28 Feb. 1169
53.	*Dilecti filii*	Pope to Henry II	626	19 Jan. 1170
54.	*Non ob gratiam*	Pope to Becket	51	27 Feb. 1164
55.	*Quod personam*	Pope to Becket	272	*c.* 1 Jan. 1167
56.	*Post discessum*	Pope to Cardinals William & Otto	307	7 May 1167
57.	*Tenemus firmiter*	Louis VII to the Pope	293	mid-late Feb. 1167
58.	*Magnificentie tue*	Pope to Henry II	273	*c.* 1 Jan.1167
59.	*Experientiam rerum*	Becket to Master Gratian	695	*post* 22 July 1170
60.	*Otiosum est*	Becket to Walter of Albano	691	*post* 22 July 1170
61.	*Sicut ad locum*	Becket to Humbald of Ostia	692	*post* 22 July 1170
62.	*Iustum est*	Becket to William of Pavia	693	*post* 22 July 1170
63.	*Si laborantem*	Becket to Cardinal Hyacinth	694	*post* 22 July 1170
64.	*Ex quo pater*	Becket to the Pope	716	Oct.–Nov. 1170
65.	*Nouit inspector*	Becket to Henry II	718	late Oct. 1170
66.	*Sciatis quod Thomas*	Henry II to the Young King	690	mid-Oct. 1170
67.	*Sciatis quod obuiam*	Henry II to Becket	722	early Nov. 1170
68.	*Oportuerat uos*	Pope to certain English and Welsh bishops	700	16 Sept. 1170
69.	*Licet commendabiles*	Pope to R. of York & H. of Durham	701	16 Sept. 1170
70.	*Illum circa*	William of Pavia to Becket	591	*c.* Dec. 1169
71.	*Gauisus est*	Cardinal Albert to Becket	703	late Sept. 1170

			Mats.	Date
72.	*Licet de uerbo*	Cardinal Theodinus to Becket	704	late Sept. 1170
73.	*Per Gunterium*	Cardinal Peter to Becket	705	late Sept. 1170
74.	*Quam feruenti*	Cardinal Hyacinth to Becket	706	late Sept. 1170
75.	*Quando paternitatis*	Humbald of Ostia to Becket	707	late Sept. 1170
76.	*Cognito et*	Cardinal Theodinus to Becket	708	late Sept. 1170
77.	*Quamuis cure*	Pope to certain English and Welsh bishops	720	24 Nov. 1170
78.	*Quamuis cure*	Pope to G. Foliot & Jocelin of Salisbury	721	24 Nov. 1170
79.	*Quam iustis*	Becket to the Pope	723	early Dec. 1170

APPENDIX II

The Rawlinson Collection

This table lists the contents of Oxford Bodl. MS Rawlinson Q.f.8, fos. 1r–122r.

Part I   *Mats.*   Date

			Mats.	Date
1.	*Sciatis quod*[1]	King Stephen to his English subjects	—	Dec. 1153
2.	*Eterna et incommutabilis*[2]	Pope to Archbishop Theobald	—	5 Oct. 1159
3.	*Quia sedis apostolice*[3]	Council of Pavia to all faithful	—	Feb. 1160
4.	*Iam dudum*	Frederick I to the Empire	100	1 July 1165
5.	*Cum clerum*	Anon. to Alexander III	99	*post* 19 May 1165
6a.	*Sicut ad uestram*[4]	Henry II to clerical subjects	—	Christmas 1159
6b.	Resumé of the Constitutions of Clarendon[5]		—	Jan. 1164
7.	*A memoria tua*	Pope to Gilbert Foliot	93	8 June 1165
8.	*Mandatum uestrum*	Gilbert Foliot to the Pope	108	late July–Aug. 1165

Part II

9.	*Desiderio desideraui*	Becket to Henry II	154	April–May 1166
10.	Treaty between Henry II and Louis VII[6]		—	May 1160
11.	*Loqui de Deo*	Becket to Henry II	152	early 1166
12.	*Si littere nostre*	Becket to Robert of Hereford	219	1165–6
13.	*Celebre prouerbium*	Becket to Jocelin of Salisbury	199	*post* 12 June 1166
14.	*Quando dominus*	Henry II to the Abbot of Citeaux	188	*c.* June 1166

[1] Cf. Rymer, *Foedera*, I.i.18.
[2] JL 10590.
[3] *MGH, Legum* IV, II, pp. 265–6.
[4] Cf. A. Saltman, 'Two early collections of the Becket correspondence and of other contemporary documents', *BIHR* XXII (1949), pp. 154–5.
[5] Ibid., pp. 155–6.
[6] Brial, *Recueil des historiens*, XVI, p. 21.

			Mats.	Date
15.	*Vestram pater*	Suffragans to the Pope	204	*c.* 24 June 1166
16.	*Appellationem*	Gilbert Foliot to Nigel of Ely[1]	—	late June 1166
17.	*Fratres mei*	Becket to Canterbury suffragans	198	*c.* 12 June 1166
18.	*Quod circa ea*	Pope to Gilbert Foliot	106	22 Aug. 1165
19.	*Etsi circa nos*	Pope to Henry II	486	*c.* 7 July 1166
20.	*Que uestro*	English clergy to Becket	205	24 June 1166
21.	*Mirandum et uehementer*	Becket to Gilbert Foliot	224	July 1166
22.	*Fraternitatis uestre*	Becket to the English clergy	223	July 1166

Part III

23.	*Dominus Cantuariensis*	Report of Gisors/Trie meeting	334	*post* 19 Nov. 1167
24.	*Venientes ad terram*	William & Otto to the Pope	342	*c.* 9 Dec. 1167
25.	*Innotuit regi*	William & Otto to Becket	343	*c.* 9 Dec. 1167
26.	*Quanta uniuerse*	Pope to William & Otto	324	22 Aug. 1167
27.	*Excellentie tue*	Pope to Henry II	395	*c.* 19 May 1168
28.	*Super discretione*	Pope to all English bishops	400	24 April 1169
29.	*Quam paterne*	Pope to Henry II	423	22 May 1168
30.	*Excessus uestros*	Becket to Gilbert Foliot	479	*c.* 13 April 1169
31.	*Vestram non debet*	Becket to the London clergy	488	*c.* 13 April 1169
32.	*Se ipsum ad penam*	Becket to William of Norwich	489	*c.* 13 April 1169
33.	*Sacrorum canonum*	Becket to Nigel of Ely	490	*c.* 13 April 1169
34.	*Et naturali*	Pope to Henry II	492	10 May 1169
35.	*Nuncios et litteras*	Norman clergy to the Pope	567	*post* 8 Sept. 1169
36.	*Illius dignitatis*	Pope to the English bishops	169	5 April 1166
37.	*Sciatis quod Thomas*	Henry II to the Young King	690	mid-Oct. 1170
38.	*Oportuerat uos*	Pope to certain English and Welsh bishops	700	16 Sept. 1170

[1] MB, *Foliot*, ep. 165.

			Mats.	Date
39.	*Licet commendabiles*	Pope to R. of York and H. of Durham	701	16 Sept. 1170
40.	*Quam iustis*	Becket to the Pope	723	early Dec. 1170
41.	*Expectans expectaui*	Becket to Henry II	153	early 1166
42.	*Vniuersis oppressis*	Pope to the English bishops	178	7 April/3 May 1166
43.	*Ex iniuncto*	Pope to clergy of Canterbury province	173	24 April 1166
44.	*Magnificentie tue*	Pope to Henry II	258	20 Dec. 1166
45.	*Pro amore Dei*	Writ of Henry II	686	22–23 July 1170
46.	*Inter scribendum*	William of Sens to the Pope	735	Jan. 1171

Part IV

Letters 47–84. This section is clearly an abbreviation of the Bodleian Archetype (cf. Appendix I), whose content and order it reproduces, except for the omission of Bodl. nos. 2, 5, 17, 20, 34–6, 40–3, 47–55, 57–63, and 66–79, and the insertion, as Rawl. 80, of Alexander III's letter *Sepe nobis* (*Mats.* 157) to Gilbert Foliot, written in late 1165 or very early 1166. Cf. p. 45, nn. 2–4 above.

Part V

85.	*Ex insperato*	JohnS to John of Poitiers	748	Jan. 1171
86.	*Immensas laudes*	Pope to Richard of Canterbury[1]	—	6 Aug. 1177

APPENDIX

87.	*More pii patris*	Innocent III to King John[2]	—	23 Jan. 1209

[1] JL 12910.
[2] Pat. Lat. CCXV, col. 1535; cf. C. R. Cheney and W. H. Semple, edd., *Selected Letters of Pope Innocent III concerning England*, NMT, London (1953), pp. 117–20.

APPENDIX III

The Vatican Archetype

The following table is dependent principally on Vatican MS Lat. 6024, fos. 72ra–139vb, which contains the earliest surviving derivative from Archetype B. The content and order of the archetype have been established by means of collation with Brit. Libr. MS Royal 13. A. xiii. The numeration of the Vat. MS has been retained.

Part I			Mats.	Date
4.	*Desiderio desideraui*	Becket to Henry II	154	April–May 1166
11.	*Que uestro*	Canterbury suffragans to Becket	205	c. 24 June 1166
13.	*Mirandum et uehementer*	Becket to Gilbert Foliot	224	July 1166
12.	*Fraternitatis uestre*	Becket to Canterbury suffragans	223	July 1166
29.	*Diu desideraui*	Henry II to R. of Cologne	213	early 1165
30.	*Et ratio iuris*	Becket to R. of Hereford & R. of Worcester	179	c. June 1166
28.	*Meminimus nos*	Becket to Gilbert Foliot	239	June 1166
31.	*Magnam de*	Ernisius and Richard of St-Victor to Robert of Hereford	220	Aug. 1166
32.	*Si curamus*	Becket to Canterbury suffragans	183	June 1166
33.	*Mittimus uobis*	Becket to all English bishops	166	May–June 1166
34.	*Abutitur ecclesie*	Becket to the Pope	246	Nov. 1166
35.	*Omnia nostra*	Becket to Conrad of Mainz	247	Nov. 1166
36.	*Si uobis aliter*	Becket to Henry of Pisa	248	Nov. 1166
37.	*Ecclesiam Anglorum*	Becket to Cardinal Hyacinth	249	Nov. 1166
38.	*Vigor sensuum*	William el. of Chartres to the Pope	192	June–Dec. 1166
39.	*Si uerum est*	Becket to Provost Robert of Aire	558	*ante* 15 Aug. 1169
40.	*Gratias agimus*	Becket to the Empress Matilda	75	Dec. 1164
41.	*Audito aduentu*	Becket to Cardinal Otto	309	July–Aug. 1167
42.	*Stylum cohibere*	Peter of St-Rémi to the Pope	352	c. Dec. 1167
43.	*Indubitanter*	Becket to Cardinal Boso	250	? early 1166

			Mats.	Date
44.	*Discretioni uestre*	Becket to Cardinal John	290	*post* 2 Feb. 1167
45.	*Miseriarum cumulus*	Becket to the Pope	331	*post* 19 Nov. 1167
46.	*Nuntium uestrum*	William & Otto to Becket	356	Oct. 1167
47.	*Venientes ad terram*	William & Otto to the Pope	342	9 Dec. 1167
48.	*Probabile quidem*	Becket to Stephen, Chancellor of Sicily	138	? early 1167
49.	*Audita promctione*	Becket to Dean Fulk of Reims	146	? 1165
50.	*Nos uobis*	Becket to Gilbert of Sempringham	148	? 1165
51.	*Multam nobis*	Becket to Richard, el. of Syracuse	405	late 1167– early 1168
52.	*Cum sanctus Job*	Carthusians to Henry II	289	Feb. 1167
53.	*Honor quem*	Louis VII to Manuel of Constantinople	597	late 1169
54.	*Longanimitatis*	Becket to the Pope	466	*post* 7 Feb. 1167
55.	*Gratias non*	Becket to Cardinal Otto	468	*post* 6 Jan. 1169
56.	*Ad illustrem*	Simon & Engelbert to the Pope	451	*post* 6 Jan. 1169
57.	*Ecclesie persecutor*	Becket to the Pope	642	Feb.–March 1168
58.	*Ecclesie Romane*	William el. of Chartres to the Pope	446	July 1168
59.	*Vobis sicut*	Alice of France to the Pope	440	July 1168
60.	*Crebrescunt*	Stephen of Meaux to the Pope	437	July 1168
61.	*Anima mea*	Becket to the Pope	643	June–July 1169
62.	*Omnis quidem*	Matthew treas. of Sens to the Pope	438	July 1168
63.	*Consolationis*	Becket to Bernard of Porto	443	June–July 1168
64.	*Gratias agimus*	Becket to Cardinal Manfred	441	June–July 1168
65.	*Consoletur uos*	Becket to Conrad of Mainz	442	June–July 1168
66.	*Nos alii*	Becket to Cardinals Humbald & Hyacinth	444	June–July 1168
67.	*Pro archiepiscopo*	Louis VII to the Pope	435	July 1168
68.	*Dilectioni uestre*	Louis VII to Cardinals Humbald and Hyacinth	439	July 1168
69.	*Qualiter in secundo*	William of Sens to the Pope	470	*post* 7 July 1169

			Mats.	Date
70.	*Sic computati*	Poitevin petition	335	Nov. 1167
71.	*Licet faciem*	Becket to Margaret of Sicily	595	late 1169
72.	*Humanitas uestra*	Becket to Richard el. of Syracuse	596	late 1169
73.	*Honor quem*	Louis VII to William of Sicily	594	late 1169
74.	*Meminisse potest*	Becket to Richard and William of Le Valasse	419	June–July 1168
75.	*Inualescunt pater*	Canons of Reims to the Pope	459	Feb. 1168
76.	*Venerabilis frater*	Henry of Reims to the Pope	458	Feb. 1168
77.	*Si causam*	Becket to the Pope	463	*post* 6 Jan. 1169
78.	*Veritas obumbrari*	Becket to William of Pavia	467	*post* 6 Jan. 1169
79.	*Desiderio*	Simon of Mont-Dieu to Cardinal Albert	465	*post* 7 Feb. 1169
80.	*Iuxta mandatum*	Simon & Engelbert to the Pope	464	*post* 7 Feb. 1169
81.	*Non turbetur*	Becket to the Canons of Pentney	485	Aug.–Sept. 1166
82a.	*Se ipsum ad penam*	Becket to William of Norwich	489	*c.* 13 April 1169
b.	*Sacrorum canonum*	Becket to Nigel of Ely	490	*c.* 13 April 1169
83.	*Vestra debuerat*	Becket to Gilbert Foliot	480	*c.* 13 April 1169
84a.	*Excessus uestros*	Becket to Gilbert Foliot	479	*c.* 13 April 1169
84b.	*Vestram non debet*	Becket to the London clergy	488	*c.* 13 April 1169
85.	*Dilectionis uestre*	Becket to Roger of Worcester	496	*c.* April 1169
86.	*Adhuc pater*	William of Sens to the Pope	498	*c.* 13 April 1169
87.	*Apostolice sedis*	Becket to the Pope	497	*c.* 13 April 1169
88.	*Vestra fraternitas*	Becket to Godfrey of St Asaph	357	? Oct. 1167
89.	*Nouerit fraternitas*	Becket to Hugh of Durham	495	*c.* 13 April 1169
90.	*Sacrorum canonum*	Becket to Rotrou of Rouen	494	*c.* 13 April 1169
91.	*Iustum est*	Becket to Geoffrey Ridel	500	*c.* 13 April 1169
92.	*Nouerit uniuersitas*	Becket to the clergy of Kent	499	*c.* 13 April 1169
93.	*Sepe quidem*	Becket to Humbald of Ostia	538	June 1169

			Mats.	Date
94.	*Nobis in aure*	Becket to William of Pavia	540	June–July 1169
95.	*Impudentie mater*	Milo of Thérouanne to the Pope	544	June 1169
96.	*Ferreum pectus*	Baldwin of Noyon to the Pope	545	June 1169
97.	*Audiuit ecclesia*	Becket to Cardinal John	541	June–July 1169
98.	*Gratias agimus*	Becket to Hugh of Bologna	542	June–July 1169
99.	*Si unum patitur*	William of Autun to the Pope	543	June 1169
100.	*Parit et alit*	Maurice of Paris to the Pope	546	June 1169
101.	*Inspectis litteris*	Becket to Roger of Worcester	551	June 1169
102.	*Acta nostrorum*	Henry of Winchester to the exiles	553	April–May 1168
103.	*Sinceritati uestre*	Becket to Henry of Winchester	549	? Sept. 1169
104.	*Ad sanctorum*	Becket to Henry of Winchester	550	early June 1169
105.	*Quot et quanta*	Becket to Christ Church	502	c. 13 April 1169
106.	*Nouit inspector*	Becket to Owen of Wales	129	1166–8
107.	*Scelerum mater*	William of Sens to the Pope	547	Aug. 1169
108.	*Apud dominum*	Matthew of Troyes to the Pope	548	Aug. 1169
109.	*Licet studia*	Becket to Gilbert Foliot	297	July–Aug. 1166
110.	*Cui plura*	Becket to Owen of Wales	125	c. March 1166
111.	*Mater tua*	Becket to David, Archd. of Bangor	127	1166
112.	*Quia ecclesiam*	Becket to the Canons of Bangor	126	1166
113.	*Apostolicis sine*	Becket to Godfrey of St Asaph	358	1166
114.	*Ecclesie pacem*	Becket to the Pope	554	Sept. 1169
115.	*A uestra non*	Master Gratian to G. Ridel, et. al.	581	c. 29 Sept. 1169
116.	*Meminit uestra*	Becket to Rotrou of Rouen	579	c. 29 Sept. 1169
117.	*Ad uestram*	Becket to the clergy of Rouen	580	c. 29 Sept. 1169
118.	*Lamentati sumus*	Becket to Christ Church	573	*post* 18 Nov. 1169
119.	*Nouit uestra*	Becket to the clergy of Kent	574	*post* 18 Nov. 1169

			Mats.	Date
120.	*Quanto maiorem*	Becket to Clarembald el. of St Augustine's	575	*post* 29 Sept. 1169
121.	*Vestra discretio*	Becket to Henry of Winchester	576	*post* 18 Nov. 1169
122.	*Vobis dilectissimi*	Becket to the London clergy	577	*post* 18 Nov. 1169
123.	*Ad pedes maiestatis*	Becket to the Pope	583	*post* 29 Sept. 1169
124.	*Clarissimi oratoris*	Becket to Humbald of Ostia	584	*post* 29 Sept. 1169
125.	*Inter emptorum*	Becket to Cardinal Hyacinth	585	*post* 29 Sept. 1169
126.	*Festinat ad*	Becket to William of Pavia	586	*post* 29 Sept. 1169
127.	*Sancta Cantuariensis*	Becket to Cardinal John	587	*post* 29 Sept. 1169
128.	*Missi sunt*	Becket to Bernard of Porto	588	*post* 29 Sept. 1169
129.	*Fraternitatem uestram*	Becket to John of Naples	589	*post* 29 Sept. 1169
130.	*Impossibile est*	Becket to William of Sens	606	*post* 18 Nov. 1169
131.	*Omnem operam*	Master Vivian to the Pope	607	*post* 18 Nov. 1169
132.	*Quantum pro*	Master Vivian to Henry II	608	*post* 18 Nov. 1169
133.	*Impiorum molimina*	Becket to Master Gratian	609	*post* 18 Nov. 1169
134.	*Que in colloquio*	Becket to Alexander & John	610	*post* 18 Nov. 1169
135.	*Gratias quas*	Becket to Froger of Seez	637	*c.* Feb.–early March 1170
136.	*Vt aliquid*	Becket to Henry of Winchester	650	March–April 1170
137.	*Discretio uestra*	Becket to Roger of York	651	March–April 1170
138.	*Nos sanctitati*	B. of Noyon & M. of Paris to the Pope	639	Feb.–March 1170
139.	*Secutus fidem*	Becket to Geoffrey of Autun	638	Feb.–March 1170
140.	*Vtinam dilecte*	Becket to Cardinal Albert	662	mid-April 1170
141.	*Nullus preter*	Becket to Master Gratian	663	mid-April 1170
142.	*Gratias agimus*	Becket to Rotrou of Rouen	661	mid-April 1170

			Mats.	Date
143.	*Trecensis comes*	Becket to the Pope	394	1164–7
144.	*Quantum sit*	Becket to Cardinal Albert	664	mid-April 1170
145.	*Ei consultissime*	Exiles to Master Gratian	665	mid-April 1170
146.	*Dirigat Dominus*	Becket to Bernard of Nevers	644	late March 1170
147.	*Infirma mundi*	Becket to Idonea	672	*c.* May 1170
148.	*Vir illustris*	Becket to Roger of Worcester	649	March–April 1170
149.	*Ad nos iterato*	Becket to English and Welsh bishops	648	March–April 1170
150.	*Illustri Flandrorum*	Becket to the Pope	559	*ante* 15 Aug. 1169
151.	*Testatur uir*	Becket to the Pope	666	*c.* May 1170
152.	*Audiat sanctissime*	William of Sens to the Pope	674	*post* 14 June 1170
153.	*Quantis calamitatibus*	Becket to Roger of York	683	*post* 14 June 1170
154.	*Calamitates matris*	Becket to Gilbert Foliot	678	late June 1170
155.	*Fraternitatem uestram*	Becket to H. of Winchester	679	late June 1170
156.	*Quot et quantas*	Becket to Christ Church	680	late June 1170
157.	*Nouit uestra*	Becket to all Canterbury deans	681	late June 1170
158.	*Quanto sacrosancta*	Becket to St Augustine's	682	late June 1170
159.	*Miserationis oculo*	Becket to the Pope	684	*post* 22 July 1170
160.	*Experientiam rerum*	Becket to Master Gratian	695	*post* 22 July 1170
161.	*Otiosum est*	Becket to Walter of Albano	691	*post* 22 July 1170
162.	*Sicut ad locum*	Becket to Humbald of Ostia	692	*post* 22 July 1170
163.	*Iustum est*	Becket to William of Pavia	693	*post* 22 July 1170
164.	*Si laborantem*	Becket to Cardinal Hyacinth	694	*post* 22 July 1170
165.	*Ex quo pater*	Becket to the Pope	716	Oct.–Nov. 1170
166.	*Nouit inspector*	Becket to Henry II	718	late Oct. 1170
167.	*Quanta mala*	Becket to the Pope	160	? 1166

			Mats.	Date
168.	*Quam iustis*	Becket to the Pope	723	early Dec. 1170
169.	*Exhortationis uestre*	Becket to Giles el. of Évreux	244	1170

Part II

			Mats.	Date
208.	*Vniuersis oppressis*	Pope to Gilbert Foliot & bishops	178	7 April/3 May 1166
209.	*Suggestum est*	Pope to Cardinals William & Otto	355	Oct. 1167
210.	*Quanta uniuerse*	Pope to Cardinals William and Otto	324	22 Aug. 1167
211.	*Quod personam*	Pope to Becket	272	*c.* 1 Jan. 1166
212.	*Post discessum*	Pope to Cardinals William and Otto	307	7 May 1167
213.	*Magnificentie tue*	Pope to Henry II	273	*c.* 1 Jan. 1167
214.	*Ad aures nostras*	Pope to the English bishops	257	1 Dec. 1166
215.	*Eam quam*	Pope to the English bishops	158	28 Jan. 1167
216.	*Sepe nobis*	Pope to Gilbert Foliot	157	late 1165– early 1166
217.	*Quoniam ad omnem*	Pope to Becket	164	7 April/3 May 1166
218.	*Quoniam ad omnem*	Pope to Canterbury prelates	165	7 April/3 May 1166
219.	*Quod minor*	Pope to Becket	94	early 1165
246.	*Illius dignitatis*[1]	Pope to the English bishops	169	5 April 1166
220.	*Etsi pro animi*	Pope to Becket	50	5 March 1164
22.	*Magnificentie tue*[2]	Pope to Henry II	476	28 Feb. 1169
221.	*Non ob gratiam*	Pope to Becket	51	27 Feb. 1164
222.	*Significatum est*	Pope to Becket	420	20 May 1168
223.	*Ego Girardus*	Oath of Gerard la Pucelle	421	*c.* 20 May 1168
224.	*Significatum est*	Pope to Louis VII	422	20 May 1168
225.	*Excellentie tue*	Pope to Henry II	395	*c.* 19 May 1168
226.	*Super discretione*	Pope to the English bishops	400	24 April 1168

[1] Owing to a change of hand after no. 219, it appears that *Illius dignitatis* was omitted from the original transcription of the Vat. MS at this point. Its true position is established by reference to Brit. Libr. MS Royal 13 A. xiii.

[2] The absence of this letter from Vat. at this point is explained by its previous occurrence in Vat. Part I; its true position is established by reference to the Royal MS, cited above.

			Mats.	Date
227.	*Ad uestre discretionis*	Pope to Simon & Bernard	424	25 May 1168
228.	*A regie serenitatis*	Pope to Henry II	404	26 April 1168
229.	*Quam paterne*	Pope to Henry II	423	22 May 1168
230.	*Decet prudentiam*	Pope to Roger of York	42	Dec.–Jan. 1163–4
231.	*Ad discretionis*	Pope to Becket	414	19 May 1168
232.	*Ad audientiam*	Pope to the English bishops	413	19 May 1168
233.	*Mirabile gerimus*	Pope to John Cumin	415	*c.* 19 May 1168
234.	*Omnino nobis*	Pope to Roger of Worcester	401	April–May 1168
235.	*Nouerit discretio*	Pope to R. of Rouen & B. of Nevers	656	12 Feb. 1170
236.	*Nouerit industria*	Pope to R. of York & H. of Durham	630	18 Feb. 1170
237.	*Quoniam in aliis*	Pope to R. of Rouen & B. of Nevers	631	23 Feb. 1170
238.	*Dilecti filii*	Pope to Henry II	626	19 Jan. 1170
239.	*Karissimus in Christo*	Pope to R. of Rouen & B. of Nevers	623	19 Jan. 1170
240.	*Quoniam ad audientiam*	Pope to the English bishops	633	26 Feb. 1170
241.	*Nouerit industria*	Pope to Josius of Tours, et. al.	634	18 Feb. 1170
242.	*Quoniam de prudentia*	Pope to Bernard of Nevers	625	*c.* 19 Jan. 1170
243.	*Quoniam de uestre*	Pope to R. of Rouen & B. of Nevers	628	April–May 1170
244.	*Quoniam de persona*	Pope to Rotrou of Rouen	624	*c.* 19 Jan. 1170
245.	*Litteras quas*	Pope to William of Sens	668	*c.* June 1170
247.	*Ex commissi*	Pope to Becket & all English bishops	632	24 Feb. 1170
248.	*Oportuerat uos*	Pope to certain English and Welsh bishops	700	16 Sept. 1170
249.	*Licet commendabiles*	Pope to R. of York & H. of Durham	701	16 Sept. 1170
250.	*Quamuis cure*	Pope to certain English and Welsh bishops	720	24 Nov. 1170
251.	*Quamuis cure*	Pope to G. Foliot & Jocelin of Salisbury	721	24 Nov. 1170
252.	*Quanto personam*	Pope to Henry II	460	9 Oct. 1168–69
253.	*Saluti regum*	Pope to Louis VII	713	*c.* Oct. 1170
254.	*Cognito ex*	Pope to Henry II	689	late Aug.–Sept. 1170

			Mats.	Date
255.	*Sacrosancta Romana*	Pope to Becket	172	24 April 1166
256.	*Si enormitates*	Pope to Becket	712	9 Oct. 1170
257.	*Cura pastoralis*	Pope to prelates in Henry II's French lands	715	13 Oct. 1170
258.	*Molestias et*	Pope to W. of Sens & R. of Rouen	710	9 Oct. 1170
259.	*Virtutis et fidei*	Pope to Becket	696	July–Aug. 1170
260.	*Anxietate cordis*	Pope to Becket	714	13 Oct. 1170
261.	*Quam gratum*	Pope to all subjects of Henry II	697	12 Oct. 1170
262.	*Audito et*	Pope to R. of Rouen & B. of Nevers	711	9 Oct. 1170
263.	*Quoniam enormitatibus*	Pope to Becket & English bishops	709	8 Oct. 1170
264.	*Quia non nunquam*	Pope to R. of Rouen & T. of Amiens	764	23 Oct. 1171

The Lambeth 'Addition'

The greater part of the letter-collections in Lambeth MS 136 and Oxford Bodl. MS 937, Parts II and III is derived from the Bodleian and Vatican Archetypes, and it is unnecessary to repeat the details of that common material here. Hence this table contains the 140 'new' letters preserved in Lamb., which constitute the Lambeth Addition. The division into Parts (a) and (b) results from collation with Bodl.B, II, which indicates that Part (a) may have existed as a separate entity. The numeration is taken from the Lambeth MS.[1] Items marked with an asterisk are also in the Vatican Archetype.

Lambeth Addition (a)			*Mats.*	Date
*87.	*Quanto personam*	Pope to Henry II	460	9 Oct. 1168 or 1169
88.	*Magnam mihi*	Arnulf of Lisieux to Becket	162	March 1165
*89.	*Et ratio iuris*	Becket to R. of Hereford and R. of Worcester	179	c. June 1166
*90.	*Meminimus nos*	Becket to Gilbert Foliot	239	c. June 1166
*91.	*Omnia nostra*	Becket to Conrad of Mainz	247	Nov. 1166
*92.	*Si uobis*	Becket to Henry of Pisa	248	Nov. 1166
*93.	*Vigor sensuum*	William el. of Chartres to the Pope	192	June–Dec. 1166
*94.	*Gratias agimus*	Becket to Empress Matilda	75	Christmas 1164
*95.	*Audito aduentu*	Becket to Cardinal Otto	309	c. June 1167
*96.	*Probabile siquidem*	Becket to Chancellor Stephen	138	early 1167
*97.	*Multam nobis*	Becket to Richard el. of Syracuse	405	late 1167– early 1168
98.	*Noscat dilectio*	Becket to a friend	534	c. Aug. 1169
*99.	*Consoletur uos*	Becket to Conrad of Mainz	442	June–July 1168
100.	*Rediit nuncius*	Becket to Conrad of Mainz	48	early Jan. 1164
*101.	*Consolationis*	Becket to Bernard of Porto	443	June–July 1168
*102.	*Nos alii*	Becket to Cardinals Humbald & Hyacinth	444	June–July 1168

[1] Except where it is faulty. Nos. 90–5 are misnumbered 89bis–94, and nos. 208–364 are misnumbered 207–363.

			Mats.	Date
*103.	Pro archiepiscopo	Louis VII to the Pope	435	June 1168
104.	A memoria tua	Pope to Gilbert Foliot	93	8 June 1165
105.	Mandatum uestrum	Gilbert Foliot to the Pope	108	July–Aug. 1165
106.	Vestram pater	Canterbury clergy to the Pope	204	c. 24 June 1166
107.	Quod circa ea	Pope to Gilbert Foliot	106	22 Aug. 1165
108.	Etsi circa nos	Pope to Henry II	486	7 July 1166
*109.	Mirandum et	Becket to Gilbert Foliot	224	July 1166
*110.	Venientes ad terram	William and Otto to the Pope	342	c. 9 Dec. 1167
111.	Innotuit regi	William and Otto to Becket	343	c. 9 Dec. 1167
*112.	Quanta uniuerse	Pope to William and Otto	324	22 Aug. 1167
*113.	Excessus uestros	Becket to Gilbert Foliot	479	c. 13 April 1169
*114.	Vestram latere	Becket to the London clergy	488	c. 13 April 1169
*115.	Se ipsum	Becket to William of Norwich	489	c. 13 April 1169
*116.	Sacrorum canonum	Becket to Nigel and Richard of Ely	490	c. 13 April 1169
117.	Et naturali	Pope to Henry II	492	10 May 1169
118.	Nuncios et litteras	Norman clergy to the Pope	567	post 8 Sept. 1169
119.	Ex iniuncto	Pope to prelates of Canterbury diocese	173	24 April 1166
120.	Magnificentie tue	Pope to Henry II	258	20 Dec. 1166
121.	Ab humane pietatis	Louis VII to the Pope	734	January 1171
*122.	Decet prudentiam	Pope to Roger of York	42	6 July 1165 or 30 Jan. 1166
123.	Sullimitati uestre	English Church to the Pope	344	29 Nov. 1167
124.	Expedit beatissime	William of Pavia to the Pope	362	Dec.–Jan. 1166–7
125.	Venerabilis frater	Cardinal Otto to the Pope	363	Dec.–Jan. 1166–7
126.	Quia te super	Account of Gisors/Trie meeting	332	post 19 Nov. 1167
127.	Honor cinguli	JohnS to Baldwin Archd. of Norwich	328	Oct.–Nov. 1167
*128.	Suggestum est	William and Otto to the Pope	355	c. Oct. 1167
*129.	Super discretione	Pope to the English bishops	400	24 April 1168
130.	Quoniam ecclesia	Pope to Holy Trinity	412	16 May 1168

			Mats.	Date
131.	*Sepius nuncios*	Henry II to the Pope	564	*post* 7 Feb. 1169
132.	*Euocati a domino*	Rotrou of Rouen to the Pope	565	*post* 8 Sept. 1169
133.	*Post nunciorum*	Bernard of Nevers to the Pope	566	*post* 8 Sept. 1169
*134.	*Quot et quanta*	Becket to Christ Church	502	*c.* 13 April 1169
*135.	*Impudentie mater*	Milo of Thérouanne to the Pope	544	June 1169
136.	*De uestro*	Henry II to Rotrou of Rouen	669	Mar.–April 1170
137.	*Licet abiectio*	Odo of Canterbury to R. of Ilchester	552	June 1169
138.	*Quod statum*	Master Vivian (MS: William of Pavia) to the Pope	563	*post* 8 Sept. 1169
*139.	*Vobis dilectissimi*	Becket to Chester (MS: Chichester) diocese	577	*post* 18 Nov. 1169
140.	*Cum nuncios*	Pope to Becket	531	19 June 1169
141.	*Ad tue discretionis*	Pope to Becket	487	21 April 1167
142.	*Nouerit celsitudo*	Maurice of Paris to the Pope	605	*post* 18 Nov. 1169
143.	*Ad aures nostras*	Pope to Becket	130	20 Feb. 1166
144.	*De absolutione episcoporum*		561	Sept. 1169

The Lambeth Addition (*b*)

231.[1]	*Quanto per carissimum*	Pope to Roger of York	310	17 June 1161
234.	*Vestre satis*	Henry II to the Pope	506	June 1169
235.	*Perseuerans in corde*	Rotrou of Rouen to the Pope	528	*ante* 15 Aug. 1169
236.	*Veritatis assertio*	L. of Westminster (MS: Abbot of Ramsey) to the Pope	519	18 March 1169
238.	*Scimus prudentie*	Rotrou of Rouen to Becket	658	*post* 5 April 1170
246.	*Regie serenitatis*	Pope to Louis VII	436	Aug.–Sept. 1168
248.	*Etsi aduersitatum*	Pope to Becket	397	30 Jan. 1168
250.	*Ex litteris*	Pope to Becket	448	9 Oct. 1168
251.	*Quoniam sub uno*	Bernard of Porto to Becket	445	Aug.–Sept. 1168
252.	*Reddite sunt*	John of Naples to Becket	291	April–May 1167

[1] The MS numeration differs by one digit from no. 208 (=MS 207) onwards, because the modern numerator omitted *Mater tua* (p. 223a). Hence, 231 = MS 230, etc.

			Mats.	Date
253.	*Deuocionis ac*	Pope to Stephen of Meaux, et. al.	143	1165–6.
254.	*Quanto personam*	Pope to Roger of York	13	11 June 1162
255.	*Venerande pater*	Becket to the Pope	27	*ante* 18 Oct. 1163
256.	*Pro illa animi*	Pope to Roger of York	41	*c.* 21 Jan. 1164
257.	*Querimonias*	Pope to Becket	43	21 Jan. 1164
*259.	*Ex commissi nobis*	Pope to Becket & bishops	632	24 Feb. 1170
264.	*Cum hii qui*	Pope to Rotrou of Rouen	698	10 Sept. 1170
268.	*Solliciti estote*	Becket to Alexander and John	612	*c.* Sept. 1169
269.	*Rex proxima*	Friend to Becket	673	*c.* 7 June 1170
274 = 119				
276.	*Tanta nos*	Gilbert Foliot to Henry II	208	July 1166
277.	*Placuit excellentie*	Gilbert Foliot to Henry II	167	May–June 1166
278.	*Veniens ad nos*	Jocelin of Salisbury to Becket	206	*c.* 24 June 1166
279.	*Ad nos usque*	Salisbury Chapter to Becket	207	*c.* 24 June 1166
280.	*Seueritatem uestram*	Gilbert Foliot to Becket	474	18 March 1169
281.	*Vestram domine*	Gilbert Foliot to Henry II	503	April–May 1169
282.	*Seueritatem domine*	Gilbert Foliot to the Pope	475	*c.* April 1169
283.	*Venerabilem fratrem*	Gilbert Foliot to Henry II	236	Nov. 1166–Jan. 1167
284.	*Mittimus ad uos*	Gilbert Foliot to Henry II	504	early June 1169
285.	*Audiui grauamen*	Henry II to Gilbert Foliot	505	June 1169
286 = 234				
287.	*Perlatum est*	Pope to Becket	180	16 May 1166
288.	*Ex litteris*	Pope to Becket	187	27 May 1167
289.	*Ex rescripto*	Pope to Becket	193	8 June 1166
291.	*Gratias ago*	Becket to all English bishops	536	July–Aug. 1169
292.	*Sciatis karissimi*	Becket to all English people	636	*c.* Nov.–Dec. 1169
294.	*Venerabilis uir*	Becket to the Pope	450	*c.* 28 Dec. 1168
301.	*De uestre sinceritatis*	Becket to Cardinal Otto	330	Sept.–Oct. 1167
302.	*Ecclesie molestias*	Becket to Albert and Theodinus	501	1166–70
303.	*Gratias habemus*	Becket to Master Gratian	533	*c.* Aug. 1169

			Mats.	Date
304.	*Mittimus ad uos*	Becket to Master Lombard	406	July–Aug. 1168
305.	*Licet temporum*	William of Pavia to Becket	311	July–Aug. 1167
306.	*Litteras celsitudinis*	Becket to William of Pavia	312	*c.* July 1167
307.	*Quanto magis*	Becket to Cardinal Hyacinth	315	*c.* July 1167
308.	Nomina excommunicatorum		507	*c.* 29 May 1169
309.	*Litteras sullimitatis*	Humbert Archd. of Bourges to Becket	308	*c.* Oct. 1167
310.	*Vt cum domino*	Master Vivian to Becket	620	*post* 27 Oct. 1169
311.	*Feruentis et*	Friend to Becket	403	March–May 1168
312.	*Hec est forma*	Friend to Becket	453	*ante* 14 Feb. 1169
313.	*In die assumptionis*	Friend to Becket	560	2–8 Sept. 1169
314.	*Quos ad me*	Henry II to William of Sens	469	*c.* Jan. 1169
315.	*Venientes ad me*	Henry II to William of Sens	570	24 Aug.–2 Sept. 1169
316.	*Significauit nobis*	William of Sens to Henry II	571	24 Aug–2 Sept. 1169
317.	*In admirationem*	William of Sens to Vivian and Gratian	572	24 Aug.–2 Sept. 1169
318.	*Duplicis rationis*	Friend to Henry II	87	*post* 2 Feb. 1165
319.	*Multas sanctitati*	Philip of Flanders to the Pope	139	? 1166
320.	*Licet non sit*	Stephen of Meaux to the Pope	614	Sept.–Oct. 1169
321.	*Quantum te*	Becket to Gilbert of Sempringham	149	June 1162–Dec. 1163
322.	*Cum illius*	Pope to the King of Scots	134	late 1165–early 1166
323.	*Quando dominus*	Henry II to the Abbot of Citeaux	188	*c.* June 1166
324.	*Discretioni uestre*	William and Otto to bishops W. of Norwich and R. of Chester	353	*c.* 9 Dec. 1167
325.	*De uestra sinceritate*	Henry II to Cistercian Chapter	568	*c.* 2 Sept. 1169
326.	*Placet nobis*	John of Naples to Henry II	396	*c.* 19 May 1168
327.	*Amicitie ratio*	William of Pavia to Gilbert Foliot	245	*c.* Oct. 1166

			Mats.	Date
331.	*Regia potest*	Becket to Henry II	462	*post* 6 Jan. 1169
332.	*Benedictus Deus*	Master Vivian to Becket	601	*ante* 11 Nov. 1169
333.	*Mandatum domini*	Becket to Simon and Bernard	452	*post* 6 Jan. 1169
334.	*Sanctis uiris*	Richard of St-Victor and Richard, *quondam* Abbot of St Augustine's, Bristol, to the Pope	471	*post* 7 Feb. 1169
337.	*Dilectioni uestre*	Becket to Stephen of Meaux	613	*c.* Sept 1169
338.	*Nouit fraternitas*	Becket to Nicholas de Mont	184	Feb.–March 1166
346.	*Formam uerborum*	Rotrou of Rouen to Henry II	340	Dec. 1167
347 = 140				
348 = 325				
349 = 316				
350 = 317				
351.	*Vt desint uires*	Master William to Becket	508	*post* 1 June 1169
352 = 281				
*353.	*Miserationis*	Becket to the Pope	684	*post* 22 July 1170
*354.	*Cognito ex*	Pope to Henry II	689	Aug.–Sept. 1170
*355.	*Anxietate cordis*	Pope to Becket	714	13 Oct. 1170
*356.	*Quam gratum*	Pope to prelates, earls, and barons throughout Henry II's territories	697	12 Oct. 1170
*357.	*Audito et*	Pope to R. of Rouen & B. of Nevers	711	9 Oct. 1170
358.	*Segnius irritant*	Friend to Ralph of Serres	685	*post* 22 July 1170
359.	*Agonem nostram*	JohnS to William of Sens	777	early 1171
360.	*Gaudendum est*	Pope to Canterbury Chapter	784	12 March 1173
361.	*Redolet Anglia*	Pope to the English clergy & people	785	12 March 1173
362.	*Qui uice beati*	Pope to Walter of Aversa	786	? April 1173
363.	*Mandamus uobis*	Pope to Albert and Theodinus	787	late 1171
364.	*Letamur nos*	Albert and Theodinus to Christ Church	788	late 1171

Additional Letters in Oxford Bodl. MS 937, Parts II and III

This table lists the items in Bodl.B, Parts II and III, which are not found in Lambeth MS 136. The numeration is taken from Bodl. B, II and III.

Bodl. B, II			*Mats.*	Date
130.	*Vestro apostolatui*	William of Sens to the Pope	740	*c.* 25 Jan. 1171
131.	*Vestre placuit*	Theobald of Blois to the Pope	736	Jan. 1171
132.	*Nouerit uestra*	Messengers to Henry II	750	28 March 1171
134.	*Comitem Flandrie*	Messenger to Becket	36	Nov.–Dec. 1163
140.	*Peruenit ad*	Pope to Becket	14	16 Aug. 1162
141.	*Si quanta*	Pope to Bangor	117	10 Dec. 1165
142.	*Quia ex defectu*	Pope to Bangor	119	9 Feb. 1166
143.	*Si quanta*	Pope to Becket	118	29 Jan. 1166
145.	*Vestre discretionis*	Cardinal Peter to Becket	39	June 1162–mid 1164
146.	*Notificamus*	Cardinal Otto to Becket	306	April–May 1167
161.	*Honor quem*	Louis VII to Emperor Manuel	597	late 1169
179.	*Honor quem*	Louis VII to William of Sicily	594	late 1169
272.	*Mirabile gerimus*	Pope to John Cumin	415	May 1168
276.	*Saluti regum*	Pope to Louis VII	713	*c.* Oct. 1170
278.	*Si enormitates*	Pope to Becket	712	9 Oct. 1170
279.	*Cura pastoralis*	Pope to French bishops	715	13 Oct. 1170
280.	*Molestias et*	Pope to R. of Rouen & W. of Sens	710	9 Oct. 1170
283.	*Quia nonnunquam*	Pope to Rouen and Amiens	764	23 Oct. 1171
284.	*Ad aures nostras*	Pope to Becket	52	1 April 1164
285.	*Quoniam te uirum*	Pope to Gilbert Foliot	81	early 1165
286.	*Et ipsa loci*	Pope to Rouen & Amiens	763	23 Oct. 1711
290.	*A memoria tua*	Becket to Roger of Worcester	303	late 1166–7
296.	*Nil nobis*	Becket to Cardinal Albert	32	*post* 1 Oct. 1163

			Mats.	Date
297.	*Sanctitati uestre*	Becket to Humbald of Ostia	30	*post* 1 Oct. 1163
300.	*Benedictus Deus*	Brother R. to G. and R.[1]	—	Feb. 1171– March 1172
301.	*Secundum formam*	William of Norwich to Becket	727	Oct.–Nov. 1170
320.	*Circa mee*	Giles of Évreux to the Pope	730	mid-Dec. 1170
321.	*Ex insperato*	John of Salisbury to John of Poitiers	748	Jan. 1171
323.	*Primo dominus*	Account of Avranches agreement	771	*c.* 21 May 1172
324.	*Inter scribendum*	William of Sens to the Pope	735	early Jan. 1171
325.	*Cum apud regem*	Arnulf of Lisieux to the Pope	738	early Jan. 1171
326.	*Qui fuerint*	Royal messengers to R. of Ilchester	751	mid-April 1171

Bodl. B, III

6.	*Quotiens optimis*	William of Ramsey to the Pope	520	*c.* 18 March 1169
7.	*Si mihi presto*	Roger of York to the Pope	765	*c.* 13 Dec. 1171
8.	*Difficile est*	Friend to a friend	619	*c.* 1169–70?
12.	*Quoniam in corpore*	Becket to Dean Fulk of Reims	86	late 1165
40.	*Mora mea*	John of Salisbury to Peter of St-Rémi	724	early Dec. 1170

[1] Possibly Richard, *quondam* Abbot of St Augustine's Bristol, to Prior Richard and Brother Guarin of St-Victor Paris. The letter was printed from this MS in Giles, EpST, no. 374: cf. Pat. Lat. 190, cols. 707–09.

Alan of Tewkesbury's additional 'Becket' letters

It is assumed that Alan of Tewkesbury had access to the same sources as the compilers of the collections in the Vatican and Lambeth Families, discussed above. In addition, however, his own basic compilation (preserved in Vatican MS Lat. 1220 [AlanT(B)]) contains a further 185 letters and documents, of which 96 were written by John of Salisbury and derive mostly from his second letter collection, and 89 were written by Becket and other authors. The following table lists the latter 89 items in the order in which they occur in AlanT(B).[1]

Book I			*Mats.*	Date
1.	*Vix mihi*	John of Poitiers to Becket	25	*post* 29 June 1163
2.	*Preuenisset*	John of Poitiers to Becket	60	22 June 1164
3.	*In fine litterarum*	'Suus' to Becket	61	*c.* July 1164
6.	*Per misericordiam*	'Suus' to Becket	54	*c.* May 1164
7.	*Nouerit uestra*	'Suus' to Becket	53	*c.* May 1164
8.	*Legitur Constantii*	'Suus' to Becket	59	Nov.–Dec. 1164
9.	*Est unde respirare*	Master Hervey to Becket	62	*c.* Sept. 1164
12.	Constitutions of Clarendon		45	Jan. 1164
13.	*Nosti quam male*	Henry II to English bishops	77	Christmas 1164
14.	*Sciatis hunc*	'Amicus' to Becket	598	Sept.–Oct. 1169
15.	*Precipio tibi*	Henry II to English sheriffs	78	Christmas 1164
16.	Constitutions of 1169		599	Nov. 1169
18.	*Littere consolationis*	Becket to the Pope	29	*post* 1 Oct. 1163
20.	*Hortatur nos*	Becket to Bernard of Porto	31	*post* 1 Oct. 1163

[1] The more accurate Lupus numeration has been adopted for convenient reference. It corresponds with that in the Vatican MS except for I.139–79 (= MS 138b–78) and III.18–98 (= MS 17bis–97).

Book I   *Mats.*   Date

22.	*Inundauerunt mala*	Becket to Cardinal Hyacinth	33	*post* 1 Oct. 1163
25.	*Excitatus precurrentis*	John of Poitiers to Becket	35	Nov.–Dec. 1163
27.	*Significauit nobis*	Pope to Canterbury suffragans	408	14 May 1174
28.	*Vix apud dominum*	Master Arnulf to Becket	84	*post* 1 April 1165
35.	*Paternitatis uestre*	John of Poitiers to Becket	103	late Aug, 1165
36.	*Super his que*	'Amicus' to Becket	92	? late 1165
39.	*Miramur plurimum*	Pope to Robert of Hereford	141	? mid-1165
43.	*Quoniam dies*	Pope to Becket	95	? 8 June 1165
44.	*Nuntium uestrum*	'Amicus' to Becket	253	*ante* 18 Nov. 1166
45.	*Super negotio*	Nicholas de Mont to Becket	254	*ante* 18 Nov. 1166
46.	*Moleste ferimus*	Nicholas de Mont to Becket	284	uncertain: 1165–9
50.	*Iuxta tenorem*	Master Hervey to Becket	96	*c.* June 1165
51.	*Significamus uobis*	Cardinal Otto to Becket	82	April 1165
53.	*Quante compassionis*	Nicholas de Mont to Becket	76	Christmas 1164
54.	*Receptis litteris*	Pope to Becket	259	*c.* 20 Dec. 1166
55.	*Quanto sincerissime*	Pope to Philip of Flanders	127	? Jan. 1166
60.	*Dilectus filius*	Pope to Dean of Orleans	135	? Jan. 1166
61.	*Inter ceteras*	Pope to Henry of Champagne	136	30 Jan. 1166
62.	*Super beneficiis*	Pope to William of Clairmarais	133	? Jan. 1166
70.	*Iamdudum innotuisse*	Frederick I, encyclical	100	1 July 1165
71.	*Sicut nouit*	Frederick I to Stavelot	97	*post* 29 May 1165
72.	*Imperator cum*	'Amicus' to Alexander III	98	*post* 29 May 1165
75.	*Rediens ad nos*	Becket to Gunther	47	early Jan. 1164
80.	*Antecessorum nostrorum*	Pope to Clarembald el. of St Augustine's	102	10 July 1165
81.	*Fidei et deuotionis*	Pope to Pontigny	91	*c.* May 1165 –66
82.	*Licet uos eam*	Pope to the Cistercians	212	Aug. 1166
83.	*Super religione*	Pope to Christ Church	131	? late 1165
84.	*Iamdiu sanctitati*	Louis VII to Becket	243	Oct. 1166
86.	*Diutius expectaui*	Master Arnulf to Becket	163	late 1165– early 1166

			Mats.	Date
87.	*Dominum merito*	'Suus Hugo' to Becket	140	? early 1165
89.	*Loquitur sapiens*	Peter of Pavia to Becket	282	*post* 2 Feb. 1167
90.	*Quanta mala*	Pope to Rotrou of Rouen	182	16 May 1166
91.	*Ad hoc pontificalis*	Pope to Becket	49	*c.* Dec. 1173
92.	*Ad audientiam nostram*	Pope to the Cistercians	150	? late 1166
102.	*Pro domino rege*	Rotrou of Rouen to the Pope	101	early July 1165
105.	*Ad nos usque*	Jocelin of Salisbury to Becket	207	*c.* 24 June 1166
111.	*Proposueram*	Gerard la Pucelle[1] to Becket	234	*c.* Feb. 1167
114.	*Curam et sollicitudinem*	Pope to Becket	145	June 1162– Dec. 1163
118.	*Quod iuxta*	Pope to Becket	197	July–Aug. 1166
138.	*Satis superque*	Becket to the Pope	195	*c.* 12 June 1166
139.	*Satis superque*	Becket to the cardinals	196	*c.* 12 June 1166
143.	*Sicut nouit*	Becket to Rotrou of Rouen	201	*c.* 12 June 1166
144.	*Peruenit ad aures*	Becket to Robert of Hereford	202	*post* 12 June 1166
145.	*Quia dominum*	Becket to Hilary of Chichester	203	*c.* 12 June 1166
146.	*Vehementer gauisi*	Nicholas de Mont to Becket	209	*ante* 24 July 1166
164.	*Ipso die*	John of Poitiers to Becket	283	*post* 2 Feb. 1167
165.	*Quomodo de nouo*	Becket to John, his clerk	285	*post* 2 Feb. 1167
166.	*Cum uestre*	Master Lombard to the Pope	292	late Feb. 1167
178.	*In otio laborioso*	Master Arnulf to Becket	233	uncertain

Book II

6.	*Proxima quinta*	'Familiaris' to Becket	339	*post* 9 Dec. 1167
7.	*Qualiter iampridem*	Pope to Becket	493	10 May 1169
43.	*Inter cetera*	Pope to Louis VII	274	*c.* 1 Jan. 1167
75.	*Suggestum est*	Pope to Henry II	98	*post* 29 May 1165

[1] Wrongly attributed to John of Salisbury in AlanT.

			Mats.	Date
79.	*Vestre pater*	Owen of Wales to Becket	121	mid-1166
80.	*Gratias uobis*	Becket to Owen of Wales	122	mid-1166
81.	*Grate suscepimus*	Becket to David of Bangor	123	mid-1166
82.	*Relatum est*	Becket to Arthur de Kargan	124	mid-1166
83.	*Perlatum est*	Becket to Bangor Chapter	128	? early 1167
109.	*Ante discessum*	Becket to Alexander and John	359	? early 1168
111.	*Dum in celebratione*	Pope to Becket	67	May–June 1163

Book III

1.	*Illustris regis*	Pope to Becket	491	? 10 May 1169
15.	*Merito dixerim*	Becket to Stephen of Meaux	582	Sept.–Oct. 1169
66.	*Que acta sunt*	Becket to the Pope	611	*post* 18 Nov. 1169
77.	*Quod de mea*	Master Gratian to Becket	615	Dec.–Jan. 1169–70

Book IV

41.	*Quante auctoritatis*	Pope to English bishops	647	? 1170
48.	*Licet uestre*	'Amicus' to Becket	655	Feb.–Mar. 1170
50.	*Quot angustias*	Becket to the Pope	590	? mid-1170

Book V

9.	*Karissime, ut quid*	Becket to John of Poitiers	454	Jan.–Feb. 1169
17.	*Per uenerabilem*	Pope to Becket	635	Jan.–Feb. 1170
33.	*Transacta dominica*	'Suus' to Becket	676	*post* 14 June 1170
53.	*Mandatum uestrum*	Messengers to Becket	717	*post* 15 Oct. 1170
65.	*Inter multiplices*	Pope to Becket	699	10 Sept. 1170
74.	*Lectis caritatis*	Becket to Earl Hugh	725	c. Oct. 1170
75.	*Quid nobis*	Becket to W. of Norwich	726	c. Oct. 1170
89.	*Ne in dubium*	Albert & Theodinus to Henry II	772	c. 21 May 1172

Variants and Emendations in Brit. Libr. MS Cotton Claudius B. II: AlanT(A)

This table contains a small selection, excerpted for illustration from the complete collation, of the variants, corrections, and intended corrections inserted in Brit. Libr. MS Cotton Claudius B. II. The variants are collated with the readings of the following MSS:

Ab   Vatican Latin MS 1220 (AlanT(B))
Ac   Cambridge Corpus Christi MS 295 (AlanT(C))
Bi   Oxford Bodl. MS 509 (Bodl. A)
Bbii   Oxford Bodl. MS 937, Part II (Bodl. B, II)
Bbiii   Oxford Bodl. MS 937, Part III (Bodl. B, III)
V   Vatican Latin MS 6024 (Vat.)
R   Brit. Libr. MS Royal 13 A. xiii (Roy.)
L   London Lambeth Palace MS 136 (Lamb.)
D   Oxford Bodl. MS Douce 287 (Douce)

Additionally, the John of Salisbury letters are collated with:

JS   Brit. Libr. MS Addit. 11506
JS*   Paris Bibl. Nat. Latin MS 8562.

Where the two MSS agree in a particular reading, the single symbol JS is used; where they disagree, or where, for JohnS letters 120–169, only the Paris MS survives, the symbol JS* is used to designate the reading of the Paris MS.

Except where indicated by the symbol m (*margin*), all variants are written superscript in the MS; italics indicate corrections inserted over erasure; and entries in Hand D are marked with the superscript D. The abbreviated forms of *uel* and *alius* (ł, uł, ał) and the omission mark (/.) are given as they occur in the MS.

	Original Reading		Variant or Correction	
(1)	**Etsi circa nos I.38**			
42rb	ecclesiam sacrosanctam	Ab Ac Bbii L	sacrosanctam ecclesiam	V D
	pocius	Ab Bbii L	uł penitus	Ac V D
	eo	Ab Bbii L	uł ea	Ac V D
	usurpans	Ab Ac Bbii L	ł (usur)pas	V (usurpes D)
	uocas	Ab Ac Bbii V L D	ł (uo)cant	

		Original Reading	Variant or Correction	
42va	diuinum	Ab Ac Bbii L	ł domini	V D
	reseruare	Ab Bbii V L D	ł (reser)uasse	Ac
	potentie		ł potestati	Ab Ac Bbii V L D
42vb	que	Ac V D	qui	Ab Bbii L
	illud	Ab Ac Bbii L D	ł istud	V

(2)   Si curamus I.94

		Original Reading	Variant or Correction	
72ra	itaque	Ab Bi Bbii	ł utique	Ac V R L
72rb	fetere	Ac Bi Bbii V R	ł fatere	Ab L
	ex		ł de	Ab Ac Bbii V R L (se Bi)
	sicut	V R Bi Bbii	ł sic	Ab Ac L
	dotandum	V R	ł donandum [donandus	Ab Ac Bi L Bbii]
72va	scinditur	V R Bi L	ł rescin(ditur)	Ab Ac
	et	V R	ł in	Ab Ac Bi Bbii L
	habuerit	V R Bi Lᶜ	ł (habue)rint	Ab Ac Bbii
	eius	V R	uł ipsius	Ab Ac Bi Bbiiⁱ L
72vb	tamen	Ac V R	ł autem	Ab Bi Bbii L
	atrocius	Ac Vᶜ R	ł acrius	Ab Bi Bbii L
	quatinus	Ab Ac Bbii V R	ł (qua)te(nus)	Bi L
	hec	V R	ł hoc	Ab Ac Bi Bbii L
73ra	ethicum	Ac V R L	ł et hinc	Ab Bi Bbii

(3)   Recepi nuper I.150 (JohnS 33)

		Original Reading	Variant or Correction	
116rb	quia	Ab Ac	/. ł quodᵐ	JS
	sua sunt	Ab Ac JS	in ex(emplari) non habetur suaᵐ	
	fidissime	Ab Ac	/. ł fidelissimeᵐ	JS
116va	confidit	Ab Ac JS	ł confugit	
117ra	cause Christi	Ab JS	ał non cause sed assertor est Christiᵐ	Ab
117rb	eludere	Ab JS	ł elidere	Ac
117va	Christi	Ac	/. ł (Christ)oᴰᵐ	JS Ab
	sint	Ab Ac	ł sunt	JS
117vb	es	Ab Ac	/. tuᵐ	JS
	ducamus	Ac	ł producamusᵐ	JS Ab
118rb	uizilliani	Ab Ac	/. (uizilia)ciᵐ (viziliazi	JS JS★)

(4)   Puer meus I.169 (JohnS 50)

131vb	( )ⁱ uensi archidiacono	(1) alio libro. Ric. pictauensi archidiaconoᴰᵐ

---

¹ Erasure.   ᶜ by correction   ⁱ inserted

Claudius B II

	Original Reading		Variant or Correction	
			(2) Magistro Reimundo pictauensi cancellario^m	
			(R. Pict. archid.[1] Ab)	
			(R. Pict. cancell.[1] JS Ac)	
131vb	( )[2]		/. sinceritati^m	JS
	(sanctitati	Ab Ac)		
132ra	est	Ab Ac	ł erit^m	JS
132rb	ethnico	Ab Ac	ł ethico^m	JS
132vb	Idem	Ab Ac	/. enim^m	JS
133ra	*erased*		*in eoque*	JS Ab
	(In eo quidem Ac)			

(5) **Venientes ad terram II.35**

160va	incitauit	Ab Bbii L D	uł animauit	Ac V R
	regis		ł illius	Ac V R
	(regi	Ab)	(eius	Bbii L D)
	dissentire		uł dissone	Ac Bbii V R L D
	(dissensione	Ab)		
	ł exemptus[3]	Ac V R D	*exscriptus*	Ab Bbii L
	erased (*om* pro		*consuetudinibus . . .*	
	maxima parte	Ab Bbii L D)	*potius*	Ac V R
	presentialiter	Ac (*om* VR)	uł utique	Ab Bbii LD
160vb	sibi	Ac V R	uł secum	Ab Bbii L D
	octabas	Ac V R	uł (octa)uas	Ab Bbii L D
	uł ita[3]	V R	*taliter*	Ab Ac Bbii L D
	quod . . . descendere		Ał: quod neces-	
	(oportebat . . . proferret		sarium . . .	
		Ac VR)	descendere^m	Ab Bbii L D
	comprehense	V R	ł annotate	Ab Bbii L D
	(comprehense uel annotate Ac)			
161ra	*erased*		*ad iudicium . . .*	
	(*om* nobis . . . audita	V R)	*iudicium*	Ab Bbii L D
	(*ins* Cepit . . . iudicium Ac)			
	multis	Ac V R	uł non paucis	Ab Bbii L D
	timentes . . . exerceret	V R	ał l(ibro): timentes . . .	
			attemptaret^m	Ab Ac Bbii L D
161rb	uergat	Ac V R	ł uertatur	Ab Bbii L D

(6) **Quod hactenus II.45 (JohnS 104)**

169ra	apłisq;[4]		/. plerisque	JS Ab Ac
	natura	Ab^c	/. nature^m	JS Ac

[1] MS(S) give(s) a fuller form of this address.   [2] erasure.

[3] Original reading inserted above correction, and cited as a variant.

[4] This is the form in the MS: it could be misread as *apostolisque* instead of the intended *a plerisque*.

	Original Reading		Variant or Correction	
169rb	patienter	Ab	/. ł patenter^m	JS Ac
	sacerdotum	Ab Ac	/. eis^m	JS
	excusasti	Ab JS^x	/. ł exercit(asti)^m	JS Ac
	curialium	Ab Ac JS^x	/. curalium^m	JS
169va	adiutores	Ab	/. auc(tores)	JS Ac^c
	om Valete	Ab Ac	/. Valete^m	JS

(7) Expectatione longa II.64 (JohnS 53)

180ra	Ba( )^1 Exoniensi( )^1 (Domno Exoniensi JS^x)		(1) In ex(emplari): Baldewino exoniensi archidiacono^{Dm}	Ac
			(2) Bartholomeo^m	JS Ab
181ra	priuilegio		ł (priuileg)ia	JS Ab Ac
181va	proueniant	JS	uł (proueni)rent	Ab Ac
	nesciat	Ab Ac	ł (nes)ciebat^m	JS
	pluribus		/. (plu)rimis^m	JS Ab Ac
181vb	quod	Ab	/. quia^m	JS Ac^c
182ra	cui	Ab Ac JS	ł qui	
182va	quarundam rerum	Ac JS	ał ł(ibro) quorundam et c'^{Dm}	Ab
182vb	non		/. Non^m	JS Ab Ac
	pateret	Ab Ac JS	ł (pate)rent	
183ra	uoluptatibus	Ab Ac JS	ł uoluntatibus	
	est	Ab	/. ergo	JS Ac^c
	uel^c	JS	ł aut	Ab Ac
183rb	nec		ł neque	JS Ab Ac

(8) Ex quo prospere II.67 (JohnS 101)

185ra	feracis	Ab Ac JS	ł ferrati	
185va	hoc uerbum	Ac JS	uł hec uerba	Ab
186ra	ei	Ab	/. fata^m	JS Ac
	suum	Ab Ac	/. sentit^m	JS
186vb	comes	Ab Ac	/. (com)ites^m	JS
	fidelitatem	Ab Ac	/. (fidelita)tes^m	JS
187ra	conuenirent	Ac	/. (conue)nerant^m	JS Ab
	teneatur	Ab Ac	/. tenetur^m	JS
187rb	exhibere		/. (exhibe)ri^m	JS Ab Ac
	oper*iosius*	Ab	/. ł operosius^m	JS Ac
187va	ante quam		ł ante quod	JS Ab Ac
	interfecerant		ł (interfece)runt	JS Ab Ac

(9) Honor cinguli II.69 (JohnS 86)

188rb	B( )^1 norwicensi		Baldewino^{Dm}	JS

^{1} Erasure. ^{c} by correction

Claudius B.II

	Original Reading		Variant or Correction	
	(B. norwicensi Ab Ac)			
	(suo Willelmo Bbii L)			
	collocato	Ab Bbii L	/. ł collato[m]	JS Ac[c]
	commouet	Ab Ac Bbii	(1) ł (commoue)rit	
			(2) (commoue)rit[m] JS	
188va	uiuit	Ab Ac[c] Bbii L	/. iure non uiuit	JS
	scismatibus	Ab Bbii L	(scismati)cis[m]	JS Ac
	membra	Ab Ac Bbii L	/. carnium[m]	JS
	recipere	Ab Ac Bbii L	ł percipere[m]	JS
	prophetie	Ab Ac Bbii L	(prophe)te[m]	JS
188vb	cita	Ab Ac Bbii L	ł (ci)to	JS

(10)   Super discretione II.70

	Original Reading		Variant or Correction	
188vb	comparetis	V R D	ł apparetis	Ab Ac Bbii L
189ra	deliquistis	V R D	ul deliquiritis	Ab Ac Bbii L
	merueritis	V R D	ł (me)ruistis	Ab Ac Bbii L
	demum	V R	ł deinde	Ab Ac Bbii L D

(11)   Quot et quanta III.17

	Original Reading		Variant or Correction	
223vb	uestram		ł nostram	Ab Ac Bbii V R L
	archiepiscopo	V R	antedicto	Ab Ac Bbii L
	deferre[d] per[a] prouinciam[b]		per prouinciam	
	nostram[c]	V R	nostram deferre	Ab Ac Bbii L
224ra	ei	R	ł illi	Ab Ac Bbii V L
224rb	decreuerat	R	ł (decre)uit	Ab Ac Bbii V L
	quoniam		ł quod (maior) sit	Ab Ac Bbii V L
	maior est	R		
224va	potestis	R	ł poteritis	Ab Ac Bbii V L
	aut episcopis		In emendatiori exemplari aut	
	obedire	V R	episcopis obedire	
			non habetur[m]	Ab Ac Bbii L
	decreuerimus	R	ul decreuimus	Ab Ac Bbii V L
	/.et[Dm][1]		ex	Ab Ac Bbii V R L
224vb	*erased* (et ne . . .		*Et ne . . .*	
	impediunt *om* R)		*impediunt*	Ab Ac Bbii V L

(12)   Actiones gratiarum III.80 [JohnS 138]

	Original Reading		Variant or Correction	
257vb	scismaticis		/. ł (scisma)tis[m]	JS[x]Ab
258ra	quod	Ab	/. eum[m]	JS[x]
	ut tam	Ab JS[x]	ał non habet ut[m]	

[1] Original reading inserted beside correction, and intended for re-insertion.
[c] by correction.

	Original Reading		Variant or Correction	
	ordinaret	Ab JSˣ	al habet ordinareᵐ	
258rb	decernat	Ab	/. ł dis(cernat)ᵐ	JSˣ
	siquid	Ab	/. ł sedᵐ	JSˣᵐ

(13)   Excellentie tue IV.3

269ra	beneuolentiam		uł aurem	Ab Ac Bi Bbiii
	nostram	V R	beniuolam	L D
	uidetur	V R L D	ł uidebitur	Ab Ac Bi Bbii
	pugnare	Ac Bi Bbii V R L	ł uenire	(*om* Ab)
	asseuerent	V R L	uł assererent	Ab Ac Bi Bbii D
269rb	tuam	V R L	ł suam	Ab Ac Bi Bbii D

269rb

Original Reading	Variant or Correction
animum tuum mitigabit et te inspiratione sua dignabitur, dedimus in	In emendatiori exemplari ita habetur: animum tuum mitigare dignabitur, dedimus in
mandatis V R L	mandatisᵐ Ab Bi Bbii
(... mitigare dignabit Ac)	
(... serenare dignabitur D)	

	iterum	V R Lᶜ D	ł interim	Ab Ac Bi Bbii
269rb	poteris	Ac Bi Bbii V R L D	ł potestis	Ab
269va	uerba	V R	ł uerbum	Ab Ac Bi Bbii L D
	procederent	V R Lᶜ D	uel presiderent	Ab Ac Bi Bbii
	taliter	Ac V R D	uł aliter	Ab Bi Bbii L
	multiplicitati	V R	ł mutabilitate	Ab Ac Bi Bbii L D

Original Reading	Variant or Correction
quod specialiter propter honorem tuum fecimus imputare V R (quod propter honorem fecimus et sub tali spe imputare D)	In emendatiori exemplari ita habetur: quod ob honorem tuum et sub spe tali fecimus imputare et ceteraᵐ Ab Ac Bi Bbii L

(14)   Quam paterne IV.5

270rb	ac	V R D	ł et	Ab Ac Bi Bbii L
	alibi		ł alias	Ab Ac Bi Bbii V R L D

Original Reading	Variant or Correction
uenerabilis frater noster bellicensis episcopus et dilectus filius noster prior cartusiensis. uiri Ac¹ V R	In emendatiori exemplari ita habetur: dilecti filii nostri prior de monte dei et frater bernardus de corilo. uiri et ceteraᵐ Ab Ac² Bi Bbii L D

	ut	V R D	uł et	Ab Ac Bi Bbii L

(15)   Dilecti filii V.I

300va	quam	Bi V R	ł quando	Ab Ac Bbiiᶜ L
	ł quod³	V R	*qui*	Ab Ac Bi Bbii Lᶜ

¹ This is the original reading in Ac.
² Inserted as an alternative reading in Ac.
³ Original reading inserted above correction, and cited as variant.
ᶜ by correction

Claudius B. II

	Original Reading		Variant or Correction	
	pro	V R	ł in	Ab Ac Bi Bbii L
	suprascripte	V R	ł (supra)dicte	Ab Ac Bi Bbii L
300vb	augeatur	V R	uł adaugeatur	Ab Ac^c Bi Bbii L
	fauente	Bi	ł faciente	Ab Ac Bbii V R L
	eos	Ac Bi Bbii V R L	ł nos	Ab

(16) Karissimus in Christo V.3

	Original Reading		Variant or Correction	
301va	habuerunt (habuerint Bbii)	Ab Bi V (Bbii)	ł habuerit	Ac R
	et	V R	ł ac	Ab Ac Bi Bbii L
	Quod ... suscipere (*marked* B) Verumtamen ... complere (*marked* A)	V R	Nota quod in emendatiori exemplari uersus sequentis istum precidit^m	Ab Ac Bi Bbii L
	uestram	R	ł nostram	Ab Ac Bi Bbii V L
301vb	uoluerit	V R	ł uelit	Ab Ac Bi Bbii L
	nulla	Ac Bi V R	ł nullatenus	Ab Bbii ^cL
302ra	ipsius	V R	ł illius	Ab Ac Bi^c Bbii L
	tractauerunt	Ab Ac Bi Bbii L	ł (tracta)runt	V R
	condigne	V R	ł congrue	Ab Ac Bi Bbii L

(17) Quoniam de uestre V.4

	Original Reading		Variant or Correction	
302rb	semoto	V Bi	ł re(moto)	Ab Ac L
302va	occasione	V	ł excusatione	Ab Ac Bi L
	scripta	Ab V	pre(scripta)^c	Ac Bi L
302vb	habeatis	Bi	ł adhibeatis	Ab Ac^c V L

(18) Oportuerat uos V.69

	Original Reading		Variant or Correction	
333va	et	Ab Ac Bi Bbii V R L D	ł ex	
	iniquis	V R D	ł antiquis	Ab Ac Bi Bbii L
	iam	V R D	/. autem	Ab Ac Bi Bbii L
	uero	R L D	ł enim (autem Ab V)	Ac Bi Bbii
333vb	fuerit	Ab Ac Bi Bbii R L D	ł fuerat	V

(19) Quam iustis V.77

	Original Reading		Variant or Correction	
338ra	ł associatis¹ erased (sibi complicibus suis V R Ac D)	Ac V R D	*accitis sibi saresberiensi et aliis*	Ab Bi
338rb	concedens	Ac V R	uł cedens	Ab Bi (D reddens)
	amici	Ac^c Bi V R D	ł inimici	Ab

¹ Original reading cited as variant
^c by correction

	Original Reading		Variant or Correction	
338va	londoniensis	V R	/.et saresberi- ensis[Dm]	Ab Ac Bi D
	Elegerunt	V R	uł (Elege)rant	Ab Ac Bi D
338vb	exarmati	V R	ł in(armati)	Ab Ac Bi D
	archidiaconum	Ab Ac Bi V R D	ł (archidiacon)em	
339ra	iuri parituros	V R	ł se uestro mandato	Ab Ac Bi D
	Nunc exemplari ita inuenitur: Nos ... Quod cum et c(etera)[m] V R		*cum consilio ...* *Quod cum* (*D agrees with neither version*)	Ab Ac Bi

(20) Qui fuerunt primi V.89

347rb	Nuntius ricardi pictauensis archidiaconi (*om heading*	D)	ał l(ibro) Nuntius regis ricardo picta- uensi archidiacono[Dm] Ab Ac Bbii[1]	
	fuerunt	Ab Ac Bbii	ł (fue)rint[m]	
	om. suam		/.suam	Ab Ac Bbii D
347va	pichun (Pichim Pichun	Ab Ac Bbii D)	piiun[m]	
347va	sed salesberiensis ... et a domino papa		Sed Salesberiensis et cetera usque a domino papa in alio exemplari scripta non fuerunt[m] *om* Sed ... papa Ab Ac Bbii D	
	uenire		ł apperire	Ab Ac Bbii D
347vb	mandato	Ab Ac Bbii D	ł iudicio	
	suo	Ab Ac Bbii D	ł domini pape	
	mandato	Bbii D	uł iudicio	Ab Ac
	crederent	Bbii	uł (crederen)tur	Ab Ac D
	reportaturos	Ab Bbii D	(reportatu)ri	Ac
348ra	excepto ... eius		excepto dunelmensi usque ad Nam nuntius eius et cetera in alio exemplari non sunt[m] *om* excepto ... mancipauerit Ab Ac Bbii D	
	portebit		ł oportet	Ab Ac Bbii D

[1] The heading in Bbii reads: 'Exemplum litterarum quas Ricardo pictauensi
archidiacono miserunt amici sui explorantes in curia quenam futura esset conditio
regis et suorum post mortem sancti Thome.'

The Douce Collection

This table is dependent on Oxford Bodl. MS Douce 287, fos. 46va–101vb

			Mats.	Date
1.	*Celebre prouerbium*	Becket to Jocelin of Salisbury	199	12 June 1166
2.	*Quoniam de honestate*	Pope to Gilbert of London	37	9 Nov. 1163
3.	*Desiderio desideraui*	Becket to Henry II	154	April 1166
4.	*Loqui de Deo*	Becket to Henry II	152	early 1166
5.	*Si littere*	Becket to Robert of Hereford	219	1165
6.	*A memoria*	Pope to Gilbert of London	93	8 June 1165
7.	*Mandatum uestrum*	Gilbert of London to the Pope	108	July–Aug. 1165
8.	*Quod circa ea*	Pope to Gilbert of London	106	22 Aug. 1165
9.	*In colligendo*	Gilbert of London to the Pope	110	late 1165
10.	*Fratres mei*	Becket to Canterbury suffragans	198	c. 12 June 1166
11.	*Vestram pater*	Canterbury suffragans to the Pope	204	c. 24 June 1166
12.	*Que uestro pater*	Canterbury suffragans to Becket	205	c. 24 June 1166
13.	*Ad audientiam tuam*	Becket to the Pope	74	mid-Nov. 1164
14.	*Medicine potius*	Anon. to the Pope & cardinals	73	late Oct. 1164
15.	*Magnificentie tue*	Pope to Henry II	258	20 Dec. 1166
16.	*Mirandum et uehementer*	Becket to Gilbert of London	224	July 1166
17.	*Fraternitatis uestre*	Becket to Canterbury suffragans	223	July 1166
18.	*Multiplicem nobis*	Gilbert of London to Becket	225	late 1166
19.	*Placuit excellentie*	Gilbert of London to Henry II	167	May–June 1166
20.	*Mandatum domini*	Gilbert of London to Henry II	107	Aug.–Sept. 1167
21.	*Venerabilem fratrem*	Gilbert of London to Henry II	236	1166–7
22.	*Discretioni uestre*	William & Otto to Norwich & Chichester	353	Summer 1167
23.	*Anima nostra*	Anon. to the Pope	354	Sept.–Oct. 1167

			Mats.	Date
24.	*Venientes ad terram*	William & Otto to the Pope	342	9 Dec. 1167
25.	*Sublimitati uestre*	English Church to the Pope	344	29 Nov. 1167
26.	*Quoniam de honestate*	Pope to Gilbert of London	37	9 Nov. 1163
27.	*Litteras quas*	Pope to Becket	34	26 Oct. 1163
28.	*Vniuersis oppressis*	Pope to English bishops	178	3 May 1166
29.	*Ex iniuncto nobis*	Pope to English bishops	173	24 April 1166
30.	*Censum domine*	Gilbert of London to Henry II	111	1166–73
31.	*Tanta nos*	Gilbert of London to Henry II	208	July 1166
32.	*Si curamus esse*	Becket to English bishops	183	May–June 1166
33.	*Peruenit ad patrem*	Gilbert of London to bishops	147	1166–70
34.	*Nouerit Deus*	Becket to Jocelin of Salisbury	235	Oct.–Nov. 1166
35.	*Dominus Cantuariensis*	G. of London to Jocelin of Salisbury	477	March 1169
36.	*Ad aures nostras*	Pope to English bishops	257	1 Dec. 1166
37.	*Vestram scimus*	English Church to Becket	345	Nov. 1167
38.	*Ad uestram pater*	Gilbert of London to the Pope	569	Nov.–Dec. 1167
39.	*Scitis karissime*	G. of London to W. of Norwich	146	*c.* Nov. 1167
40.	*Placet nobis*	John of Naples to Henry II	396	Feb.–May 1168
41.	*Amicitie ratio*	William of Pavia to G. of London	245	Oct. 1166
42.	*Excellentie tue*	Pope to Henry II	395	19 May 1168
43.	*Quoniam te*	Pope to Gilbert of London	81	early 1165
44.	*Super discretione*	Pope to English bishops	400	24 April 1168
45.	*Etsi circa nos*	Pope to Henry II	486	7 July 1166
46.	*Quam paterne*	Pope to Henry II	423	22 or 24 May 1168
47.	*Seueritatem uestram*	Gilbert of London to Becket	474	18 March 1169
48.	*Excessus uestros*[1]	Becket to G. of London	479	April 1169
49.	*Vestram non debet*[1]	Becket to London clergy	488	13 April 1169
50.	*Se ipsum ad penam*[1]	Becket to William of Norwich	489	13 April 1169
51.	*Vestram domine*	Gilbert of London to Henry II	503	April–May 1169
52.	*Seueritatem domine*	Gilbert of London to the Pope	475	*c.* March–April 1169
53.	*Non potest*	Robert, Archd. of Oxford to G. of London	510	late May 1169

[1] The text of this letter is omitted.

			Mats.	Date
54.	*Mittimus ad uos*	Gilbert of London to Henry II	504	early May 1169
55.	*Multis curarum*	G. of London to R. Archd. of Oxford	509	June 1169
56.	*Audiui grauamen*[1]	Henry II to Gilbert of London	505	early May 1169
57.	*Vestre satis*	Henry II to the Pope	506	early May 1169
58.	*Perseuerans in corde*	R. of Rouen to the Pope	528	June 1169
59.	*Postquam dominus*	London Chapter to the Pope	518	*post* 18 March 1169
60.	*Apostolo domine*	Henry of Stratford to the Pope	526	June 1169
61.	*Apostolica doctrina*	William of Holy Trinity London to the Pope	527	June 1169
62.	*Expedit beatissime*	William of Pavia to the Pope	362	Dec. 1167–Jan. 1168
63.	*De nobilitatis*	Anon. to Anon.	514	Summer 1169
64a.	*Si quis inuentus*	1169 decrees[2]	—	Aug. 1169
64b.	*Dicetis super*	Instructions to judges[3]	—	1170
65.	*Super appellationis*	Anon. to Gilbert of London	515	1169
66.	*Et naturali*	Pope to Henry II	492	10 May 1169
67.	*Nouerit discretio*	Pope to R. of Rouen & B. of Nevers[4]	656	12 Feb. 1170
68.	*Quod tibi*	Pope to Gilbert of London	627	12 Feb. 1170
69.	*Sicut monet*	R. of Rouen to all England	659	c. 5 April 1170
70.	*Vniuersitati uestre*	R. of Rouen to London diocese	660	c. 5 April 1170
71.	*Illius dignitatis*	Pope to English bishops	169	5 April 1166
72.	*Formam uerborum*	Rotrou of Rouen to Henry II	340	Dec. 1167
73.	*Hoc petimus*	Becket to Vivian & Gratian	604	c. 16 Nov. 1169
74.	*Pro amore Dei*	Henry II's promise at Fréteval	686	22 July 1170
75.	*Expectans expectaui*	Becket to Henry II	153	early 1166
76.	*Sciatis quod*	Henry II to the Young King	690	Aug.–Sept. 1170

[1] First sentence only, ending 'in te'.

[2] Cf. D. Knowles, A. Duggan, and C. N. L. Brooke, 'Henry II's Supplement to the Constitutions of Clarendon', *EHR* (1972), pp. 764–71.

[3] Cf. MB, *Foliot*, Appendix VII, no. 5.

[4] Incorrectly addressed to Rotrou of Rouen and Bartholomew of Exeter, possibly as a result of confusing the abbreviated forms 'B. Niuern.' and 'B. Exon.'.

			Mats.	Date
77.	*Cum hii qui*	Pope to Rotrou of Rouen	698	10 Sept. 1170
78.	*Licet commendabiles*	Pope to R. of York & H. of Durham	701	16 Sept. 1170
79.	*Oportuerat uos*	Pope to certain English bishops	700	16 Sept. 1170
80.	*Quam iustis*	Becket to the Pope	723	early Dec. 1170
81.	*Cum apud regem*	Arnulf of Lisieux to the Pope	738	Jan. 1171
82.	*Miseranda rumorum*	William? to Hugh of Durham	741	*post* 25 Jan. 1171
83.	*Qui fuerunt*	Messenger to R. of Ilchester	751	mid-April 1171
84.	*Venturi sunt*	Anon. to Gilbert of London	756	early June 1171
85.	*Nouerit maiestas*	Messengers to Henry II	750	28 March 1171
86.	*Quantis tribulationibus*	W. of Ramsey to the Pope	521	*post* 18 March 1169
87.	*Vestre maiestati*	A. of Chertsey to the Pope	522	June 1169
88.	*Nonne pater*	A. of St Osyth's to the Pope	525	June 1169
89.	*Cum apud summum*	S. of Holy Trinity to the Pope	758	early 1171
90.	*Scriptum est*	C. of Llanthony to the Pope	523	June 1169
91.	*Et ipsa loci*	Pope to Rotrou of Rouen & Theobald of Amiens	763	23 Oct. 1171
92.	*Fraternitati uestre*	Pope to Rotrou of Rouen and Theobald of Amiens	767	27 Feb. 1172
93.	*Licet in proposito*	Pope to Jocelin of Salisbury	768	30 March 1172

Minor Collections

A. The Faustina Collection: Brit. Libr. MS Cotton Faustina B.I, fos. 2r–11va

			Mats.	Date
1.	*Et uera incommutabilis*[1]	Pope to all English bishops	—	13 Dec. 1159
2.	*Quia sedis apostolice*[2]	Encyclical from Pavia	—	Feb. 1160
3.	*Sacra scriptura*[3]	Cardinals to Frederick I	—	Dec. 1159
4.	*Cum Christus*[4]	Frederick I to Henry II	—	28 Oct. 1159
5.	*Benedictus Deus*[5]	Arnulf of Lisieux to the Pope	—	Oct.–Dec. 1159
6.	*Susceptis uestre*[6]	Philip of l'Aumône to the Pope	—	1160
7.	*Licet commendabiles*	Pope to R. of York & H. of Durham	701	16 Sept. 1170
8.	*Oportuerat uos*	Pope to certain English and Welsh bishops	700	16 Sept. 1170
9.	*Quam iustis*	Becket to the Pope	723	early Dec. 1170
10.	*Que uestro*	English clergy to Becket	205	c. 24 June 1166
11.	*Mirandum et uehementer*	Becket to Gilbert Foliot	224	July 1166
12.	*Ab humane pietatis*	Louis VII to the Pope	734	Jan. 1171
13.	*Vestro apostolatui*	William of Sens to the Pope	740	Jan. 1171
14.	*Vestre placuit*	Theobald of Blois to the Pope	736	Jan. 1171
15.	*Redolet Anglia*	Pope to all England	785	12 March 1173

B. *The Vallicelliana Appendix :* Rome Bibl. Vallicelliana MS B.60, fos. 73ra–101rb

1.	Constitutions of Clarendon		45	Jan. 1164
2.	*Desiderio desideraui*	Becket to Henry II	154	April–May 1166

[1] JL 10602; cf. Wilkins, *Concilia*, II, pp. 432–3.
[2] *MGH, Legum* IV. I, pp. 265–6.
[3] This letter in favour of Alexander III is otherwise unknown; for the text, taken from this MS, cf. W. Holtzmann, 'Quellen und Forschungen zur Geschichte Friedrich Barbarossas (Englische Analekten I)', *Neues Archiv*, XLVIII (1930) pp. 398–400.
[4] Pat. Lat. CXC, cols. 1058–9; cf. *MGH, Legum* IV, I, p. 254.
[5] *Arnulf of Lisieux*, ep. 24.   [6] Pat. Lat. CC, cols. 1359–61.

			Mats.	Date
3.	*Fratres mei*	Becket to Canterbury suffragans	198	*c.* 12 June 1166
4.	*Que uestro*	English clergy to Becket	205	*c.* 24 June 1166
5.	*Vestram pater*	Suffragans to the Pope	204	*c.* 24 June 1166
6.	*Mirandum et uehementer*	Becket to Gilbert Foliot	224	July 1166
7.	*Si littere*	Becket to Robert of Hereford	219	1165
8.	*Ad aures nostras*	Pope to Becket	52	1 April 1164
9.	*Precipio tibi*	Henry II to English sheriffs	78	Christmas 1164
10.	*Illius dignitatis*	Pope to all English bishops	169	5 April 1166
11.	*Licet commendabiles*	Pope to R. of York & H. of Durham	701	16 Sept. 1170
12.	*Oportuerat uos*	Pope to certain English bishops	700	16 Sept. 1170
13.	*Quam iustis*	Becket to the Pope	723	early Dec. 1170
14.	Passio sancti Thome[1]		748	Jan. 1171
15.	*Apostolatui uestro*	William of Sens to the Pope	740	Jan. 1171
16.	*Ab humane pietatis*	Louis VII to the Pope	734	Jan. 1171
17.	*Vestre placuit*	Theobald of Blois to the Pope	736	Jan. 1171
18.	*Eram magnificentie*	Anon. to the Pope	737	Jan. 1171
19.	*Qui fuerunt primi*	Royal messenger to R. of Ilchester	751	mid-April 1171
20.	*Fraternitati uestre*	Pope to Bourges & Nevers	753	24 April 1171
21.	*Et ipsa loci*	Pope to Rouen and Amiens	763	23 Oct. 1171
22.	*Quoniam expectare*	Albert & Theodinus to William of Sens	774	*c.* 21 May 1172
23.	*Redolet Anglia*	Pope to all England	785	12 March 1173

C. The Titus Collection: Brit. Libr. MS Cotton Titus D. XI, fos. 3r–41v

1.	*Expectans expectaui*[2]	Becket to Henry II	153	early 1166
2.	*Desiderio desideraui*	Becket to Henry II	154	April–May 1166
3.	*Que uestro*	English clergy to Becket	205	*c.* 24 June 1166
4.	*Mirandum et uehementer*	Becket to Gilbert Foliot	224	July 1166
5.	*Fraternitatis uestre*	Becket to his suffragans	223	July 1166
6.	*Fratres mei*	Becket to his suffragans	198	*c.* 12 June 1166
7.	*Si curamus*	Becket to all English bishops	183	May–June 1166
8.	*Sciatis karissimi*	Becket to all English bishops	636	Dec. 1169

[1] Adapted from John of Salisbury's letter, *Ex insperato*.
[2] The text begins defectively with the words 'Recedens a uia . . .'

TABLE 1

Schedule of letters used by Edward Grim

This table lists the letters included in or appended to Edward Grim's Life of St Thomas, together with their numerical location in Robertson's *Materials* (*Mats.*), and collates them with the Bodleian Archetype (Bodl.: cf. Appendix I and Oxford Bodl. MS 509), the Vatican Archetype (Vat.: cf. the reconstruction in Appendix III and Vatican MS Lat. 6024), and Alan of Tewkesbury's Recension II (AlanT(B): Vatican MS Lat. 1220).

A. Letters included in the text	*Mats.*	Bodl.	Vat.	AlanT(B)
1. *Fratres mei*	198	8	—	I.96
2. *Illius dignitatis*	169	48	—	(IV.49)*
3. *Que uestro*	205	15	11	I.126
4. *Mirandum et*	224	—	13	I.108
5. *Desiderio desideraui*	154	2	4	I.64
6. *Quam iustis*	723	79	168	V.73
†7. *Licet commendabiles*	701	69	249	V.67
†8. *Oportuerat uos*	700	68	248	V.66
†9. *Fratres mei*	198	8	—	I.96
B. Letters appended to the text				
1. *Apostolatui uestro*	740	—	—	V.82
2. *Ab humane pietatis*	734	—	—	V.78
3. *Vestre placuit*	736	—	—	V.81
4. *Eram magnificentie*	737	—	—	—
†5. *Qui fuerint primi*	751	—	—	V.84
†6. *Fraternitati uestre*	753	—	—	—
†7. *Et ipsa loci*	763	—	—	V.85
8. *Quoniam expectare*	774	—	—	—
†9. *Redolet Anglia*	785	—	—	V.93
†10. *Decens credendum*	—	—	—	—
†11. *Ecclesie uestre*	808	—	—	—

* Not found in AlanT(B), but occurs in AlanT(A) with the note 'non est inter ordinatas'.

† These items are found only in the Vespasian copy of Grim: Brit. Libr. MS Cotton Vespasian E.x.

TABLE 2

Schedule of letters used by William of Canterbury

This table lists the letters quoted or cited in William of Canterbury's Life of St Thomas, together with their numerical location in Robertson's *Materials* (*Mats.*), and collates them with the Bodleian Archetype (Bodl.: cf. Appendix I and Oxford Bodl. MS 509), the Vatican Archetype (Vat.: cf. Appendix III and Vatican MS Lat. 6024), and Alan of Tewkesbury's Recension II (AlanT(B): Vatican MS Lat. 1220).

A. Letters quoted at length	*Mats.*	Bodl.	Vat.	AlanT(B)
1. *Meminerit excellentia*	72	—	—	—
2. *Fraternitatis uestre*	223	16	12	I.127
3. Constitutions of Clarendon	45	—	—	I.12
4. Constitutions of 1169	599	—	—	I.16
5. *Mandatum uestrum*	108	—	—	I.38
6. *Non ob gratiam*	51	54	221	I.5
7. *Eam quam*	158	44	215	I.160
8. *Fratres mei*	198	8	—	I.96
9. *Celebre prouerbium*	199	3	—	I.100
10. *Quia te super*	332	—	—	II.27
11. *Quoniam de uestre*	628	33	243	V.4
12. *Nouerit industria*	629	38	—	V.7
13. *Nouerit industria*	630	39	236	V.8
14. *Illius dignitatis*	169	48	—	(IV.49)*
15. *Super his que*	255	34	—	II.41
16. *Sciatis quod Thomas*	690	66	—	V.43
17. *Oportuerat uos*	700	68	248	V.66
18. *Licet commendabiles*	701	69	249	V.67
19. *Quam iustis*	723	79	168	V.73
B. Letters quoted briefly				
20. *Solliciti de statu*	322	21	—	II.22
21. *Desiderio magno*	314	22	—	(II.24)*
22. *Post discessum*	307	56	212	II.23
23. *Magnificentie tue*	476	52	—	III.3
24. *Sepius nuntios*	564	—	—	III.20

		Mats.	Bodl.	Vat.	AlanT(B)
25.	*Euocati a domino*	565	—	—	III.21
26.	*Karissimus in Christo*	623	32	239	V.3

C. Letters merely cited

27.	*Quanta mala*	182	—	—	I.90
28.	*A memoria tua*	93	—	—	I.37
29.	*Mandatum uestrum*	108	—	—	I.38

* Not found in AlanT(B), but occurs in AlanT(A) with the note 'non est inter ordinatas'.

TABLE 3

Schedule of letters used by William FitzStephen

This table lists the letters quoted or cited in William FitzStephen's *Life* of St Thomas, together with their numerical location in Robertson's *Materials* (*Mats.*), and collates them with the Douce Collection (Douce: cf. Appendix VIII and Oxford Bodl. MS Douce 287), the Bodleian Archetype (Bodl.: cf. Appendix I and Oxford Bodl. MS 509), the Vatican Archetype (Vat.: cf. Appendix III and Vatican MS Lat. 6024), and Alan of Tewkesbury's Recension II (AlanT(B): Vatican MS Lat. 1220).

A. Letters quoted at length	*Mats.*	Douce	Bodl.	Vat.	AlanT(B)
1. *Excessus uestros*	479	48	—	84a	III.39
2. *Vestram non debet*	488	49	—	84b	III.43
3. *Audiui grauamen*	505	56	—	—	III.47
4. *Se ipsum ad penam*	489	50	—	82a	III.44
5. *Pro amore Dei*	686	74	—	—	—
6. *Sciatis quod Thomas*	690	76	66	—	V.43
7. *Hoc petimus*	604	73	—	—	—

B. Letters very briefly quoted or merely cited

1. *Nosti quam male*	77	f.46rb	—	—	I.13
2. *Precipio tibi*	78	f.46rb	—	—	I.15
3. *Desiderio desideraui*	154	3	2	4	I.64
4. *Fraternitatis uestre*	223	17	16	12	I.127
5. *Mirandum et uehementer*	224	16	—	13	I.108
6. *Mandatum uestrum*	108	7	—	—	I.38
7. *Mittimus uobis*	166	—	—	33	I.121
8. *Vniuersis oppressis*	178	28	43	208	I.32
9. *Placuit excellentie*	167	19	—	—	I.123
10. *Satis superque*	195	—	—	—	I.138
11. *Fratres mei*	198	10	8	—	I.96
12. *Quoniam ad omnem*	165	—	46	218	I.120
13. *Sacrosancta Romana*	172	—	—	255	I.115
14. *Ex iniuncto*	173	29	—	—	I.116

		Mats.	Douce	Bodl.	Vat.	AlanT(B)
15.	*In apostolice sedis*	170	—	—	—	—
16.	*Tanta nos*	208	31	—	—	I.131
17.	*Ad discretionis*	414	—	—	231	IV.16
18.	*Illustris regis*	491	—	—	—	III.1
19.	Constitutions of 1169	599	64	—	—	I.16
20.	*Sciatis karissimi*	636	—	—	—	IV.47
21.	*Vestram pater*	204	11	—	—	I.128
22.	*Que uestro*	205	12	15	11	I.126
23.	*Ex commissi*	632	—	—	247	IV.43
24.	*Quoniam ad audientiam*	633	—	—	240	IV.42
25.	*Oportuerat uos*	700	79	68	248	V.66
26.	*Licet commendabiles*	701	78	69	249	V.67
27.	*Quam iustis*	723	80	79	168	V.73
28.	*Impossibile est*	606	—	—	130	III.61
29.	*Omnem operam*	607	—	—	131	III.62

TABLE 4

Schedule of letters cited by Herbert of Bosham

This table lists the letters cited in Herbert of Bosham's Life of St Thomas, together with their numerical location in Robertson's *Materials* (*Mats.*), and collates them with the Bodleian Archetype (Bodl.: cf. Appendix I and Oxford Bodl. MS 509), the Vatican Archetype (Vat.: cf. Appendix III and Vatican MS Lat 6024), and Alan of Tewkesbury's Recension II (AlanT(B): Vatican MS Lat. 1220).

		Mats.	Bodl.	Vat.	AlanT(B)
1.	Constitutions of Clarendon	45	—	—	I.12
2.	*Ad aures nostras*	52	—	—	I.26
3.	*Sciatis quod*	71	—	—	—
4.	*Nosti quam male*	77	—	—	I.13
5.	*Precipio tibi*	78	—	—	I.15
6.	*Celebre prouerbium*	199	3	49	I.100
7.	*Vestram pater*	204	—	—	I.128
8.	*Que uestro*	205	15	11	I.126
9.	*Fraternitatis uestre*	223	16	12	I.127
10.	*Sacrosancta Romana*	172	—	255	I.115
11.	*Carissimus in Christo*	623	32	239	V.3
12.	*Ex commissi*	632	—	247	IV.43
13.	*Quoniam ad audientiam*	633	—	240	IV.42
14.	*Oportuerat uos*	700	68	248	V.66
15.	*Licet commendabiles*	701	69	249	V.67
16.	*Anxietate cordis*	714	—	260	V.29

TABLE 5

Schedule of letters quoted by Guernes de Pont-Sainte-Maxence

This table lists the letters quoted by Guernes de Pont-Sainte-Maxence in his metrical French Life of St Thomas, together with their numerical location in Robertson's *Materials* (*Mats.*), and collates them with the Bodleian and Vatican Archetypes and AlanT(B).

		Mats.	Bodl.	Vat.	AlanT(B)
1.	Constitutions of Clarendon	45	—	—	I.12
2.	Constitutions of 1169	599	—	—	I.16
3.	*Expectans expectaui*	153	5	—	I.65
4.	*Desiderio desideraui*	154	2	4	I.64
5.	*Que uestro*	205	15	11	I.126
6.	*Mirandum et uehementer*	224	—	13	I.108
7.	*Sciatis quod Thomas*	690	66	—	V.43
8.	*Quam iustis*	723	79	168	V.73

TABLE 6

Schedule of letters contained in Roger of Crowland's *Quadrilogus*

The following table lists the letters inserted into Roger of Crowland's expansion of *Quadrilogus II*, together with their numerical location in Robertson's *Materials* (*Mats.*), and collates them with the earliest and fullest version of Alan of Tewkesbury's collection of Becket letters (AlanT(A): Brit. Libr. MS Cotton Claudius B.II). The table is based on Paris Bibl. Nat. MS Lat 5372, fos. 15vb–123rb, the most complete surviving copy of Roger's work.

Book I		*Mats.*	AlanT(A)	Date
1a.	*Vix mihi*	25	I.1	*c.* Oct. 1163
1b.	Constitutions of Clarendon	45	12a	Jan. 1164
1c.	Constitutions of 1169	599	12e	Nov. 1169
1d.	*Ad aures nostras*	52	22	1 April 1164
2.	*Littere consolationis*	29	14	Oct. 1163
3.	*Hortatur nos*	31	16	Oct. 1163
4.	*Nichil nobis*	32	17	Oct. 1163
5.	*Etsi circa nos*	486	38	7 July 1165
6.	*Ad hoc pontificalis*	49	88	Dec.–Jan. 1163–4
7.	*Excitatus precurrentis*	35	21	Nov.–Dec. 1163
8.	*Legitur constantii*	59	8	Nov.–Dec. 1164
9.	*Est unde respirare*	62	9	*c.* Sept. 1164
10.	*Etsi pro animi*	50	4	5 March 1164
11.	*Non ob gratiam*	51	5	March–April 1164
12.	*Preuenisset tarditatem*	60	2	22 June 1164
13.	*Per misericordiam*	54	6	May 1164
14.	*Ex quo partes*	55	20	March 1164
15.	*Comitem Flandrie*	36	19	Nov.–Dec. 1163
16.	*Litteras quas*	34	13	26 Oct. 1163
17.	*Quod minor*	94	45	early 1165
Book II				
18.	*Medicine potius*	73	25	late Oct. or mid-Nov. 1164

		Mats.	AlanT(A)	Date
19.	*Ad audientiam tuam*	74	I.26	mid-Nov. 1164
20.	*Magnam mihi*	162	82	March 1165
21.	*Loquitur sapiens*	282	86	? late 1166
22.	*Dominum merito*	140	84	early 1165
23.	*Cum dominum papam*	85	27	*post* 2 Feb. 1165
24.	*Ex relatione*	115	29	late 1165
25.	*Litteras uestras*	185	—	Aug.–Sept. 1165
26.	*Nosti quam male*	77	12b	Christmas 1164
27.	*Precipio tibi*	78	12d	Christmas 1164
28.	*Licet faciem*	595	53	*c.* 1169
29.	*Probabile quidem*	138	52	? early 1167
30.	*Quoniam in corpore*	86	43	1165
31.	*Quanto sincerissime*	137	51	early 1166
32.	*Inter ceteras*	136	57	30 Jan. 1166
33.	*Super beneficiis*	133	58	late 1165
34.	*Licet tibi*	155	64	Aug. 1165
35.	*Si littere nostre*	219	36	1165
36.	*Si curamus*	183	94	*c.* June 1166
37.	*Expectabam litteras*	80	30	*c.* Nov. 1164
38.	*Breuiloquio*	603	62	early 1166
39.	*Gratias agimus*	75	48	Dec. 1164
40.	*Quante compassionis*	76	49	Dec. 1164
41.	*Moleste ferimus*	284	42	mid-1166
42.	*Miramur plurimum*	141	35	mid-1165
43.	*Antecessorum*	102	77	10 July 1165
44.	*Tamquam ex iniuncto*	158	160	28 Jan. 1167
45.	*A memoria tua*	93	33	8 June 1165
46.	*Mandatum uestrum*	108	34	late July–Aug. 1165
47.	*Sacrosancta Romana*	172	110	24 April 1166
48.	*Ex iniuncto*	173	I.111	24 April 1166
49.	*Quoniam ad omnem*	164	114	7 April/3 May 1166
50.	*Vniuersis oppressis*	178	28	7 April/3 May 1166
51.	*Et ratio iuris*	179	112	*c.* June 1166
52.	*Meminimus nos*	239	117	June 1166–Jan. 1167
53.	*Mittimus uobis*	166	116	May–June 1166
54.	*Tanta nos*	208	118	*post* 30 June 1166
55.	*Placuit excellentie*	167	119	*ante* 18 Nov. 1166
56.	*Nos uobis alia*	148	71	? May–June 1166
57.	*Relatum est*	124	II.84	mid-1166
58.	*Quanto uobis*	144	I.108	? June 1162–Dec. 1163
59.	*Celebre prouerbium*	199	97	*post* 12 June 1166

		Mats.	AlanT(A)	Date
60.	Loqui de Deo	152	I.59	early 1166
61.	Expectans expectaui	153	61	early 1166
62.	Desiderio desideraui	154	60	April–May 1166
63.	Conquesti sumus (Quando dominus)	188	—	c. June 1166
64.	Diu desideraui	213	65	Feb.–Mar. 1165
65.	Imperator cum	98	69	post 29 May 1165
66.	Iamdudum innotuisse	100	67	1 July 1165

Book III

67.	Fratres mei	198	93	c. 12 June 1166
68.	Sicut nouit	201	143	c. 12 June 1166
69.	Satis superque	195	139	c. 12 June 1166
70.	Que uestro	205	123	c. 24 June 1166
71.	Vestram pater	204	127	c. 24 June 1166
72.	MS has number but no letter			
73.	Fraternitatis uestre	223	125	July–Aug. 1166
74.	Mirandum et uehementer	224	124	July 1166
75.	Licet ex more	194	140	late June 1166
76.	Litteras quas	231	161	July 1166
77.	Ex rescripto	193	149	8 June 1166
78.	Quod iuxta officii	197	113	July–Aug. 1166
79.	Fidei et deuotionis	91	78	c. May 1165–66
80.	Licet uos eam	212	79	Aug. 1166
81.	Tamdiu sanctitati	243	81	Oct. 1166
82.	Abutitur ecclesie	246	129	Nov. 1166
83.	Indubitanter credimus	250	137	? 1166
84.	Ecclesiam Anglorum	249	132	Nov. 1166
85.	Vigor sensuum	192	II.72	? June–Dec. 1166
86.	Ad aures nostras	257	3	1 Dec. 1166
87.	Receptis litteris	259	I.50	20 Dec. 1166
88.	Magnificentie tue	258	II.4	20 Dec. 1166
89.	Tenemus firmiter	293	60	late Feb. 1167
90.	Mittimus sanctitati	286	51	post 2 Feb. 1167
91.	Si de exilio	295	61	late Feb. 1167
92.	Licet temporum	311	10	July–Aug. 1167
93.	Solliciti de statu	322	23	c. Sept. 1167
94.	Quanto magis	315	15	summer 1167
95.	Quomodo de nouo	285	I.165	post 2 Feb. 1167
96.	Inter optimam	288	II.22	post 2 Feb. 1167
97.	Cum uestre	292	I.166	late Feb. 1167

		Mats.	AlanT(A)	Date
98.	*Post discessum*	307	II.25	7 May 1167
99.	*Quanta uniuerse*	324	31	22 Aug. 1167
100.	*Inter cetera*	274	28	*c.* 1 Jan. 1167
101.	*Quod personam*	272	1	*c.* 1 Jan. 1167
102.	*Magnificentie tue*	273	2	*c.* 1 Jan. 1167
103.	*Miseriarum cumulus*	331	37	*post* 19 Nov. 1167
104.	*Innotuit regi*	343	36	*c.* 9 Dec. 1167
105.	*Mittimus sanctitati*	348	50	*post* 14 Dec. 1167
106.	*Sublimitati uestre*	344	38	29 Nov. 1167
107a.	*Venientes ad terram*	342	35	*c.* 9 Dec. 1167
107b.	*Si salutationis*	333	126	*post* 19 Nov. 1167

Book IV

		Mats.	AlanT(A)	Date
108.	*Expectatione longa*	263	II.64	Oct. 1166
109.	*Vnde amantissimi*	351	42	Dec. 1167
110.	*Quod hactenus*	431	45	late 1167
111.	*Qualiter iampridem*	493	8	11 May 1168
112.	*Excellentie tue*	395	IV.3	19 May 1168
113.	*Placet nobis*	396	4	19 June 1168
114.	*Anima mea*	643	16	June–July 1168
115.	*Remittimus sanctitati*	407	II.58	July–Aug. 1168
116.	*Misero uerba*	287	II.52	*post* 2 Feb. 1167
117.	*Quanta mala*	182	IV.330	16 May 1166
118.	*Etsi aduersitatum*	397	II.108	30 Jan. 1168
119.	*Ecclesie persecutor*	642	IV.15	Feb.–Mar. 1168
120.	*Consolationis uestre*	443	17	June–July 1168
121.	*Nos alii uerbis*	444	20	June–July 1168
122.	*Consoletur uos*	442	19	June–July 1168
123.	*Pro archiepiscopo*	435	23	July 1168
124.	*Vobis sicut*	440	24	July 1168
125a.	*Crebrescunt pater*	437	25	July 1168
125b.	*Ecclesie Romane*	446	II.63	July 1168
126.	*Omnis quidem*	438	IV.26	July 1168
127.	*Postquam priores*	411	I.179	June–July 1168
128.	*Ad discretionis*	424	IV.1	25 May 1168
129.	*Ad uestre discretionis*	414	21	19 May 1168
130.	*Regie serenitatis*	436	59	Sept. 1168
131.	*A regie sublimitatis*	404	2	26 April 1168
132.	*Quam paterne*	423	5	22 May 1168
133.	*Longanimitatis*	466	7	*post* 2 Feb. 1169
134.	*Veritas obumbrari*	467	31	Jan. 1169

		Mats.	AlanT(A)	Date
135.	*Gratias non quas*	468	IV.8	*post* 6 Jan. 1169
136.	*Si causam*	463	14	*post* 6 Jan. 1169
137.	*Venerabilis frater*	458	29	Feb. 1169
138.	*Qualiter in secundo*	470	9	*post* 7 Feb. 1169
139.	*Ad illustrem*	451	10	*c.* 6 Jan. 1169
140.	*Sanctis uiris*	471	30	*post* 7 Feb. 1169
141.	*Quod de mea*	615	III.77	late 1169–early 1170
142.	*In otio laborioso*	233	I.178	? mid-1166
143.	*Quanto personam*	460	III.11	9 Oct. 1168/69
144.	*Ad audientiam*	413	IV.35	19 May 1168
145.	*Significauit nobis*	408	I.23	14 May 1174
146.	*Quante auctoritatis*	647	IV.47	1170
147.	*Decet prudentiam*	42	I.75	6 Aug. 1165
148.	*Super religione*	131	80	late 1165
149.	*Audiens tibi*	368	II.46	? late 1167–9
150.	*Meminisse potest*	366	57	1165–7

Book V

		Mats.	AlanT(A)	Date
151.	*Apostolice sedis*	497	III.75	13 April 1169
152.	*Adhuc pater*	498	78	*c.* 13 April 1169
153.	*Excessus uestros*	479	39	*c.* 13 April 1169
154.	*Expectauimus longo*	237	I.95	Aug.–Sept. 1166
155.	*Sacrorum canonum*	494	III.70	*c.* 13 April 1169
156.	*Se ipsum ad penam*	489	44	*c.* 13 April 1169
157.	*Vestram domine*	503	42	*c.* April–May 1169
158.	*Seueritatem uestram*	474	I.120	*post* 18 March 1169
159.	*Seueritatem domine*	475	122	*c.* April 1169
160.	*Mittimus ad uos*	504	III.46	early June 1169
161.	*Ad sanctorum*	550	94	June 1169
162.	*Gratias ago*	536	IV.38	July–Aug. 1169
163.	*Inspectis litteris*	551	III.87	July 1169
164.	*Quot et quanta*	502	17	*c.* 13 April 1169
165.	*Doleo dilectissimi*	535	19	*c.* June 1169
166.	*Audiui grauamen*	505	47	June 1169
167.	*Vestre satis*	506	48	June 1169
168.	*Perseuerans in corde*	528	49	*c.* 1 June 1169
169.	*Quotiens optimis*	520	51	*c.* 18 May 1169
170.	*Ad pedes maiestatis*	583	54	*c.* Oct. 1169
171.	*Sepe quidem*	538	79	June 1169
172.	*Potestis recolere*	294	—	1167–9
173.	*Scelerum mater*	547	88	June 1169

		Mats.	AlanT(A)	Date
174.	*Parit et alit*	546	III.86	June 1169
175.	*Si unum patitur*	543	85	June 1169
176.	*Impudentie mater*	544	16	June 1169
177.	*Illustris regis*	491	1	10 May 1169
178.	*Et naturali ratione*	492	2	10 May 1169
179.	*Sepius nuntios*	564	20	*post* 8 Sept. 1169
180.	*Nuntios et litteras*	567	23	*post* 8 Sept. 1169
181.	*Quod statum nostrum*	563	27	*post* 8 Sept. 1169
182.	*Audiat queso (Ad pedes)*	583	54	*c.* Oct. 1169
183.	*Clarissimi oratoris*	584	55	Oct. 1169
184.	*Interemptorum*	585	56	Oct. 1169
185.	*Missi sunt*	588	59	Oct. 1169
186.	*Que acta sunt*	611	66	*post* 18 Nov. 1169
187a.	*Impossibile est*	606	61	*post* 18 Nov. 1169
187b.	Constitutions of 1169	—	—	Nov. 1169
188.	*Vestra discretio*	576	52	*post* 18 Nov. 1169
189.	*Vobis dilectissimi*	577	72	*post* 18 Nov. 1169
190.	*Lamentati sumus*	573	34	*post* 18 Nov. 1169
191.	*Sciatis carissimi*	636	IV.55	*c.* Nov.–Dec. 1169

Book VI

192.	*Carissimus in Christo*	623	V.3	19 Jan. 1170
193.	*Dilecti filii*	626	1	19 Jan. 1170
194.	*Quoniam de uestre*	628	4	April–May 1170
195.	*Nouerit industria*	629	7	18 Feb. 1170
196.	*Testatur uir*	666	24	*c.* May 1170
197.	*Vtinam dilecte*	662	20	mid-April 1170
198.	*Nullus preter*	663	21	mid-April 1170
199.	*Dirigat Dominus*	644	12	late March 1170
200.	*Quante auctoritatis*	647	IV.47	?1170
201.	*Ad nos iterato*	648	V.51	March–April 1170
202.	*Discretio uestra*	651	53	March–April 1170
203.	*Miserationis oculo*	684	56	*post* 22 July 1170
204.	*Sicut ad locum*	692	50	*post* 22 July 1170
205.	*Si laborantem*	694	52	*post* 22 July 1170
206.	*Experientiam rerum*	695	48	*post* 22 July 1170
207.	*Sciatis quod Thomas*	690	44	mid-Oct. 1170
208.	*Virtutis et*	696	34	Aug. 1170
209.	*Cognito ex litteris*	689	57	Aug.–Sept. 1170
210.	*Quam gratum*	697	58	12 Oct. 1170
211.	*Gauisus est*	703	59	Sept. 1170

		Mats.	AlanT(A)	Date
212.	*Cognito et*	708	V.64	Sept. 1170
213.	*Quam feruenti*	706	62	Sept. 1170
214.	*Mandatum uestrum*	717	54	*post* 15 Oct. 1170
215.	*Ex quo pater*	716	53	Oct.–Nov. 1170
216.	*Molestias et*	710	31	9 Oct. 1170
217.	*Anxietate cordis*	714	29	13 Oct. 1170
218.	*Inter multiplices*	699	68	10 Sept. 1170
219.	*Sciatis quod obuiam*	722	45	early Nov. 1170
220.	*Preces uestras*	719	66	Oct. 1170
221.	*Licet commendabiles*	701	70	16 Sept. 1170
222.	*Oportuerat uos*	700	69	16 Sept. 1170
223.	*Quamuis cure*	720	71	24 Nov. 1170
224.	*Nouit inspector*	718	55	late Oct. 1170

Book VII

225.	*Quam iustis*	723	77	early Dec. 1170
226.	*Ab humane pietatis*	734	83	Jan. 1171
227.	*Inter scribendum*	735	85	Jan. 1171
228.	*Vestre placuit*	736	86	Jan. 1171
229.	*Agonem nostram*	777	97	Jan. 1171
230.	*Cum apud regem*	738	84	Jan. 1171
231.	*Vestro apostolatui*	740	87	Jan. 1171
232.	*Ne in dubium*	772	95	*c.* 21 May 1172
233.	*Letamur nos*	788	102	Dec. 1171
234.	*Gaudendum est*	784	98	12 March 1173
235.	*Redolet Anglia*	785	99	12 March 1173
236.	*Qui uice beati*	786	100	? April 1173

TABLE 7

Schedule of letters appended to the 1495 edition of the *Quadrilogus*

The following table lists the letters appended to J. Philippi, ed., *Vita et Processus Sancti Thome Cantuariensis Martyris Super Libertate Ecclesiastica*, Paris 1495 (*Quadrilogus I*), together with their numerical location in Robertson's *Materials*, and collates them with the Bodleian Archetype (Bodl.: cf. Appendix I and Oxford Bodl. MS 509), the Vatican Archetype (Vat.: cf. Appendix III and Vatican MS Lat. 6024), and Alan of Tewkesbury's Recension II (AlanT(B): Vatican MS Lat. 1220).

		Mats.	Bodl.	Vat.	AlanT(B)
1.	Constitutions of Clarendon	45	—	—	I.12
2.	Constitutions of 1169	599	—	—	I.16
3.	*Litteras quas*	34	—	—	I.17
4.	*Non ob gratiam*	51	54	221	I.5
5.	*Decet prudentiam*	42	—	230	I.78
6.	*Quoniam ecclesia*	412	—	—	(II.129)*
7.	*Magnificentie tue*	476	52	22	III.3
8.	*Et naturali*	492	—	272	III.2
9.	*A memoria tua*	93	—	266	I.37
10.	*Vniuersis oppressis*	178	43	208	I.32
11.	*Suggestum est*	355	—	209	II.104
12.	*Quod circa ea*	106	—	—	I.41
13.	*Super discretione*	400	—	226	II.68
14.	*Oportuerat uos*	700	68	248	V.66
15.	*Licet commendabiles*	701	69	249	V.67
16.	*Illius dignitatis*	169	48	246	(IV.49)*
17.	*Quam paterne*	423	51	229	IV.4
18.	*Quoniam de uestre*	628	33	243	V.4
19.	*Mandamus uobis*	787	—	—	V.95
20.	*Quot et quantas*	680	—	156	V.37

* Not found in AlanT(B), but occurs in AlanT(A) with the note 'non est inter ordinatas'.

		Mats.	Bodl.	Vat.	AlanT(B)
21.	Noscat dilectio	534	—	—	III.18
22.	Fratres mei	198	8	—	I.96
23.	Celebre prouerbium	199	3	—	I.97
24.	Que uestro	205	14	11	I.126
25.	Fraternitatis uestre	223	16	12	I.127
26.	Medicine potius	73	—	—	I.29
27.	Ad audientiam	74	—	—	I.30
28.	Cum clerum	99	—	—	—
29.	Desiderio desideraui	154	2	4	I.64
30.	Loqui de Deo	152	1	—	I.63
31.	Si littere	219	7	—	I.40
32.	Expectans expectaui	153	5	—	I.65
33.	Dominus Cantuariensis	334	—	—	—
34.	Venientes ad terram	342	—	47	II.28
35.	Ut aliquid	650	—	136	IV.45
36.	Quoniam in corpore	86	—	—	I.47
37.	Aggredimur rogare	—	—	—	—
38.	Anima nostra	354	—	—	II.103
39.	Ecclesie molestias	501	—	—	III.76
40.	Mirandum et uehementer	224	—	13	I.108
41.	Excessus uestros	479	—	84a	III.39
42.	Vestram non debet	488	—	84b	III.43
43.	Se ipsum ad penam	489	—	82a	III.44
44.	Sciatis karissimi	636	—	—	IV.47
45.	Quam iustis	723	79	168	V.73
46.	Gratias agimus	688	—	—	—
47.	Excellentie tue	395	50	225	IV.3
48.	Expedit beatissime	362	—	—	II.97
49.	Venerabilis frater	363	—	—	II.98
50.	Mandatum uestrum	108	—	—	I.38
51.	Vestram pater	204	—	—	I.128
52.	Sepius nuntios	564	—	—	III.20
53.	De uestro aliorumque	669	—	—	V.14
54.	Sciatis quod Thomas	690	66	—	V.43
55.	Post nuntiorum	566	—	—	III.22
56.	Euocati a domino	565	—	—	III.21
57.	Sublimitati uestre	344	—	—	II.33
58.	Licet abiectio	552	—	—	III.90
59.	Vestre placuit	736	—	—	V.81
60.	Inter scribendum	735	—	—	V.80
61.	Letamur nos	788	—	—	V.96
62.	Nouerit celsitudo	605	—	—	III.28

		Mats.	Bodl.	Vat.	AlanT(B)
63.	*De uestra sinceritate*	568	—	—	III.29
64.	*Infirma mundi*	672	—	147	V.70
65.	*Mittimus ad uos*	504	—	—	III.46
66.	*Misero uerba*	287	14	—	II.46
67.	*Cum illius sincerissime*	134	—	—	I.59

Index 1

Manuscripts

Index 2

Incipits

Index 3

Authors of Letters

Index 4

Recipients of Letters

Index 5

General Index